Investment Decisions and Financial Strategy

First Published in India by
B.R. Chawla
Heritage Publishers
4C, Ansari Road
New Delhi-110002
in arrangement with
Philip Allan Publishers Limited
Oxford OX5 4SE

British Library Cataloguing in Publication Data
Pike, R.H.
Investment decisions and financial strategy.
1. Investments
I. Title II. Dobbins, Richard
332.2 HG4521
ISBN 0-86003-537-9

Reissued 1991

PRICE :. Rs. 495-00

Typeset by Activity Limited, Salisbury
Printed and bound in Great Britain by
The Camelot Press, Southampton

Contents

Preface

Long-term investment decisions are probably the most important yet most difficult decisions facing a manager. Most investment decisions are characterised by committing cash to projects in the uncertain expectation of obtaining higher cash returns in future periods. Frequently we find that only relatively minor changes in the forecasts, upon which such decisions are based, can tip the balance between a project's acceptability or otherwise.

This book examines and discusses the theory and practice of investment and financial strategy. Practice and theory have been likened to bricks and mortar. Both are essential and both must be sound if we are to erect a worthy structure. Within the constraints of a book of this length, we have sought to provide a balance between the two rather than concentrate on one element at the expense of the other.

The book is based on the authors' extensive experience in lecturing in financial management to undergraduate and MBA students and to managers. Much of the empirical work described in the book is drawn from the authors' own research based upon extensive discussions with managers.

We have aimed in the book to provide a thorough grounding in the basic concepts matched with an understanding of the practical aspects. It is hoped that the reader will be able to reflect upon how decisions are made and, perhaps, how they can be improved. Wherever possible, we have adopted descriptive or graphical approaches to the subject, mathematical analysis only being employed where it is regarded as more appropriate.

Worked examples are provided throughout the book, applying theory to practical problems. Further problems are presented at the end of each chapter, many of which are relevant professional accounting examination questions.

We see the book as being primarily applicable to undergraduate and MBA students and professional accounting students. Managers should also find it to be of value in understanding the investment and financial operations of their own organisations.

Finally, we wish to thank the publishers for their patience, and Mrs Kath Pike and Miss Kay Sutcliffe for typing from our manuscripts and tapes.

Richard Pike FCA, MA, PhD
Richard Dobbins FCCA, MSc, PhD

Management Centre
University of Bradford

March 1985

1

Overview

Investment and Financing Decisions

This book is concerned with investment and financing decisions in business organisations. These two broad areas for decision making are at the heart of financial management theory and practice. Let us first be clear what we mean by these decisions.

The *investment decision*, sometimes referred to as the capital budgeting decision, is the decision to acquire assets. Most of these assets will be *real assets* employed within the business to produce goods or services to satisfy consumer demand. Real assets may be tangible, such as land and buildings, plant and equipment, and stocks, or intangible, such as patents, trademarks and 'know-how'. Sometimes a firm may choose to invest in *financial assets* outside the business in the form of short-term securities and deposits. The basic problems facing the finance manager concerning investment are:

1. How much should the firm invest?
2. In which specific projects should the firm invest?

A considerable part of this book is devoted to these very issues.

The *financing decision* addresses the problems: how much should be raised to fund the firm's operations (both existing and proposed), and what is the best mix of financing in relation to the overall value of the firm? In the same way that a firm can hold financial assets such as shares and loan deposits, it can also sell claims on its own real assets, in the form of shares, loans, lease obligations, and so on.

The Financial Manager as an Intermediary

The financial manager, whether a corporate treasurer in a multinational company or the sole trader of a small business, performs a vital function by acting as a *financial intermediary* between financial markets and the firm. To perform this task properly he requires a clear grasp of both the firm's operations *and* the workings and theory of financial markets. The diagram in Figure 1.1 outlines the essential role of the financial manager.

All transactions that result in financial assets and financial liabilities constitute the *financial markets*. Some of these transactions are conducted

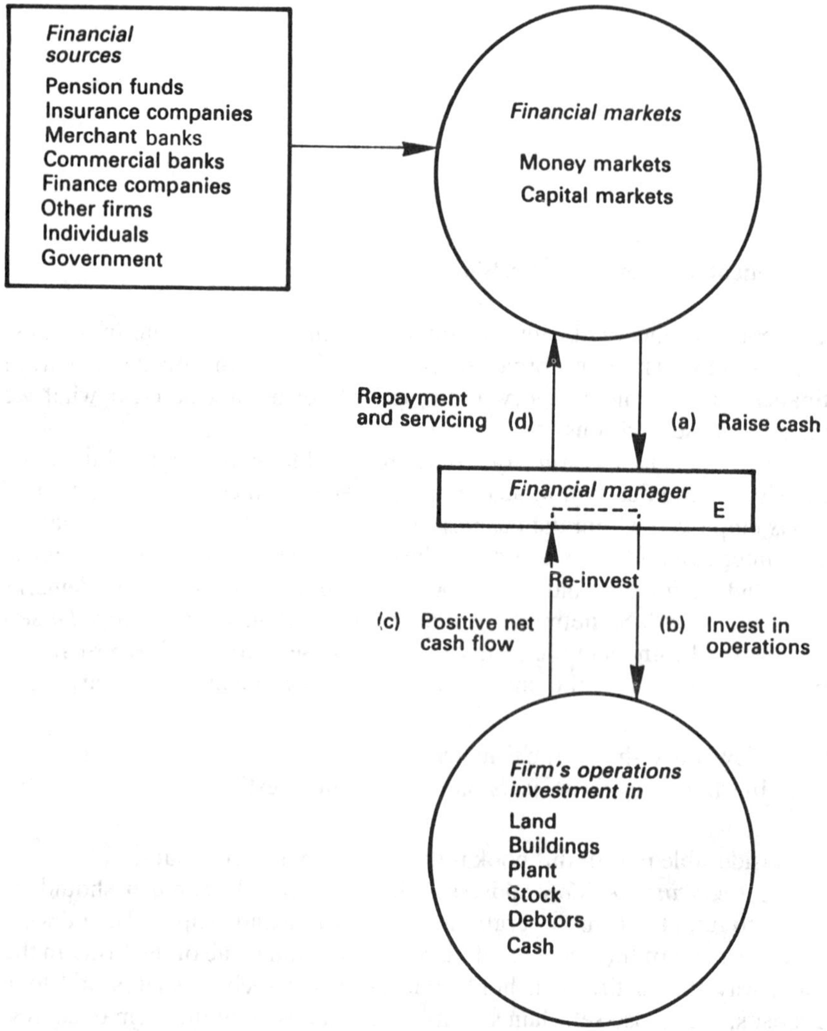

Figure 1.1 The Financial Manager as an Intermediary

through institutions such as the London Stock Exchange, while others arise through credit agreements for hire purchase, leasing, loans, and other such facilities. Collectively, the financial markets provide a mechanism through which the financial manager has access to a wide range of financing sources. Financial institutions, such as pension funds and insurance companies, are the major contributors, but individuals and government agencies also provide important sources of finance.

As shown in transaction (a) in Figure 1.1, the financial manager raises cash by selling claims on its existing or future assets on the money markets and capital markets. The former trades in financial assets and liabilities having a maturity of less than one year; the latter deals in financial transactions exceeding one year. He then uses the cash to fund the proposed level of real investment in the firm's operations (b). If the investment decisions turn out to be successful they will, in total, generate a positive cash flow from operations (c). This surplus is then used in two ways: first, it will service existing financial obligations in the form of dividends, interest etc. and eventually make repayment (d); secondly, it may be reinvested in the firm to replace existing assets or expand operations.

What is Capital Budgeting?

We said in the previous section that the financial manager is faced with the problems of how much to invest and in which specific projects to invest. This naturally leads us to the all-important topic of *capital budgeting*. Capital budgeting is the art of investing in assets whose worth exceeds their cost. A fuller explanation is provided in Chapter 2. At this stage we would simply make the point that capital budgeting is not a mechanistic process which, if properly operated, guarantees successful investments. One firm may appear to practise all the best investment evaluation methods and yet still perform less satisfactorily than another firm which is blissfully ignorant of such methods. Why should this be? Because the prosperity of a business depends more on its ability to *create* profitable investment opportunities than on its ability to *appraise* them. Successful investment programmes depend on the creativity, enthusiasm, experience and judgement of the managers responsible for finding, shaping and evaluating projects.

Why is Investment Important?

Before adding to the already vast literature on investment, it is worth summarising the reasons why the subject merits the attention it attracts. As far as the firm is concerned, investment not only presents the businessman with the most important decision he has to make, but also with one of the hardest. The decisions he takes as to the size and form of investment will affect the operating environment of the firm for the remainder of the investment's life. The quality of such decisions will, therefore, largely determine the future prosperity and health of the firm.

For the economy as a whole, aggregate investment sanctioned in the current period is a major factor in determining aggregate demand and hence the level of employment. In the longer term, the current volume of investment orders determines the economy's future productive capacity and, ultimately, the growth in living standards. It is hardly surprising that a country such as Japan, which has consistently invested some 30 per cent of its Gross Domestic Product, ranks higher in growth leagues than the UK and the USA, each with investment of around 15 per cent GDP. Investment both generates growth by increasing capital per worker and is itself stimulated by growth, as rapid growth produces buoyant expectations in a self-sustaining process.[1]

Goal of the Firm

Before we can construct an investment decision model, we must first agree upon the goal, or possibly combination of goals, of the firm. In this book we assume that the goal of the firm is to create as much wealth as possible for its shareholders. Given this objective, any financing or investment decision expected to improve the value of the shareholder's stake in the firm is acceptable.

Let it be said at the outset that the above goal may well be at odds with the reader's views and, indeed, with the views of many practising managers. In recent years a wide variety of goals has been suggested for the firm, from the traditional goal of profit maximisation to include goals relating to earnings per share, sales, employee welfare, manager satisfaction, survival, and the good of society. It has also been questioned whether management seeks to *maximise*, by seeking optimal solutions, or to *satisfice*, by seeking satisfactory solutions.

Empirically, it seems that maximisation of shareholders' wealth is not the only goal of management — nor is it the most important. Managers are more interested in profitability than in wealth creation. A recent survey asked finance directors in the largest UK companies to rank specified goals in order of importance. A summary of results is provided in Table 1.1. It will be seen that maximisation of shareholder wealth comes a poor fourth, only around 18 per cent of respondents seeing it as a 'very important' goal. Many US studies support this finding (e.g. Petty *et al.* 1975). Maximisation of shareholder wealth, then, is not so much a reflection of how investment and financing decisions are made, but rather a normative goal for how firms *should* operate. Wherever this goal conflicts with other important considerations, the conflict must be examined and, where possible, resolved.

Table 1.1 The Importance of Financial Objectives for a Company

	Mean[1]	*Very important* (%)
Maximise percentage return on assets	4.35	58.4
Maximise earnings or earnings per share	4.05	43.8
Target share of market	3.28	18.3
Maximise share price	3.15	17.9
Target earnings per share growth rate	2.98	12.3
Other	1.40	1.0

Source: Pike (1986)
Note: [1]Higher number indicates greater importance.

One such conflict arises because of the separation of ownership from management. Shareholders may exert only limited influence over the investment and financial strategies of companies. Accordingly, managers may be more concerned with their own welfare than that of their shareholders' and adopt low-risk survival strategies and 'satisficing' decision behaviour. Such conflict has been explored by Jensen and Meckling (1976) who developed a theory of the firm under *agency* arrangements. Managers are, in effect, agents for the shareholders and are required to act in their best interests. To ensure that the agents make optimal decisions it is necessary to offer appropriate incentives and institute necessary controls. Incentives may take the form of bonuses, stock options and perquisites given in relation to how closely management decisions accord with shareholders' interests. In firms where ownership and operational control are almost entirely separate, management is more likely to pursue other goals. Shareholders may be willing to incur the costs of monitoring management activity to assess the extent to which managers' actions accord with shareholder wealth-maximising behaviour.

Application of Financial Theory

To what extent is financial theory directly applicable to the world of commerce and industry? It is often said that a good theory should be empirical rather than speculative. So, can the student of finance apply the theory to develop successful investment and financing strategies? The extent to which financial theory will provide superior decisions must rest on the degree of realism in the assumptions underlying the theory. It is therefore beneficial to consider at the outset the main assumptions upon which much of financial theory rests.

Assumptions of Pure Finance Theory

Financial theory in its purest form assumes the following:

(i) All markets — not just capital markets — are perfectly competitive.
(ii) Information is perfect and costless; transaction costs are zero.
(iii) No taxes exist.
(iv) Investors prefer more consumption to less consumption.
(v) Shareholder-managers do not use their voting rights to reap benefits from being managers.

These assumptions lead naturally to certain propositions. Firstly, only shareholders are interested in the firm. A perfect labour market implies that managers and workers can always find another equally attractive job. Secondly, shareholders are only interested in maximising the market value of their shareholdings. Given perfect, costless information, managers are perfectly controlled by the shareholders to implement value-maximising strategies. Thirdly, as will be discussed in subsequent chapters, the pursuit of shareholder wealth is achieved by instructing managers to invest only in those projects which are worth more than they cost. Financing strategies, whether concerning dividends, capital structure or leasing, are irrelevant as they do little to increase shareholders' wealth.

Most people would agree that the assumptions underlying the neoclassical theory of finance summarised above are at odds with reality. Information is imperfect; transaction costs and information costs may be sizeable. Markets are frequently highly imperfect; management will usually have a good deal of interest in the firm — interest which may well conflict with that of shareholders. Managers have far from complete knowledge on such things as the set of feasible financing strategies available, their cash flow patterns and impact on market values. Shareholders are even less well informed. Taxation policy, bankruptcy costs and other factors can have a major influence on financial strategies. Throughout this book we shall attempt to discuss the theoretical developments which take account of such imperfections. It is to be hoped that a clearer understanding of the concepts, together with an awareness of the degree of realism in their underlying assumptions, will enable the reader to make sound and successful investment and financial decisions in practice.

To summarise the discussion to date: the assumed objective of the firm, so far as concerns investment and financing decisions, is to *increase shareholder wealth*. Wealth is represented by the value of the shareholder's stake in the business which, in turn, is a reflection of the firm's investment and financing decisions.

Development of the Book

The book is divided into four parts. Section A considers the investment decision and related aspects. Emphasis is given to evaluation mechanics and the extent to which the techniques available are consistent with shareholders' interests. Because the future benefits derived from projects are not known with certainty, investment appraisals necessarily involve risk analysis. Consequently, projects should be viewed in terms of their expected returns and risks. Two chapters are devoted to risk measurement. The first considers the uncertainty inherent in the investment proposal itself, while the second views risk from the shareholder's perspective.

Investments may be classified in a variety of different ways. For the purposes of this book, we consider four different forms of investment: normal capital projects (e.g. scale expansion proposals), replacement projects, working capital investment, and mergers. Although very different in some aspects, these investment opportunities can be evaluated in the same general manner.

Section B considers the firm's financing decisions. It examines whether, and to what extent, the financial manager can improve the value of his firm by altering the financing mix and dividend policy. A related issue is the leasing decision. When does it pay to lease assets rather than purchase them? Although investment decisions and financing decisions are dealt with in separate sections in this book, the two are inextricably connected. The final chapter in this section examines the adjusted present value approach as a means of solving investment and financing decisions simultaneously.

While sections A and B deal mainly with the concepts underlying investment and financing decisions, section C is devoted to the more practical aspects. Attention is paid to the investment practices found in UK firms and the extent to which they differ from the recommended approach outlined in section A. No matter how complex the theoretical model, it can never embody all the complexities found in the business world. The fact that theory and practice differ is not, therefore, a simple matter of establishing which is right and which is wrong.

A much neglected area in capital budgeting is the resource allocation process. A chapter is devoted to how investments are conceived, channelled through the capital budgeting process, implemented and eventually monitored. Many of the investment methods discussed in the book lend themselves to computer applications. The final section provides the output of four such programmes which are listed in the appendices.

Questions

1. Discuss the reasons why investment is important (a) to the firm and (b) to the economy.
2. What do you understand by the *investment* decision and the *financing* decision?
3. Provide three examples of *real* assets and *financial* assets.

4. Discuss the role of the financial manager.
5. Why is the goal of maximising owners' wealth a helpful one in analysing capital investment decisions? How realistic do you view this goal? What other goals may also need to be considered?

Note

1. We must add that investment alone does not guarantee economic growth. Profitable opportunities must be identified and exploited.

References

Jensen, M. C. and Meckling, W. H. (1976) 'Theory of the firm: managerial behavior, agency costs and ownership structure', *Journal of Financial Economics*, October.

Petty, J. W., Scott, D. F. and Bird, M. M. (1975) 'The capital expenditure decision-making process of large corporations', *The Engineering Economist*, Spring.

Pike, R. H. (forthcoming) 'Owner–manager conflict and the role of the payback method', *Accounting and Business Research*.

Further Reading

Donaldson, G. (1963) 'Financial goals: management versus stock holders', *Harvard Business Review*, May–June.

Findley, C. M. and Whitmore, G. A. (1974) 'Beyond shareholder wealth maximisation', *Financial Management*, Winter.

Gordon, M. J. (1981) 'Interest in a corporation of its management, workers, and country', in G. J. Derkinderen and R. L. Crum, *Readings in Strategy for Corporate Investment*, Pitman.

Weston, J. F. and Brigham, E. F. (1979) *Managerial Finance*, Holt, Rinehart and Winston.

Section A

Investment Evaluation and Decision Making

2

The Measurement of Wealth

In the first chapter we described the art of capital budgeting as the ability to create wealth by finding investments which are worth more than they cost. We now turn our attention to the issue of how wealth should be measured. To do this we will consider:

1. the meaning of 'wealth' and the important role it plays in the decision making process;
2. the time-value of money which underlies the discounted cash flow concept;
3. the application of the net present value investment decision rule.

Measurement of Wealth

Financial management theorists generally assert that the objective of the firm is to create as much wealth as possible. Wealth is created when the market value of the outputs exceeds the market value of the inputs, i.e. the investment is *worth* more than it *costs*. Expressed mathematically:

$$V_j = W_j - I_j$$

The wealth or value (V_j) created by investment j is the difference between the worth (W_j) and the initial cost (I_j) of that investment. This leads to a decision rule: accept a project if—

$$W_j - I_j > 0$$

i.e., accept the investment proposal if its worth is *greater* than its cost. This is the same as saying: accept the project if V_j, the wealth created by the investment, is *positive*. This — in a nutshell — is what good investment decision making is all about. Nothing could be simpler in concept — the problems emerge only when we probe more deeply into how, in practice, these concepts are to be measured. In most instances, the initial expenditure incurred on an investment undertaken is clear-cut: it is what we pay for it. This usually includes the cash paid to the supplier of the asset plus any other costs involved in making the project operational. The problems really start in measuring the worth of the investment project. What an asset is worth has little to do with what it cost or what value is placed on it in the firm's balance sheet. A machine standing in the firm's books at £20,000 may be worth far more if it is essential to the manufacture of a highly profitable product, or far less than this if rendered obsolete through the advent of new technology. In order to measure its worth we need to consider the *value of the current and future benefits* arising from the investment. Wherever possible, these benefits should be expressed in terms of *cash flows*. Sometimes (as will be discussed later) it is impossible to quantify benefits so conveniently.

Time-Value of Money

Present wealth is not simply the sum of the cash expected to arise at different times in the future. An important principle is that the value of money is time dependent — £1 now is worth *more* than £1 tomorrow or at some future time. Four reasons can be given for this:

1. *Inflation* Under inflationary conditions the value of money, expressed in terms of its purchasing power over goods and services, declines.
2. *Risk* £1 now is certain, whereas £1 receivable tomorrow is less certain. This 'bird-in-the-hand' principle is extremely important in investment appraisal.
3. *Personal Consumption Preference* Many individuals have a strong preference for immediate rather than delayed consumption. The promise of a bowl of rice next week counts for little to the starving man.
4. *Investment Opportunities* Even when the above reasons are ignored, the fact still remains that money — like any other desirable commodity — has a price. Given the choice of £100 now or the same amount in one year's time, it is always preferable to take the £100 now because it could be invested over the next year at (say) 6 per cent interest rate to produce £106 at the end of one year. If 6 per cent is the best risk-free return available, then you would be indifferent to

receiving £100 now or £106 in one year's time. Expressed another way, the *present value* of £106 receivable one year hence is £100.

There is, of course, a spectrum of interest rates to be found listed in the financial press. This variation in rates of interest arises predominantly because of uncertainty surrounding the future and imperfections in the capital market. To simplify our understanding of the time-value of money concept let us 'assume away' these realities. In our make-believe world the lender knows with certainty the future cash flow arising from the project for which finance is sought, and can borrow or lend on a perfect capital market. The latter implies that:

(i) relevant information is freely available to all participants in the market;
(ii) no transaction costs or taxes are involved in using the capital market;
(iii) no participant (borrower or lender) can influence the market price for funds.

The net result is that the corporate treasurer of ICI cannot raise funds any more cheaply than the owner of a small business. A single market rate of interest prevails, which we shall term i. Borrowers and lenders will base time-related decisions on this unique market rate of interest.

Compounding and Discounting

The process of *compounding* provides a convenient way of adjusting for the time-value of money. An investment in the capital market of £V_o now gives rise to a cash flow of £V_o $(1 + i)$ after one year, £V_o $(1 + i)^2$ after two years, and so on. In general, the future value (FV_n) of £V_o invested for n years at a compound rate of interest of i% will be:

$$FV_n = £V_o(1 + i)^n$$

Now try this example: find the future value of £100 invested for six years at a compound rate of interest of 10 per cent, using the compounding formula

$$\begin{aligned} FV_6 &= £100\,(1 + 0.10)^6 \\ &= £177.16 \end{aligned}$$

This is demonstrated in Table 2.1.

Undoubtedly, it is of interest to know how much will be received when the investment is withdrawn. It is much more relevant to the current situation if the above is expressed in terms of *present* rather than future

Table 2.1

Year	*Amount at start of year* (£)		*Interest rate* (i = *10%*)		*Future value* (£)
1	100	×	1.10	=	110
2	110	×	1.10	=	121
3	121	×	1.10	=	133.1
4	133.1	×	1.10	=	146.41
5	146.41	×	1.10	=	161.05
6	161.05	×	1.10	=	177.16

value. Taking the formula $FV_n = V_o (1 + i)^n$ and dividing both sides by $(1 + i)^n$, we derive:

$$PV = V_o = \frac{FV_n}{(1 + i)^n}$$

which can be read as the present value of cash flow FV receivable in n years' time. This is the process of *discounting* future sums to their present values. Applying the present value formula to check the previous example, the present value of £177.16 receivable six years hence, discounted at 10 per cent, should be £100:

$$PV = \frac{£177.16}{(1 + .10)^6} = £100$$

An individual should not pay more than £100 today for an investment offering a certain return of £177.16 after six years, assuming a 10 per cent market rate of interest.

Let us now consider the application of the present value method within a decision-making context.

Example

Ron Devie, a well-known soccer manager, has recently been offered a lucrative contract of £50,000 for the next three years to manage an overseas football team. He estimates that in taking up such an appointment he would lose in the region of £30,000 a year, that being his present salary and other promotional income. He also estimates that it would take him about a year following his return to find a club offering at least as good a salary as his present one. Assuming the market rate of interest is 15 per cent, would the move increase his present wealth?

Devie is presented with a straight financial choice between 'staying put' or taking up the new appointment. He should evaluate these two options to ascertain which offers the highest present value of the future income for the next four years.

Option 1: stay put

$$PV = \frac{30,000}{(1.15)} + \frac{30,000}{(1.15)^2} + \frac{30,000}{(1.15)^3} + \frac{30,000}{(1.15)^4}$$
$$= £85,650$$

Option 2: new appointment

$$PV = \frac{50,000}{(1.15)} + \frac{50,000}{(1.15)^2} + \frac{50,000}{(1.15)^3} + \frac{0}{(1.15)^4}$$
$$= £114,160$$

The new offer produces present wealth of £114,160. This is an increase in wealth of £28,510 over the decision to stay with his present club. In terms of wealth maximisation, therefore, the move makes sense, but he must then weigh against this any non-financial considerations that might be involved in such a move.

Net Present Value

As previously stated, the assumed objective of the firm is to create as much wealth as possible for the owners through the efficient use of existing and future resources. To create wealth now, the present value of all future cash inflows must exceed the present value of all anticipated cash outflows.

Most decisions involve both costs and benefits. Typically, investment decisions involve an initial capital expenditure followed by a stream of cash receipts and disbursements in subsequent periods. The net present value (NPV) method is applied to evaluate the desirability of investment opportunities and is defined as follows:

$$NPV = \frac{X_1}{1 + K} + \frac{X_2}{(1 + K)^2} + \frac{X_3}{(1 + K)^3} + \cdots\cdots + \frac{X_n}{(1 + K)^n} - I$$

The above may be summarised as:

$$NPV = \sum_{t=1}^{n} \frac{X_t}{(1 + K)^t} - I$$

where

X_t = the net cash flow arising at the end of year t

K = the minimum required rate of return on the investment (i.e. the discount rate)
I = the initial cost of the investment
n = the project's life.

In other words, a project's net present value is determined by summing the discounted net cash flows at a rate which reflects the cost of an equivalent investment on the capital market, and deducting the initial outlay. (The Greek letter Σ, or sigma, denotes the sum of all values in a particular series.) This leads to development of the Net Present Value Rule: wealth is maximised by *accepting all projects that offer positive net present values* when discounted at the required rate of return for each investment.

Examination of the main elements in the NPV formula reveals that most are largely externally determined. For example, in the case of an investment in a new piece of manufacturing equipment, management has relatively little influence over the price paid, the life expectancy, or the discount rate. These elements are determined, in the main, by the price of capital goods, the rate of new technological development, and the returns required by the capital market. Management's main opportunity for wealth creation lies in its ability to implement and manage the project in such a manner as to generate strong positive net cash flows over the project's economic life. For this reason, two firms may invest in the same equipment but obtain very different annual cash flows.

A simple example will serve to demonstrate how the NPV method is applied. The management of Conners Ltd is currently evaluating an investment costing £1,000. Anticipated net cash inflows are £600 received at the end of Year 1, and £600 received at the end of Year 2. The firm operates in a low risk industry and divides its various projects into three categories: class A, where the risk is low and the required rate of return is 10 per cent; class B, where the risk is average for the industry and the required rate of return is 13 per cent; and class C, where risk is higher and the required rate of return is 16 per cent. Evaluating the project from the NPV viewpoint, and using the NPV formula given above will provide the estimates illustrated in Table 2.2, which shows the NPV of the project under each of the three risk classifications.

If the project is classified as low risk, the cash flows are discounted at a rate of 10 per cent. The Year 1 cash flow has a present value of £540 and the Year 2 cash flow has a present value of £500. The present value of the inflows is therefore £1,040 and, after deducting the initial outlay which has a present value of £1,000, the project has a net present value of £40. The project should be accepted; it has a positive NPV. It does in fact create wealth. If the projected cash flows are achieved, the market value of the firm should rise by £40. On the other hand, if the project is classified as high risk, the cash inflows are discounted at a rate of 16 per cent and the NPV is estimated at −£40. The project is unacceptable; it has a negative NPV. Its

Table 2.2 Net Present Value of a Project

Risk class	*Discount rate*	*Present value of cash inflows Yr 1*	*Yr 2*	*Cost*	*NPV*
A	10%	£540	£500	£1,000	£40
B	13%	£530	£470	£1,000	£00
C	16%	£520	£440	£1,000	−£40

acceptance would have the effect of reducing the firm's market value by £40. Clearly, it would not be wise to exchange £1,000 today for future cash flows having a present value today of only £960. If the project is classified as average risk, the discount rate used is 13 per cent, yielding a NPV of £0. The project is just acceptable; it yields 13 per cent. From this simple example, we can draw three important conclusions:

1. project acceptability depends upon cash flows and risk;
2. the present value of a given expected cash flow decreases with time;
3. the higher the risk of a given set of expected cash flows (and the higher the applied discount rate), the lower will be its present value, that is, the present value of a given expected cash flow decreases as its risk increases.

Present Value Formulae and Tables

The present value concept is not difficult to apply in practice. Much of the tedium of using formulae and power functions can be eased enormously by using the discount tables provided at the back of this book. The remainder of this chapter is devoted to explaining the various present value formulae and discount tables, and illustrating how they can be applied to investment problems. Throughout, we shall use the symbol X to denote annual cash flow and i to denote the interest rate (or discount rate).

Present Value

The present value of £X receivable in n years is calculated from the expression

$$PV = \frac{X}{(1 + i)^n}$$

Example: Calculate the present value of £1,000 receivable in 10 years' time, assuming a discount rate of 12%.

$$PV = \frac{1000}{(1.12)^{10}} = £321.97$$

From the table in Appendix A, the discount factor for $n = 10$ and $i = 12\%$ is 0.32197.

$$PV = 1000 \times 0.32197 = £321.97$$

The present value of £1,000 receivable 10 years hence, discounted at 12%, is £321.97.

Present Value of Perpetuities

Frequently an investment pays a fixed sum each year for a specified number of years. A series of annual receipts or payments is termed an *annuity*. The simplest form of annuity is the *perpetuity*. For example, certain government stocks offer a fixed annual income but there is no obligation to repay the capital. The return on such stocks is found by dividing the annual interest by the present value of the stock (i.e. the current price). From this we can compute the present value of a perpetuity:[1]

$$PV \text{ perpetuity} = \frac{X}{i}$$

Example
Great-aunt Bessie has notified her solicitor that she wishes to leave you an annual sum of £1,000 a year. Assuming an interest rate of 10%, how much of her estate must be set aside for this purpose? The answer is £10,000:

$$PV \text{ perpetuity} = \frac{1000}{0.1} = £10{,}000$$

Suppose that your benevolent great-aunt now wishes to compensate for inflation estimated to be at 5% per annum. The formula can be adjusted to allow for growth in the annual amount:[2]

$$PV = \frac{X}{i - g}$$

As long as the growth rate is less than the interest rate, we can compute the new present value required. In this case it is £20,000.

$$PV = \frac{1000}{0.10 - 0.05} = £20{,}000$$

Present Value of Annuities

The above perpetuities were special cases of the annuity formula. To find the present value of an annuity, we can first use the perpetuity formula and deduct from it the years outside the annuity period. For example, if an annuity of £100 is issued for 20 years at 10%, we would find the present value of a perpetuity of £100 using the formula

$$PV = \frac{X}{i} = \frac{100}{0.10} = £1{,}000$$

Next, find the present value of a perpetuity for the same amount, *starting* at year 20 using the formula

$$PV = \frac{X}{i(1+i)^t} = \frac{100}{0.10(1+0.10)^{20}} = £148.64$$

The difference will be

$$PV \text{ of annuity} = \frac{X}{i} - \frac{X}{i(1+i)^t}$$
$$= 1{,}000 - 148.64 = £851.36$$

The present value of an annuity of £100 for 20 years discounted at 10% is £851.36.

The formula may be simplified to

$$PV \text{ of annuity} = X\left[\frac{1}{i} - \frac{1}{i(1+i)^t}\right]$$

Using the table in Appendix B, the annuity factor for $n = 20$ and $i = 10\%$ is 8.5136.

$$PV \text{ of annuity} = £100 \times 8.5136 = £851.36$$

The annuity discount factor has many other uses. Consider the following example: a new investment costing £3,250 is expected to produce net cash receipts of £1,000 for the next five years. Assuming a 10% discount rate, is the investment worthwhile? The present value annuity factor for 5 years at 10% is 3.791.

	£
Present value of future benefits = £1,000 × 3.791 =	3,791
Less initial investment outlay	3,250
Net present value	541

The project offers a positive NPV and should be accepted. Suppose your boss now asks you to determine the minimum acceptable annual cash receipts to make the project acceptable. In effect, this means that the present value of the annuity can fall to the initial investment of £3,250 to give a zero net present value.

Break-even annual cash receipt = 3,250/3.791 = £857

The annual future benefits could fall as low as £857 before the investment ceases to be viable.

Summary

The objective of the firm is to create as much wealth as possible by the effective use of its existing and future resources. In assessing capital projects, managers should follow the net present value rule, which states that a project is acceptable if the present value of anticipated cash flows exceeds the present value of anticipated cash outflows. Two important lessons were discussed:

1. project acceptability depends on cash flows and the perceived risk of those cash flows;
2. the present value of an expected cash flow decreases with time.

Although it is essential for the student of finance to understand the mathematics of net present value, discount tables will normally be employed for adjusting cash flows for the time-value of money.

Questions

1. Define the main elements in the capital budgeting decision.
2. Give four reasons why £1 now is worth more than £1 tomorrow.
3. What do you understand by the net present value rule?
4. Explain the difference between accounting profit and cash flow.

Use the discount tables in the appendices to solve the following problems:

5. Calculate the present value of £1,000 receivable 12 years hence, assuming the discount rate (cost of capital, percentage interest rate, discount factor, capitalisation rate) to be 12 per cent.
6. Calculate the present value of £623 receivable in 8 years' time plus £1,092 receivable 8 years after that, assuming an interest rate of 7 per cent.
7. Calculate the present value of a ten-year annuity of £100, assuming an interest rate of 20 per cent.
8. Calculate the present value of £250 receivable annually for 21 years plus £1,200 receivable after 22 years, assuming an interest rate of 11 per cent.
9. A firm is considering the purchase of a machine which will cost £20,000. It is estimated that annual savings of £5,000 will result from the machine's installation, that the life of the machine will be 5 years, and that its residual value will be £1,000. Assuming the required rate of return to be 10 per cent, what action would you recommend?
10. Calculate the net present value of projects *A* and *B*, assuming discount rates of 0 per cent, 10 per cent and 20 per cent.

	A	*B*
	£	£
Initial outlay	1,200	1,200
Cash receipts:		
Year 1	1,000	100
Year 2	500	600
Year 3	100	1,100

Which is the superior project at each level of discount rate? Why do they not all produce the same answer?

11. The directors of Yorkshire Autopoints are considering the acquisition of an automatic car-washing installation. The initial cost and setting-up expenses will amount to about £140,000. Its estimated life is about 7 years, and estimated annual accounting profit is as follows:

Year	1	2	3	4	5	6	7
Operational cash flow	£30,000	50,000	60,000	60,000	30,000	20,000	20,000
Depreciation	20,000	20,000	20,000	20,000	20,000	20,000	20,000
Accounting profit	10,000	30,000	40,000	40,000	10,000	–	–

At the end of its 7-year life, the installation will yield only a few pounds in scrap value. The company classifies its projects as follows:

	Required rate of return
Low risk	20 per cent
Average risk	30 per cent
High risk	40 per cent

Car-washing projects are estimated to be of average risk.

(a) Should the car-wash be installed?

(b) List some of the popular errors made in assessing capital projects.

Notes

1. This formula derives from the present value formula

$$PV = \frac{X}{1+i} + \frac{X}{(1+i)^2} + \frac{X}{(1+i)^3} + \ldots.$$

Let $X/(1+i) = a$ and $1/(1+i) = b$. We now have

(i) $PV = a(1 + b + b^2 + \ldots.)$

Multiplying both sides by b gives us

(ii) $PVb = a(b + b^2 + b^3 + \ldots.)$

Subtracting (ii) from (i) we have

$$PV(1-b) = a$$

Substituting for a and b,

$$PV\left(1 - \frac{1}{1+i}\right) = \frac{X}{1+i}$$

Multiplying both sides by $(1 + i)$ and rearranging, we have

$$PV = \frac{X}{i}$$

2. In note 1 we obtained

$$PV(1-b) = a$$

Redefining $b = (1+g)/(1+i)$ and keeping $a = X/(1+i)$,

$$PV\left(1 - \frac{1+g}{1+i}\right) = \frac{X}{1+i}$$

Multiplying both sides by $(1 + i)$ and rearranging, we have

$$PV = \frac{X}{i-g}$$

Further Reading

Brealey, R. and Myers, S. (1984) *Principles of Corporate Finance*, McGraw-Hill.

Dean, J. (1954) 'Measuring the productivity of capital', *Harvard Business Review*, January–February.

Levy, H. and Sarnat, M. (1982) *Capital Investment and Financial Decisions*, Prentice-Hall.

3

The Investment–Consumption Decision

We suggested in the previous chapter that managers should base investment decisions on the net present value criterion: accept all projects which offer a positive net present value. It is now necessary to justify this claim by presenting the theoretical case as to why the NPV rule makes sense both for the firm and its owners.

There are really only three basic financing decisions available to individuals and shareholders:

1. *Consumption decisions:* How much of the resources available should be spent on immediate consumption?
2. *Investment decisions:* How much of the resources available should I forego *now* in the expectation of *increased* resources at some time in the future? How should such decisions be made?
3. *Financing decisions:* How much cash should I borrow or lend to enable me to carry out the above investment and consumption decisions?

Clearly, these decisions are interrelated and should not, therefore, be viewed in isolation. To simplify our discussion we will initially consider only investment and consumption decisions, assuming that a capital market does not exist (or if it does, we do not have access to it).

Individuals are faced with the choice of how much of their wealth should be *consumed* immediately and how much should be *invested* for consumption at a later date. This applies equally to the young child with his pocket money, the undergraduate with his grant, the businessman with his capital, and the shareholder with his investment portfolio. All these cases involve a trade-off between immediate and delayed consumption. We are primarily concerned with how managers should reach investment decisions. Cash generated from business operations can be utilized in two ways: it can be distributed to the shareholders in the form of a dividend, or reinvested within the business. At least once each year the directors decide how much of the shareholders' wealth to distribute in the form of dividends and how much to withhold for investment purposes, such as building up stock levels or purchasing new equipment. The shareholders, who ultimately control the company, will only be willing to forego a higher *present* level of consumption (in the form of dividends) if they expect an even greater *future* level of consumption. It is this willingness to give up consumption now with the aim of increasing future consumption which characterises investment decisions.

Assumptions

In order to present a conceptual framework for the NPV rule it is first necessary to make certain simplifying assumptions that allow us to portray in two-dimensional form the essential features of the investment–consumption decision model. The basic assumptions are:

1. Only two periods are considered — the present period (t_o) and the next period (t_1). This two-period model implies that investments involve an immediate cash outlay in t_o in return for a cash benefit in the following period, t_1.
2. Investors are wealth maximisers.
3. All decision-relevant information is known with certainty.
4. Investment projects are entirely independent of each other and are divisible.

Two other assumptions are made which will be subsequently lifted:

5. No capital market exists for lending or borrowing funds.
6. The firm is owner-managed. In other words, management and ownership are not different individuals or groups.

The reader will recognise that these assumptions are hopelessly unrealistic in the actual setting within which investment decisions are taken in practice. Nonetheless, unless the logic of the net present value approach is first understood within this highly-simplified setting, it is doubtful whether its relevance and limitations can be fully grasped within the complex real world of business.

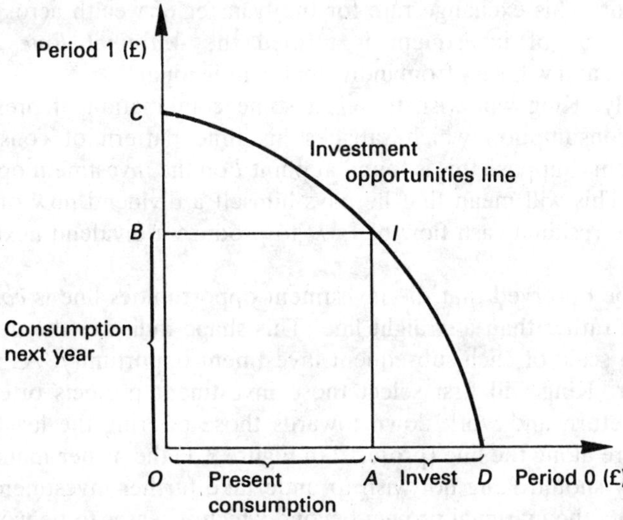

Figure 3.1 Investment – Consumption Decision

Graphical Approach

David King is the owner-manager of King Ltd. The graph in Figure 3.1 illustrates the range of consumption possibilities open to him. The curve *CD* is the investment opportunities line, representing the physical investments available to the firm. At one extreme, King may decide to spend all his wealth this year by liquidating the company and receiving £*D*. Obviously, this will leave him with no wealth left in the business next year. As King is willing to forego increasing amounts of present consumption, he transfers wealth to the next period, the maximum investment being £*D* which would yield £*C* consumption next year.

How should King proceed to make investment decisions under the assumptions laid down? He requires a criterion for judging between cash today and cash receivable next year. In effect, he requires a *rate of exchange for the transfer of wealth across time*. Suppose King requires a minimum of £112 receivable next year to induce him to give up £100 now: his rate of exchange would be $112_{t1}/100_{t0}$ or 1.12/1. This represents a premium for delayed consumption of one year of

$$112/100 - 1 = 0.12 \text{ or } 12\%$$

This exchange rate between today's money and tomorrow's money is not static—it will change with the level of present consumption sacrificed. King may be willing to forego the first £100 of potential dividend in return for an additional 12 per cent next year, but to persuade him to delay the consumption of a further £100 will probably require something in excess of

12 per cent. This exchange rate for the transfer of wealth across time at various levels of investment is termed the *Marginal Rate of Time Preference*, and will vary from individual to individual.

Typically, King will wish to select some combination of present and delayed consumption which satisfies his time pattern of consumption requirement. Suppose this is found at point *I* on the investment opportunities line. This will mean that he pays himself a dividend now of £*A* and invests the residual cash flow of £*AD* to produce a dividend next year of £*B*.

It will be observed that the investment opportunities line is *concave* to the origin rather than a straight line. This shape indicates the decreasing returns to scale of each subsequent investment opportunity. As a wealth maximiser, King will first select those investment projects offering the greatest return and work down towards those offering the least return. Somewhere along the line (project *I* in Figure 3.1) the owner-manager will stop. Why should King not wish to undertake further investment? Point *I* represents the marginal project beyond which it ceases to be worthwhile to invest — the marginal return from the next £1 in investment would not be sufficient to compensate for the sacrifice involved in giving up a further £1 in dividends. For King, *I* represents the point where the *marginal return on investment equals his marginal rate of time preference*.

Investor Attitude

Individuals are not homogeneous in their attitudes towards investment–consumption decisions. In our simple example of a single owner-manager it is possible to describe in graphical form King's preferences for money expenditures at different points in time by *utility curves*. Utility curves, in this context, indicate all possible combinations of consumption in the two periods considered which offer constant utility, or welfare. The form of the utility function can be seen in Figure 3.2. At any point along any utility curve the owner is indifferent to (i.e. equally satisfied with) the trade-off between present and future consumption. The owner can only obtain a higher level of satisfaction if the investment opportunities are such as to permit a shift from one level of utility to a higher level (e.g. from *U*1 to *U*2).

The slope at any point along a utility curve indicates the owner's marginal rate of time preference between present and future consumption. Using Figure 3.2, it is possible to identify that point on the investment opportunities line which derives the maximum utility for the owner. This is located at point *I* — the point of tangency between the investment opportunities line and the highest utility curve. In other words, this point is where the owner's marginal rate of time preference equals the return on the marginal investment project undertaken by the firm. It makes no sense

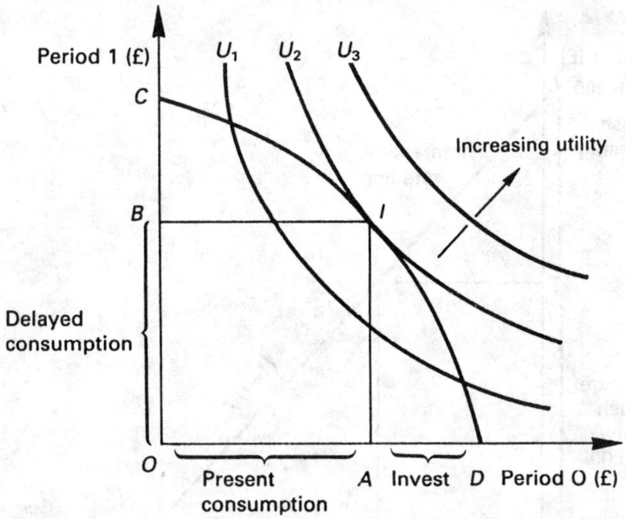

Figure 3.2 Determining the Level of Investment for an Owner-Manager in the Absence of Capital Markets

for our owner-manger, David King, to invest beyond this point as the investment returns will not satisfy the minimum return he requires for further delaying consumption.

Borrowing and Lending Opportunities

So far, under our highly simplistic assumptions, our owner-manager, King, is given only two decisions — consumption and investment decisions. The more he invests, the less he can consume now and vice versa. This ignores the third choice open to him, namely the *financing decision*. Where capital markets exist, individuals and firms can buy and sell not only *real* assets (i.e. fixed and current) but also *financial* assets. As we saw in Chapter 2, when perfect capital markets are introduced (i.e. no borrower can influence the interest rate, all traders have equal and costless access to information, no transaction costs or taxes) there will be a single market rate of interest for both borrowing and lending.

The existence of a capital market permits owners to transfer wealth across time in a manner different from the investment–consumption pattern of the firm. This is depicted by the interest rate line *LK* in Figure 3.3 which represents the exchange rate between current and future cash flows under perfect capital market conditions. Its slope is $1 + r$, where r denotes the single period rate of interest. If S represents the present cash flow for a firm, by lending all of it on the capital market the firm could increase its future cash flows by $(1 + r)S$ or £TL. Conversely, by borrowing against the firm's

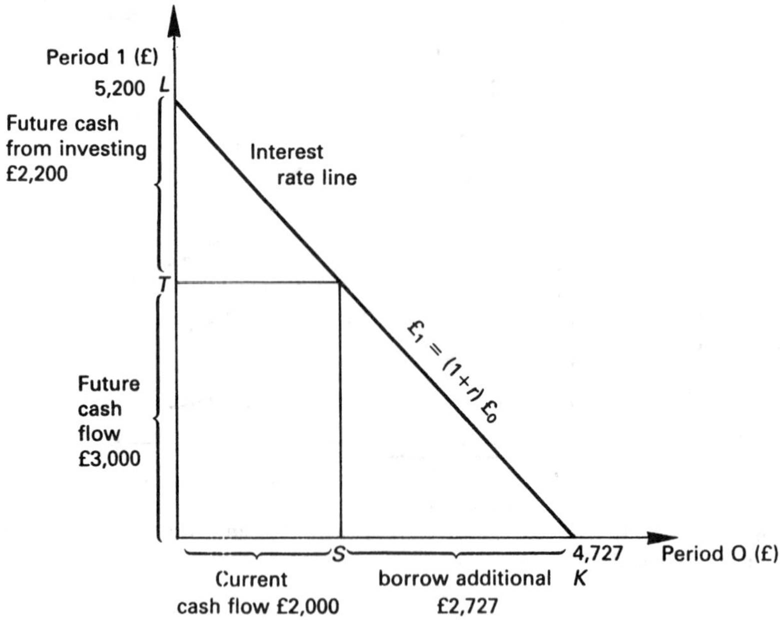

Figure 3.3 Transfer of Wealth across Time by Borrowing and Lending

future cash flow of £T, it could increase its present consumption by $T/(1 + r)$ or £SK.

It is probably easier to illustrate the above by a numeric example. King has £2,000 in cash and will receive £3,000 in cash next year. If these are the only transactions involved and the market rate of interest is 10%, he could invest the whole £2000 on the capital market to yield 2,000 (1 + 0.10), or £2,200 next year, in addition to the £3,000 he will already receive. This gain is represented by LT in Figure 3.3. Alternatively, he could borrow from the capital market against his future cash flow of £3,000 to produce 3,000/(1 + 0.10) or £2,727 today, i.e. SK. Thus King would have a maximum present cash flow of £2,000 + £2,727 = £4,727, available for immediate consumption in the form of dividends.

Separating Ownership from Management

The introduction of *financial* investment opportunities is extremely important for two reasons: firstly, it enables the owner to achieve a higher level of utility than would otherwise be possible; and secondly, it enables us to devise an investment criterion satisfying both managers and shareholders alike. Most firms are characterised by a large number of shareholders (owners), few of whom are actively involved in the management of the firm. It would obviously be an impossible task for managers to evaluate investment decisions on the basis of the personal investment–consumption preferences of all the shareholders. Happily, the existence of capital markets renders any such foolhardy attempt unnecessary. Managers do not need to devise the firm's investment schedule such that its cash flows match shareholders' preferred time patterns of consumption. The task of the manager is to maximise present value by accepting all investment proposals offering a return at least as good as the market rate of interest.

This criterion maximises the current wealth of the shareholders who can then transform that wealth into whatever time pattern of consumption they require. This they can do by lending or borrowing on the capital market until their marginal rate of time preference equals the capital market rate of interest. This *Separation Theorem*[1], as it is usually termed, leads to the following decision rules:

1. Corporate management should invest in projects offering positive net present values when discounted at the capital market rate.
2. Shareholders should borrow or lend on the capital market to produce the wealth distribution which best meets their personal time pattern of consumption requirements.

We can now incorporate in Figure 3.4 the interest rate line and investment opportunities line of Figures 3.3 and 3.2. Suppose David King's business is acquired by Stuart Prince, but King remains as manager, agreeing to act in the new owner's interests. Ownership and management are now separate. How will this influence decision making? The answer depends on the availability of capital markets.

In the absence of capital markets the firm should invest up to project I, where the marginal rate of return on investments *equals* the new owner's marginal rate of time preference as reflected in the slope of the utility curve U_1 at I. This would result in £A being distributed this year to Prince (in dividends) and £AD being invested to provide £B wealth next year. With the introduction of financing opportunities afforded by the capital market, the firm can increase its level of investment to project E — where the interest rate line LK is tangential to the investment opportunities line. At this point all investments offering a return at least as high as the market rate of interest are accepted. They all offer positive net present values. Prince now receives a lower dividend of £F this year and a higher dividend of £G next year.

However, Prince is short of cash, having just acquired the new business. By borrowing or lending on the capital market he can now transform this wealth distribution which maximises the value of the firm into whatever time pattern of consumption he desires. In Figure 3.4 this is found for our shareholder at point M, where the interest rate line is tangential to the utility curve U_2. Prince's strong preference for cash leads him to borrow £FR to produce a total consumption in the present year of £R and £S in the next. The

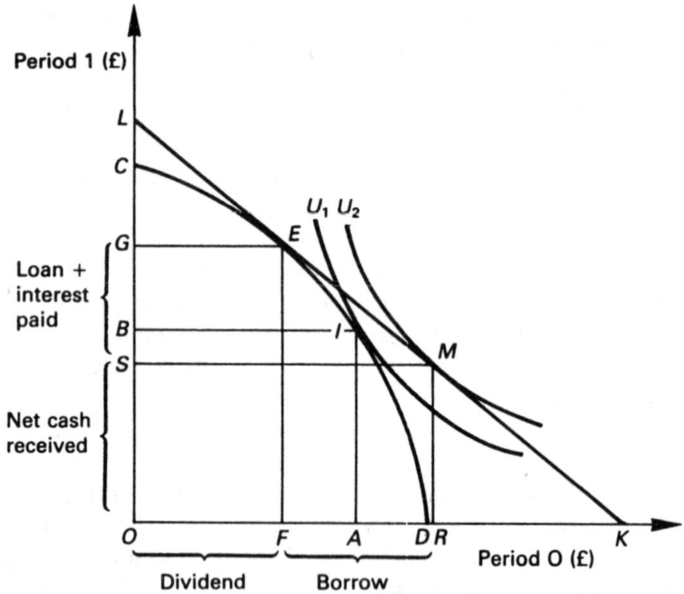

Figure 3.4 Real and Financial Investment Opportunities

company will still pay a dividend of £*G* next year, of which £*GS* will be used by Prince to repay the loan plus interest. Thus, by lending or borrowing on the capital market, the owner has been able to attain a higher utility curve (U_2) and present level of consumption than would otherwise have been possible. At the same time, management has continued to evaluate investment projects using the net present value rule. Let us now apply the foregoing to a worked numerical example.

Example

Joe Baker is the sole proprietor of Baker Enterprises, a new business with only one asset of £4,000 cash. Figure 3.5 portrays the investment opportunities available to the firm (curved line) and the interest rate line (straight line), representing the exchange rate between the present and next year. All investments are of one-year duration. Baker is looking for a current dividend of £1,500.

1. How much should the firm invest in real assets?
2. What is the interest rate?
3. What is the net present value of this level of investment?
4. What is the value of the company after making this investment?
5. How much will Baker receive next year?

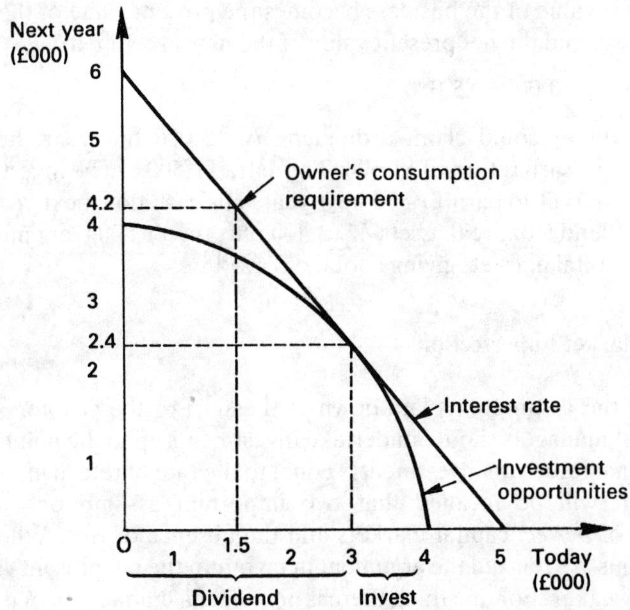

Figure 3.5 Investment and Financing Opportunities for Baker Enterprises

Solution

1. The maximum the firm can invest is the £4,000 cash available (ignoring the possibility of borrowing against higher expected cash flows). However, the firm should invest only up to the point where the marginal rate of return on investment equates with the interest rate. This would mean a dividend of £3,000 today and an investment of £1,000 (i.e. £4,000 – £3,000). It simply is not worth the firm investing beyond this amount as these projects offer negative net present values.
2. The interest rate is found by relating present wealth to next year's wealth:

   6,000/5,000 = 1.20

   The interest rate is therefore 20 per cent.
3. Cash flow from the £1,000 investment programme is £2,400. The net present value is:

   NPV = (£2,400/1.20) – £1,000
   = £2,000 – £1,000
   = £1,000

   This represents an internal rate of return on these projects of 1,000/1,000 = 100 per cent. Alternatively, the present value of £2,000 can be found by reference to the interest rate line (£5,000 – £3,000).

4. The new value of the business becomes the present value of the existing cash asset and the net present value of the new investment:

   £4,000 + £1,000 = £5,000

5. While Baker could claim a dividend of £3,000 this year, he is only requiring a cash return of £1,500. The extra £1,500 can be invested in the capital market to earn £1,800 next year. His cash flow next year will be the dividend from real assets of £2,400 plus the £1,800 from money lent to the capital market, giving a total of £4,200.

Capital Market Imperfections

Based on the assumptions laid down at the start of the chapter, we have shown that managers should undertake investments up to the point at which the marginal return on investment is equal to the rate of return in the capital market. It will be recalled that two important assumptions were the existence of *perfect* capital markets and the absence of risk. Where these assumptions are relaxed the argument in favour of the net present value rule becomes weaker. For one thing there is no longer a unique rate of interest in the capital market, but a range of interest rates varying with the status of borrower, the amount required and the perceived riskiness of the investment. Risk will be the subject of subsequent chapters. At this stage all that need be said is that a project's return should be compared with the rate of return on investments in the capital market of *equivalent risk* — the greater the investment risk, the higher the required rate of return.

Our concern here is with capital market imperfections where these are such that the borrowing rate is substantially higher than the lending rate. When this is the case the two-period investment model will look something like Figure 3.6. The steeper line represents the interest rate for the borrower and the flatter line represents the lending rate. The existence of two different interest rates gives rise to two different points on the investment opportunities line *CD*. Prospective borrowers, having to pay a higher rate of interest for funds, would prefer the company to invest only £*BD* this year (i.e. up to project *Y*). However, prospective lenders will require the company to discount at the lower lending rate leading to a much greater investment of £*AD*, with investment *X* being the marginal project.

There is no simple solution to the investment–consumption decision when capital market imperfections prevail. Fortunately, in the UK and the USA the capital markets are highly competitive and function fairly well so that differences between lending and borrowing rates are minimised.

Summary

In this chapter we have examined, with the aid of a series of two-period

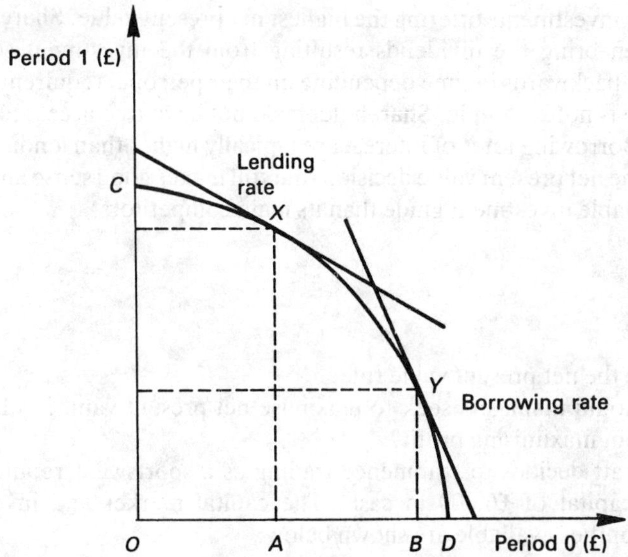

Figure 3.6 Investment Decisions in Imperfect Capital Markets

investment–consumption models, why the net present value makes sense for investment decision purposes. This logic can be summarised as follows:

1. Managers are assumed to act in the best interest of the owners or shareholders.
2. This they can do by seeking to increase shareholders' wealth in the form of maximising cash flows through time. There is a rate of exchange between current and future wealth which is reflected in the market rate of interest.
3. Managers should undertake all projects up to the point at which the marginal return on the investment is equal to the rate of interest on equivalent financial investments in the capital market. This is exactly the same as the net present value rule: accept all investments offering positive net present values when discounted at the equivalent market rate of interest. The result is an increase in the market value of the firm and thus in the market value of the shareholders' stake in the firm.
4. Management need not concern itself with shareholders' particular time patterns of consumption or risk preferences. In well-functioning capital markets shareholders can borrow or lend funds to achieve their personal consumption requirements. Furthermore, by carefully combining risky and safe investments they can achieve the desired risk characteristics for those consumption requirements.

The net present value concept permits efficient separation of ownership and corporate management. Managers should select that package of investments offering the highest net present value. Shareholders should then bring the dividends resulting from the investment schedule forward or backwards in time depending on their personal requirements. In reality, life is not so simple. Shareholders do not have free access to capital markets. Borrowing rates of interest are typically higher than lending rates. Even so, the net present value decision rule still makes good sense and offers a more reliable investment guide than its main competitors.

Questions

1. What is the net present value rule?
2. Why should managers seek to maximise net present value? Is business not about maximising profit?
3. Ron Bratt decides to commence trading as a sportswear retailer, with initial capital of £6,000 in cash. The capital market and investment opportunities available are shown below:

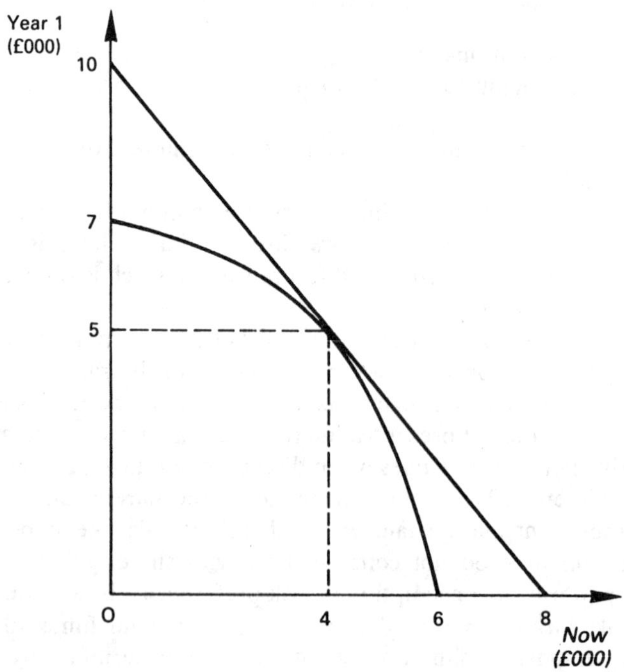

You are required to calculate:
   (i) how much the firm should invest in real assets;
   (ii) the market rate of interest for the business;
   (iii) the average rate of return on investment;

(iv) the net present value of the investment;
(v) the value of the firm after this level of investment;
(vi) next year's dividend if Bratt only requires a current dividend of £3,000.

4. What are the assumptions underlying the two-period investment–consumption model?
5. How does the net present value rule permit the separation of ownership from management?
6. Packers Ltd has been offered a contract to manufacture a batch of chemicals. The company's managers estimate that it will take two years to produce the chemicals. The price offered is £235,000 expressed in current pounds sterling. This price will be increased in line with increases in the Retail Price Index during the contract period, and the adjusted amount will be paid in full when the chemicals are delivered at the end of two years.

   Production of the chemicals will require the following resources:

   (1) A machine will be purchased immediately for £75,000 for exclusive use on this contract. The machine will have a two-year life and no scrap or resale value.
   (2) Ten men who are currently employed by the company will each work for two years on production of the chemicals. The total cost of employing one man is currently £6,000 per annum, based on wage rates which have recently been agreed for the coming year. The managers expect to negotiate wage rates at the end of one year; as a result, they expect that total employment costs for the second year of the contract will rise by a factor of 1.25 multiplied by the rate of increase in the Retail Price Index. (For example, if the Retail Price Index increases by 8%, total employment costs will rise by 8% × 1.25, which equals 10%). You may assume that all employment costs are payable on the last day of the year to which they relate.

       If the chemicals contract is not accepted, there will be no work within the company for the ten men during the coming two years and they will be made redundant. The company will incur a net redundancy cost of £200 for each man payable immediately. The managers expect new orders after two years and the company will re-employ the ten men at the end of the second year. Administrative and advertising costs associated with the re-employment are expected to be £500 per man. This amount will not be affected by inflation during the next two years.
   (3) 2,000 units of raw material *D* will be needed immediately and 2,000 units will be needed at the end of one year. Packers Ltd has 2,000 units of *D* in stock. These units originally cost £18 per unit and have a current replacement cost of £20 per unit. The company has

no use for material *D* other than on the contract offered, and if the contract is rejected, the units in stock will be disposed of at an immediate cost of £1.50 per unit. (The material is highly specialised and cannot be resold.) The cost of buying material *D* is expected to rise during the coming year by a factor of 1.5 multiplied by the rate of increase in the Retail Price Index.

Packers Ltd has a money cost of capital of 15% per annum, which is not expected to be affected by any future change in the rate of inflation. The managers estimate that the Retail Price Index will increase at a rate of 10% per annum compound during the next two years.

You are required to:

(i) calculate the net present value of the contract which has been offered to Packers Ltd;

(ii) estimate, to the nearest one per cent, the rate of increase in the Retail Price Index over the next two years at which the net present value of the contract is zero;

(iii) outline the arguments for and against the indexation of input and output prices in long-term contracts from the point of view of both the buyer and the seller.

Ignore taxation. (ICA, PE II, July 1983)

Notes

1. The Separation Theorem was first noted by J. Tobin (1958) in 'Liquidity preference as behavior toward risk', *Review of Economic Studies*, February, pp. 65–86.

Further Reading

Fama, E. F. and Miller, M. H. (1972) *The Theory of Finance*, Holt, Rinehart and Winston.

Fisher, I. (1965) *The Theory of Interest*, Augustus M. Kelley.

Hirshleifer, J. (1958) 'On the theory of optimal investment decisions', *Journal of Political Economy*, August.

4

Techniques of Capital Investment Appraisal

Several techniques are available which help managers to identify those projects which *make money*...*satisfying consumer wants*...in *competitive markets*. In this book we propose that the objective of the firm is to create a positive cash flow, the selling value of its outputs being greater than the cash paid for its inputs. We also propose that the maximum benefit to society is achieved when companies strive to satisfy consumer wants rather than have the 'needs' of society dictated by the government. We further advocate competitive markets which offer a choice and satisfy consumer wants. Without offering any lengthy treatise in defence of the capitalist system, we suggest that such a system results in the greatest amount of created wealth. It is not necessarily a 'fair' system, and therefore we find that all capitalist systems do have amounts of state involvement to a greater or lesser extent.

The net present value approach to measuring the wealth created by investment projects was discussed in Chapter 2. In this chapter we introduce some of the other commonly used managerial techniques for assessing capital projects. We give brief explanations of the use of the following techniques:

1. Net present value
2. Internal rate of return or yield
3. Profitability index or cost benefit ratio
4. Payback period
5. Discounted payback period
6. Return on capital employed

7. Effect on earnings per share

Financial management theorists assert that the objective of the firm is to create as much wealth for consumption as possible. *Wealth is created* when *the market value of the outputs exceeds the market value of the inputs*. In assessing capital projects, managers should follow the *net present value rule* which states that a project is acceptable if the present value of anticipated incremental cash inflows exceeds the present value of the anticipated incremental cash outflows. Studies of managerial behaviour reveal that managers pursue objectives relating to sales, market share, number of employees, growth in assets, return on capital employed, increasing earnings per share, and their own personal satisfaction. However, we still insist that the fundamental objective of industrial and commercial enterprises is the creation of wealth, the production of consumable goods and services which are worth more than they cost, the management of projects which are worth more than they cost, the creation of a positive cash flow, the making of money satisfying consumer wants in competitive markets.

Managers create wealth by ensuring that the market value of the firm's outputs is greater than the market value of its inputs. Cash flows in from customers, and cash flows out to suppliers of goods, labour, services, and capital items. All projects can be assessed by calculating the net cash flows accruing to the firm, using the net present value rule, after taking into account the risk and timing of cash flows associated with the project. We will again consider the net present value approach against which other techniques will be compared.

1. Net Present Value

The objective of the firm is to create wealth by using existing and future resources to produce goods and services now and in the future with greater value than the resources consumed. To create wealth now, the present value of anticipated cash inflows must exceed the present value of all anticipated cash outflows. The net present value (NPV) of a project is the sum of all future cash flows discounted at the required rate of return minus the present value of the cost of the investment. The NPV rule is illustrated as follows:

$$NPV = \sum_{t=1}^{n} \frac{R_t}{(1 + k)^t} - C$$

where R_t = expected net cash inflows, k = the required rate of return on the project, C = the immediate capital outlay (or alternatively the present value of all capital outlays). Put into words, the net present value (NPV) of a project is the sum (Σ) of all anticipated net cash inflows

(R_t) from year 1 ($t = 1$) to the end of the project life (n), discounted at the project's required rate of return (k), less the cost of investing in the project (C). The following simple example will be used to illustrate the application of all the techniques discussed in the chapter.

Investment opportunity The initial capital outlay to finance an investment opportunity is £100. It is anticipated that the project will yield net cash inflows of £60 at the end of year 1 and £60 at the end of year 2. The firm operates in an industry in which three classes of project are available: class A where the project risk is low and the required rate of return is 10 per cent; class B where the risk is average for the industry and the required rate of return is 13 per cent; and class C where the risk is fairly high and the required rate of return is 16 per cent. We are required to evaluate the project assuming that it is, firstly, a class A project; secondly, class B; and thirdly, class C. The NPV formula will provide the guidelines as to whether or not the project should be accepted.

$$\text{Class A NPV} = \frac{60}{1+0.1} + \frac{60}{(1+0.1)^2} - 100$$
$$= 54 + 50 - 100 = 4$$

$$\text{Class B NPV} = \frac{60}{1+0.13} + \frac{60}{(1+0.13)^2} - 100$$
$$= 53 + 47 - 100 = 0$$

$$\text{Class C NPV} = \frac{60}{1+0.16} + \frac{60}{(1+0.16)^2} - 100$$
$$= 52 + 44 - 100 = (4)$$

If the project is low risk, the £60 anticipated at the end of year 1 is discounted at 10 per cent, giving a present value of £54. The £60 expected at the end of year 2 has to be brought back to the present at 10 per cent, giving a present value of only £50. The cash flows anticipated from the investment have a present value of £104, whereas the cost of buying into the project is only £100. The project is therefore a *wealth-creating opportunity* with a present value of £4. The project is worth more than its cost. The project offers a positive cash flow. It appears that acceptance of the project will result in the company making money satisfying consumer wants in competitive markets.

From the calculations we can see one of the important messages of the net present value approach. Cash now is worth more than cash expected in the future. £60 today is worth £60 today, £60 expected in one year's time discounted at 10 per cent is worth £54 today, £60 anticipated in two years' time is worth £50 today, and so on. If the project is classified as a Class B project, it has a zero NPV. The project yields 13 per cent. Discounting at 13 per cent yields a zero net present value. If the required rate of return on the project is 13 per cent, it is just about worthwhile. Again we can see that cash flows in the future are worth less than immediate cash balances. £60 anticipated in one year's time discounted at 13 per cent has a present value of £53, reducing to £47 if the cash flow is expected in two years' time. If the project is categorised as class C, it has a negative NPV. Discounting at 16 per cent, the cash flows have a present value of only £96 which compares unfavourably with the initial outlay of £100. The project is unacceptable if the required rate of return is 16 per cent. The present value of the cash inflows is less than the present value of the outflow.

From the above calculations we can also appreciate the second important lesson of the NPV formula. *The higher the risk of a cash flow, the lower is its present value*. We can see that £60 expected in two years' time has a present value of £50 discounting at 10 per cent, £47 discounted at 13 per cent, and £44 discounted at 16 per cent. We can therefore note that the present value of a cash flow decreases with both time and risk. The further we go into the future, the lower is the present value of an anticipated cash flow. The higher the risk of an anticipated cash flow, the lower will be its present value. The results of our calculations are repeated in Table 4.1.

Table 4.1 Net Present Value of a Project

Risk class	*Discount rate*	*Present value of cash inflows* *Yr 1*	*Yr 2*	*Cost*	*NPV*
A	10%	£54	£50	£100	−£4
B	13%	£53	£47	£100	£0
C	16%	£52	£44	£100	−£4

Again, if the project is classified as low risk, then the cash flows are discounted at 10 per cent. The Year 1 cash flow has a present value of £54 and the Year 2 cash flow has a present value of £50. The present value of the inflows is £104 and, after deducting the initial outlay which has a present value of £100, the project has a net present value of £4. The project should be accepted; it has a positive NPV; it creates wealth. Given the projected cash flows, the market value of the firm should rise by £4. On the other hand, if the project is classified as fairly high risk, the cash inflows are discounted at 16 per cent, and the NPV is estimated at £4 negative. The project is therefore unacceptable; it has a negative NPV. Its acceptance would have the effect of reducing the firm's market value by £4. Clearly, it would not be wise to exchange £100 today for future cash flows having a present value of only £96. If the project is classified as average risk, then the discount rate used is 13 per cent, yielding an NPV of £0. The project is just acceptable. It *yields* the expected 13 per cent. From this example we can draw three important conclusions:

(i) Project acceptability depends upon cash flows and risk.
(ii) The present value of a given expected cash flow decreases with time.
(iii) The higher the risk of a given set of expected cash flows (and therefore the higher the discount rate), the lower will be its present value. The present value of a given expected cash flow decreases as its risk increases.

2. *Internal Rate of Return*

The NPV rule offers a theoretically sound answer to the accept/reject problem. An alternative approach is to calculate an investment's *internal rate of return* (IRR), sometimes called the *yield*. The internal rate of return is the rate of return which equates the anticipated net cash flows with the initial outlay. To calculate the IRR, it is necessary to solve the following formula for R:

$$0 = \sum_{t=1}^{n} \frac{R}{(1 + r)^t} - C$$

where r is the rate of return which gives a zero NPV, all the other symbols being the same as for the NPV formula. A project is acceptable if its yield or IRR is greater than the required rate of return on the project. In our example k represented the required rate of return. In the vast majority of cases the IRR method of appraising capital projects gives exactly the same accept/reject decision as NPV. Projects with positive net present values will have values of r greater than k. In the case of the example already used, the project's yield is 13 per cent:

$$\frac{60}{(1 + 0.13)} + \frac{60}{(1 + 0.13)^2} - 100 = 0$$

If the project is categorised as class A, it is acceptable because the yield of 13 per cent is greater than the required rate of return of 10 per cent. If the project is classified as B, it is just acceptable. The project would be rejected as a class C project because it earns less than 16 per cent. We always recommend managers to use the NPV method because it is easier to handle than IRR. Without the use of a computer the yield calculation can be laborious. There are other problems with IRR which we discuss in the appendix to this chapter. Chapter 15 discusses why the IRR method is so popular among managers.

3. *Profitability Index (Cost–Benefit Ratio)*

A third and equally correct method for assessing capital expenditure decisions is the Profitability Index, sometimes called the *Cost–Benefit Ratio*. The Profitability Index (PI) is the present value of anticipated net future cash flows *divided* by the initial outlay.

$$PI = \frac{\sum_{t=1}^{N} Rt/(1 + k)^t}{C}$$

The only difference between the NPV and PI methods is that when using the NPV technique the initial outlay is *deducted* from the present value of anticipated cash flows, whereas with the PI approach the initial outlay is *divided* into the present value of anticipated cash flows. A project is acceptable if its profitability is greater than one. Clearly, a project offering a PI greater than one must also offer a net present value which is positive. In our example:

$$\text{Class A PI} = \frac{60(1.736)}{100} = 1.04$$

$$\text{Class B PI} = \frac{60(1.668)}{100} = 1.00$$

$$\text{Class C PI} = \frac{60(1.605)}{100} = 0.96$$

If we are considering a class A project, the profitability index is greater than one and the project is acceptable. As a class B project, the project is just acceptable having a profitability index of 1.00. At 16 per cent the profitability index is 0.96 which is less than one and the project would appear to be unacceptable. The profitability index method gives exactly the same accept/reject indication offered by the net present value formula. We shall return to this measure of investment performance in Chapter 9 when considering the approach to be adopted when there is insufficient capital to finance all the projects required.

4. Payback Period

The NPV rule provides a good guideline to assist managers in making sensible wealth-creating decisions. However, there are several other techniques for assessing capital projects which may give misleading indications as to whether or not an investment should be accepted. Other popular methods examine the project payback period, the discounted payback period, the return on capital employed, and the effect on earnings per share. The payback period is the length of time required to recover the initial investment. In our example, the payback period is two years if the cash flows are received at the end of year 1 and year 2. By the end of year 2 the sum of £120 is expected, which more than recovers the initial outlay. If the cash flows were receivable on a monthly basis, the payback period would be approximately one and two-thirds years. Given the estimated payback period, is the project acceptable? Clearly, we do not have enough information to make a decision because we do not know whether or not the project is wealth-creating. The payback method is inadequate because it involves the subjective establishment of an acceptable payback period — frequently cited as two and a half years. Payback period is often criticised as an appraisal method because it may ignore big payoffs beyond the payback point. Most managers, however, are eminently sensible people who do not ignore big payoffs beyond the cut-off point. The payback period is used to test a manager's gut reaction to a project. It gives the manager a 'feel' as to the length of time cash is at risk. As will be seen in Chapter 15, the payback period is very popular with managers, and when applied intelligently, combines well with the NPV method.

5. *Discounted Payback Period*

The discounted payback period is different from the payback period only in that the payback period is calculated *after* discounting the cash flows. For all projects with orthodox cash flows, it will therefore always be longer than the payback period which ignores discounting. From Table 4.1 we can see that the payback period for the class A project is just under two years, for the B classification exactly two years, and for the C classification the project never achieves payback. As with the payback period, the method suffers from our inability to decide an appropriate period for payback. The discounted payback method does not indicate whether or not an investment makes money satisfying consumer wants in competitive markets.

6. *Return on Capital Employed*

Return on capital employed (ROCE), or accounting rate of return, is widely used as an indicator of performance. Managers use a great many ratios to give a feel for the performance of the business. Ratios offer rules of thumb for helping managers in four areas:

(i) in comparing this year's performance with last year's performance;
(ii) in comparing the company's performance with that of its competitors;
(iii) in comparison of actual performance with targeted performance;
(iv) in making financial plans.

We should not use return on capital employed, which is only one rule of thumb, for making decisions as to the acceptability or otherwise of projects. Return on capital employed is simply accounting profit measured as a percentage of capital employed. The ratio ignores cash flow, ignores the timing of cash flows, and ignores risk. We can see the ROCE for our project in Table 4.2. The annual cash flow is £60. Assuming that the initial investment is written off on a straight-line basis, depreciation would be £50 in year 1 and £50 in year 2. Accounting profit is therefore £10 in each year. The capital employed of £100 falls to £50 at the end of year 1 and to zero at the end of year 2. The average capital employed is therefore £75 in year 1 and £25 in year 2. The project therefore offers a return on capital employed of 13.3 per cent in the first year and 40 per cent in the second year. Is the project acceptable? We cannot make a decision on the basis of this information alone. It does not indicate whether or not the project is wealth-creating.

Table 4.2 ROCE and EPS Effect

Year	*1*	*2*
Net cash flow	£60	£60
Depreciation	£50	£50
Accounting profit	£10	£10
Average capital employed	£75	£25
ROCE	13.3%	40%
Number of shares	100	100
EPS	10p	10p

7. *Effect on Earnings Per Share*

Earnings per share is calculated by dividing accounting profit by the number of shares in issue. Again, this calculation ignores cash flow, timing and risk. It is another widely-used ratio indicating the amount of accounting profit a company has earned in one year for each share issued by the company. In our example, let us assume that the company issues 100 shares of £1 each to finance the project. From Table 4.2 we can see that the company has 100 shares in year 1, and 100 shares in year 2. Accounting profit is £10 in each period, and therefore the earnings per share amount to 10p in year 1 and 10p in year 2. Is the project acceptable? Again, we cannot make a decision because the EPS effect does not indicate whether or not a project is making money satisfying consumer wants in competitive markets. It does not tell us whether the cash flows generated by the project are worth more than the present value of the cash outlays. The acceptability of a project depends on anticipated cash flows, the timing of those cash flows, and the riskiness of the cash flows. We therefore conclude that Payback Period, Discounted Payback Period, ROCE, and EPS Effect have serious shortcomings as techniques for assessing capital projects. They may well give an incorrect go/no go indication.

A Note on Net Annual Benefit

We occasionally encounter a calculation referred to as net annual benefit. An enterprise may consider investing £100 and incurring annual expenses amounting to £20. How much must the enterprise (perhaps a public utility) charge to customers each year to earn 13 per cent on investment? The net cash flow required to give a zero NPV at 13 per cent is:

$$\text{NCF}\ (1.668) = £100$$

$$\text{NCF} = \frac{£100}{1.668} = £60$$

The gross cash flow charged to customers must therefore be £80: £20 to cover annual payments, plus £60 net cash flow. The net annual benefit indicates the amount needed to be charged annually to customers to achieve a target yield.

Application of Capital Budgeting Techniques

To conclude this chapter, we introduce an investment problem to illustrate how each of the techniques discussed above may be applied and interpreted. (The reader may wish to examine the output of computer program 1 in Chapter 18 which calculates the same investment criteria.)

Question

The following estimated cash flows relate to a project.

Year	*1*	*2*	*3*	*4*
Incremental cash inflows	£14,000	22,000	14,000	10,000
Incremental cash outflows	£ 6,000	14,000	6,000	4,000
Net cash flow	£ 8,000	8,000	8,000	6,000

An immediate cash investment in plant is required amounting to £20,000. The firm's policy is to depreciate the initial cost of a project in equal instalments over its estimated life. The project is to be financed by the issue of 20,000 ordinary shares of £1 each.

A Calculate:

1. The net present value of the project
2. The project internal rate of return/yield
3. The cost–benefit ratio/profitability index
4. Payback period
5. Discounted payback period
6. The annual return on capital employed
7. The annual earnings per share

The required rate of return on the project is estimated at 14 per cent.

B Does the project appear to be an acceptable one?

C How would your calculations be affected if the firm used a different depreciation method?

Answer

A 1. Net present value

$$8{,}000(2.322) + 6{,}000(0.592) - 20{,}000 = \underline{£2{,}128}$$

2. Internal rate of return

$$19\%\quad 8{,}000(2.140) + 6{,}000(0.499) - 20{,}000 = \underline{£114}$$

$$20\%\quad 8{,}000(2.106) + 6{,}000(0.482) - 20{,}000 = \underline{£(260)}$$

The above approximate yields have been found by trial and error. By interpolation:

$$19 + \frac{114}{374} = \underline{19.3\%} \quad \text{OR} \quad 20 - \frac{260}{374} = \underline{19.3\%}$$

The yield on the project is therefore 19.3 per cent.

3. Cost benefit ratio/profitability index

$$\frac{22{,}120}{20{,}000} = 1.1$$

4. Payback period

	Cash Flow	
	£	
Year 1	8,000	
2	8,000	
3	8,000	2½ years
4	6,000	

If the cash flows accrue at the end of each year, the payback period is three years. Assuming the cash flows accrue evenly throughout the year, the payback period is two and a half years.

5. Discounted payback period

		14%		£	
Year 1	8,000	(0.877)	=	7,016	
2	8,000	(0.769)	=	6,152	
3	8,000	(0.675)	=	5,400	
4	6,000	(0.592)	=	3,552	3.4 years
				22,120	

The discounted payback period lies between three and four years.

6. Annual return on capital employed (£):

Yr.	*Cash Flow*	*Depreciation*	*Accounting profit*	*Average book value*	*Annual return*
1	8,000	5,000	3,000	17,500	17.1%
2	8,000	5,000	3,000	12,500	24.0%
3	8,000	5,000	3,000	7,500	40.0%
4	6,000	5,000	1,000	2,500	40.0%

If we depreciate the initial cost of the investment on a straight-line basis over its estimated useful life, the £20,000 initial investment will be depreciated at £5,000 per annum. In year 1, the average book value of the investment falls from £20,000 to £15,000, an average of £17,500. In year 2, the book value of the investment falls from £15,000 to £10,000, an average of £12,500. The average investments in years 3 and 4 are £7,500 and £2,500. The annual depreciation charge of £5,000 is deducted from the annual cash flows to give accounting profit figures of £3,000 for years 1, 2 and 3, and £1,000 in year 4. Accounting profit as a percentage of average book value is 17.1 per cent in year 1, 24.0 per cent in year 2, and 40 per cent in years 3 and 4.

7. Annual earnings per share

	Accounting profit	*Earnings per share*	*Cash flow*	*CFPS*
	£		£	
Year 1	3,000	15p	8,000	40p
2	3,000	15p	8,000	40p
3	3,000	15p	8,000	40p
4	1,000	5p	6,000	30p

The number of shares is constant throughout the project at 20,000. Dividing 20,000 into the annual accounting profit gives earnings per share statistics of 15p in years 1, 2 and 3, and 5p in year 4. If we ignore the annual depreciation charge and use cash flow instead of accounting profit, we arrive at cash flow per share (CFPS) statistics of 40p in years 1, 2 and 3, and 30p in year 4.

B The project is acceptable. The net present value is positive at £2,128. The internal rate of return/yield is 19.3 per cent, which is greater than the required rate of return of 14 per cent. The cost/benefit ratio (profitability index) is 1.1, which is greater than unity. We can therefore conclude that, using discounted cash flow techniques, the project appears to be a wealth-creating opportunity. The payback period is 2½ years, and the discounted payback period 3.4 years. We cannot tell from payback period calculations whether or not the project is wealth-creating. However, it does appear to give managers a feel for the length of time corporate cash is at risk. We leave managers to decide whether the calculated payback periods are acceptable.

Calculation of average return on capital employed does not enable us to make a decision. Return on capital employed is one part of ratio analysis. Ratio analysis provides many rules of thumb by which managers can measure corporate performance against targets. Ratios can be used as aids to financial statement planning. They can be used to compare one firm with other firms in the same industry. Finally, ratios can be plotted over time to give an indication of the company's financial history. Since return on capital employed ignores cash flow, the timing of cash flow and the risk of the project, it cannot be used as a technique for accepting and rejecting investment proposals. Similarly, with calculations of earnings per share and cash flow per share, we cannot determine whether or not the project is acceptable. Earnings per share and cash flow per share are accounting statistics which, like many other statistics, can help to provide a feel for a company's financial history. They cannot be used as techniques for accepting and rejecting investment opportunities.

C Depreciation policies do not influence our decision. Depreciation is ignored in net present value, internal rate of return and profitability index calculations. Accounting profit is a concept, not a fact. Accountants have the difficult responsibility of measuring annual profit. Cash flow and profit are very different. In measuring profit in the Profit and Loss Account, accountants deduct the invoiced cost of sales and depreciation from the periodic invoiced sales. Accounting profit is therefore based on invoices, not cash. Accounting policies must be established for estimating depreciation, valuing stock, estimating bad debt provisions, treatment of research and development, estimating profit on long-term contracts, estimating after-sales service costs and accrued expenses, treatment of extraordinary items and prior-year adjustments, and estimating future taxation. We do not use these estimates of accounting profit in discounted cash flow calculations. A change from straight-line depreciation to some other method of depreciation would not affect our recommendation in any way.

Use NPV and Payback

We always make a final recommendation that managers should use NPV and payback. Use NPV because it gives the best indication of a project's contribution to shareholder wealth. Use payback because managers insist that it gives them the correct 'feel' for a project. Those of us who used to spend a good deal of time trying to persuade managers to surrender their allegiance to payback have long since abandoned all hope. So take note of the payback period — just in case the academics have got it all wrong! A number of academic papers has recently been published in defence of payback. See, for example, Boardman *et al.* (1982); Mepham (1975); Weingartner (1969); and Pike (1986).

Ranking Problems and Mutually-Exclusive Projects

In the examples we considered earlier, net present value, internal rate of return and profitability index all gave the same answer to the 'accept or reject' problem. This is the usual case. Projects with positive net present values have profitability indices greater than one, and internal rates of return greater than the required rate of return. However, some awkward problems can arise when we try to rank projects and when we try to make decisions between mutually-exclusive projects.

1. Project Size

Consider the following mutually-exclusive investment opportunities, assuming that the firm's required rate of return is 14 per cent.

Project		*A*	*B*
Initial outlay		£10,000	£5,000
Cash flows	Year 1	6,000	3,000
	2	6,000	3,000
	3	6,000	3,000
Rankings			
	NPV	3,932	1,966
	IRR	36.3%	36.3%
	PI	1.393	1.393

The present value of project A's cash flows is £6,000 (2.322) = £13,932, and the present value of project B's cash flows is £3,000 (2.322) = £6,966. Both projects are equally profitable because £10,000 yielding £6,000, £6,000, and £6,000 is the same as £5,000 yielding £3,000, £3,000 and £3,000. The internal rate of return on both projects is 36.3 per cent, but A is a bigger project. It has a higher net present value, and therefore creates more wealth than project B. If an investor has £10,000 to invest, all funds can be invested in project A. Alternatively, £5,000 can be invested in project B, and £5,000 can be invested elsewhere. We could then compare the present values of two investment schedules of £10,000 each.

Clearly, it would be possible to generate imaginary projects whereby project A has the higher net present value and project B the higher internal rate of return. All we would need to do in our example is to imagine a small increase in the cash flows expected from project B. Its net present value would increase only slightly above £1,966 but not to as much as £3,932; however, its internal rate of return would be greater than 36.3 per cent, which is higher than the internal rate of return offered by project A. Which project should we accept? Project A would have a higher net present value, but project B would have the higher internal rate of return and profitability index. The object of the exercise is to create as much wealth as possible, and we should therefore recommend acceptance of project A. However, if project B can be coupled with a second project having a greater NPV than £1,966, we should accept investment schedule B which would have a greater NPV than the £3,932 associated with investment schedule A.

2. *Multiple Solutions to IRR*

It is possible to devise situations in which multiple solutions are possible for solving the internal rate of return equation.

Example A project is expected to yield the following cash flows:

		(£)
Initial outlay	0	−100,000
Year	1	+360,000
	2	−431,000
	3	+171,600

Internal rates of return of 10 per cent, 20 per cent and 30 per cent offer multiple solutions as follows:

$$(10\%) - 100 + 360\,(0.909) - 431\,(0.826) + 171.6\,(0.751) = 0$$
$$(20\%) - 100 + 360\,(0.833) - 431\,(0.694) + 171.6\,(0.579) = 0$$
$$(30\%) - 100 + 360\,(0.769) - 431\,(0.592) + 171.6\,(0.455) = 0$$

Multiple solutions occur where there are changes of sign. In our example there are three changes in sign — from negative cash flow at the start to positive in year 1, negative in year 2 and positive in year 3. The occurrence of multiple solutions to the IRR formula can cause considerable anxiety for managers. It may even be the case that no internal rate of return can be found. Under these circumstances we cannot easily use the internal rate of return method for assessing projects and use of net present value is to be preferred. At each stage of investment the net present value method is recommended because it measures increases or reductions in shareholder wealth, and it does not offer multiple solutions.

3. *The Pattern of Cash Flows*

Consider the following mutually-exclusive investment opportunities:

Project		*A*	*B*
		£	£
Initial outlay		1,200	1,200
Cash flows	Year 1	1,000	100
	2	500	600
	3	100	1,100

Project A offers cash flows which total £1,600 over three years. The three years' cash flows on project B total £1,800. At very low required rates of return project B will have a higher net present value. For example, as Table 4.3 shows, if the required rate of return is zero, project B has a positive net present value of £600, whereas the NPV of project A is only £400. However, the biggest cash flow on project B is expected in year 3. As we increase the required rate of return, the present value of the £1,100 receivable on project

Table 4.3

DCF rate	*NPV*	
%	*A(£)*	*B(£)*
0	400	600
5	292	388
11	180	180
15	114	64
20	38	(64)
25	(29)	(173)
30	(89)	(267)

B falls. At 11 per cent, both projects have a positive net present value of £180. Beyond 11 per cent, A has the higher net present value because its largest cash flow of £1,000 does not suffer as much as the £1,100 receivable in year 3 on project B. In the unlikely event of these two projects existing in the real world, it appears difficult at first to decide which project should be accepted. In fact, managers must decide on the required rate of return on each project: if the required rate of return is 5 per cent, project B is preferred; if the required rate of return is 15 per cent, project A is preferred. If the required rate of return is 11 per cent, a manager would be indifferent as to which project is accepted.

It would be quite wrong to rank mutually-exclusive projects according to their internal rates of return. The graph in Figure 4.1 reveals that, while project A has a higher IRR than project B, it may not necessarily produce the greater net present value. However, the IRR method can be adapted to provide precisely the same ranking as the NPV method.

Let us begin by examining the *differences* between the cash flows of the two projects shown in Table 4.4.

Project A offers positive differential cash flows over project B of £900 in year 1, but negative differential cash flows of £100 in year 2 and £1,000 in year 3. What is the consequence of accepting A? In present value terms, it is the differential cash flows gained and sacrificed by choosing A, discounted at the cost of capital. Table 4.4 shows this to be £16 at a 10 per cent cost of capital. Project B ranks above project A because it is estimated to create an additional £16 in present-value terms.

Alternatively, we could calculate the IRR on the *differential* cash flows. In the above example the IRR is approximately 11 per cent. This return represents the point at which the two NPV curves intersect, as shown in Figure 4.1. If the cost of capital were 11 per cent, the two projects would have identical ranking and the company could choose either one. In fact, the cost of capital is 10 per cent which, on Figure 4.1, is to the left of the intersection point showing B to have the greater NPV. In this case, project B is marginally preferred to project A.

This gives rise to the four general steps involved in evaluating internal

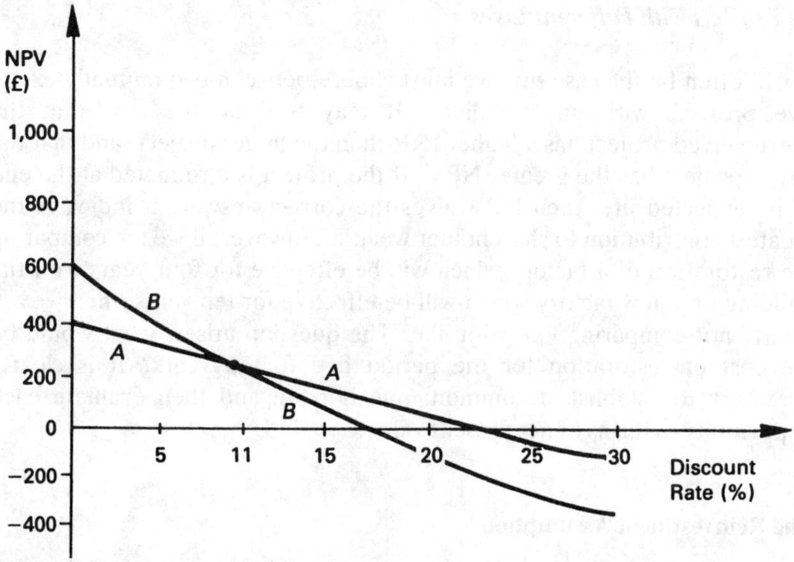

Figure 4.1

Table 4.4

Year	A (£)	B (£)	A − B (£)	Present value 10% (£)
0	−1,200	−1,200	0	0
1	1,000	100	900	+818
2	500	600	−100	−983
3	100	1,100	−1,000	−751
				−16

1. Calculate the IRR for each project.
2. If both projects have IRRs in excess of the cost of capital, calculate the IRR on the differential cash flows.
3. If the differential cash flow IRR is *greater* than the cost of capital, accept the project with the *smaller* IRR.
4. If the differential cash flow IRR is *smaller* than the cost of capital, accept the project with the *greater* IRR.

It will be seen that this approach is somewhat complicated, and involves calculating the differential cash flows between each competing project, of which there may be many. This is why we strongly advocate the more direct net present value approach.

4. Projects with Different Lives

It will often be the case that we must choose between two mutually-exclusive projects with unequal lives. It may well be the case that the shorter-lived project has a higher IRR than the larger project, and that the larger project has the greater NPV. If the project is terminated at the end of its expected life, then NPV gives the correct answer. It indicates the greatest contribution to shareholder wealth. However, if we are comparing the restoration of a factory which will be effective for four years with the building of a new factory which will be effective for ten years, then we are clearly not comparing like with like. The question arises: what would be the cost of restoration for the period five to ten years? It is clearly necessary to establish a common time horizon and then evaluate each opportunity in terms of net present value.

The Reinvestment Assumption

Many writers assert that the internal rate of return method of project appraisal assumes that incoming cash flows are reinvested at the internal rate of return. We do not accept this argument. The internal rate of return or yield is simply the rate of return which equates anticipated cash flows with the initial outlay. In our little example at the beginning of this chapter, we evaluated a project offering £60 in year 1, and £60 in year 2, the initial outlay being £100. The yield or internal rate of return on the project is 13 per cent. If we assume that the £60 cash inflows are placed on a bank deposit at 8 per cent, the internal rate of return is still 13 per cent. If the incoming cash flows are donated to charity, paid out as dividends, reinvested in risky projects, or simply placed on current account the internal rate of return is still 13 per cent — regardless of the destination of the incoming cash flows. In short, there is no reinvestment assumption. The yield is the number which equates anticipated cash flows with the initial outlay. It is the number which would give a zero net present value if it were the required rate of return.

A more apt description would be the *opportunity cost of capital* assumption. We have already seen that the NPV method assumes that the cash flows associated with projects have an opportunity cost equal to the capital market rate of return. The IRR approach assumes that the opportunity cost of capital is comparable, not with an equivalent investment in the capital market, but with a hypothetical investment in a project offering returns identical to the project under consideration. While there may well be other projects offering equally high — if not higher — returns in competitive markets, the IRR of one project should not be used to judge the acceptability of other projects. These other projects are available regardless of whether or not the firm accepts the particular project under consideration.

Questions

1. List the techniques for assessing capital projects.
2. The directors of Palendromics PLC are considering the acquisition of a new machine. The initial cost and setting-up expenses will amount to about £140,000. Its estimated life is about four years, and estimated annual accounting profit is as follows:

Year	*1*	*2*	*3*	*4*
Operational cash flow	90,000	90,000	100,000	50,000
Depreciation	50,000	30,000	40,000	20,000
Accounting profit	40,000	60,000	60,000	30,000

At the end of its four-year life, the installation will yield only a few pounds in scrap value. The company classifies its projects as follows:

	Required rate of return
Low risk	16 per cent
Average risk	24 per cent
High risk	30 per cent

(a) List some of the popular techniques for assessing capital.
(b) Should the new machine be acquired?

3. Parsifal Ltd is a private company whose ordinary shares are all held by its directors. The chairman has recently been impressed by the arguments advanced by a computer salesman, who has told him that Parsifal will be able to install a fully operational computer system for £161,500. This new system will provide all the data currently being prepared by a local data-processing service. This local service has a current annual cost of £46,000. According to the salesman, annual maintenance costs will be only £2,000 and if properly maintained the equipment can be expected to last 'indefinitely'.

   The Chairman has asked the company accountant to evaluate whether purchase of the computer system is worthwhile. The accountant has spoken to a friend who works for a firm of management consultants. She has told him that Parsifal would probably have to employ two additional members of staff at a total cost of about £15,000 per annum and that there would be increased stationery and other related costs of approximately £4,000 per annum if Parsifal purchased the computer system. She also estimates that the useful life of the system would be between 6 and 10 years, depending upon the rate of technological change and changes in the pattern of the business of Parsifal. The system would have no scrap or resale value at the end of its useful life.

The company accountant has prepared a net present value calculation by assuming that all the annual costs and savings were expressed in real terms and that the company had a real cost of capital of 5% per annum. He chose this course of action because he did not know either the expected rate of inflation of the cash flows or the cost of capital of Parsifal Ltd. All cash flows, except the initial cost of the system, will arise at the end of the year to which they relate.

You are required to:

(a) estimate, using the company accountant's assumptions, the life of the system which produces a zero net present value;
(b) estimate the internal real rate of return arising from purchase of the computer system, assuming that the system will last
  (i) for 6 years
  (ii) indefinitely;
(c) estimate the value of the annual running costs (maintenance, extra staff, stationery and other related costs) that will produce a net present value of zero, assuming that the system will last for 10 years;
(d) discuss how the company accountant should incorporate the information from parts (a), (b) and (c) above in his recommendation to the directors of Parsifal Ltd as to whether the proposed computer system should be purchased;
(e) discuss how the company accountant could improve the quality of his advice.

Ignore taxation. (ICA, PE II, July 1984)

References

Boardman, C. M., Reinhart, W. J. and Celec, S. E. (1982) 'The role of the payback period in the theory and application of duration to capital budgeting', *Journal of Business Finance and Accounting*, Winter.

Mepham, M. J. (1975) 'A payback interpretation of the annuity tables', *The Accounting Review*, October.

Pike, R. H. (1986) 'Owner–Manager conflict and the role of the payback method', *Accounting and Business Research* (forthcoming).

Weingartner, H. M. (1969) 'Some new views on the payback period and capital budgeting decisions', *Management Science*, August.

Further Reading

Alchien, A. (1955) 'The rate of interest, Fisher's rate of return over costs, and

Keynes' internal rate of return', *American Economic Review*, December.

Bierman, H. and Smidt, S. (1957) 'Capital budgeting and the problem of reinvesting cash proceeds', *Journal of Business*.

Dudley, C. L. (1972) 'A note on reinvestment assumption in choosing between net present value and internal rate of return', *Journal of Finance*, September.

Hoskins, C. G. (1974) 'Benefit cost ratios versus net present value: revisited', *Journal of Business Finance and Accounting*, Summer.

Lerner, E. M. and Rappaport, A. (1968) 'Limit DCF in capital budgeting', *Harvard Business Review*, September-October.

Longbottom, D. and Wiper, L. (1978) 'Necessary conditions for the existence of multiple rates in the use of the internal rate of return', *Journal of Business Finance and Accounting*, Winter.

Mao, J. C. T. (1966) 'The internal rate of return as a ranking criterion', *Engineering Economist*, Winter.

Renshaw, E. F. (1957) 'A note on the arithmetic of capital budgeting decisions', *Journal of Business*, July.

Sarnat, M. and Levy, H. (1969) 'The relationship of rules of thumb to the internal rate of return', *Journal of Finance*, June.

Solomon, E. (1956) 'The arithmetic of capital budgeting decisions', *Journal of Business*, April.

Weingartner, M. H. (1963) 'The excess present value index — a theoretical basis and critique', *Journal of Accounting Research*, Autumn.

Weingartner, M. H. (1969) 'Some new views on the payback period and capital budgeting decisions', *Management Science*, August.

5

Capital Budgeting Applications

The preceding chapters have covered most of the important concepts involving capital investment appraisals. In this chapter we bring these concepts together by applying them to a variety of different practical investment problems. In particular, we deal with two commonly-found problems:

(1) how should replacement or cost-saving projects be evaluated, and
(2) how do we handle tax in project analyses?

The Replacement Decision (1)

Question

At the beginning of 1984 your company purchased a machine for £50,000. It was estimated that the life of the machine would be twelve years with no residual value, and straight-line depreciation was charged on this basis. At the end of 1985 an improved model becomes available at a cost of £70,000, against which a trade-in allowance of £30,000 will be given in respect of the old machine. The new machine has an expected life of ten years with no residual value, and the accountant intends to charge straight-line depreciation as before. It is estimated that the new machine will produce 500,000 units of finished goods per annum, compared with the

400,000 produced by the old machine. In order to dispose of these the overall selling price will be reduced from £1.1 to £1. Furthermore, additional advertising expenditure of £30,000 will need to be incurred in each of the first three years. As a result of the increased activity, the production engineer's salary will be increased by £2,250 per annum. However, it is anticipated that the higher sales will cause a fall of 40,000 units per annum in the sales of a competing product made by the company (selling at £0.75) as a result of which salesmen's commissions will fall by £1,800 per annum. The company installing the machine will make a maintenance call at the end of year 1 at a standard charge of £300. It is expected that direct costs of production of the main product will fall from £0.7 to £0.6 per unit and that factory overhead will increase by an additional £10,000 per annum as the result of purchasing the new machine. The direct costs of the competing product are £0.5 per unit and no other costs or receipts will be changed if the new machine is acquired. The required rate of return on the project is 10 per cent.

(a) You are required to advise the company as to whether or not the new machine should be acquired.
(b) In what way would your answer be different if the trade-in allowance on the machine were reduced to £20,000?
(c) How would your answer change if depreciation on the new machine were charged at 20 per cent on the reducing balance method?

Ignore taxation. Assume that all cash flows, except the payment for the new machine, are paid or received at the end of the year.

Answer (£)

(a)	*(1)* *1986*	*(2)* *1987*	*(3)* *1988*	*(4)* *1989*	...	*(10)* *1995*
Incremental income:						
Sales receipts	60,000	60,000	60,000	60,000	...	60,000
Commission	1,800	1,800	1,800	1,800	...	1,800
Cost of 'other product'	20,000	20,000	20,000	20,000	...	20,000
	81,800	81,800	81,800	81,800	...	81,800
Incremental cash outflows:						
Advertising	30,000	30,000	30,000	–		–
Salary	2,250	2,250	2,250	2,250	...	2,250
Maintenance	300	–	–	–		–
Sales losses	30,000	30,000	30,000	30,000	...	30,000
Overheads	10,000	10,000	10,000	10,000	...	10,000
Increased production costs	20,000	20,000	20,000	20,000	...	20,000
	92,550	92,250	92,250	62,250	...	62,250
Net cash flow	(10,750)	(10,450)	(10,450)	19,550	...	19,550

Year	1	(10,750)	(0.909)	=	(9,772)
	2	(10,450)	(0.826)	=	(8,632)
	3	(10,450)	(0.751)	=	(7,848)
	4	19,550	(0.683)	=	13,353
	5	19,550	(0.621)	=	12,141
	6	19,550	(0.564)	=	11,026
	7	19,550	(0.513)	=	10,029
	8	19,550	(0.467)	=	9,130
	9	19,550	(0.424)	=	8,287
	10	19,550	(0.386)	=	7,546
					45,260
Less initial outlay					40,000
			NPV		5,260

The project is *acceptable*. It has a *positive net present value* of £5,260. We do not reproduce the laborious calculations, but the internal rate of return on the project is 11.45 per cent, which is greater than the required rate of return of 10 per cent. The profitability index is 1.13, which is greater than 1.0. Although DCF techniques suggest that this project is acceptable, we should add a cautionary note that many managers would not accept this project because the payback period is between six and seven years.

(b) If the trade-in allowance is reduced to £20,000, the NPV is negative: NPV = 45,260 − 50,000 = £(4,740). A £10,000 reduction in the trade-in allowance reduces the net present value by £10,000, from £5,260 positive to £4,740 negative. The internal rate of return falls to 8.83 per cent, and the profitability index to 0.91. The project is therefore unacceptable.

(c) A change in depreciation method does not affect cash flow, and our recommendation is unchanged.

The Replacement Decision (2)

Question

On your recommendation your company purchased an electronic device to reduce variable costs. The cost was £17,000 and the equipment was purchased exactly one year ago. Its expected life was four years and its expected scrap value at the end of its life £1,000. Accounting policy stipulated that the asset should be written off over its useful life on a straight-line basis, i.e. at £4,000 per annum, so that its present book value is £13,000. You have investigated the potential of new equipment currently being marketed at £20,000 which you feel will reduce variable costs by a further £5,000 per annum. The expected life of the machine is three years with a residual value of £2,000. Your informal approach to the vendors has revealed that a trade-in allowance of £7,000 will be offered for the old equipment. You have recommended the installation of the new device to the finance committee and now receive the following memo:

'Sir,

On your recommendation we recently spent £17,000 on some equipment. You apparently now require us to spend a further £20,000. Please note the following very carefully:

1. The cost of the machine (£20,000) is more than the savings it will generate (3 multiplied by 5 equals 15).
2. Purchase of the new item will increase the annual depreciation charge from £4,000 to £6,000 per annum, a fact which is ignored in your £5,000 per annum savings figure.
3. There will be a considerable loss of disposal (£13,000 book value less £7,000 cash equals a loss of £6,000). This year's accounts will simply not stand it.

We regret that we must reject your proposal. There is obviously no chance of the investment yielding the 10% return we must earn on such an investment.'

Present a statement to the finance committee suggesting a rational decision.

Answer

			£
Initial outlay (£20,000 − £7,000)			13,000
Cash flows	Year 1	5,000 (0.909)	4,545
	2	5,000 (0.826)	4,130
	3	6,000 (0.751) (5,000 + 2,000 − 1,000)	4,506
		NPV of cash flows	13,181
		NPV of project	181

'Sirs,

The net present value of the above project is positive. It is a wealth-creating opportunity which should result in an *increase in the value of the firm* of £181. Although this is clearly not a very exciting prospect, it does appear to be a profitable project. The initial outlay is £13,000, not £20,000 as suggested in your memo. I agree that the annual depreciation charge will increase from £4,000 to £6,000, but *depreciation charges do not affect cash flows*. Discounted cash flow techniques are concerned with cash flow and risk. I agree there will be a book loss on disposal of the existing electronic device, but the object of the exercise is to create wealth, not to present appealing financial statements. Although balance sheets do not show the market value of the company or the market value of its assets, clearly the balance sheet figure of £13,000 is greater than the net realisable value of the asset which is only £7,000. On the basis of the net present value calculation, I suggest that the project is marginally worthwhile.'

The Importance of Taxation

Shareholder *wealth is maximised at the after-tax level*. It is essential to take taxation into account when estimating incremental cash flows. Some economists tend to dismiss taxation as a *market imperfection*. We agree that projects should make economic sense, regardless of the tax effects. However, we repeat that shareholder wealth is maximised at the after-tax level, and we must therefore consider the tax implications in capital expenditure analysis.

There are three very important points to be made when managers consider projects:

1. Sales income is taxable after deducting allowable expenses incurred for the purposes of carrying on the trade, e.g. wages, materials, stationery, postage, telephone;
2. *Depreciation is a non-allowable expense for tax purposes*, which must be added back to the net profit figure when calculating assessable profits for corporation tax in the case of companies, and income tax in the case of sole traders and partners;
3. For tax purposes, *capital allowances* are given on plant and equipment, industrial buildings, motor vehicles, etc. Managers are often confused by published accounts which do not show capital allowances computations. These are calculated outside the financial accounts and are not made available to shareholders.

A *first-year allowance* has been available for many years at the rate of 100 per cent on plant, equipment, vans and lorries, regardless of whether new or used. The 100 per cent rate was applicable until 13 March 1984. For expenditure incurred after that date the rate was reduced to 75 per cent. It reduces to 50 per cent for expenditure incurred after 1 April 1985, and to zero from 1 April 1986. In addition, a 25 per cent writing-down allowance, calculated on a reducing-balance basis, is available for the year following the first-year allowance. For many years motor vehicles have attracted only a writing-down allowance of 25 per cent per annum, restricted to a maximum of £2,000 per annum. A 75 per cent initial allowance was available on new industrial buildings until 13 April 1984. A 4 per cent annual allowance was available on cost, the final 1 per cent being written off in year seven. The initial allowance was reduced to 50 per cent for the period after 13 April 1984 but ending on 31 March 1985. It is reduced to 25 per cent for the year ending 31 March 1986, and will then be reduced to zero. On the disposal of a capital item, *a balancing allowance or balancing charge* may arise for tax purposes. If the written-down tax value is greater than the disposal value, a balancing allowance will arise. If the tax written-down value is lower than the sale value, this will give rise to a balancing charge. In practice, the tax payable on the balancing charge can be delayed by deducting the balancing charge from the pooled written-down values of pooled assets.

It must be remembered that to get the benefit of tax allowances, the sole trader or limited company must be in a tax-paying position. Where the tax payer is in a temporary non-tax-paying position, provisions are available for carrying back capital allowances and for carrying them forward to future years. As a final note, we should point out that capital allowances are given for expenditure during an account period. We can therefore understand why many managers seek out capital expenditure opportunities at the end of the accounting period. The tax benefit is received sooner than the tax benefit on expenditure incurred during the earlier part of an accounting period.

Sole traders and partners do not pay corporation tax. They pay income tax at rates varying from zero per cent for low income earners to as much as 60 per cent for those with high incomes. Corporate profits are assessable to corporation tax. The small-company rate is 30 per cent, small companies being those earning assessable profits up to £100,000. Marginal relief is available for profits up to £500,000. Large companies have been subject to corporation tax at 52 per cent for many years. Recent proposals are that the rate should fall to 50 per cent for 1983/84; 45 per cent for 1984/85; 40 per cent for 1985/86; and 35 per cent for 1986/87 and thereafter. The year end for corporation tax purposes is 31 March.

The Tax Factor

Question

On 21 December 1979 you are considering the replacement of a machine purchased on 1 January 1978 for £70,000. Its replacement cost is £84,000. The 1978 machine had an estimated life of six years and an estimated residual value of £14,000. A trade-in allowance of £25,000 has been offered against the new machine. The company's year end is 31 December and the machine could be purchased immediately and be operating within a few days. The firm depreciates plant on a straight-line basis. The 1979 machine will produce incremental output generating sales income of £65,000 per annum for four years, after which time it is expected to realise £15,000. Increased running and maintenance costs will be £36,000 per annum.

The firm claims the 100 per cent first-year allowance on plant. Assume the corporation tax rate is 52 per cent, and that tax is payable about one year after the company generates its cash flows. The after-tax required rate of return on plant replacement decisions is 16 per cent.

If the new machine is acquired, what will be the book profit or loss on disposal? Should the new machine be acquired?

Answer

$$\text{Book loss on disposal} = 70{,}000 - \frac{2(70{,}000 - 14{,}000)}{6} - 25{,}000 = £26{,}333.$$

The book loss on disposal is irrelevant when calculating net present value.

Cash flow: Year	*0* *1979* £	*1* *1980* £	*2* *1981* £	*3* *1982* £	*4* *1983* £	*5* *1984* £
Incremental sales		65,000	65,000	65,000	65,000	
Incremental costs		(36,000)	(36,000)	(36,000)	(36,000)	
Operational cash flow		29,000	29,000	29,000	29,000	
Taxation		–	(15,080)	(15,080)	(15,080)	(15,080)
After-tax operational cash flow		29,000	13,920	13,920	13,920	(15,080)
100% FYA		43,680				
Tax on disposal		(13,000)				(7,800)
Disposal price					15,000	
Lost disposal price					(14,000)	
Tax saved thereon						7,280
Initial outlay	59,000					
	(59,000)	59,680	13,920	13,920	14,920	(15,600)
Discount factor 16%	(1.000)	(0.862)	(0.743)	(0.641)	(0.552)	(0.476)
NPV = £12,520 =	(59,000)	51,444	10,343	8,923	8,236	(7,426)

The net present value is *positive*, and acceptance is recommended, provided that taxable profits are available against which the capital allowances can be set. Tax relief is available at 52 per cent on the full £84,000 cost of the new machine, which is £43,680. A balancing charge arises on disposal of the old machine amounting to 52 per cent of £25,000, i.e. £13,000. A *balancing charge* also arises on disposal of the new machine in year 4, although the company does save tax amounting to £7,280 on the sacrificed disposal price of the old machine. The project has a positive net present value of £12,520. A major incentive in its acquisition is the 100 per cent first-year allowance. Depreciation charges do not enter into our calculations, since depreciation is a non-cash expense which has no effect on cash flows nor on the company's tax position.

Recent Tax Changes

Kildwick Engineering Company Ltd

Ted Beddis is managing director of Kildwick Engineering Company Ltd. The company's year end is 31 March and it is anticipated that the company will pay corporation tax for the foreseeable future at the small-company rate of 30 per cent. In February 1984 Ted is considering the acquisition of a CNC (computer numerically controlled) machine which will cost £100,000, and can generate incremental cash inflows of about £35,000 per annum for the following four years. At the end of this period the machine can be sold for approximately £20,000. Ted could delay acquisition until February 1985, or February 1986, with no foreseeable effect on cash flow estimates. The after-tax required rate of return on such a project is 18 per cent. Calculate the net present value of the project in February 1984, February 1985 and February 1986 taking into account that the first-year allowance of 100 per cent will reduce to 75 per cent and then to 50 per cent.

Answer (£)

February 1984

Year end	31.3.84	31.3.85	31.3.86	31.3.87	31.3.88	31.3.89
Incremental cash inflows		35,000	35,000	35,000	35,000	
Corporation tax (30%)			(10,500)	(10,500)	(10,500)	(10,500)
Operational cash flows		35,000	24,500	24,500	24,500	(10,500)
Cost	(100,000)					
Residual value					20,000	
Corporation tax (30%)						(6,000)
FYA 100% (Purchased Feb. 1984)		30,000				
Undiscounted net = £42,000	(100,000)	65,000	24,500	24,500	44,500	(16,500)
	(1.000)	(0.847)	(0.718)	(0.609)	(0.516)	(0.437)
NPV = £3,317 =	(100,000)	55,055	17,591	14,920	22,962	(7,211)

The incremental cash flows of £35,000 per annum are taxed at 30 per cent approximately one year after the company's year end. The initial outlay of £100,000 attracts a 100 per cent first-year allowance, giving a tax saving at 30 per cent of £30,000 approximately one year later. At the end of the project's life cash amounting to £20,000 is received as residual value. This gives rise to a balancing charge at 30 per cent payable approximately one year later. The undiscounted cash flows amount to a net £42,000, the discounting reducing the undiscounted cash flows to a net present value of £3,317. The importance of the 100 per cent first-year allowance is obvious: a tax saving amounting to £30,000 is made about one year after acquisition.

February 1985 (£)

Year end	31.3.85	31.3.86	31.3.87	31.3.88	31.3.89	31.3.90
Incremental cash inflows		35,000	35,000	35,000	35,000	
Corporation tax (30%)			(10,500)	(10,500)	(10,500)	(10,500)
Operational cash flows		35,000	24,500	24,500	24,500	(10,500)
Cost	(100,000)					
Residual value					20,000	
FYA (75%)		22,500				
WDA (25%) Tax savings			1,875	1,406	1,055	(2,836)
Undiscounted net = £42,000	(100,000)	57,500	26,375	25,906	45,555	(13,336)
	(1.000)	(0.847)	(0.718)	(0.609)	(0.516)	(0.437)
NPV = £1,095 =	(100,000)	48,703	18,937	15,777	23,506	(5,828)

If acquisition is delayed until February 1985, the first-year allowance is reduced from 100 per cent to 75 per cent. In subsequent years a 25 per cent writing-down allowance can be claimed on the outstanding balance. Over the life of the project tax allowances amounting to £80,000 are available, giving a tax saving amounting to £24,000.

Tax Savings on Capital Allowances

Accounting period year ended	*Capital allowances* £	*Tax saving at 30%* £	*Date saved*
31.3.85	75,000	22,500	31.12.85, i.e. y/e 31.3.86
31.3.86	6,250	1,875	31.12.86, i.e. y/e 31.3.87
31.3.87	4,688	1,406	31.12.87, i.e. y/e 31.3.88
31.3.88	3,516	1,055	31.12.88, i.e. y/e 31.3.89
31.3.89	(9,454)	(2,836)	31.12.89, i.e. y/e 31.3.90
	80,000	24,000	

If the machine is acquired for £100,000 and subsequently sold for £20,000, the company obtains relief over the life of the project on £80,000. The effect of reducing the first-year allowance is to push the cash savings further into the future, giving a lower net present value for the project. The undiscounted net cash flows remain exactly the same at £42,000, but the present value of those cash flows is lower as the tax savings are pushed further into the future. The effect is to reduce the net present value from £3,317 to £1,095, a reduction of £2,222.

February 1986 (£)

Year end	31.3.86	31.3.87	31.3.88	31.3.89	31.3.90	31.3.91
Incremental cash inflows		35,000	35,000	35,000	35,000	
Corporation tax (30%)			(10,500)	(10,500)	(10,500)	(10,500)
Operational cash flows		35,000	24,500	24,500	24,500	(10,500)
Cost	(100,000)					
Residual value					20,000	
FYA (50%) } WDA (25%) } Tax savings }		15,000	3,750	2,813	2,109	328
Undiscounted net = £42,000	(100,000)	50,000	28,250	27,313	46,609	(10,172)
	(1.000)	(0.847)	(0.718)	(0.669)	(0.516)	(0.433)
NPV = (£1,127) =	(100,000)	42,350	20,284	16,634	24,050	(4,445)

In February 1986 the first-year allowance will be only 50 per cent, followed by writing-down allowances of 25 per cent in subsequent years. Operational cash flows, cost and residual value remain the same, but the tax savings on capital allowances are delayed.

Tax Savings on Capital Allowances

Accounting period year ended	*Capital allowances* £	*Tax saving @ 30%* £	*Date saved*
31.3.86	50,000	15,000	31.12.86, i.e. y/e 31.3.87
31.3.87	12,500	3,750	31.12.87, i.e. y/e 31.3.88
31.3.88	9,375	2,813	31.12.88, i.e. y/e 31.3.89
31.3.89	7,031	2,109	31.12.89, i.e. y/e 31.3.90
31.3.90	1,094	328	31.12.90, i.e. y/e 31.3.91
	80,000	24,000	

Again, capital allowances amounting to £80,000 are given over the life of the project, resulting in tax savings at 30 per cent amounting to £24,000. Undiscounted net cash flows are exactly the same at £42,000, but the delayed effect of capital allowances results in a negative net present value of £1,127. The effect of delayed capital allowances is to reduce net present values. We emphasise that the capital allowances have value when the company is in a tax-paying position, or at least expects to be in a tax-paying position in the foreseeable future. When a company does not expect to be able to make use of capital allowances, leasing should be seriously considered. This is discussed in Chapter 13.

A Few Additional Comments

Tax and the Misallocation of Resources

We have already stated that shareholder *wealth is maximised at the after-tax level*, and that managers must consider the tax aspect in project appraisal. A cautionary note should be added that some projects may be made worthwhile by the tax incentives. This may be desirable for shareholders and may even be the intention of successive governments. However, we suggest that projects should be particularly desirable when they create wealth, taking only the economic aspects into account.

Abandonment Value

How much will it cost to *escape from or abandon a project*? This is an important question not asked often enough by managers, who are naturally optimistic about their chosen investment schedules. There is a temptation to take on long leases, enter into long-term contracts, purchase plant, equipment and computers, and take on additional fixed costs. We encourage managers to take on *variable costs rather than fixed costs* in the early stages of a new project, and to enter into leasing agreements and other contracts which can be terminated without penalty. Managers should strive to control project expenditures in such a way that the cost of abandonment is low. We keep on reminding managers that most new products and projects fail!

Working Capital Management

Additional investment in *working capital* should be justified in terms of wealth creation just like any other investment opportunity. Cash outflows into additional stock and additional debtors are investments which must be justified in terms of additional cash expected to be received from customers in the future. Cash flow can be stated as $R — W — I$, where R is additional cash from sales receipts, W is additional wages and other operational expenditures, and I is new investment. The NPV formula states that additional I must be justified in terms of additional expected $R - W$ in future periods.

Working capital decisions are often completely ignored in financial management texts because the additional investment in working capital and its ultimate recovery are taken into account in cash flow forecasts, the bottom line 'net after-tax operational cash flow' giving the numbers which are discounted at the after-tax required rate of return. Managers express concern at the omission of working capital from the literature. They see one of their major areas of concern apparently somewhat neglected. In controlling working capital, managers use *ratio analysis*—stock turnover, credit periods allowed to customers, credit periods allowed by suppliers. These rules of thumb are useful in controlling the level of working capital for any level of activity. Ratios can be compared with the past, compared with competitors, examined against targets, and used as an aid to financial statement planning. We should all bear in mind that increases in working capital are investments which must be justified in terms of additional net operational cash flow discounted at the required rate of return to give positive net present values.

Questions

1. The directors of Heckhuddfax Engineering Ltd are considering the acquisition of a new CNC machine which could generate incremental cash inflows and outflows as follows:

Year	*1*	*2*	*3*	*4*	*5*
Income	£60,000	80,000	80,000	60,000	30,000
Expenditure	£30,000	40,000	40,000	30,000	20,000
Incremental cash flow before tax	£30,000	40,000	40,000	30,000	10,000

The immediate initial outlay to acquire the CNC machine and set it up for operations is estimated at £50,000. (For financial accounting purposes, new machinery is depreciated on a straight-line basis.) The corporate planning team has categorised all projects as follows:

	Risk	*After tax required rate of return*
A	Low	15%
B	Average	25%
C	High	30%

The facility under consideration is expected to be of interest to existing customers and the riskiness of the project no greater than average. The company pays tax at 52% almost one year after earning its cash flow, and the residual value of the CNC machine after five years is estimated at £18,000.

(a) Present data showing whether or not the acquisition is wealth-creating.
(b) List the techniques for assessing capital projects. Why is NPV generally recommended?

2. Mr Cowdrey runs a manufacturing business. He is considering whether to accept one of two mutually-exclusive investment projects and, if so, which one to accept. Each project involves an immediate cash outlay of £100,000. Mr Cowdrey estimates that the net cash inflows from each project will be as follows:

	Project A	*Project B*
Net cash inflow at end of:	£	£
Year 1	60,000	10,000
Year 2	40,000	20,000
Year 3	30,000	110,000

Mr Cowdrey does not expect capital or any other resource to be in short supply during the next three years.

You are required to:

(a) prepare a graph to show the functional relationship between net present value and the discount rate for the two projects (label the vertical axis 'net present value' and the horizontal axis 'discount rate');
(b) use the graph to estimate the internal rate of return of each project;
(c) on the basis of the information given, advise Mr Cowdrey which project to accept if his cost of capital is (i) 6% (ii) 12%;
(d) describe briefly any additional information you think would be useful to Mr Cowdrey in choosing between the two projects;
(e) discuss the relative merits of net present value and internal rate of return as methods of investment appraisal.

Ignore taxation. (ICA, PE II, July 1981)

3. Nebraska Ltd is a wholesaler of travelling aids. The company employs a large number of sales representatives, each of whom is supplied with a company car. Each sales representative travels approximately 40,000 miles per annum visiting customers. The directors of Nebraska Ltd wish to continue their present policy of always buying new cars for the sales representatives but they wonder whether their present policy of replacing the cars every three years is optimal. They believe that keeping the cars longer than three years would result in an unacceptable unreliability and wish to consider whether a replacement period of

either one year or two years would be better than the present three-year period. The company's fleet of cars is due for replacement in the near future.

The cost of a new car, at current prices, is £5,500. Resale values of used cars which have travelled similar mileages to those of Nebraska Ltd, are £3,500 for a one-year-old car, £2,100 for a two-year-old car and £900 for a three-year-old car, all at current prices. Running costs at current prices, excluding depreciation, are as follows:

	Road fund licence and insurance	*Fuel, maintenance repairs, etc.*
	£	£
During 1st year of car's life	300	3,000
During 2nd year of car's life	300	3,500
During 3rd year of car's life	300	4,300

The directors of Nebraska Ltd expect that the cost of new cars and the resale value of used cars will increase in the future at an annual compound rate of 5%. They expect running costs to increase at 15% per annum compound. Nebraska Ltd has a money cost of capital of 20% per annum. The Retail Price Index has increased at 10% per annum for a number of years, and is expected to continue doing so.

Running costs and resale proceeds are paid or received on the last day of the year to which they relate. New cars acquired for use from the start of one year are purchased on the last day of the previous year, at prices prevailing during that previous year. Assume that all 'current prices' given above have been operative for almost one year and are due to change shortly. Subsequently all prices will change annually.

You are required to:

(a) prepare calculations for the directors of Nebraska Ltd showing whether they should replace sales representatives' cars every one, two or three years;

(b) discuss how investment appraisal procedures are affected by the existence of high rates of inflation.

Ignore taxation. (ICA, PE II, December 1981)

4. The profits of Curzio Ltd for the year to 31st December 1981 were £24,000 on annual sales of £120,000 — the same result as in the previous two years. During this period Curzio Ltd has been operating at 75% of maximum productive capacity. This capacity has been unchanged for the past two years and is expected to remain so.

The lack of growth is thought to be due in part to the recession and in part to the company's aggressive credit policies. The directors believe that the worst of the recession is over and that the next three years will see some growth in sales. Optimistic, most likely, and pessimistic growth rates are estimated to be 25% per annum (probability 0.2), 12.5% per annum (probability 0.4) and 5% per annum (probability 0.4) respectively. Beyond the three-year growth period sales are expected to stabilise and to be constant for the indefinite future.

The marketing director believes that for the optimistic, most likely and pessimistic predictions, the above annual growth rates can be increased to 35%, 20% and 10% respectively if Curzio Ltd changes its credit and collection policies. His proposed changes are (i) to give a 2½% discount on all sales paid within the month, and (ii) to allow the average debt collection period to increase from 1.75 months of sales revenues to 2.4 months of sales revenues. These policy changes are expected to result in 40% of invoiced sales being subject to discount and in bad debts rising from a negligible level to 2% of invoiced sales.

Profits before interest and taxes for the year $(t + 1)$ have been observed to follow the relationship

$$P_{(t+1)} = P_{(t)} + 0.25\,(S_{(t+1)} - S_{(t)})$$

where $S_{(t+1)}$ and $S_{(t)}$ represent the net sales revenues (i.e. after deduction of bad debts and discounts allowed) arising in years $(t - 1)$ and (t) respectively.

You are required to:

(a) prepare a statement showing the profits for the following three years under both policies;

(b) point out the other factors which should be considered when contemplating changes in working capital policies.

Ignore taxation. (ICA, PE II, July 1982)

5. Mr Colorado is a map retailer. His business has operated at a constant level for many years; sales have been £14,500 per month, purchases have represented 60% of sales and overhead costs have been £4,000 per month, all directly variable with the amount of sales. The business has no fixed assets.

One half of sales are paid for as they are made. The remainder are on credit. Mr Colorado offers no cash discount for early payment and credit customers pay, on average, two months after the date of sale.

All purchases are on credit. Mr Colorado's suppliers each offer 2½% cash discount for payment within one month and at present Mr Colorado takes advantage of the cash discount offered for all purchases. Fixed overhead costs are paid in the month in which they arise.

Mr Colorado estimates that his bank overdraft at 31st December 1981 will amount to £14,800 and that his stock at the same date will be £18,500.

The present limit on Mr Colorado's overdraft is £15,000. He is now expecting a steady expansion in his business from 1st January 1982 and is concerned that he might exceed his overdraft limit if he does not change his present policy for giving and taking credit. Mr Colorado expects his sales in January 1982 and in subsequent months to increase at a monthly compound rate of 2% indefinitely.

Mr Colorado is considering whether to offer his credit customers 2½% cash discount for payment within one month of sale. If he does so, he expects that all credit customers will take advantage of the discount, which will be available in respect of all credit sales made on or after 1st January 1982. He is also considering whether to delay paying his suppliers until two months after the date of purchase for purchases made on or after 1st January 1982. In addition, he wishes to increase his stock level so that he always has sufficient stock to meet sales requirements for three months at predicted levels.

Mr Colorado currently pays 2½% interest per month on his bank overdraft, calculated on the balance at the beginning of each month. This rate of interest is expected to continue indefinitely. You may assume that all receipts and payments are made on the last day of the month.

You are required to:

(a) predict Mr Colorado's bank balance or overdraft at 31st March 1982 under both his present and proposed policies for giving and taking credit;

(b) comment on the figures you have calculated in (a) and describe and justify how you would evaluate the long-term effects of the alternative credit policies on Mr Colorado's business. (Note: You are *not* required to calculate the long-term effects.)

Ignore taxation. (ICA, PE II, December 1981)

6. Blue Jays Ltd manufactures several types of knitwear, which it sells to a variety of retail outlets. The company expects to suffer a temporary shortage of funds during the first three months of 1984 and its directors are considering three alternative means of meeting the shortfall, as follows:

(1) Delay payments to trade creditors in respect of purchases of wool. At present, Blue Jays Ltd receives a cash discount of 2½% in return for settlement of creditors' invoices within one month of the invoice date. It takes advantage of this discount in respect of all invoices received. The proposed policy would involve payment of 50% of invoices (by value) at the end of two months and 50% at the end of three months.

(2) Offer discounts to trade debtors. At present, Blue Jays Ltd offers no cash discount for early settlement of invoices. On average, 10% of debtors pay one month after invoice date, 36% two months after

invoice date and 50% three months after invoice date. 4% of trade debts are bad. The proposed policy would be to offer a discount of 3% for payment within one month of the invoice date. If the policy were implemented, the directors expect that 50% of debtors would pay one month after invoice date, 22% two months after invoice date and 25% three months after invoice date. 3% of trade debts would be bad.

(3) Undertake short-term borrowing. Overdraft facilities are available from the company's bankers at an interest cost of 1% per month. Short-term borrowing could be undertaken to meet all of the expected shortfall or just the shortfall remaining after the implementation of either or both of the two alternatives described above.

If either of the first two alternatives were adopted, it would be applied only to invoices received or issued in January, February and March 1984. Thereafter, Blue Jays Ltd would revert to its existing policies.

The actual and expected sales of Blue Jays Ltd for the nine months from October 1983 to June 1984 are as follows:

			£
Actual sales:	October	1983	250,000
	November	1983	250,000
Expected sales:	December	1983	200,000
	January	1984	200,000
	February	1984	160,000
	March	1984	140,000
	April	1984	140,000
	May	1984	140,000
	June	1984	160,000

Wool is purchased, and the manufacture of knitwear takes place, in the month before sale. For all types of knitwear, the cost of wool is equal to 30% of selling price. All invoices for sales or purchases are issued or received by Blue Jays Ltd on the last day of the month to which they relate.

You are required to:

(a) prepare calculations showing the effect on the cash flows of Blue Jays Ltd on a month by month basis if the company

(i) delays payments to creditors in respect of January, February and March wool purchases;

(ii) offers discounts to trade debtors in respect of January, February and March sales;

(b) prepare calculations showing whether either delaying payments to creditors or offering discounts to debtors is worthwhile;

(c) draft a note for the directors of Blue Jays Ltd advising them on any matters not included in your calculations in (a) and (b) above, which they should consider in arriving at their decision on whether to change temporarily their existing policies relating to trade creditors and trade debtors.

Ignore taxation. (ICA, PEII, December 1983)

6

The Cost of Capital[1]

Few business projects can be started without funds. Funds play the role in the financial system that energy plays in the physical system. Just as energy is needed to move a physical system, so funds are needed to start up a business project. Funds are seldom free; funds have an opportunity cost. If the funds committed to a given project were not used in that project they would almost certainly have alternative uses. If these alternative uses of the funds were to provide the investor with a positive return, this return would be the opportunity cost of the funds used in the project. The *cost* of the funds (or capital) used up in financing a project is, therefore, one of the key concepts in financial management.

Throughout this chapter we shall consider the cost of capital within the context of a single risk-class business. In other words, we assume that the project under evaluation has the same risk characteristics as the business as a whole. The required rate of return for projects with differing risk complexions will be the subject of Chapter 8.

Calculating the Cost of Capital

It might be thought that calculating the cost of the capital entering into a project evaluation is a relatively simple matter. Once the volume of funds required is known, the user can consult the provider of funds to find out how much he will be charged for borrowing this amount. This rate, adjusted possibly for tax, is the cost of capital of the project. For example, a company invests in a new machine tool costing £100,000, and it raises the money as a fixed interest, five-year loan at 15% p.a. The company's tax rate is 35%. The cost of capital for this project might be thought to be $15.00 \times 0.65 = 9.75\%$ per annum.

Unfortunately, this simple calculation seldom provides a correct measure of the cost of capital. The reason for this apparent anomaly is that a corporation rarely negotiates the financing of each investment project as a separate operation. Normally the company treasurer raises a large 'tranche' of funds and these funds are used up on a number of projects. The funds of the company at any one time can, therefore, be regarded as a *pool* of funds into which additional funds are pumped at various times and out of which funds are drawn to finance projects. As will be seen later, this pool of funds (entered on the liabilities side of the balance sheet) can have an *optimal mix*, the optimal debt–equity mix being such as to minimise the company's cost of capital. We therefore assume that when this pool of funds moves away from the optimal debt–equity mix the next tranche of funds pumped into the pool will restore the pool to the optimal mix. The key point is that the cost of each tranche of funds is *not* the cost of capital of a project financed at the same time as this tranche of funds is raised. The relevant cost of capital for an investment project is the weighted average cost of capital of all the funds in the pool at the time the investment in the project is made, where all projects are of average risk.

In the above example a fixed interest loan of £100,000 for five years at 15% p.a. is not the relevant cost of capital to use when evaluating the project. The fact that the entire tranche consists of a fixed interest loan suggests that the funds pool had been undergeared and needed to be topped up with a fixed interest loan to bring it back to an optimal mix of debt and equity. If the net of tax cost of the fixed loan is 9.75% p.a. and the average, net of tax, cost of capital in the pool is 12% p.a. it would be quite wrong to use the former percentage as a cut-off rate in evaluating the project. If the individual cost of each injection of capital into the pool were taken as the cut-off rate for evaluating investment projects, this cut-off rate would jump up or down depending upon the marginal cost of capital entering the pool. This is clearly an incorrect procedure. The relevant cost of capital in investment decisions, where all rpojects are of average risk, is the weighted average cost of capital in the funds pool.

Calculating the Weighted Average Cost of Capital

How then do we calculate the weighted average cost of capital in the funds pool? First, let us assume that the correct debt–equity mix is close to being optimal. This means that the firm cannot reduce its cost of capital significantly by changing the mix. The procedure to be adopted is as follows:

1. Identify each existing source of capital, ordinary shares, preference shares, debentures, etc.
   Note that what is sometimes incorrectly called 'free' capital, such as trade credit, is excluded from the calculations.
2. Find the current *market* value (not book value) of each source of capital. Calculate the percentage of the total value of funds derived from each source. This percentage gives us the *weight* to be applied to each source of capital.
3. Calculate the current net of tax cost of each source of capital.
4. Calculate the weighted average cost of capital by multiplying the cost of each source of funds by its relative weight and summing the resulting figures.

Example

The financing of XYZ PLC is as follows on a given date:

	£m		
	Market value	*Book value*	*Cost*[1] *%*
Ordinary shares and retained earnings	60	100	15
Preference shares	10	6	12
Debentures 'A'	30	30	8
Debentures 'B'	15	10	9

Note: [1]Based on market values, net of tax.

We calculate this company's average weighted cost of capital as follows:

Source of finance	(*a*) *Market value* (*£000*)	(*b*) *%*	(*c*) *Cost* (*net of* tax)	(*d*) (*b*) × (*c*)
Ordinary shares	60	52	15	7.80
Preference shares	10	9	12	1.08
Debentures 'A'	30	26	8	2.08
Debentures 'B'	15	13	9	1.17
	115	100		12.13

The weighted average cost of capital for this company is approximately 12%.

Some Qualifications

The above method of calculating a company's cost of capital is widely used in British industry, but we must make certain qualifications as to its use. These are as follows:

1. It is assumed that the current capital structure is optimal, or not far from being optimal. In other words, it is assumed that the company's current cost of capital cannot be reduced much by altering the existing capital structure.
2. It is assumed that any project being evaluated is *marginal*, in the sense that it is not so large that its financing might require a restructuring of the funds pool. If a project is very large relative to the existing size of the company, we would have to guess the likely weights and costs of each source *after* the finance is raised and the project implemented. In practice this is very difficult to do with any degree of accuracy.
3. It is assumed that the new project being evaluated is of the same *risk class* as the current portfolio of projects. If it is of a different risk class, this fact may affect the cost of one or all of the existing sources of capital. A very risky project might persuade the existing providers of finance that the company is moving into a riskier environment. They will thus add a risk premium to the existing cost of finance.

These qualifications would not apply to a good number of investment projects. Where they do apply, alternative procedures may need to be adopted to calculate the cost of capital.

The Cost of Individual Sources of Capital

We will now examine the problem of calculating the cost of the individual sources of finance. We will examine the costing of three sources, fixed interest loan, preference share, retained earnings and new equity capital.

Fixed Interest Loans This is the cost of fixed interest debt in the ratio of the annual interest payment, net of tax, to the current market value of the debt. For example, if a company raises £800,000 of debt for ten years at 12% p.a., the current cost of the debt is: 96,000/800,000 = 12% gross of tax, and (96,000 × 0.65)/800,000 = 7.8% net of tax, assuming a tax rate of 35%. If the market rate of interest should fall thus increasing the market value of the debt to £900,000, the cost of debt capital will fall to (96,000 × 0.65)/900,000 = 6.93%. Issue costs, such as legal or advertising costs, can also reduce the amount raised from the debt issue, thus increasing the cost of debt.

The component cost of debt in the weighted average cost of capital is usually, but not always, the net of tax cost. Note that we use the current cost of new debt, not the average cost of past tranches of debt. The cost of debt for irredeemable loan stock currently priced at par is thus:

$$Kd = (i \times t)/(D - E)$$

where

Kd = cost of debt
i = periodic interest payment
t = 1 — the marginal rate of tax
D = current market value of the debt
E = expenses of issue

Qualifications on Tax Adjustment The cost of debt was reduced by the tax charge on the assumption that the company's tax bill would be reduced by the interest paid, an allowable charge against tax. If the company does not make sufficient profits to affect the tax charge or is a non-profit making organisation, the cost of debt must be calculated gross, not net, of tax.

Preference Shares Preference shares, like debt, require a fixed periodic service charge to be paid by the company issuing them. Normally they are less risky to issue than debt since, if the periodic dividend is not paid, it is cumulated forward. In the case of debt, unpaid interest is likely to result in bankruptcy proceedings being initiated by the lender. However, the interest on preference shares is not allowable against tax and so this form of finance is often considered to be a more expensive form of finance than debt. The calculation of the cost of preference shares is similar to that for debt except that no deduction from the dividend is made for tax. A company issues 500,000 £1 preference shares at 12% p.a. The cost is therefore 60,000/50,000 = 12%. However, this calculation assumes that the issue itself was costless. This is most unlikely. Legal, advertising and underwriting costs may take, say, 5% of the face value. The true cost of the preference shares is thus 60,000/(500,000 – 25,000) = 12.6%.

The equation for calculating the cost of preference capital is:

$$Kp = d/(P - E)$$

where

Kp = cost of preference capital
d = periodic dividend paid
P = current value of preference capital
E = expenses of issue

Equity New equity finance can come from two sources: the first source is *internal* to the firm, namely, the earnings of profits retained in the business, that is, the proportion of profits not paid out to shareholders in the form of dividend. The second source of equity finance is external to the firm: this consists of funds raised in the form of 'rights issues'. The existing shareholders are invited to subscribe to a new flotation of ordinary shares in the company. We will first consider the cost of retained earnings.

Retained Earnings The holder of an ordinary share in a company need not retain that share. He can sell it on the stock exchange. This option being available, the shareholder will sell his share unless it provides him with 'adequate' return. The retained earnings must earn sufficient return to satisfy the existing marginal shareholder, that is, sufficient return to persuade the shareholder to retain the share in his portfolio. The cost of equity capital is that *minimum* return sufficient to satisfy the earning requirements of the holder of the marginal share. How do we measure the return expected by the marginal shareholder? There are two ways of tackling this measurement problem. The first approach is to look at the past performance of the share: the growth in earnings in past years. It seems reasonable to assume that existing shareholders will expect this growth of earnings in the future. An alternative approach is to use the capital asset pricing model outlined in Chapter 8 to estimate the risk-adjusted rate of return expected by the market on this share.

The Growth Model If we assume that dividends in the future will grow at a constant rate of $g\%$, the rate of return expected by the market will be:

$$Ke = \frac{d}{p} + g$$

where

Ke = rate of return on ordinary share required by the marginal shareholder
d = expected dividend
p = market price of share
g = expected growth in dividends

If the share achieves a return of $Ke\%$ in the following period the value of the share will remain unchanged on the stock market.

Thus, if an ordinary share has the following characteristics—

current dividend = 30p
market price = 240p
expected growth of dividends = 5%

then

$$\text{expected return} = \frac{30}{240} + 0.05 = 17.5\%$$

The main problem in practice lies in the accurate measurement of g. The average growth over the last five to ten years is normally taken as a proxy for the future growth of dividends. However, if a change in the rate of growth of earnings is expected, it would be wiser to use the predictions put forward by financial forecasters as the best measure of g. Whichever method we use for measuring g, the rate Ke will give us the cost of retained earnings to enter into our average weighted cost of capital model.

Raising External Equity Finance The cost of external equity finance is the same as the cost of retained earnings except for the fact that external finance incurs flotation costs such as legal, advertising and underwriting fees. In the case of small value issues these costs can be substantial, reaching perhaps 10% of the gross value of the equity issue. The cost of external equity financing is therefore:

$$Ke = \frac{d}{(p - e)} + g$$

where

Ke = the return required by the market on external equity financing
d = dividend expected to be paid in first year
p = issue price of share
e = expenses of share issue
g = expected growth in dividends

Thus, if a rights issue has the following characteristics —

expected dividends = 50p
issue price = 400p
issue expenses = 40p
expected growth of dividends = 10%

the required return will be:

$$Ke + \frac{50}{(400 - 40)} + 0.10 = 23.9\%$$

The Capital Asset Pricing Approach The cost of equity capital is determined by the required return of the investor. If the investor achieves his required return, the value of the equity share will remain unchanged on the stock market. If it is less, the share will fall in value; if greater, the share will rise in value. The expected return on the share is, therefore, the key to calculating the cost of equity capital. In Chapter 8 we shall discuss the logic behind the capital asset pricing model (CAPM). The CAPM provides an alternative approach to calculating the returns the market expects from a given share. The CAPM approach splits the return on a share into two parts. The first part represents the current return on a close to riskless investment. The second part is a surplus return representing a premium on the risk attached to that particular share, i.e.:

$$E = R + (S - R)B$$

where

E = expected return on share
R = current return on riskless investment
S = current return on share of average risk
B = beta of share

As will be discussed later, the beta represents the relative riskiness of the return on the particular share. For example, if a relatively riskless government stock earns a return of 10% net of tax and a share of average riskiness earns 18%, the expected returns on three shares with the following betas would be as follows:

Share	*Beta*	
A	0.3	Gold share
B	1.1	Chemicals
C	2.2	Microcomputers

Share
A: 10 + (18 − 10) 0.3 = 12.4%
B: 10 + (18 − 10) 1.1 = 18.8%
C: 10 + (18 − 10) 2.2 = 27.6%

From these calculations it can be seen that the holders of the microcomputer company C expect a great deal from their share so far as earnings is concerned. The cost of equity capital to company C is high because the typical project is associated with a very high expected rate of return. Whichever method — growth model or CAPM — is used, the resulting figure provides the cost of capital for the equity component for the weighted average cost of capital calculation. However, the CAPM approach includes an allowance for risk in the cost of capital calculation. The growth model does not.

Depreciation If the reader studies the flow of funds statement provided by most major companies in their statement of annual accounts, he will find depreciation listed as a major source of funds. Depreciation, however, was not included in the average cost of capital calculation set out above. The reason for this apparent anomaly is that if the company is optimally financed, the cost of the depreciation funds will be approximately equal to the existing average cost of capital. Therefore, the addition of depreciation will not alter the average cost of capital calculation. The cost of depreciation is the same as the average cost of capital since the depreciation fund is assumed to be drawn from each source of funds proportionately to its optimal mix. If this were not so it would upset the optimal mix. If the funds were not invested but returned to finance providers, they would have to be returned in proportion to the existing mix, otherwise the optimal mix of funds would be disturbed. The cost of depreciation funds is thus the same as the weighted average cost of the funds from the funds pool.

Conditional Sources of Capital

We argued above that the cost of funds raised at the same time as a project is undertaken should not be used as the cost of funds invested in the project. There is one important exception to this rule. If the funds are made available only on condition that the given project is undertaken, the cost of funds for such a project should be calculated independently. The cost of the company pool of funds should not be used. The most obvious example of conditional sourcing of funds is in development areas or certain foreign investments. Cheap funds, below the current market price, are frequently provided by government or nationalised industries for investment in development areas. If a company is considering such an investment, it should take this cheaper cost of privileged funds into account when calculating the net present value of the project. (See APV in Chapter 14.)

Gearing and the Cost of Capital

Earlier in this chapter we provided a method for calculating the cost of individual sources of capital, such as new equity and debt.

A crucial assumption behind these calculations i that the debt–equity mix, both before and after the injection of new funds, is reasonably optimal. By 'reasonably optimal' we mean that a change in the debt–equity mix would not, by itself, alter the weighted average cost of capital by a significant amount. If a change in the debt–equity *does* alter the weighted average cost of capital the cost of each source of funds cannot be calculated independently. For example, an increase in debt might increase the cost of existing equity capital. Research into the effect of gearing on the cost of capital has

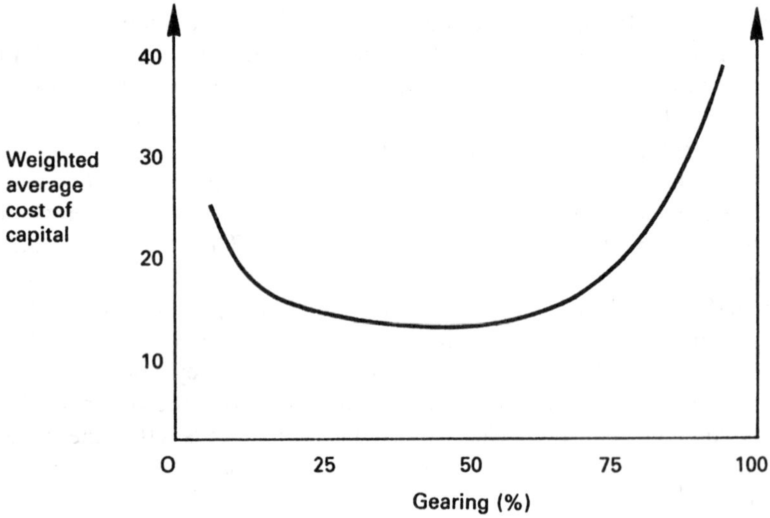

Figure 6.1 The Effect of Gearing on the Cost of Capital. (Note that over a wide range of gearing % the average cost of capital is little affected.)

disclosed that, over a wide range of gearing, the proportion of debt has relatively little effect on the cost of capital (see Fox 1977). As illustrated in Figure 6.1 the cost of capital schedule is saucer-shaped with regard to gearing. So long as the existing gearing of the company is inside the flat portion of the saucer and the new gearing ratio is also within this portion, then the calculations described above are viable. If, however, the gearing ratio before or after the injection of new funds is outside the flat portion of the saucer, the change in gearing can significantly alter the weighted average cost of funds and this fact must be taken into account by calculating the weighted average cost of capital *after* the injection of the new funds.

Example: Gearing Effect on Cost of Capital

Let us assume that the debt–equity mix has little effect on the average cost of capital if debt makes up 30% to 60% of total financing. The average cost of capital calculation might then look something like this for various levels of gearing:

% of debt in total financing	*Weighted average cost of capital* (%)
0	20
10	15
30	12
50	12
70	14
90	30

We can call the range from 30% to 60% the 'optimal range' of gearing. A financial manager can operate within this range and not unduly affect his cost of capital. This fact is reassuring. The problem is not to find the optimal mix of debt–equity but to *avoid* the non-optimal mixes at either end of the gearing spectrum. Empirical support for this advice is provided in Table 6.1. This table shows the *book-value* gearing of a range of UK companies in various industries. Note that each industry does not zero in on a specific gearing ratio. The gearing ratios are scattered over a wide range in each industry although there is a slight tendency to cluster around a central value (Fox 1977). We conclude that, over a wide range of gearing, the proportion of debt in a company's capital structures has little effect on a company's cost of capital.

The following example illustrates much of the discussion to date on estimating the cost of capital. Gibson plc currently (31st December 1985) has a share capital of two million ordinary shares, each with a nominal value of 25p and a current market price of 95p *ex div*. The company pays a single dividend each year which has risen steadily from 6p in 1975 to 14p in 1985. Gibson plc currently has 400,000 10 per cent loan stock, redeemable 31st December 1987, with a market value of £90 per cent *ex interest*. Taxation relief is available on interest at 50 per cent in the following year.

Cost of Equity

The cost of equity is estimated as the expected dividend yield plus the expected growth rate, that is:

$$Ke = \frac{d(1 + g)}{p} + g$$

Historically, the compound rate of growth in dividends over the past ten years has been:

$$\sqrt[10]{\frac{14 \text{ pence}}{6 \text{ pence}}} = 1.088 \text{ or } 8.8\%$$

Assuming this rate can be maintained, the estimated cost of equity,

$$Ke = \frac{14(1.088)}{95} + 0.088 = 0.248, \text{ say } 25\%$$

Cost of Loan Stock

The simple approach would be to find the after-tax interest yield, that is

Table 6.1 Analysis of Current Gearing Percentages of Quoted Companies by 'Industry' Category

Industry Category	*No. of companies in category = 100%*	*Gearing percentage ranges* 0–9		10–19		20–29		30–39		40–49		50–74		75–100	
Aircraft	8	12.5	1	25.0	2	–	–	25.0	2	25.0	2	12.5	1	–	–
Motor vehicle mfg and distribution	76	1.3	1	2.6	2	10.5	8	30.3	23	18.4	14	36.9	28	–	–
Motor vehicle accessory mfg and distribution	78	15.4	12	19.2	15	15.4	12	23.1	18	14.1	11	11.5	9	1.3	1
Chemicals and plastics	99	15.2	15	22.2	22	22.2	22	14.1	14	16.2	16	10.1	10	–	–
Breweries, wines, spirits and drinks	79	7.6	6	19.0	15	27.8	22	22.8	18	13.9	11	8.9	7	–	–
Building materials and aggregates	205	10.7	22	18.5	38	20.0	41	23.0	47	15.1	31	12.2	25	0.5	1
Construction and building	149	17.5	26	15.4	23	13.4	20	16.1	24	13.4	20	21.5	32	2.7	4
Cinema, TV and entertainment	59	28.8	17	25.4	15	20.3	12	15.3	9	5.1	3	5.1	3	–	–
Drapery and stores	219	16.9	37	16.4	36	17.8	39	20.6	45	16.0	35	10.5	23	1.8	4
Electrical engineering	57	15.8	9	26.3	15	17.6	10	21.0	12	8.8	5	10.5	6	–	–
Light electrical, electronics, radio & TV	91	16.5	15	18.7	17	16.5	15	23.0	21	12.1	11	12.1	11	1.1	1
Iron and steel	34	5.9	2	20.6	7	17.6	6	20.6	7	14.7	5	20.6	7	–	–
Shipbuilding and heavy engineering	74	17.6	13	18.9	14	20.2	15	13.5	10	14.9	11	14.9	11	–	–
Machine tools	39	28.2	11	12.8	5	12.8	5	20.6	8	12.8	5	12.8	5	–	–
General engineering	378	22.2	84	20.1	76	15.3	58	18.5	70	13.8	52	9.0	34	1.1	4
Food and groceries	157	12.7	20	12.7	20	23.0	36	17.2	27	15.9	25	17.2	27	1.3	2
General services	114	14.0	16	13.2	15	17.5	20	21.1	24	17.5	20	14.9	17	1.8	2
Hotels and catering	53	7.6	4	13.2	7	5.7	3	26.4	14	30.2	16	16.9	9	–	–
Industrial and commercial durable	197	15.7	31	16.8	33	20.8	41	20.3	40	13.2	26	11.7	23	1.5	3
Industrial and commercial non-durable	165	15.8	26	17.0	28	21.2	35	21.2	35	13.9	23	10.3	17	0.6	1
Oils	16	31.3	5	18.7	3	18.7	3	6.3	1	12.5	2	12.5	2	–	–
Printing, publishing and newspapers	81	19.8	16	19.8	16	19.8	16	18.4	15	11.1	9	11.1	9	–	–
Paper and packing	47	12.8	6	17.0	8	19.1	9	23.4	11	21.3	10	4.3	2	2.1	1
Shipping	46	17.4	8	13.1	6	6.5	3	21.7	10	13.1	6	28.2	13	–	–
Shoes and leather	46	19.5	9	17.4	8	15.2	7	21.7	10	10.9	5	13.1	6	2.2	1
Wool textiles	49	10.2	5	20.4	10	22.4	11	12.3	6	14.3	7	20.4	10	–	–
Non-wool textiles	183	15.8	29	13.1	24	21.9	40	20.8	38	18.6	34	9.8	18	–	–
Tobacco	9	–	–	11.1	1	22.2	2	22.2	2	33.4	3	11.1	1	–	–
Transport and distribution	62	17.7	11	14.5	9	11.3	7	29.1	18	14.5	9	12.9	8	–	–
Total	2,870	15.9	457	17.1	490	18.0	518	20.2	579	14.9	427	13.0	374	0.9	25

Source: Fox (1977)

$$Kd = \frac{10 - 5}{90} = 5.6\%$$

However, this is the formula for irredeemable loans and would be quite wrong in our case where redemption is only two years away. We need to find the internal rate of return for the cash flows that the loan produces. On each £100 of loan stock we have the following cash flows:

	1985	*1986*	*1987*	*1988*
Loan issue	90			
Gross interest		−10	−10	
Tax relief			5	5
Loan repayment			−100	
	90	−10	−105	5

The IRR for this stream of cash flows is approximately 12%.
The weighted average cost of capital is:

$$WACC = \frac{KeVe + KdVd}{Ve + Vd}$$

where the value of equity, *Ve*, = 2 million × 95p = £1.9 million and the value of loan stock, *Vd*, = 0.4 million × 90/100 = £0.36 million

$$WACC = \frac{25 \times £1.9 \text{ million} + 12 \times £0.36 \text{ million}}{£1.9 \text{ million} + £0.36 \text{ million}}$$

$$= 22.9, \text{ say } 23\%.$$

Cost of Capital and Inflation

The previous discussion has assumed that the rate of inflation over the period of the project under analysis is zero. An annual zero rate of inflation is unusual. Since 1932, in the UK, a zero rate of inflation over one year has never occurred. A positive rate of inflation is the norm. In the UK this has varied, on an annual calculation, from 1% to 26% between 1945 and 1985. How do we incorporate inflation into the cost of capital calculation? There are two approaches to this problem. First we can remove the effects of inflation from *both* the cost of capital and the estimated cash flows. We calculate the NPV or yield *net* of inflation. The alternative approach is to represent both the cost of capital and the cash flows *gross* of inflation. It is generally agreed by financial analysts that the latter approach is the better one. Note that the cost of capital and the cash flows must *both* be calculated net or gross of inflation. A common error in investment calculations is to calculate one of these factors, say the cost of capital, gross of inflation, and the other, the cash flow, net of inflation. This is clearly an incorrect procedure.

Removing Inflation Allowance from Cost of Capital

In an earlier section of this chapter the current market cost of various sources of capital was calculated: loans, preference shares, equity shares, etc. All these costs were gross of inflation. By 'gross of inflation' we mean that the providers of funds raise the real return they require by a fraction to allow for the expected average rate of inflation over the period during which the funds are made available. For example, suppose that a fixed interest loan is provided for five years at a real rate of 4% per annum. The lender expects inflation to average 7% per annum over this period. The nominal rate the lender will ask on the loan is therefore (1.04) (1.07) − 1 = (1.113 − 1) = 11.3%. The formula for converting a real rate to a nominal inflation adjusted rate is:

$$i = (1 + r)(1 + f) - 1$$

where

i = nominal rate gross of inflation
r = real rate of interest
f = expected rate of inflation over period of loan

The cost of capital calculations in the earlier part of this chapter provided market rates gross of inflation. Therefore, to calculate the cost of capital net of inflation, we must use the equation:

$$r = \frac{(1 + i)}{(1 + f)} - 1$$

If the cost of capital, gross of inflation, is calculated to be 15% and the expected rate of inflation over the given period is 9%, the net of inflation, or *real* cost of capital, is:

$$r = \frac{(1.15)}{(1.09)} - 1 = 0.055 = 5.5\%$$

Note that a simple subtraction of the expected inflation rate from the cost of capital rate, gross of inflation, will not give an accurate calculation of the real rate — although the result will seldom be more than 1% out.

Estimating Expected Inflation over a Future Period

The previous calculations would seem to require that the analyst must estimate the average rate of inflation over a future period. Actually, the required estimate is much less rigorous. The analyst need only estimate *market expectations* as to average inflation over a future period. In the UK certain government bonds are available, the return on which depends on future inflation. The current value of these bonds compared to similar non-inflation-proofed bonds gives a good estimate of market expectations as to future average inflation. An alternative option is to take the *average* of various predictions on inflation for the period in question put forward by several economic forecasting agencies.

The 'Net of Inflation' Approach

We are now in a position to calculate the NPV or yield on a project net of inflation. The cash flows are set out in £ values of a given year. Normally the £ values are as at the beginning of the project. The rate of discount applied to this net cash flow is the cost of capital of the company net of inflation. An example is provided in Table 6.2.

Table 6.2 Discount Cash Flow Evaluation

DCF evaluation (net of inflation)	*£ values of a given year*			
	Total	1	2	3
Expected cash flow (net of inflation)	1,351.0	176.0	840.0	335.0
discount at 10%	1,105.9	160.0	694.2	251.7
DCF evaluation with cash flow and discount rate gross of inflation at 5% per annum	*£ values of a given year*			
	Total	1	2	3
Expected cash flow (gross of inflation)	1,499.0	185.0	926.0	388.0
discount at 15.5%	1,105.9	160.2	694.0	251.8

Calculation of the inflation-adjusted discount rate:
$(1.10)(1.05) - 1 = 15.5\%$

Note: DCF evaluations using a single inflation rate arrive at the same value so long as the cash flows and discount rate are *both* expressed gross or net of inflation.

The 'Gross of Inflation' Approach

The alternative approach to incorporating inflation into project evaluation is to set out the cash flows *gross* of inflation. Since the market based cost of capital already incorporates an allowance for estimated future inflation, there is no need to adjust this figure. Adjusting the estimated cash flows for future inflation raises an important question. Should the future cash flows be adjusted by a single index or a series of indices, representing expected inflation on each of the various items making up the cash flow? Accountants will recognise this problem as being similar to the key controversy in the debate on inflation accounting. The single index represents the current purchasing power approach (CPP), the multiple index represents the current cost accounting approach (CCA). We have no intention of reviewing this complex debate here. We simply alert the reader to the similarity between the two situations.

Do we Get a Different Answer?

Will the 'net' and 'gross' approaches to inflation adjustment give different answers to project evaluation? If the single index method is used the answer is no. The adjustment to the discount rate exactly counterbalances the adjustment to the future cash flows. The net present value is the same in both cases (see Table 6.2). If, however, different indices are used to adjust the various items making up the cash flows, the resulting NPV will not be the same since the inflation adjustment applied by the lenders to the cost of capital is unlikely exactly to counterbalance the average inflation adjustment to the various cash flows. This is an unresolved problem.

Which is the Better Method?

The use of a series of indices will provide a stream of budgeted cash flows which are closer to the actual cash flows of the project. The DCF cash flow projection will be, in effect, a cash budget for the project. The alternative method, particularly with regard to tax calculations, will not provide a cash budget. Thus the CCA approach which uses a series of inflation indices to gross up the cash flows and uses current market values to calculate the gross of inflation cost of capital, would seem to provide the most practical approach to the inflation adjustment problem.

Some Qualifications

This chapter has explained a method of calculating a company's weighted average cost of capital. This method can be used over a wide range of conditions. However, as we pointed out earlier, the method is based on a series of assumptions, and if those assumptions are violated, the weighted average cost of capital calculations may produce an incorrect result. The implicit assumptions behind the calculations are as follows:

1. The financial market generating the market values used in the calculation is reasonably efficient.
2. The capital structure, that is the debt–equity mix, both before and after the injection of new capital, is in the optimal range. The definition of 'optimal range' was explained earlier in this chapter.
3. The capital project being evaluated is of the same 'risk class' as the existing portfolio of projects being run by the company.
4. The new project under evaluation is *marginal* in the sense that it will not effect significant changes in the financial market's view of the company. Obviously, points (2) and (3) above are specific aspects of this condition.

If the first condition as to the market being efficient is breached, the theory expounded in this chapter falls. The other conditions can be surmounted, but only at the price of making the cost of capital calculation more complicated.

Questions

1. What is meant by the 'opportunity cost' of funds?
2. If funds are raised to finance a given project, why might the cost of these funds not be the cost of funds to charge to the project?
3. What is meant by the 'optimal mix' of funds financing a company?
4. Describe the procedures for calculating the weighted average cost of capital.
5. Why is it recommended to use market values rather than book values of sources of capital when calculating the WACC?
6. 'It is assumed that the project being evaluated is (a) marginal, and (b) of the same risk class as that of other company projects.' Explain.
7. Set down and explain the equation for calculating the cost of debt entering into a company's cost of capital pool.
8. Is the cost of retained earnings the same as the cost of new equity finance?
9. How is g, the growth of dividends, estimated in the growth model of the cost of equity?
10. How does the capital asset pricing model differ from the growth model approach to estimating the cost of equity finance? Why is the CAPM more comprehensive?
11. Using the following data calculate the expected return on equity on this share:

    Return on 'riskless' stock 6%

Return on average share	12%
Beta of share	1.5%

12. When is the weighted average cost of capital the appropriate discount rate?
13. What are 'conditional' sources of capital? How do they affect the cost of funds calculation?
14. How does gearing affect the cost of capital? Why would the conventional WACC calculations be incorrect if gearing was not within the 'optimal' range?
15. Describe the two approaches to handling expected inflation when calculating the WACC.
16. How can we find an objective measure of market expectations as to expected future inflation?
17. The directors of Osmin plc are considering opening a factory to manufacture a new product. Detailed forecasts of the product's expected cash flows have been made, and it is estimated that an initial capital investment of £2.5 million is required. The company's current (31st December 1981) authorised share capital consists of 4 million ordinary shares, each with a nominal value of 25p. During the last five years the number of shares in issue has remained constant at 3 million, and the market price per share at 31st December 1981 is 135p *ex div*. The company pays only one dividend each year (on 31st December) and dividends for the last five years have been as follows:

Year	*1977*	*1978*	*1979*	*1980*	*1981*
Dividend per share (pence)	10.0	10.8	11.6	13.6	13.6

Osmin plc currently has in issue 800,000 8% debentures redeemable on 31st December 1985. The current market price of these debentures is £82.5 ex interest, and the interest is payable in one amount each year on 31st December. The company also has outstanding a £900,000 bank loan repayable on 31st December 1989. The rate of interest on this loan is variable, being fixed at 1½% above the bank's base rate which is currently 15%.

You are required to:

(a) calculate the weighted average cost of capital (WACC) for Osmin plc as at 31st December 1981;

(b) explain briefly to the directors of Osmin plc what assumptions they are making if the WACC calculated in (a) above is used to discount the expected cash flows of the project;

(c) describe the practical problems that might be encountered when attempting to compute the WACC for a large UK listed company.

Ignore taxation. (ICA, PE II, July 1982)

18. Redskins plc is a holding company owning shares in various subsidiary companies. Its directors are currently considering several projects which will increase the range of the business activities undertaken by Redskins plc and its subsidiaries. The directors would like to use discounted cash flow techniques in their evaluation of these projects but as yet no weighted average cost of capital has been calculated.

Redskins plc has an authorised share capital of 10 million 25p ordinary shares, of which 8 million have been issued. The current *ex div* market price per ordinary share is £1.10, a dividend of 10p per share having been paid recently. The company's project analyst has calculated that 18% is the most appropriate after-tax cost of equity capital. Extracts from the latest balance sheets for both the group and the holding company are given below:

	Redskins plc and subsidiaries (£000)	*Redskins plc (£000)*
Issued share capital	2,000	2,000
Share premium	1,960	1,960
Reserves	3,745	708
Shareholders' funds	7,705	4,668
Minority interests	895	–
3% Irredeemable debentures	1,400	–
9% Redeemable debentures	1,500	1,500
6% Loan stock	2,000	2,000
Bank loans	1,540	600
Total long term liabilities	6,440	4,100

All debt interest is payable annually and all the current year's payments will be made shortly. The current *cum interest* market prices for £100 nominal value stock are £31.60 and £103.26 for the 3% and 9% debentures respectively. Both the 9% debentures and the 6% loan stock are redeemable at par in ten years' time. The 6% loan stock is not traded on the open market, but the analyst estimates that its effective pre-tax cost is 10% per annum. The bank loans bear interest at 2% above base rate (which is currently 11%) and are repayable in six years. The effective corporation tax rate of Redskins plc is 46%.

You are required to:

(a) calculate the effective after-tax weighted average cost of capital as required by the directors;

(b) discuss the problems that are encountered in the estimation of a company's weighted average cost of capital when the following are used as sources of long term finance:

  (i) bank overdraft
  (ii) convertible loan stock;

(c) outline the fundamental assumptions that are made whenever the weighted average cost of capital of a company is used as the discount rate in net present value calculations.

Ignore personal taxation. (ICA, PE II, July 1983)

19. The directors of Red Sox plc wish to calculate the cost of the company's equity capital for various decision-making purposes. To investigate the sensitivity of their calculations they have used two models, the (Gordon) dividend growth model and the capital asset pricing model, to calculate the cost of equity capital. A dividend of 10p per share has recently been paid by the company and the current market price of the ordinary shares is 100p per share. Analysts have forecast that the expected return on the stock market in the near future will be 0.15 (i.e. 15%) per annum with a standard deviation of return of 0.50 (i.e. 50%); the return on a risk-free security is expected to be 0.05 (i.e. 5%) per annum. The covariance of Red Sox's returns with the market over the past five years has been estimated as 0.25 on an annualised basis; the covariance is expected to rise to 0.275 in the future due to changes in the asset composition of the company. Dividend growth rates, on an annual basis, for the past ten years have been as follows:

Years	*Dividend Growth Rate*
1974–1978	5% per annum
1979	14% per annum
1980–1983	10% per annum

Government controls restricted actual dividend growth to 5% per annum between 1974 and 1978, but were lifted at the beginning of 1979. It is generally believed to be highly unlikely that dividend controls will be reintroduced in the foreseeable future.
You are required to:

(a) estimate the cost of equity capital of Red Sox plc using both the (Gordon) dividend growth model and the capital asset pricing model;
(b) comment upon the results of your answer to (a) above;
(c) discuss the likely impact of an increase in the rate of inflation upon a company's cost of equity capital.

Ignore taxation. (ICA, PE II, December 1983)

20. Bailey Ltd is developing a new product, the Oakman, to replace an established product, the Shepard, which the company has marketed successfully for a number of years. Production of the Shepard will cease in one year whether or not the Oakman is manufactured. Bailey Ltd has recently spent £75,000 on research and development relating to the Oakman. Production of the Oakman can start in one year's time. Demand for the Oakman is expected to be 5,000 units per annum for the first three years of production and 2,500 units per annum for the subsequent two years. The product's total life is expected to be five years.

Estimated unit revenues and costs for the Oakman, at current prices, are as follows:

	£	£
Selling price per unit		35.00
less Costs per unit:		
Materials and other consumables	8.00	
Labour (see (1) below)	6.00	
Machine depreciation and overhaul (see (2) below)	12.50	
Other overheads (see (3) below)	9.00	
		35.50
Loss per unit		0.50

(1) Each Oakman requires two hours of labour, paid £3 per hour at current prices. The labour force required to produce Oakmans comprises six employees, who are at present employed to produce Shepards. If the Oakman is not produced, these employees will be made redundant when production of the Shepard ceases. If the Oakman is produced, three of the employees will be made redundant at the end of the third year of its life, when demand halves, but the company expects to be able to find work for the remaining three employees at the end of the Oakman's five-year life. Any employee who is made redundant will receive a redundancy payment equivalent to 1,000 hours' wages, based on the most recent wage rate at the time of the redundancy.

(2) A special machine will be required to produce the Oakman. It will be purchased in one year's time (just before production begins). The current price of the machine is £190,000. It is expected to last for five years and to have no scrap or resale value at the end of that time. A major overhaul of the machine will be necessary at the end of the second year of its life. At current prices, the overhaul will cost £60,000. As the machine will not produce the same quantity of Oakmans each year, the directors of Bailey Ltd have decided to spread its original cost and the cost

of the overhaul equally between all Oakmans expected to be produced (i.e. 20,000 units). Hence the combined charge per unit for depreciation and overhaul is £12.50: (£190,000 + £60,000) ÷ 20,000 units.

(3) Other overheads at current prices comprise variable overheads of £4.00 per unit and head office fixed costs of £5.00 per unit, allotted on the basis of labour time.

All wage rates are expected to increase at an annual compound rate of 15%. Selling price per unit and all costs other than labour are expected to increase in line with the Retail Price Index. The Retail Price Index is expected to increase in the future at an annual compound rate of 10%. Corporation tax at 52% on net cash income is payable in full one year after the income arises. A one hundred per cent first-year tax allowance is available on the machine. Bailey Ltd has a money cost of capital, net of corporation tax, of 20% per annum.

Assume that all receipts and payments will arise on the last day of the year to which they relate. Assume also that all 'current prices' given above have been operative for one year and are due to change shortly. Subsequently all prices will change annually.

You are required to:

(a) prepare calculations, with explanations, showing whether Bailey Ltd should undertake production of the Oakman;

(b) discuss the particular investment appraisal problems created by the existence of high rates of inflation.

(ICA, PE II, July 1981)

Note

1. This chapter has been contributed by Professor T. W. McRae.

Reference

Fox, R. B. (1977) 'Corporate leverage — a study', M.Sc. dissertation, University of Bradford.

Further Reading

Arditti, Fred D. (1973) 'The weighted average cost of capital: some questions on its definition, interpretation and use', *Journal of Finance*, 28, September, pp. 1001–1007.

Bromwich, M. (1969) 'Inflation and the capital budgeting process', *Journal of Business Finance*, Autumn.

Ezzell, John R. and Porter, R. Burr. (1976) 'Flotation costs and the weighted average cost of capital', *Journal of Financial and Quantitative Analysis*, 11, September, pp. 403–414..

Foster, E. M. (1970) 'The impact of inflation on capital budgeting decisions', *Quarterly Review of Economics and Business Studies*, 10, No. 3, Autumn.

Grinyer, John R. (1976) 'The cost of equity, the C.A.P.M. and management objectives under uncertainty', *Journal of Business Finance and Accounting*, 3, Winter, pp. 101–121.

Modigliani, Franco and Miller, M. H. (1958) 'The cost of capital, corporation finance and the theory of investment', *American Economic Review*, 48, June, pp. 261–297.

Mare, R. D. de la (1975) 'An investigation into the discounting formulae used in capital budgeting', *Journal of Business Finance and Accounting*, 2, No. 2, Summer.

Robichek, Alexander A. and McDonald, John G. (1965) 'The cost of capital concept: potential use and misuse', *Financial Executive*, 33, June pp. 2–8.

Woods, J. R. (1975) 'The cost of capital raised by way of a rights issue', *Investment Analyst*, September, pp. 20–29.

7

Risk and Investment Evaluation

An essential characteristic of investment decision making is orientation to the future — a future which, by its very nature, is uncertain. In earlier chapters we said very little about risk. In fact, some investment evaluation techniques appear to assume that risk can be ignored. As this assumption is relaxed, investment evaluation becomes increasingly complex. The risk dimension to capital budgeting, however, is a crucial factor in the valuation of assets, and we ignore it at our peril. Indeed, it is quite feasible that acceptance of a profitable but highly risky investment proposal may increase the perceived riskiness of the total business and result in an actual reduction in the value of the firm. Nowhere is the gap between theory and practice wider than in the area of risk analysis. Our investment survey of large UK companies revealed that, while 96 per cent of firms surveyed conducted a formal financial evaluation on investment proposals, only 37 per cent included any formal analysis of risk within that evaluation.

This chapter considers the more important approaches to the analysis and evaluation of risk within the capital budgeting decision framework. It commences by defining the various forms of risk discussed in this book and examining investors' attitudes towards risk. This is followed by a description of the main statistical methods for measuring project risk within single-period and multiperiod frameworks. A variety of risk analysis techniques will then be discussed. These fall conveniently into methods intended to *describe* or highlight risk and methods *incorporating* project riskiness within the net present value formula. The chapter concludes by examining the extent to which the methods discussed are found in business organisations.

What is Risk?

At the outset we need to clarify our terms:

Certainty Perfect certainty arises when expectations are single-valued, that is, a particular outcome will arise rather than a range of outcomes. Is there such a thing as a certain investment? Probably not, but some investments come fairly close to it. For example, an investment in three-month Treasury bills will, subject to the Bank of England keeping its promise, provide a precise return on redemption.

Risk and Uncertainty Strictly speaking, risk and uncertainty are not synonymous. *Risk* refers to the set of unique consequences for a given decision which can be assigned probabilities, while *uncertainty* implies that it is not possible to assign probabilities.

The most obvious example of risk is the one in six chance of obtaining a six from a single die. Another example is the fuel consumption per mile for a particular model of car, based on manufacturer's tests. For most investment decisions, however, empirical evidence is hard to find. Managers are then forced to make *subjective* probabilities where objective statistical evidence is not available. A manager with little prior experience of launching a particular product in a new market can still subjectively assess the risks involved based on the information available to him. Because subjective probabilities may be applied to investment decisions in a manner similar to objective probabilities, the distinction between risk and uncertainty is not critical, in practice, and the two are often used interchangeably.

Risk may be classified into a number of types. A clear understanding of the different forms of risk is useful in the evaluation and monitoring of capital projects:

Business Risk This is the variability in operating earnings before interest and tax are deducted. A firm's business risk depends, in large measure, on its *operating leverage* (the proportion of fixed costs to variable costs). The decision to become more capital intensive generally leads to an increase in the proportion of fixed costs within the cost structure. In turn, this increase in operating leverage leads to greater variability in operating earnings.

Financial Risk This is the risk, over and above business risk, which results from the use of debt. Financial leverage is increased by taking on more debt, thereby incurring more fixed-interest charges and increasing the variability in net earnings. Financial risk is considered more fully in a later chapter.

Project Risk This is the variability in the capital project's expected cash flows. In general, the greater the uncertainty in relevant markets, technologies, and factor costs, the greater the degree of project risk.

Portfolio Risk This is the variability in shareholders' returns. As we shall see in the next chapter, investors can significantly reduce their variability in earnings by holding carefully selected investment portfolios.

It is important to recognise the distinction between the *prediction* of likely events and the *course of action* that may stem from such predictions. Consider the following prediction: 'My car is unlikely to pass the MOT test next month.' It would have been preferable if the forecaster had stated more precisely just how unlikely this was by expressing the subjective probability in the outcome of the prediction. For example: 'There is a 75% probability that my car will fail the MOT test next month.' This prediction of the degree of certainty surrounding the likelihood that my car will remain legally roadworthy gives rise to a number of possible courses of action:

1. getting the car repaired;
2. selling it before the test date;
3. doing nothing in the hope that the car passes the test.

Each of these different options gives rise to different cash considerations and qualitative assessments. Investment decisions are only as good as the information upon which they rest. Relevant and useful information is central in predicting the degree of risk surrounding future economic events and in selecting the best investment option.

Expected Net Present Value

To what extent is the net present value criterion relevant in the selection of risky investments? Consider the case of the businessman contemplating three options with very different degrees of risk. The distribution of possible outcomes for these options is given in Table 7.1.

Table 7.1

Investment	*NPV* £		*Probability*		*Expected NPV* £
A	9,000	×	1	=	9,000
B	−10,000	×	0.2	=	−2,000
	10,000	×	0.5	=	5,000
	20,000	×	0.3	=	6,000
			1.0		9,000
C	−55,000	×	0.2	=	−11,000
	10,000	×	0.5	=	5,000
	50,000	×	0.3	=	15,000
			1.0		9,000

Clearly, while the NPV criterion is appropriate for investment option *A*, where the cash flows are certain, it is no longer appropriate for the risky investment options *B* and *C*, at least without adaptation. The whole range of possible outcomes may be considered by obtaining the mean of the NPV distribution weighted by the probabilities of occurrence. The NPV rule may then be applied by selecting projects offering the highest *expected* net present value. In our example, all three options offer the same expected NPV of £9,000. Should the businessman view all three as equal? The answer to this question lies in the businessman's attitude towards risk, for while the expected outcomes are the same the possible outcomes vary considerably. Thus, although the expected NPV criterion provides a single measure of profitability which may be applied to risky investments, it does not, by itself, provide an acceptable decision criterion.

Attitude to Risk

Businessmen prefer less risk to more risk for a given return. In other words they are *risk averse*. This is best grasped by introducing the important concept of *utility*, or subjective satisfaction. In general, a businessman derives less utility from gaining an additional £1,000 than he foregoes in losing £1,000. This is based on the concept of diminishing marginal utility which holds that as wealth increases, marginal utility declines at an increasing rate. Thus the utility function for risk averters is concave as shown in the graph of Figure 7.1. As long as the utility function of the decision maker can be specified, this approach may be applied in reaching investment decisions.

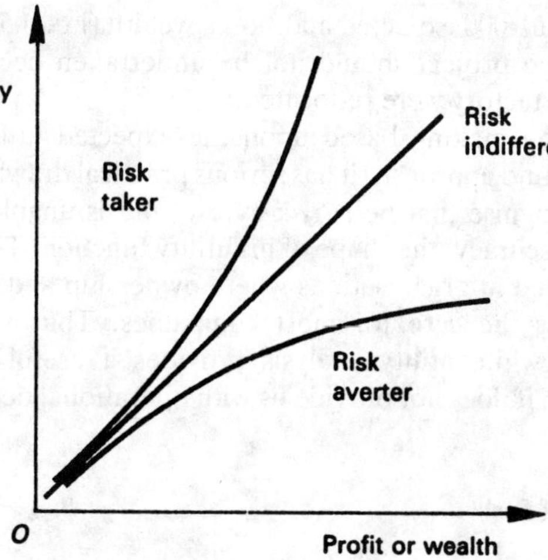

Figure 7.1 Risk Profiles

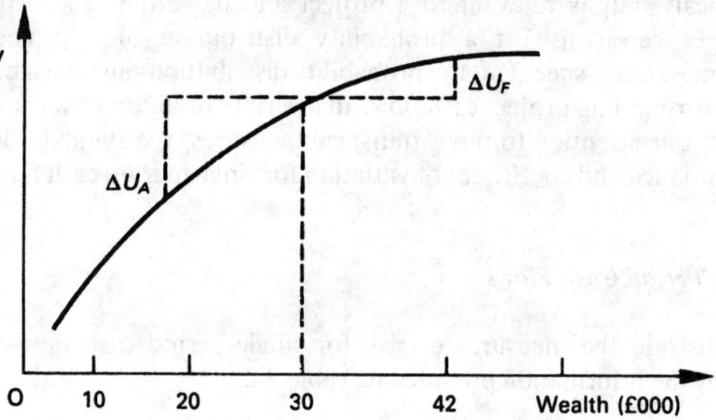

Figure 7.2 Risk Averse Utility Function

Example

A business currently worth £30,000 has an opportunity to relocate its factory to larger premises. It is estimated that there is a 50% probability of increasing its value by £12,000 and a similar probability that value will fall by £10,000. The owner's utility function is outlined in Figure 7.2. The concave slope shows that the owner is risk averse. The gain in utility (ΔU_F) as a result of the favourable outcome of £42,000 is less than the fall in utility (ΔU_A) resulting from the adverse outcome of only £20,000.

The conclusion to be drawn, therefore, is that although the investment proposal offers £1,000 expected additional wealth (i.e. 0.5 × £12,000 + 0.5 × −£10,000) the project should not be undertaken because total utility would fall if the factory were re-located.

While decision making based upon the expected utility criterion is a conceptually sound approach, it has serious practical drawbacks. A decision maker may recognise that he is risk averse, but is unable to define, with any degree of accuracy, the shape of his utility function. This becomes even more complicated in organisations where ownership and management are separated, as is the case for most companies. Thus we are forced to recognise that while utility analysis provides a useful insight into the problem of risk, it does not provide us with operational decision rules.

Measurement of Risk

Identification of the probabilities of future uncertain outcomes, although difficult, is rarely impossible. With the little knowledge the manager may have concerning the future, and by applying past experience backed by historical analysis relevant to a project and its setting, the experienced manager can construct a probability distribution of a project's cash outcomes. Once specified, the probability distribution can then measure the risks surrounding project cash flows in a variety of different ways. We shall restrict our attention to three statistical measures: the standard deviation, semivariance and coefficient of variation for single period cash flows.

Single Period Cash Flows

To illustrate the measures of risk for single-period cash flows we shall employ the information provided in Table 7.2.

Table 7.2

State of economy	*Probability of outcome*	*Cash flow (£)* A	B
Strong	0.2	700	550
Normal	0.5	400	400
Weak	0.3	200	300

Standard Deviation

We have already seen that expected value is not by itself an acceptable criterion because it omits important information — the dispersion (risk) of

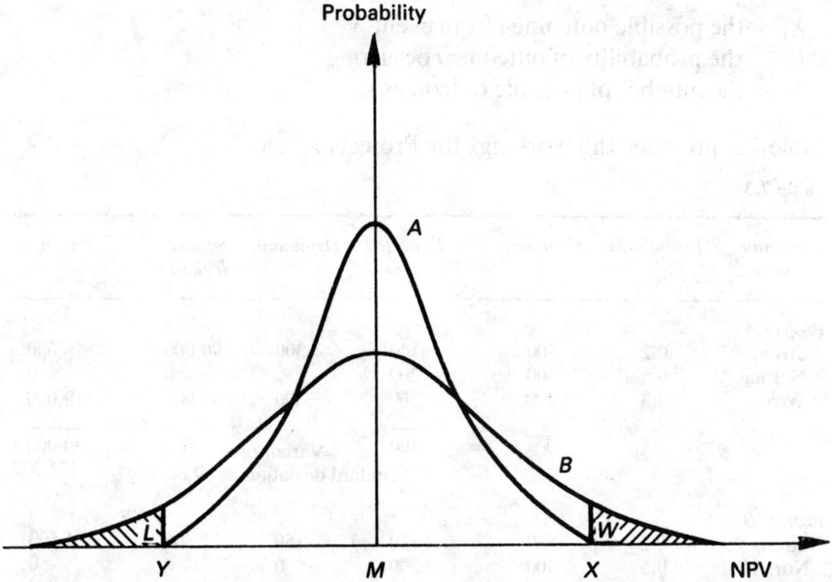

Figure 7.3

the outcomes. We know that different people behave differently in risky situations. Consider projects A and B and their NPV distributions in Figure 7.3.

Both projects have the same expected NPV but project B has greater dispersion. The risk averter will choose A since he wants to minimise risk. The risk taker will choose B because the NPV of project B has a chance (W) of being higher than X — which project A cannot offer — but also a chance (L) of being lower than Y.

It is impossible to predict people's choice without knowing their attitudes to risk. In general, people don't like risk. Hereafter we make a reasonable assumption: people are risk averters. The standard deviation is a measure of the dispersion; the wider the dispersion, the higher the standard deviation. The expected value of cash flows is given by the equation:

$$\bar{X} = \sum_{i=1}^{N} P_i X_i$$

and the standard deviation of the cash flows:

$$\sigma = \sqrt{\sum_{i=1}^{N} P_i (X_i - \bar{X})^2}$$

where

$\bar{X}$ = the expected value of event X

X_i = the possible outcome i from event X
P_i = the probability of outcome i occurring
N = the number of possible outcomes

Table 7.3 provides the workings for Projects A and B.

Table 7.3

Economic state	*Probability*	*Outcome*		*Expected value*	*Deviation*	*Squared deviation*		*Variance*
Project A								
Strong	0.2	700		140	300	90,000		18,000
Normal	0.5	400		200	0	0		0
Weak	0.3	200		60	−200	40,000		12,000
		$\overline{X_A}$	=	400	Variance =	σ_A^2	=	30,000
					Standard deviation =	σ_A	=	173.2
Project B								
Strong	0.2	550		110	150	22,500		4,500
Normal	0.5	400		200	0	0		0
Weak	0.3	300		90	−100	10,000		3,000
		$\overline{X_B}$	=	400	Variance =	σ_B^2	=	7,500
					Standard deviation =	σ_B	=	86.6

Alternatively,

$$\overline{X_A} = 700\ (0.2) + 400\ (0.5) + 200\ (0.3) = 400$$
$$\sigma_A = \sqrt{0.2\ (700 - 400)^2 + 0.5\ (400 - 400)^2 + 0.3\ (200 - 400)^2}$$
$$= 173.2$$
$$\overline{X_B} = 550\ (0.2) + 400\ (0.5) + 300\ (0.3) = 400$$
$$\sigma_B = \sqrt{0.2\ (550 - 400)^2 + 0.5\ (440 - 400)^2 + 0.3\ (200 - 300)^2}$$
$$= 86.6$$

Applying the formulae, we obtain an expected cash flow of £400 for both project A and project B. If the decision maker had a neutral risk attitude he would view the two projects equally favourably. As, however, he is likely to be risk averse, it is appropriate to examine the standard deviations of the two probability distributions. Here we see that project A, with a standard deviation twice that of project B, is more risky and hence less attractive. No doubt the reader could have deduced this fact simply by observing the distribution of outcomes and noting that the same probabilities apply to both projects. Observation cannot, however, tell us by how much one project is riskier than another.

Semivariance

Some writers have argued[1] that, while deviations above the mean may be viewed favourably by businessmen, it is only 'downside risk' that is considered in the decision process. Downside risk is best measured by the semivariance, a special case of the variance, given by the formula:

$$SV = \sum_{j=1}^{K} P_j (X_j - \bar{X})^2$$

where

SV = semivariance
j = all values of X which are less than the expected value
K = number of outcomes which are less than the expected value

Applying the semivariance to the previous example in Table 7.3, the downside risk relates exclusively to the 'weak' state of the economy:

$$SV_A = 0.3\,(200 - 400)^2 = £12{,}000$$
$$SV_B = 0.3\,(300 - 400)^2 = £3{,}000$$

Once again project *B* is seen to have a much lower degree of risk. In both cases the semivariance accounts for 40 per cent of the project variance.

Coefficient of Variation

It is not altogether satisfactory to make direct comparison between projects on the basis of *absolute* risk measures such as those previously defined. Where projects differ in scale, a more valid comparison is found by applying a *relative* risk measure such as the coefficient of variation.[2] This is calculated by dividing the standard deviation by the expected value of net cash flows as in the equation:

$$CV = \frac{\sigma}{\bar{X}}$$

In our example from Table 7.3 this gives the following coefficients:

Project *A* 173.2/400 = 0.43
Project *B* 86.6/400 = 0.22

As in this case both projects have the same expected cash flows the outcomes are no different from the previous two measures — in all three cases project *B* has a significantly lower degree of risk but the same expected value. In the next example, however, the two projects under review are different in scale.

	Standard deviation		*Expected value*		*Coefficient of variation*
Project *P*	1,000	÷	10,000	=	0.1
Project *Q*	2,000	÷	40,000	=	0.05

Although the absolute measure of dispersion (the standard deviation) is greater for project *Q*, few businessmen would regard it as of greater risk than project *P* because of the significant difference in the expected values of the two investments. The coefficient of variation reveals that *Q* actually offers the lower amount of risk per £1 of expected value.

Mean–Variance Rule

Given the expected return and the measure of dispersion (variance or standard deviation), it is possible to formulate the operational rule commonly referred to as the mean–variance rule. This rule states that project *X* will be preferred to project *Y* if at least one of the following conditions apply:

(i) the expected return of *X* exceeds that of *Y* and the variance is equal to or less than that of *Y*; or

(ii) the expected return of *X* exceeds or is equal to the expected return of *Y* and the variance is less than that of *Y*.

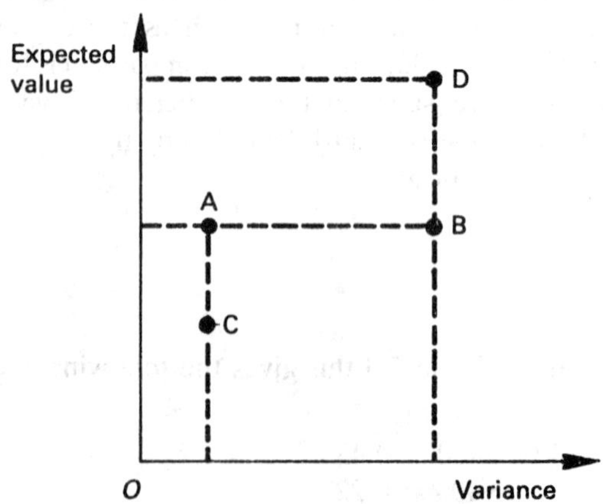

Figure 7.4

This is illustrated in Figure 7.4. Projects *A* and *D* are always preferable to projects *C* and *B* respectively because they offer a higher return for the same degree of risk. In addition, *A* is preferable to *B* because for the same expected return it incurs lower risk. The importance of the mean–variance rule is that it is applicable to all risk averters regardless of their particular utility functions. What this rule cannot do, however, is distinguish between projects where both expected returns and risk differ (projects *A* and *D* in Figure 7.4). This important aspect will be discussed in Chapter 8.

Multiperiod Cash Flows

So far our analysis of risk has assumed single-period investments. We have conveniently ignored the fact that typically investments are multiperiod and hence our analysis must be based on net present values. As risk is to be specifically evaluated, cash flows should be discounted at the risk-free rate of interest reflecting only the time value of money. To include a risk premium within the discount rate when risk is already considered separately amounts to double counting and typically understates the true net present value. The expected NPV of an investment project is found by summing the present values of the expected net cash flows and deducting the initial investment outlay. Thus, for a two-year investment proposal:

$$\overline{NPV} = \frac{\overline{X}_1}{1 + r} + \frac{\overline{X}_2}{(1 + r)^2} - I$$

where

$\overline{NPV}$ = expected NPV
$\overline{X}_1$ = expected value of net cash flow in year 1
$\overline{X}_2$ = expected value of net cash flow in year 2
I = investment outlay
r = risk-free rate of interest

Independent Cash Flows

A major problem in the calculation of the standard deviation of a project's NPVs for multiperiod projects lies in the fact that the cash flows in one period are typically dependent, to some degree, on the cash flows of earlier periods. Assuming for the present that cash flows for our two-period project are statistically *independent*, the total variance of the NPV is equal to the discounted sum of the annual variances. This is illustrated by the following example: assume a project with a two-year life has an initial cost of £500 and the possible payoffs and probabilities outlined in Table 7.4. Applying the standard deviation and expected value formulae already discussed, we obtain:

Table 7.4

Probability	*Year 1 cash flow (£)*	*Year 2 cash flow (£)*
0.1	100	200
0.2	200	400
0.4	300	600
0.2	400	800
0.1	500	1000

	Year 1	*Year 2*
Expected value	£300	£600
Standard deviation	£109	£219

Assuming a risk-free discount rate of 10 per cent, the expected NPV is:

$$\overline{NPV} = \frac{300}{(1.10)} + \frac{600}{(1.10)^2} - 500$$

$$= £268$$

The standard deviation of the entire proposal is found by discounting the annual variances to their present values, applying the equation:

$$\sigma = \sqrt{\sum_{t=1}^{N} \frac{\sigma_t^2}{(1+r)^{2t}}}$$

In our simple case this is:

$$\sigma = \sqrt{\frac{\sigma_1^2}{(1+r)^2} + \frac{\sigma_2^2}{(1+r)^4}}$$

$$= \sqrt{\frac{12,000}{(1.1)^2} + \frac{48,000}{(1.1)^4}}$$

$$= £206$$

The project therefore offers an expected NPV of £268 and a standard deviation of £206.

Perfectly Correlated Cash Flows[3]

At the other extreme to the statistical independence assumption between periods is the assumption that the cash flows in one year are entirely dependent upon the cash flows achieved in previous periods. When this is the case, cash flows are said to be perfectly correlated. Any deviation in one year from forecast directly affects the accuracy of subsequent forecasts. The effect of cash flows being correlated over time is that the standard deviation of the probability distribution of net present values increases. The standard deviation of a stream of cash flows perfectly correlated over time is:

$$\sigma = \sum_{t=1}^{N} \frac{\sigma}{(1 + i)^t}$$

Returning to the example in Table 7.4, but assuming perfect correlation of cash flows over time, the standard deviation for the project is:

$$\sigma = \frac{109.5}{1.1} + \frac{219.1}{(1.1)^2}$$
$$= £280.6$$

Thus the risk associated with this two period project is £280.60, assuming perfect correlation. Reference back to the calculation assuming independence of cash flows gives a lower standard deviation of £206. Obviously this difference would be considerably greater for longer-lived projects.

Interpreting Results

While our decision maker is interested to know the degree of risk associated with a given project, his fundamental concern is 'Will this project produce a positive net present value?' Risk analysis can go some way to answering this question. If a project's probability distribution of expected NPVs is approximately normal, we can estimate the probability of failing to achieve at least zero NPV. In the previous example the expected NPV was £268. This is then standardized by dividing it by the standard deviation using the formula:

$$S = \frac{X - \overline{NPV}}{\sigma}$$

where X is in this case zero. Thus we have in the case of the independent cash flow assumption:

$$S = \frac{0 - 268}{206}$$
$$= -1.30 \text{ standard deviation}$$

Reference to normal distribution tables reveals that there is a 0.0968 probability that the NPV will be zero or less. Accordingly there must be a

1 −0.0968 or 90.32 per cent probability of the project producing an NPV in excess of zero. The decision maker can then subjectively relate this risk with his particular utility function before reaching a decision.

In reality, few projects are either independent or perfectly correlated over time. How then should the standard deviation of the net present values be computed? It will be clear that the answer lies somewhere between the two, and will be based on the formula for the independence case but with an additional term for the covariance between annual cash flows.

Risk Analysis Methods

Two broad approaches may be adopted for handling the risk dimension within the investment decision process. The first approach attempts to *describe* the riskiness of a given project, either using various applications of probability analysis or some simple method. The second approach aims to *incorporate* the investor's perception of project riskiness within the NPV formula. We now turn our attention to the various techniques available which help describe investment risk.

Sensitivity Analysis

In principle, sensitivity analysis is a very simple concept, used to locate and assess the potential impact of risk on a project's profitability. It does not aim to quantify risk, but rather to identify factors that are potentially risk-sensitive. Sensitivity analysis merely provides the decision maker with answers to a whole range of 'what if' questions. For example: what is the NPV if selling price falls by 10 per cent? What is the IRR if the project's life is only three years, not five years as expected? What is the level of sales revenue required to break-even in net present value terms?

Sensitivity graphs permit the plotting of net present values (or IRRs) against the percentage deviation from the expected value of the factor under investigation. This is illustrated by the sensitivity graph in Figure 7.5 depicting the potential impact of deviations from the expected values of a project's variables on NPV. When everything is unchanged, the NPV is 2,000. However, NPV becomes zero when market size decreases by 20% and price decreases by 5%. This shows that the profitability is very sensitive to price change. Similarly, a 10% increase in discount rate will make the NPV equal to zero while fixed costs must increase to 25% in order to make the project unprofitable. Therefore the project is more sensitive to discount rate than fixed costs. The sensitivity of NPV to each factor is reflected by the slope of the sensitivity line.

Sensitivity analysis is widely used because of its simplicity and ability to focus on particular estimates. It can identify the critical factors which have

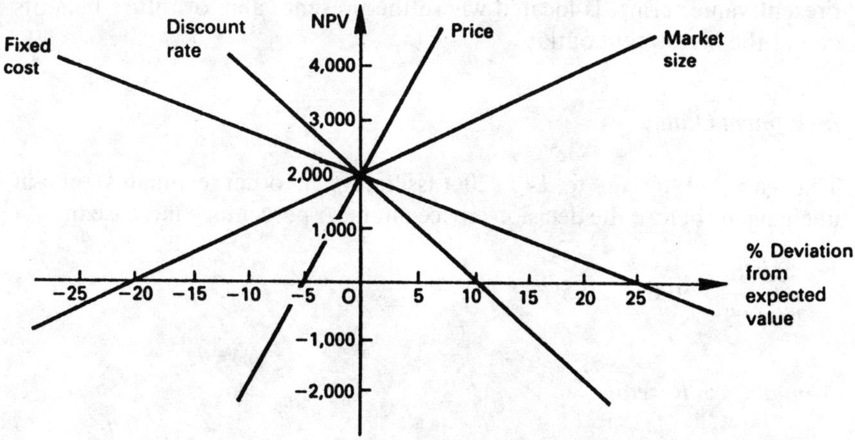

Figure 7.5 Sensitivity Graph

greatest impact on a project's profitability. It does not however actually evaluate risk; the decision maker must still assess the probability of occurrence for these deviations from expected values. The above approach is sometimes referred to as deterministic sensitivity analysis. Probabilistic sensitivity analysis is described in the next section.

An application of sensitivity analysis is illustrated in the following example: the accountant of Poltech plc has put together the cash flow forecasts for a new product with a four-year life involving capital investment of £200,000 to produce a net present value, at a 10 per cent discount rate, of £40,920. His basic analysis is given below:

Unit data	£	£
Selling price		20
less Materials	6	
Labour	5	
Variable costs	1	
		12
Contribution		8
Annual sales		12,000
Total contribution		96,000
less Additional fixed costs		20,000
Annual net cash flow		76,000
Present value — 4 years at 10%:		
76,000 × 3.17		240,920
less Capital outlay		200,000
Net present value		40,920

Which factors are most critical to the decision? The break-even point, in net present value terms, is located where the present value of future benefits equals the investment outlay.

Investment Outlay

This can rise by up to £40,920 (assuming all other estimates remain unchanged) before the decision advice alters. A percentage increase of

$$\frac{40{,}920}{200{,}000} \times 100 = 20.5\%$$

Annual Cash Receipts

The break-even position is reached when annual cash receipts multiplied by the annuity factor equal the investment outlay:

$$\frac{£200{,}000}{3.17} = £63{,}091$$

This is a percentage fall of $\dfrac{76{,}000 - 63{,}091}{76{,}000} \times 100 = 17.0\%$

Annual fixed costs could increase by the same amount of £12,909 or

$$\frac{12{,}909}{20{,}000} \times 100 = 64.5\%$$

Annual Volume

The break-even annual contribution is £63,091 + £20,000 = £83,091.

Volume to break-even is $\dfrac{£83{,}091}{£8} = 10{,}386$

a decline of $\dfrac{12{,}000 - 10{,}386}{12{,}000} \times 100 = 13.5\%$

Selling price can fall by:

$\dfrac{96{,}000 - 83{,}091}{12{,}000} = £1.07$ per unit: a decline of

$$\frac{1.07}{20} \times 100 = 5.4\%$$

Variable costs can rise by:

$$\frac{1.07}{12} \times 100 = 8.9\%$$

Discount Rate

The break-even annuity factor is $\frac{200{,}000}{76{,}000} = 2.63$

Reference to the present value annuity tables for four years shows this to be an IRR of 19%. The error in cost of capital calculation could be as much as 9 percentage points before it affects the decision advice.

Sensitivity analysis, as applied in the above example, discloses that selling price and variable costs are the two most critical variables in the investment decision. The decision maker must then decide (subjectively or objectively) the probabilities of such changes occurring, and whether he is prepared to accept the risk involved.

Simulation Approach

Monte Carlo simulation is an operations research technique with a variety of business applications. One of the first writers to apply the simulation approach to risky investments was David B. Hertz who, in a *Harvard Business Review* article, described the approach adopted by his consultancy firm in evaluating a major expansion of the processing plant of an industrial chemical producer. This approach involved constructing a mathematical model which captured the essential characteristics of the investment proposal throughout its life as it encountered random events. A simulation model considers the following exogenous (input) variables which are subject to random variation.

Market-related factors
1. Market size
2. Market growth rate
3. Selling price of product
4. Market share captured by the firm

Investment-related factors
5. Investment outlay
6. Useful life of investment
7. Residual value of the investment

Cost-related factors
8. Variable operating unit cost
9. Fixed costs

Probability distributions are assigned to each of these variables, based upon

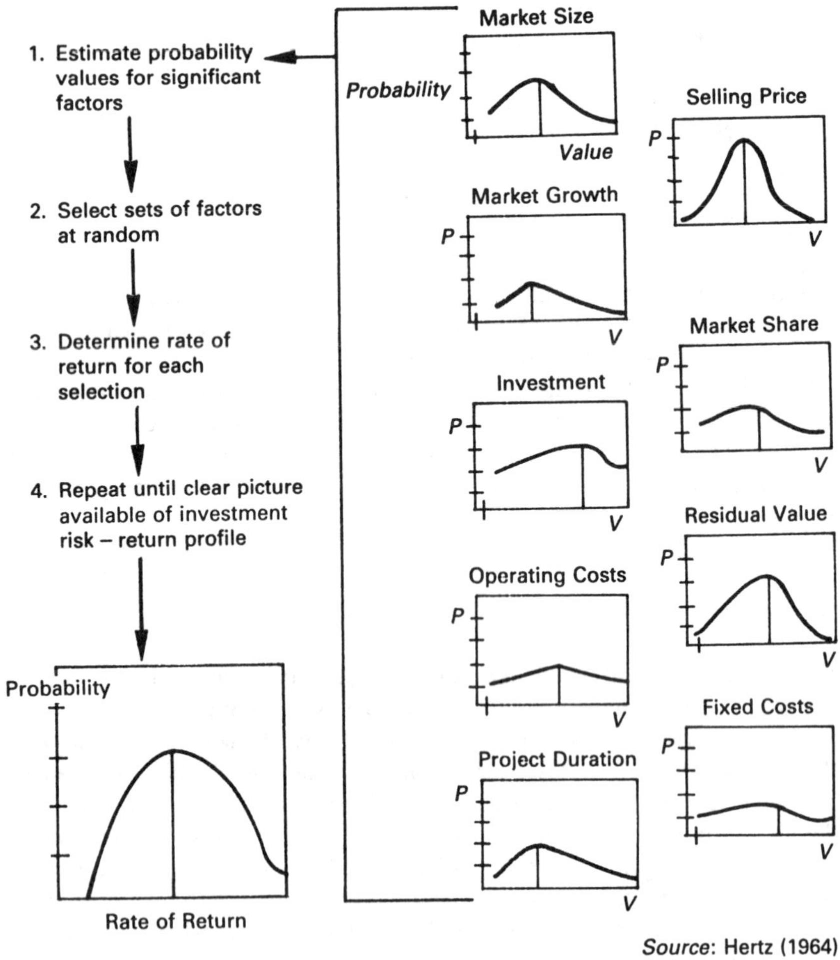

Figure 7.6 Simulation for Investment Planning

management's perception of the probability of occurrence, as shown in Figure 7.6.

The next step is to determine the net present value that will result from a random combination of the exogenous factors involved. For example, suppose the market share factor has the following distribution:

Market Share (%)	*Probability*
6	0.10
7	0.25
8	0.30
9	0.25
10	0.10

Applying these probabilities we can say that out of a possible total of 100, if a random number is generated between 0 and 10, this simulates a market share of 6 per cent. If a random number is generated between 11 and 35, this simulates a market share of 7 per cent, and so on. This process of simulation is conducted on all variables to produce, after discounting, the net present value of the proposal based on that trial run. The process is repeated many times for each of the nine variables, eventually producing enough outcomes to construct the probability distribution for the proposal's net present value. Comparison is then possible between mutually exclusive projects whose NPV probability distributions have been calculated in this manner (Figure 7.7). It will be observed that project *A*, with a higher expected NPV and lower risk dominates project *B*.

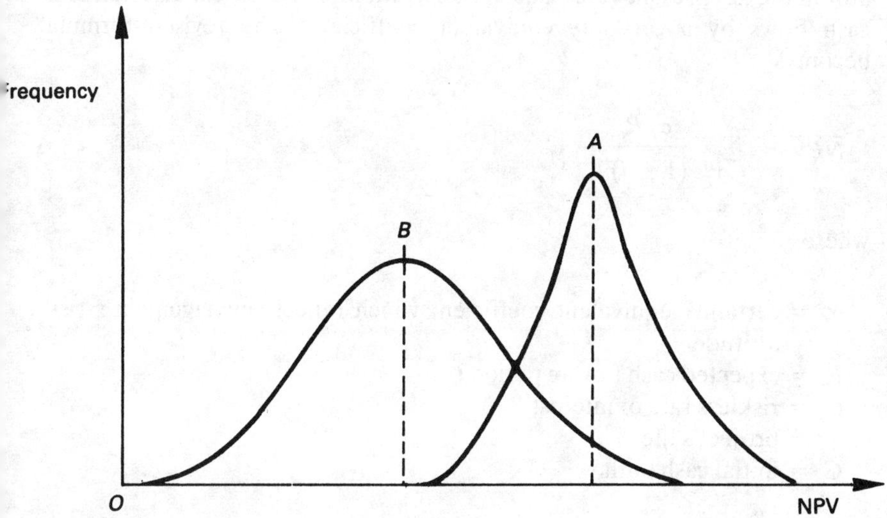

Figure 7.7

A number of simulation programmes are available to the user. One such is provided in Program 4 (see Chapter 18). Why then is it so rarely employed?

1. The simple model described above assumes the economic factors are independent. Clearly many of these factors (e.g. market share and selling price) are statistically dependent. To the extent that dependency exists among variables, it must be specified. Such interrelationships are not always clear and are frequently complex to model.
2. Managers are required to specify probability distributions for the exogenous variables. Few managers are able or willing to accept the demands required by the simulation approach.

Adjusting for Risk

Two approaches are commonly used to incorporate risk within the NPV formula:

Certainty Equivalent Method

This conceptually appealing approach permits adjustment for risk by incorporating the decision maker's utility risk preference into the capital investment decision. The certainty equivalent method adjusts the numerator in the net present value calculation by multiplying the expected annual cash flows by a certainty equivalent coefficient. The revised formula becomes

$$\overline{NPV} = \sum_{t=1}^{N} \frac{\alpha_t \bar{R}_t}{(1 + i)^t} - C$$

where

α_t = certainty equivalent coefficient which reflects management's risk attitude
$\bar{R}_t$ = expected cash flow in period t
i = riskless rate of interest
n = project's life
C = initial cash outlay

The numerator (αR_t) represents the figure that management would be willing to receive as a certain sum each year in place of the uncertain annual cash flow offered by the project. The greater is management's aversion to risk, the nearer the certainty equivalent coefficient approaches zero. Where projects are of normal risk for the business, and the cost of capital and risk-free rate of interest are known, it is possible to determine the certainty equivalent coefficient.

Example

Calculate the certainty coefficient for a normal risk project with a one-year life and an expected cash flow of £5,000 receivable at the end of the year. The company has a cost of capital of 12% and the risk-free rate of interest is 6%.

Solution

The present value of the project, using the cost of capital as the discount rate, is as follows:

$$PV = \frac{£5,000}{1 + 0.12} = £4,464.28$$

Using this present value and substituting the risk-free interest rate for the cost of capital we obtain the certainty equivalent coefficient:

$$\frac{\alpha \cdot £5,000}{1 + 0.06} = £4,464.28$$

$$\alpha = \frac{(£4,464.28)\ (1.06)}{£5,000}$$

$$= 0.9464$$

The management is, therefore, indifferent as to whether it receives an uncertain cash flow one year hence of £5,000 or a certain cash flow of £4,732 (i.e. £5,000 × 0.9464).

Risk-Adjusted Discount Rate

Whereas the certainty equivalent approach adjusted the numerator in the NPV formula, the risk-adjusted discount rate adjusts the denominator:

$$\overline{NPV} = \sum_{t=1}^{N} \frac{\overline{R_t}}{(1 + r)^t} - C$$

where r is the risk-adjusted discount rate based on the perceived degree of project risk. The higher the perceived riskiness of a project, the greater the risk premium to be added to the risk-free interest rate. This results in a higher discount rate and, hence, a lower net present value.

Although this approach has a certain intuitive appeal, its relevance depends very much on how risk is perceived to change over time. The risk-adjusted discount rate assumes that the risk premium grows over time at an exponential rate. Consider the case of a manufacturer of confectionery currently appraising a proposal to launch a new product which has had very little pre-launch testing. It is estimated that this proposal will produce annual cash flows in the region of £100,000 for the next five years, after which product profitability declines sharply. As the proposal is seen as a high-risk venture, a 12 per cent risk premium is incorporated in the discount rate. The risk-adjusted cash flow, before discounting at the risk-free discount rate is, therefore, £89,286 in year 1 (£100,000/1.12) falling to £56,743 in year 5 (£100,000/$(1.12)^5$).

To what extent does this method reflect the actual riskiness of the annual cash flows for years 1 and 5? Arguably, greatest uncertainty surrounds the initial launch period. Once the initial market penetration and subsequent repeat orders are known, the subsequent sales are relatively easy to forecast. Thus, in this example, a single risk-adjusted discount rate is a poor proxy for the impact of risk on value over the project's life, because risk does not increase exponentially with the passage of time.

Relationship between Certainty Equivalent and Risk-Adjusted Rate Approaches

We have seen that both the certainty equivalent and risk-adjusted discount rate approaches attempt to incorporate project risk within the NPV formula. The certainty equivalent formula is:

$$PV = \sum_{t=1}^{n} \frac{\alpha_t R_t}{(1+i)^t}$$

where α_t represents the measure of investors' degree of risk aversion, the relationship being:

$\alpha < 1$ risk aversion
$\alpha = 1$ risk neutral
$\alpha > 1$ risk taking

The risk-adjusted discount rate formula is:

$$PV = \sum_{t=1}^{n} \frac{R_t}{(1+r_t)^t}$$

where r_t is the appropriate discount rate which reflects the riskiness of cash flow in period t.

Assuming a constant discount rate r, the two approaches should give the same present value of cash flow for each period:

$$\frac{R_1}{1+r} = \frac{\alpha_1 R_1}{1+i} \quad \cdots\cdots \quad \frac{R_t}{(1+r)^t} = \frac{\alpha_t R_t}{(1+i)^t}$$

This implies that

$$\alpha_1 = \frac{1+i}{1+r} \quad \cdots\cdots \quad \alpha_t = \left(\frac{1+i}{1+r}\right)^t$$

So a constant risk-adjusted discount rate is equivalent to the certainty equivalent coefficient α_t where

$$\alpha_t = \left(\frac{1+i}{1+r}\right)^t$$

Assuming both the discount rate and certainty equivalent coefficient are constant over time, the net present value of risky cash flows must be the same, as shown below:

$$NPV = \sum_{t=1}^{n} \frac{R_t}{(1+r)^t} = \sum_{t=1}^{n} \frac{\alpha R_t}{(1+i)^t} = \alpha \sum_{t=1}^{n} \frac{R_t}{(1+i)^t}$$

This implies that:

$$\alpha = \frac{\sum_{t=1}^{n} R_t/(1+r)^t}{\sum_{t=1}^{n} R_t/(1+i)^t}$$

where α is the weighted average coefficient of certainty equivalent of the project.

Example

A project with a certain immediate cash outlay of £3,000 offers uncertain cash receipts of £2,000 in years 1 and 2. The risk-free rate of interest is 10 per cent. Management estimates the risk premium for this investment to be a further 10 per cent, giving a risk-adjusted discount rate of 20 per cent. Applying the *NPV* formula:

$$\begin{aligned} NPV &= -£3{,}000 + \frac{£2{,}000}{1.2} + \frac{£2{,}000}{(1.2)^2} \\ &= -£3{,}000 + £1{,}667 + £1{,}388 \\ &= £55 \end{aligned}$$

Discounting at the risk-free interest rate gives

$$\begin{aligned} NPV &= -£3{,}000 + \frac{£2{,}000}{1.1} + \frac{£2{,}000}{(1.1)^2} \\ &= -£3{,}000 + £1{,}818 + £1{,}653 \\ &= £471 \end{aligned}$$

The certainty equivalent coefficient is the relationship between the sum of the present values of the risky cash flows discounted at risk-adjusted and risk-free rates.

$$\alpha = \frac{£1{,}667 + £1{,}388}{£1{,}818 + £1{,}653} = \frac{£3{,}055}{£3{,}471}$$
$$= 0.88$$

Applying the certainty equivalent method with this coefficient produces the same *NPV* as above of £55.

$$NPV = -£3{,}000 + \frac{0.88\ (2{,}000)}{1.1} + \frac{0.88\ (2{,}000)}{(1.1)^2}$$
$$= -£300 + 1{,}600 + 1{,}455$$
$$= £55$$

It was noted at the start of the chapter that for most UK companies formal risk analysis does not form part of the investment decision process. Table 7.5 shows the percentage of firms using risk analysis techniques in 1975 and 1980. Two observations are drawn from these findings. First, that although the gap between theory and practice is immense in this regard, the trend is towards greater use of risk analysis methods. Second, that the techniques adopted tend to be simple, rule-of-thumb methods. Sensitivity analysis does not aim to analyse risk, but locates the potential impact of risk on project profitability. Shortening payback period and increasing the discount rate for risk projects are traditional rule-of-thumb approaches.

Table 7.5 Percentage of Firms using Risk Analysis Techniques (150 firms)

	1980	*1975*
Sensitivity analysis	38	24
Risk-adjusted rate	36	33
Shortening payback period	31	23
Probability analysis	12	8

Note: Many firms use more than one method.
Source: Pike (1982) *Capital Budgeting in the 1980s*, ICMA, Occasional Paper Series.

Why are so few managers prepared formally to analyse risk? Responses from the same survey suggest that risk is too dificult and costly to quantify and too complicated for managers to understand.

'Risk analysis is not popular with managers, partly because they find it

> difficult to grasp and partly because they have little information on which to assess the risk parameters.'

> 'We have used risk appraisal using probability but it is time consuming, to some extent the probability assessments reflect subjective judgements anyway and finally few people really understand it.'

Consequently an informal, more qualitative approach is adopted:

> 'Risk judgement is built into the commercial factors affecting the project. It is not analysed mathematically — this is merely playing with figures.'

> 'Any assessment of risk is completely subjective. Senior management can often be confused by either a range of possible outcomes or an attempt to assess the probability distribution.'

In those firms where risk analysis is conducted, its main purpose appears to be to make the decision maker aware of the risks he is taking:

> 'My Board must know the probable chances of success of any proposal.'

> 'Good for getting "feel" for uncertainty, and for forcing project sponsors/estimators to think about how wrong they could be.'

Summary

Risk is an important element in virtually all investment decisions. Because most businessmen are risk-averse, preferring less risk to more, the identification, measurement and, where possible, reduction of risk should be a central feature in the decision-making process. The evidence, however, suggests that firms conducting risk analysis are in the minority. This does not mean that the risk dimension is totally ignored by other firms; rather, they choose to handle project risk by less objective methods such as experience, feel or intuition.

In this chapter we have defined what is meant by risk and examined a variety of ways of measuring it. The probability distribution, giving the probability of occurrence of each possible outcome following an investment decision, is the concept underlying most of the methods discussed. Measures of risk, such as the standard deviation and cooefficient of variation, indicate the extent to which actual outcomes are likely to vary from the expected value. The semivariance is another useful measure of risk which may better simulate the decision maker's perceptions since it weights negative variations more heavily than positive variations. Other viable techniques for risk analysis include Monte Carlo simulation and sensitivity analysis.

Finally, the certainty equivalent and risk-adjusted rate of return approaches were introduced as ways by which the net present value formula may be adjusted to account for risk. In the following chapter this notion will be developed to show how the capital asset pricing model provides a means for determining a market-adjusted discount rate suitable for determining the net present value of risky investments.

Questions

1. Explain the importance of risk in capital budgeting.
2. What do you understand by the following:
   (i) risk
   (ii) uncertainty
   (iii) risk aversion
   (iv) expected value
   (v) standard deviation
   (vi) semi-variance
   (vii) mean-variance rule
3. Explain the distinction between project risk, business risk, financial risk and portfolio risk.
4. Why is it not always appropriate to judge projects solely on the basis of expected net present values?
5. Project *X* has an expected return of £2,000 and a standard deviation of £400. Project *Y* has an expected return of £1,000 and a standard deviation of £400. Which project is more risky?
6. Explain the relationship between the risk-adjusted discount rate and the certainty equivalent approach.
7. What do you understand by Monte Carlo simulation? When might it be useful in capital budgeting?
8. The 'woodpulp' project has an initial cost of £13,000 and the firm's risk-free interest rate is 10 per cent. If certainty equivalents and net cash flows for the project are as below, should the project be accepted?

Year	*Certainty Equivalents*	*Net Cash Flows* (£)
1	0.90	8,000
2	0.85	7,000
3	0.80	7,000
4	0.75	5,000
5	0.70	5,000
6	0.65	5,000
7	0.60	5,000

9. The NPV probability distributions for projects *X* and *Y* are given below:

Probability	*Project X* (£)	*Project Y* (£)
0.2	2,000	0
0.6	3,000	3,000
0.2	4,000	6,000

Calculate the expected NPV, the standard deviation, and coefficient of variation for each project. Which of these mutually exclusive projects would you accept?

10. Mystery Enterprises has a proposal costing £800. Using a 10 per cent cost of capital, compute the expected NPV, standard deviation and coefficient of variation assuming independent interperiod cash flows.

Probability	*Year 1* *Net cash flow* (£)	*Year 2* *Net cash flow* (£)
0.2	400	300
0.3	500	400
0.3	600	500
0.2	700	600

11. Recalculate the previous problem, assuming perfectly dependent cash flows.
12. Check your answers to questions 10 and 11 using the computer program in the Appendix.
13. Mikado plc is considering launching a new product involving capital investment of £180,000. The machine has a four-year life and no residual value. Sales volumes of 6,000 units are forecast for each of the four years. The product has a selling price of £60 and a variable cost of £36 per unit. Additional fixed overheads of £50,000 will be incurred. The cost of capital is 12½% p.a. Present a report to the directors of Mikado plc giving:

    (i) the net present value;
    (ii) the percentage amount each variable can deteriorate before the project becomes unacceptable;
    (iii) a sensitivity graph.

14. The directors of Statham Ltd are considering which two of three possible investment projects the company should accept. Each project will last for one year and returns will depend on which of three economic environments prevails during that year. Each project requires the same level of investment. The directors estimate returns for the year and the probabilities of the three possible environments as follows:

Environment	*Probability of environment*	*Estimated returns*		
		Project 1	*Project 2*	*Project 3*
A	0.2	22%	16%	36%
B	0.4	22%	21%	22%
C	0.4	22%	26%	15%

For each economic environment, the percentage return from project 2 is equivalent to that expected from the company's other activities and to that expected from holding a well diversified market portfolio. The

investment in each pair of projects will be equivalent to 10% of the company's total investment.
You are required to:

(a) prepare calculations for the directors of Statham Ltd showing which two projects should be accepted;
(b) write a report to the directors of Statham Ltd explaining the basic principles involved in your calculations and discussing the implications of those principles for investment appraisal.

Ignore taxation. (ICA, PE II, July 1981)

15. The directors of Astros plc are considering the purchase and exploitation of a disused tin mine which is being offered for sale for £50,000. A review of the mine's history shows that the total amount of pure tin that can be extracted depends upon the type of rock formations in the area and that only the following three possibilities exist:

Rock type	*Total tin output*	*Probability*
A	240 tonnes	0.4
B	120 tonnes	0.4
C	72 tonnes	0.2

If Astros purchases the mine, the first year of ownership will be spent in making the mine and associated smelting plants operational, at a cost of £95,000 payable at the end of the year. Production will start at the beginning of the second year of ownership, when the output of pure tin will be 2 tonnes per month, whatever the type of rock formations. This production rate will remain unchanged until the mine is exhausted. During the first year of production, the directors expect that the resale value of the tin will be £9,900 per tonne and that labour and other production costs will be £187,000. These revenues and costs are expected to rise by 10% per annum in subsequent years. These cash flows can be assumed to occur at the end of the year in which they arise. Special mining equipment will also be purchased at the beginning of the first year of production at a cost of £48,000. This equipment will be sold immediately on the cessation of production, at an amount expected to equal its purchase price, less £200 for every tonne of tin produced during its life. Other revenues from the sale of the mine at the end of production are expected to equal the closure costs exactly.

Astros plc has received permission from the present owners of the mine to carry out a geological survey of the area. The survey would cost £10,000 and would reveal for certain the type of rock formations in the area and hence how much tin could be produced from the mine.

Astros plc has a money cost of capital of 21% per annum for this type of project.
You are required to:

(a) calculate the expected net present value of purchasing the mine, assuming that the geological survey is *not* undertaken;
(b) advise the directors of Astros plc whether or not they should commission the geological survey.

Ignore taxation. (ICA, PE II, December 1983)

16. Idaho Ltd designs and manufactures toys. A typical toy has a commercial life of three years. Heavy initial advertising generally leads to relatively high sales during the first two years of a toy's commercial life but there is often a substantial decline in demand during the final year. The level of demand for a toy over its life depends on product acceptance. The marketing department of Idaho Ltd has just completed an analysis of the demand for the most recent 200 types of toy marketed by the company. The analysis indicates that of the 200 types of toy, 50 enjoyed an above-average demand throughout their commercial lives, 120 an average demand and 30 a below-average demand.

Idaho Ltd has recently developed a new toy, the Oregon. Development costs amounted to £3,500 and have just been paid. The marketing department has made the following estimates of sales for the Oregon:

	Sales Revenue		
	Year 1	*Year 2*	*Year 3*
	(£)	(£)	(£)
If demand is above average	24,000	50,000	16,000
If demand is average	14,000	34,000	8,000
If demand is below average	5,000	18,000	5,000

Variable costs will amount to 30% of sales revenue. Sales revenue will be received and variable costs will be paid on the last day of the year in which they arise.

If Oregons are produced, a special machine will have to be purchased at the start of year 1 at a cost of £19,000, payable at the time of purchase. The machine will have a scrap value at the end of the product's life of £1,000, receivable one year after the last year in which production takes place.

If purchased, the machine will be installed in an unused part of one of Idaho Ltd's factories. The company has been trying to let this unused factory space at a rent of £1,600 per annum. Although there now seems no chance of letting the space during year 1, there is a 60% chance of letting it for two years at the beginning of year 2, and a 50% chance of letting it for one year at the beginning of year 3, provided that it has not been let at the beginning of year 2. Any rental receipts will be received annually in advance.

Fixed costs, which include depreciation of the special machine on a straight line basis, are expected to amount to £7,000 per annum. These costs are all specific to the production of Oregons and, with the exception of depreciation, will be paid on the last day of the year in which they arise.

Advertising expenses will be paid on the first day of each year and will amount to £3,000 at the start of year 1, £2,000 at the start of year 2 and £1,000 at the start of year 3. Idaho Ltd has a cost of capital of 20% per annum.

You are required to:

(a) prepare calculations showing whether Idaho Ltd should produce Oregons, assuming that the decision will be based on expected present values;
(b) outline the limitations of expected present values as a criterion for making investment decisions under uncertainty;
(c) discuss the relative merits of other criteria which might be used for making investment decisions under uncertainty.

Ignore taxation. (ICA, PE II, December 1981)

Notes

1. James Mao (1970) 'Survey of capital budgeting: theory and practice', *Journal of Finance*, May, pp. 349–360.
2. We would not suggest that the coefficient of variation is always preferable. See for example Levy and Sarnat (1982) *Capital Investment and Financial Decisions*, 2nd edn, Prentice-Hall, p. 230.
3. This same example is used in the computer program output in Chapter 17.

Further Reading

Bierman, H. Jr. and Hass, J. E. (1973) 'Capital budgeting under uncertainty: a reformulation', *Journal of Finance*, March.

Gitman, L. J. (1977) 'Capturing risk exposure in the evaluation of capital budgeting projects', *The Engineering Economist*, Summer.

Hertz, D. B. (1964) 'Risk analysis in capital investment', *Harvard Business Review*, 42, January–February.

Hillier, F. S. (1963) 'The derivation of probabilistic information for the evaluation of risky investments', *Management Science*, April.

Hirshleifer, J. (1965) 'Investment decision under uncertainty: choice — theoretic approaches', *Quarterly Journal of Economics*, November.

Knight, F. H. (1921) *Risk Uncertainty and Profit*, Houghton Mifflin.

Lessard, D. R. and Bower, R. S. (1972) 'An operational approach to risk screening, *Journal of Finance*, June.

Lewellen, W. G. and Long, M. S. (1972) 'Simulation vs. single-value estimates', *Decision Sciences*, vol. 3.

Magee, J. F. (1964) 'How to use decision trees in capital investment', *Harvard Business Review*, September–October.

Mao, J. C. T. and Helliwell, J. F. (1969) 'Investment decisions under uncertainty: theory and practice', *Journal of Finance*, May.

Miller, E. M. (1978) 'Uncertainty-induced bias in capital budgeting', *Financial Management*, Autumn.

Myers, S. C. (1976) 'Postscript: using simulation for risk analysis', in S. C. Myers (ed.), *Modern Developments in Financial Management*, Praeger.

Rappaport, A. (1967) 'Sensitivity analysis in decision making', *Accounting Review*, July.

Reinhardt, V. E. (1973) 'Break-even analysis for Lockheed's Tri-Star: an application of financial theory', *Journal of Finance*, September.

Robichek, A. A. and Van Horne, J. C. (1967) 'Abandonment value in capital budgeting', *Journal of Finance*, December.

8

Risk–Return Measurement and Modern Portfolio Theory

Introduction

One of the most difficult problems facing the financial manager is the estimation of individual project risk. Investment appraisal involves the forecasting of project cash flows and discounting at some rate which reflects the economic risk of the project. In this chapter we outline the big new ideas emerging from modern portfolio theory, and try to use the theory to develop ways of estimating the required rates of return on projects of different risk.

Portfolio theory has undergone a revolution in the last thirty years. A trade-off between risk and return has been postulated and illustrated by the capital-asset pricing model. Total risk is shown to be made up of *market risk* and *specific risk*. Market risk is unavoidable because it arises from movements in the economy as a whole. The specific or unique risk relating to individual companies and projects can be removed by *diversification*, and efficient capital markets will therefore offer no rewards for specific risk. Diversification thus makes sense for investors because they can avoid specific risk. We introduce the market model, the security market line, and the Markowitz approach to diversification.

The Capital Asset Pricing Model

Modern portfolio theory teaches that there is a trade-off between risk and return. For many years, investment advisers and investment managers focused on returns with the occasional caveat 'subject to risk'. As risk was not understood, not a great deal could be said. Modern portfolio theory (MPT) concentrates on risk at least as much as return. In fact, MPT could be described as risk management, rather than return management. We can make decisions about the risks we are prepared to take but we cannot make decisions about the returns we shall achieve, as these are decided by factors beyond our control, although we would anticipate that the higher the risk the higher should be the expected return. For example, borrowing money from the bank in order to invest in equities which promise an expected return considerably higher than the bank rate of interest may result in considerable gain, but, there is a high risk of substantial loss if equity prices fall. On the other hand, if you place your initial investment in a clearing bank deposit account, the risk of loss is just about zero, but you do expect the return to be the given (low) rate of interest. We would expect other investments, such as unit trusts and quoted ordinary shares, to offer higher returns than bank deposits or government securities because the returns they offer are more volatile, that is, risky. In a rational world we should expect a clear trade-off between risk and return and the most widely acclaimed description of this trade-off is the *capital asset pricing model* (CAPM), which is derived from the *security market line* (SML) depicted in Figure 8.1

Portfolio (or security) expected returns are measured along the vertical axis and portfolio (or security) risk is measured along the horizontal axis. Portfolio returns include dividends and capital appreciation. The most widely used measure of *portfolio risk is beta*, which is a measure of the market sensitivity of returns. It represents the extent to which the return of an individual security or portfolio moves with some broad-based market index representative of the total economy. For the time being, Figure 8.1 shows that there is a trade-off between risk and return and that the trade-off is positive and linear, each incremental increase in risk being associated with an increase in expected return.

Some investments are virtually zero risk. For example, the return of three-month Treasury bills can be considered as riskless, the probability of default by the government being zero. The return of such *risk-free investments* is represented by R_F. They offer a small positive return for zero risk. For those who prefer to play for higher returns and accept the associated higher risk, there is the market for quoted ordinary shares (equities, common stocks). The portfolio M represents the total economy. It is a weighted average of all quoted equities and is generally referred to as the market portfolio. If we invest in this portfolio we expect to earn the return on the market, R_M. This theoretical portfolio is important in the theory of portfolio management because it is a *perfectly diversified portfolio*. It is almost certain that nobody ever holds this particular portfolio, but a widely diversified equity portfolio could approximate to the *market portfolio*. Let us assume for the time being that this is the only equity portfolio in which

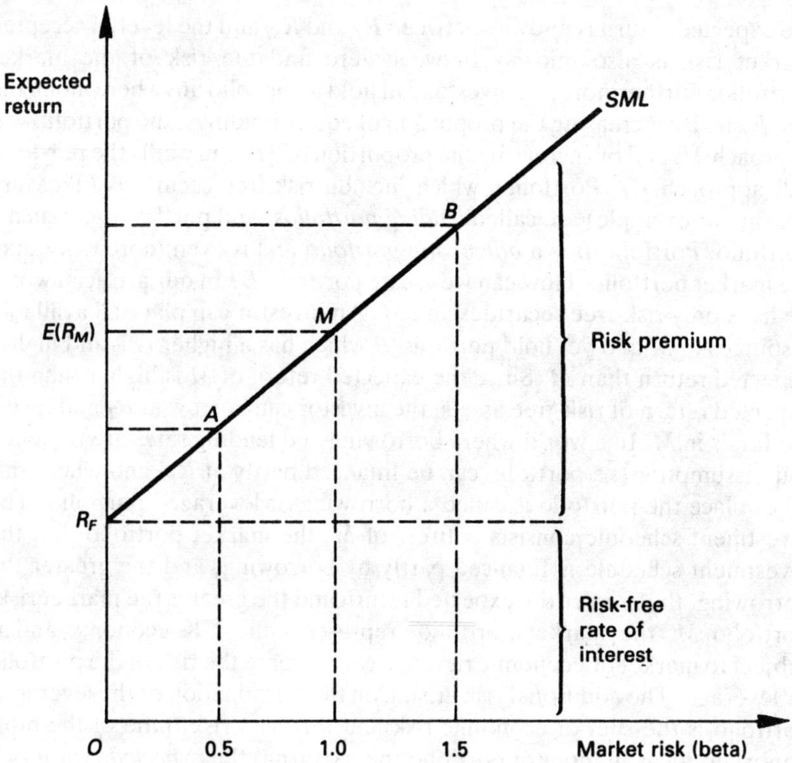

Figure 8.1 The Security Market Line (SML)

investors are interested. It is more risky than the risk-free investment because returns in the stock market are far more volatile than returns of three-month Treasury bills. We know that it is possible to make and lose a great deal of money playing the stock market. Even a casual glance at historic share price movements leads us to conclude that prices are highly volatile. The trade-off between risk and return implies that rational investors expect a higher return for investing in the market portfolio than investing in risk-free assets. They will not always get the higher return, but they must always expect it, otherwise rational investors would switch from equities to Treasury bills.

Having identified R_F and R_M we can now seek out some investment opportunities. The extremely risk-averse investor might choose to place all his or her funds into risk-free assets, while another investor might invest in the market portfolio expecting a higher return for accepting greater market risk. Now what should an investor do who wishes to achieve portfolio *A* in Figure 8.1? Portfolio *A* offers an expected return greater than R_F but less than R_M. The answer is that the investor can hold a mix of Treasury bills and equities. If half the funds are invested in risk-free securities and half *M*, then the expected return is midway between R_F and R_M and the level of accepted market risk is also midway between zero and the risk of the market portfolio. Furthermore, an investor can hold a portfolio anywhere along the line R_FM. By increasing the proportion of equity holdings, the portfolio will approach M, and by increasing the proportion of Treasury bills the portfolio will approach R_F. Portfolios which include risk-free securities (Treasury bills in our example) are called *lending portfolios*, and portfolio A is such a portfolio. Portfolio B is a *borrowing portfolio* and is even more risky than the market portfolio. How can we create portfolio B? In our artificial world we have only risk-free securities and M. An investor can place all available resources in M and yet hold portfolio B which has a higher risk and higher expected return than M. Since the expected return of M is higher than the expected return of risk-free assets, the investor can borrow at R_F and invest the funds in M. In a world where borrowing and lending rates are the same (our assumption), a portfolio can be financed partly at R_F, and where this takes place the portfolio is called a borrowing or leveraged portfolio. The investment schedule consists entirely of M, the market portfolio, but the investment schedule is financed partly by borrowing, and the greater the borrowing, the greater the expected return and the greater the market risk. Portfolio M, the market portfolio, represents the UK economy and is subject to market or economic risk. We can increase the risk of the portfolio by leverage. The additional risk arising on the introduction of the leveraged portfolio is the sum of economic risk and financial risk. One of the most important ideas in modern portfolio theory is that the *expected return of a portfolio is directly related to the riskiness of the portfolio*. Furthermore, *portfolio risk can be measured by beta*.

We shall return to beta very shortly. For the time being, let us end this introductory section with the capital asset pricing model which states that the expected return of a portfolio is made up of R_F, the risk-free reward for time, plus a premium for accepting market risk:

$$E(R_p) = R_F + \beta_p[E(R_M) - R_F]$$

where $E(R_p)$ is the expected return of the portfolio, R_F is the risk-free rate of interest, β_p is the portfolio beta (*market sensitivity index*), $E(R_M)$ is the expected return of the market portfolio and $[E(R_M) - R_F]$ is the market risk premium.

If the risk-free rate of interest is 6 per cent and the expected return of the market portfolio is 15 per cent, the expected return of the portfolio is clearly a linear function of beta. For portfolio betas of (1) 0, (2) 0.5, (3) 1.0, (4) 1.5, and (5) 2, the expected returns are:

(1) $E(R_p) = 6 + 0(15 - 6) = 6$ per cent
(2) $E(R_p) = 6 + 0.5(15 - 6) = 10.5$ per cent
(3) $E(R_p) = 6 + 1.0(15 - 6) = 15$ per cent

(4) $E(R_p) = 6 + 1.5(15 - 6) = 19.5$ per cent
(5) $E(R_p) = 6 + 2.0(15 - 6) = 24.0$ per cent

The security market line in Figure 8.1 demonstrates the trade-off between market risk and expected return. The capital-asset pricing model enables us to estimate the expected return of a portfolio given R_F, R_M and beta. For the time being we invite readers to imagine how the CAPM can be applied in assessing the risk of individual projects.

Return

Positive returns are welcome. This is what investment is all about: delayed consumption and risk-taking in the expectation of greater opportunities for consumption (returns) in the future. We expect rewards for delayed consumption, R_F, and something extra for taking risks, $[E(R_M) - R_F]$. Investors have always been extremely aware of returns which, as far as investment in equities is concerned, come in two forms: dividends and capital gains. The return of an individual investment or portfolio can be measured as follows:

$$R_t = \frac{P_t - P_{t-1} + D_t}{P_{t-1}}$$

where R_t is the periodic return, P_t is the price at the end of the period, P_{t-1} is the price at the start, and D_t is the dividend received at the end of the period. For example, if the value of a portfolio is 100 at the beginning of a period, and 120 at the end of the period after receiving a dividend of 10, the return of the portfolio is 30 per cent:

$$R_t = \frac{120 - 100 + 10}{100} = 30 \text{ per cent}$$

The traditional approach to investment management concentrated on returns and methods of achieving positive returns. A 20 per cent expected return might be considered as acceptable 'subject to risk', although risk was generally not measured. The modern approach focuses on risk.

Risk

Risk is the one-in-six rule. It relates to the volatility of an expected outcome, the dispersion or spread of likely returns around the expected return. In Figure 8.2 the expected return of a project is 16 per cent. From statistics we know that for 68 per cent of the time the actual return will lie within one

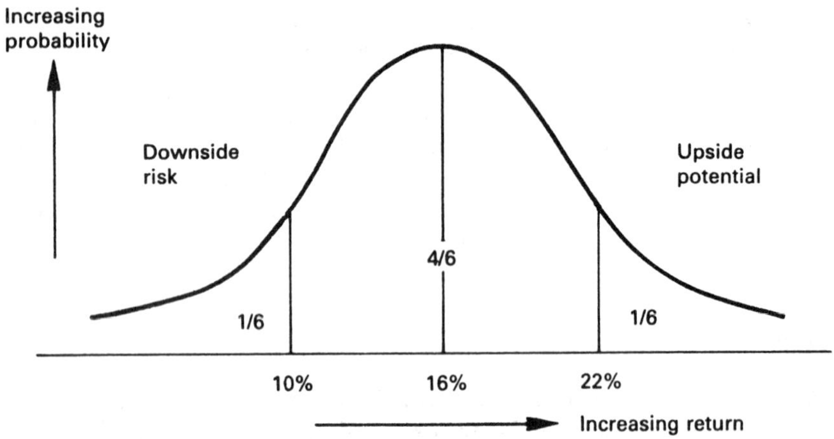

Figure 8.2 Risk: The One-in-Six Rule

standard deviation of the expected return. The standard deviation is a measure of dispersion or spread. Approximately four out of six actual outcomes should, on average, lie within one standard deviation of the expected outcome. In Figure 8.2, four out of six outcomes should, on average, lie between 10 per cent and 22 per cent, 6 per cent being the standard deviation. This is the good news. The bad news is that two times in six the outcome can be expected to lie outside one standard deviation. On average, one time in six the outcome will be above 22 per cent, and this is generally referred to as *upside potential*. Unfortunately, one time in six the actual return should be less than 10 per cent and this is generally referred to as *downside risk*. This is the one-in-six rule. Investors do not like risk, and the greater the riskiness of returns of an investment, the greater will be the return expected. There is a trade-off between risk and return which must be reflected in the required rates of return of investment opportunities.

The standard deviation (or variance, which is the standard deviation squared) measures the total risk of an investment. It is not necessary for an investor to accept the *total risk* of an individual security. Investors can and do diversify. Some of the risk associated with individual investments can be avoided by diversification, and Figure 8.3 shows how some of the total risk associated with individual securities can be avoided by diversification. Investment in a single security implies acceptance of total risk. It is not advisable for investors to put all their funds into a single investment as this exposes them to more risk than is necessary for the expected return. Figure 8.3 shows that if we increase the number of investment holdings from 1 to 2, 3, 4 and so on, we achieve considerable portfolio risk reduction. This happens because the surprise bad news for one company is offset by surprise good news for another company. These good and bad shocks specific to individual companies cancel out each other. Company *A* launches a

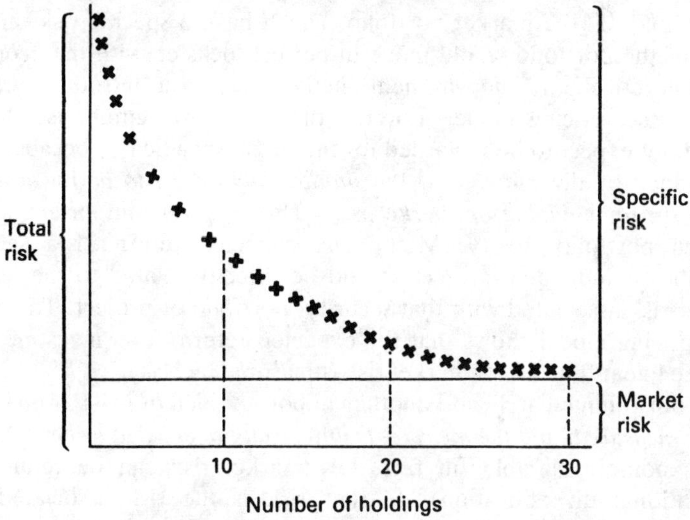

Figure 8.3 Risk Reduction by Diversification

successful new product while Company *B* launches a failure. Company *C* has a sudden damaging strike, while Company *D* makes a breakthrough in design. Company *E* learns that its products are dangerous to health, while Company *F* wins a large government contract. These events are *specific* to individual companies and are unrelated to general movements in the economy. These specific events generally cancel out, and the result of *diversification* is reduction in portfolio volatility, that is, *reduction in portfolio risk*. As the number of holdings approaches 20 or 30, a good deal of total risk is removed by diversification, and this risk which can be removed by diversification is called *specific risk*, because it is specific to individual companies. *Specific risk* is sometimes called *diversifiable risk*, *unique risk*, *avoidable risk* or *non-market risk*, and one of the very important ideas in modern portfolio theory is that investors should not expect to be rewarded for taking on risk which can be avoided. They should expect to be rewarded only for *unavoidable* or market risk.

Not all risk can be removed by diversification. To some extent the fortunes of all companies move with the economy. Changes in the money supply, interest rates, exchange rates, taxation, the prices of commodities, government spending and overseas economies tend to affect all companies to some greater or lesser extent. The risk associated with movements in the economy is generally referred to as *market risk*, but it is sometimes referred to as non-diversifiable, systematic or unavoidable risk. In Figure 8.3 a great deal of specific risk is removed by holding ten securities, some extra risk reduction is achieved by holding eleven to twenty securities, and thereafter only a small amount of risk is removed. Eventually, by holding a weighted average of all securities we could remove all specific risk. At this point we would hold *M*, the market portfolio, which has no specific risk, and the value of the portfolio would move in perfect lockstep with the economy. This theoretical portfolio was mentioned earlier, in our introduction to the capital asset pricing model. For the time being we emphasise that we should not expect to be rewarded for taking on specific risk because it can be avoided by diversification. *We should only expect to be rewarded for taking on unavoidable or market risk*. This is a very important idea in modern portfolio theory (MPT): the expected return of a security, portfolio or individual project should be directly related to the level of market risk associated with that security, portfolio or project. The capital asset pricing model shows that the expected return of an investment is a positive linear function of market risk (measured by *beta*).

We must immediately add another important idea of MPT. *Market risk can be measured, and the measure is universally referred to as beta*. Market risk is non-diversifiable (in fact, UK market risk can be reduced by international diversification). Market risk is the risk associated with general movements in the economy and affects all quoted companies to some greater or lesser extent. Unfortunately, there is no readily available measure of general movements in the economy on a day-to-day basis. With a view to measuring the market risk of individual securities and portfolios it is therefore necessary to find a benchmark representing the economy. Such a benchmark in the UK is the broad-based Financial Times all-share index. Using this broad-based index as a surrogate for the UK economy, it is possible to measure the extent to which returns of portfolios and individual securities move with unanticipated changes in general economic conditions.

Figure 8.4 shows the change in the periodic returns of three hypothetical securities plotted against changes in the periodic returns of the Financial Times (FT) all-share index. Let us suppose that the return of a security rises by 10 per cent when the return of the index rises by 10 per cent and that when the return of the market falls by 10 per cent, the return of the individual security also falls by 10 per cent. If these periodic returns are plotted, the line of best fit through all the points would be a 45° line as shown for security *B*. *The slope of the line as measured by beta* would be one. *The beta coefficient is therefore the measure of a security's market risk*. It is a market sensitivity index indicating the extent to which periodic returns of an individual security move with periodic returns of the market. A high risk investment, such as security *C*, might have a beta of two (security *C* might be an investment in a hire purchase or property company). Its periodic return rises by 20 per cent or falls by 20 per cent when the return of the all-share index rises or falls, respectively, by only 10 per cent. Security *A* is an example of an investment in a low risk company. It might be a tea or snuff company, and its periodic return rises or falls by 5 per cent when the market rises or falls, respectively, by 10 per cent. It has a beta of 0.5.

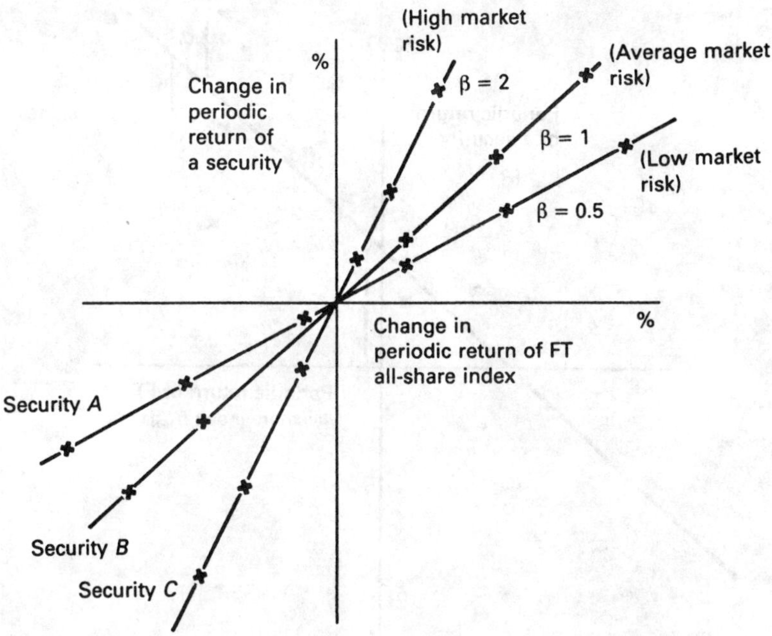

Figure 8.4 Measuring Security Betas

Beta is therefore a market sensitivity index. It measures the extent to which, on average, the periodic return of a security or portfolio moves with the market. Betas are important in MPT because the theory suggests that expected returns are directly related to the level of accepted market risk as measured by beta. The beta of a portfolio is the weighted average of the betas of individual securities making up the portfolio. Furthermore, these betas are now available from several UK sources including the Risk Measurement Service at the London Business School.

In Figure 8.4 all co-ordinates lie on straight lines which pass through the origin. Periodic returns of individual securities *A*, *B* and *C* move directly with changes in the market return, but we would not expect this to occur in the real world. Securities offer specific returns as well as market returns so that we should not expect the points to fall exactly on a straight line.

In Figure 8.5 the periodic returns of an individual security, R_i are plotted against the periodic returns of the FT all-share index, R_M. The co-ordinates do not lie exactly on the line of best fit because, as already indicated, companies earn not only returns associated with general movements in the economy but also specific returns associated with corporate decisions and events affecting only the individual company or its industry. The characteristic line, as illustrated in Figure 8.5, suggests that there is a linear relationship between the periodic return of an individual security R_i and periodic returns of the market, R_M, and also that the return of the security does not move exactly with the market return. Using least-squares

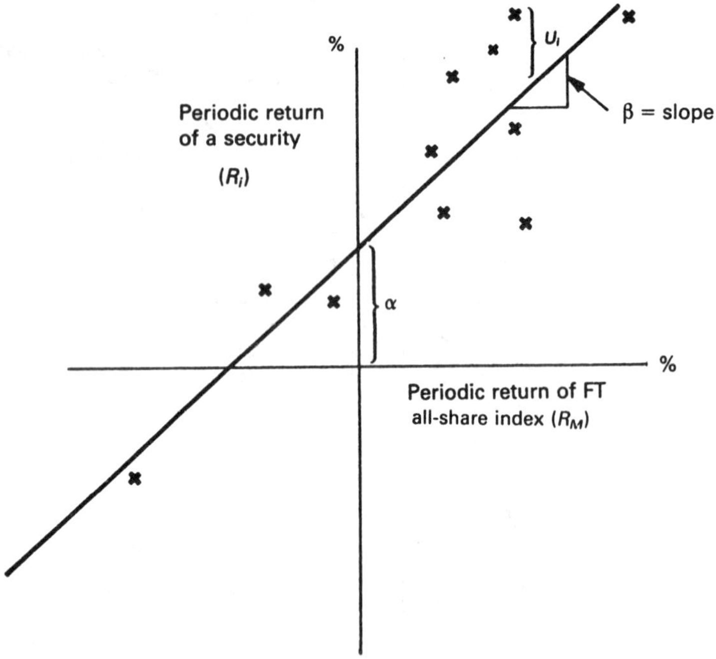

Figure 8.5 The Characteristic Line

regression analysis, a line of best fit is plotted through the co-ordinates. The relationship between R_i and R_M is given by the market model:

$$R_i = \alpha_i + \beta_i R_M + U_i$$

where R_i is the return of an individual security, α_i is the value of the intercept, β_i is the slope of the characteristic line, and U_i is a random error term. The beta for a security is given by:

$$\beta_i = \frac{\text{Cov.}\ (r_i r_m)}{\sigma_m^2}$$

where Cov.$(r_i r_m)$ is the covariance of returns on security i with returns on the stock market, m, and σ_m^2 is the variance of the returns on the stock market.

Beta indicates the average sensitivity of returns of an individual security to the market return, and is a measure of the market or systematic risk of a security (or portfolio). As the co-ordinates do not fall exactly on the line of best fit, an error term, U, is introduced to represent the unexplained security return. The specific returns arise because of events affecting the company rather than events affecting the total economy, and are represented by α as well as U. In Figure 8.5, α is the intercept on the vertical axis and represents, on average, the portion of a security's return which is not associated with general movements in the economy. Alpha therefore represents the average return of an individual security when the return of the market index is zero.

We can summarise that the total return of a security is the sum of the systematic return and the unsystematic or specific return. The systematic or market return is $\beta_i R_M$ and the specific or unsystematic return is measured by α_i plus U_i. We can also reiterate from Figure 8.3 that the total risk of a security is the sum of specific risk and market risk, and that specific risk can be removed by diversification. We should not expect competitive markets to reward investors for taking risks which they can avoid, and we should therefore expect rewards to be related only to market risk.

Diversification

Spreading the risk, or diversification, makes good sense for investors. It removes specific, diversifiable, unique, non-market risk. This was illustrated in Figure 8.3. Diversification does not remove market risk (other than by international diversification). The purchaser of a share in a quoted company gets two investments for the price of one — an investment in the UK economy and an investment in the company earning returns unique to the company. One of the attractive features of MPT is that it explains the way in which shareholders have always behaved. They have always held diversified portfolios. Modern portfolio theory suggests that diversification is rational, given that investors should take on only that part of risk for which they expect to be rewarded.

The pioneering work in modern portfolio theory, and risk quantification in particular, is attributable to Harry Markowitz (1952). Some thirty years ago he suggested that for any given level of risk the rational investor would select the maximum expected return, and that for any given level of expected return the rational investor would select the minimum risk. Before Markowitz, investment analysts talked about maximising returns — subject to risk. Harry Markowitz laid down the cornerstones of modern portfolio theory by measuring risk.

Let us suppose that the stock market is made up of 100 quoted equities. With a view to developing a series of possible or attainable portfolios it would be necessary to estimate the expected return of each security. *The expected return of any portfolio or mix of equities would be a weighted average* of the expected returns of each security in the portfolio. *Risk is more complicated because it is not a weighted average.* First, it would be necessary to estimate the variance (or standard deviation) of the expected return for each security. This is a measure of volatility or total risk. For 100 equities we would be faced with the difficult task of estimating 100 variances or standard deviations. Secondly, it would be necessary to estimate how returns of every individual security would move or covary with every other individual security. This is obviously an extremely difficult task but we would expect returns of securities in the same industry to move in the same direction, while returns of investments in different industries would not move in lockstep. In fact, we would clearly expect to reduce total risk or variance by diversification. As already discussed, we would not expect to remove risk completely, but we would expect to remove or significanly reduce specific or non-market risk.

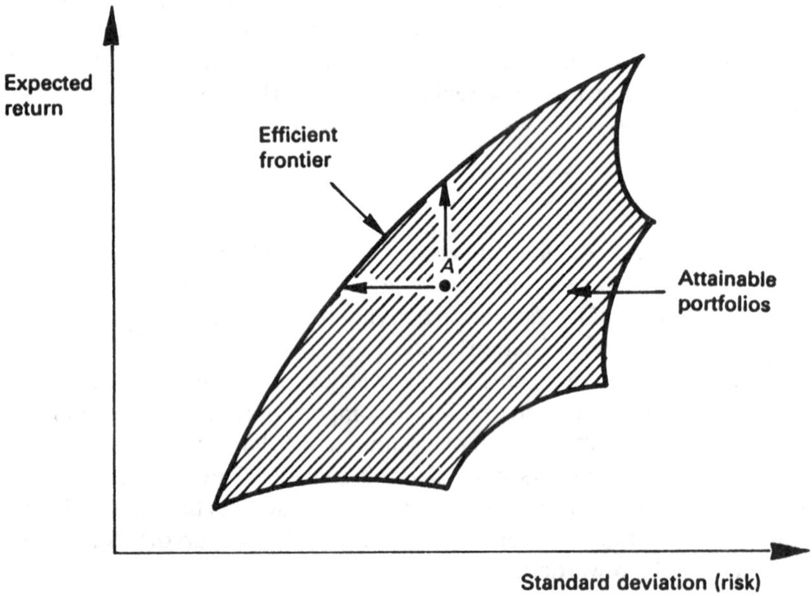

Figure 8.6 Markowitz Mean-Variance Approach to Diversification

In Figure 8.6 the shaded area represents the set of portfolios which can be generated with the available equities. Each portfolio is *attainable*, though not necessarily desirable. For example, portfolio *A* is an attainable but inefficient portfolio. It is possible to accept the total risk associated with portfolio *A* and move vertically upwards to find a portfolio on the efficient frontier offering a higher expected return for the same risk. Alternatively, for the expected return associated with portfolio *A*, it is possible to move horizontally to the left and find a portfolio on the *efficient frontier* offering the same expected return for lower risk. One of the maxims of the Markowitz approach is that the rational investor prefers maximum expected return for any level of risk, and the minimum risk for any level of expected return. The efficient frontier in Figure 8.6 identifies those portfolios offering the maximum expected return for any level of risk and those portfolios offering minimum risk for any level of expected return. Having identified the efficient set of portfolios, the investor can select that portfolio on the efficient frontier which satisfies his or her risk–return preference.

Unfortunately, a great deal of data is required for the above approach to portfolio construction. For 100 securities we need 100 expected returns, 100 variances and no less than 4,950 correlation coefficients between returns of different securities. For 1,000 securities we require 1,000 expected returns, 1,000 variances and 499,500 correlation coefficients. This is indeed a daunting task. Nevertheless, the Markowitz mean-variance approach provided important insights into portfolio management, diversification and risk management. With a view to simplifying the computations and reducing the quantity of data required for the Markowitz approach, later theorists such as Sharpe (1963), Lintner (1965) and Tobin (1958) side-stepped the difficult task of estimating covariances between all securities. This was achieved by including risk-free securities in the analysis, identifying the *market portfolio* on the Markowitz efficient frontier, and generating a market sensitivity (beta) for each security. The market sensitivity index or beta became accepted as the appropriate measure of portfolio risk, rather than total risk as measured by variance or standard deviation. Since part of total risk, that is, specific risk, can be diversified away, portfolio returns should be related directly to unavoidable or market risk. In short, the computational difficulties of correlating the returns of all securities with each other were overcome by measuring the sensitivity or return of each security to the market return.

The reader should recognise that we are again discussing *the capital asset pricing model*. The Markowitz approach, as illustrated in Figure 8.6, deals with all-equity portfolios. Once we introduce the risk-free rate of interest we can generate the capital market line as illustrated in Figure 8.7, from which it is possible to derive the security market line. The Markowitz efficient frontier of all-equity portfolios is shown in Figure 8.7. We now add R_F, the zero risk small positive return of three-month Treasury bills, and draw a line which just touches the Markowitz efficient frontier at M, the market portfolio. *The only portfolio which has no specific risk at all is M, the weighted average of all equities.* This is the only efficient all-equity portfolio once we introduce risk-free assets. Investors may hold the market at M or invest some of their funds in risk-free assets. For those investors who seek an even higher risk than the market, it is possible to add financial risk to economic risk by borrowing and investing in M. As the market portfolio has no specific risk, all portfolios along *the capital market line* (CML) are theoretically efficient in that they have no specific risk, and the expected return of any portfolio along the CML is a function of the total risk of the portfolio. *The security market line* (SML), which relates expected return to beta for individual securities and portfolios, may be derived from the CML. We can now use *the capital asset pricing model* to estimate any portfolio as follows:

$$E(R_p) = R_F + \beta_p[E(R_M) - R_F]$$

The expected return of a portfolio is equal to the risk-free rate of interest plus a premium for market risk. The higher the beta the greater the risk premium.

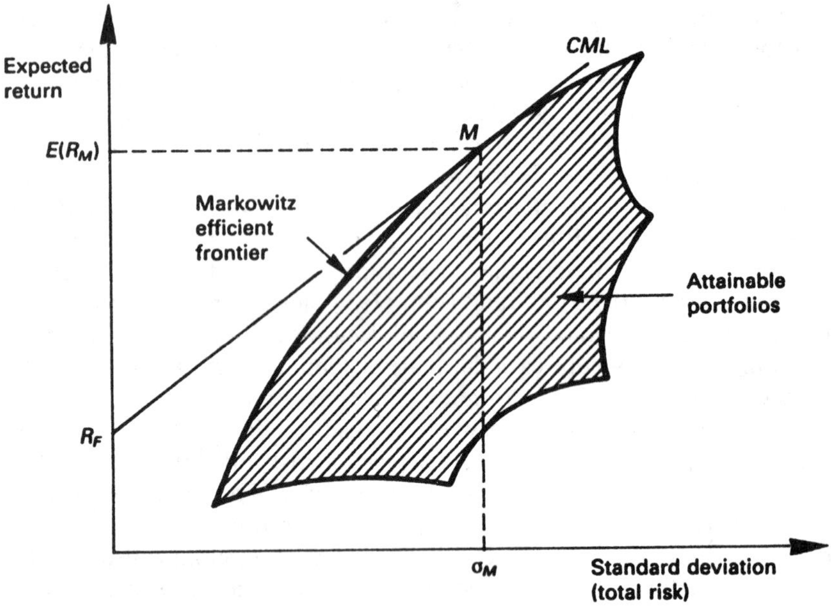

Figure 8.7 The Capital Market Line

If R_F is 6 per cent and $E(R_M)$ is 15 per cent, the risk premium for the market is 9 per cent. A portfolio with a beta of 0.5 has an average expected return of 10.5 per cent and a portfolio with a beta of two has an average expected return of 24 per cent.

The Efficient Market Hypothesis

One of the most important ideas in modern portfolio theory is the efficient market hypothesis (EMH). The EMH suggests that *share prices fully reflect all available information, any new or shock information being immediately incorporated into the share price*. In highly competitive markets, such as the New York Stock Exchange or London Stock Exchange, we should expect prices fully to reflect anticipations. A great many individuals and financial institutions participate in the market and they buy and sell with real money. They have access to a great deal of information such as economic forecasts, stockbrokers' reports, newspaper articles, investment advisory services and company reports. They know the current market price of all quoted securities and have access to past price movements. Many have access to computers, and some even use risk measurement services. In such highly competitive and well-informed markets, we should expect prices to reflect fully all available information, and we should expect prices to adjust very rapidly to any new or shock information.

This apparently simple hypothesis, to the extent that it holds in the real world, has very powerful implications for investment analysis and corporate management. The hypothesis is impossible to test directly, as we would need to know the market's anticipated net operational cash flows and anticipated required rates of return for all future periods, and also all information relevant to security prices and the way this information is reflected in prices. It is therefore necessary to design tests of the hypothesis based on available information and available statistical techniques. Tests of the EMH are generally made under the assumptions of zero transaction costs, no taxation, free access to all available information for all traders, and agreement among them as to the implications of information for security prices. A great deal of evidence supports the hypothesis, such evidence appearing in three forms: the weak, the semi-strong and the strong. *Weak* form tests of the EMH are concerned with the extent to which historic share prices can be used to predict future prices, and a great deal of evidence suggests that such footsteps cannot predict the future. *Semi-strong* form tests attempt to measure the extent to which share prices fully reflect all publicly available information. Investors anticipate and react to publicly available information relating to stock splits, earnings announcements, dividend announcements, forecasts, and large block trades. Most of the research suggests that it is extremely difficult to earn excess returns using publicly available information. Finally, *strong* form tests are designed to discover whether share prices reflect all information, even information which is not available to the public. The studies are generally concerned with the stock market performance of professional investors and fund managers, and most of the evidence suggests that the professionals do not have access to techniques enabling them to earn returns greater than returns expected for the level of accepted market risk.

Some evidence against the EMH is available. Stock market specialists and corporate insiders have monopolistic access to information which, on occasions, enables them to earn superior returns. Furthermore, there is some evidence that some people do have better forecasting ability than the rest of us. It is therefore possible to beat the EMH — but it is extremely difficult. Modern stock markets do appear to be efficient in that share prices do reflect all available information, any new information being very rapidly incorporated into the share price in an unbiased way by the competitive trading activities of many investors.

The efficient market hypothesis is extremely bad news for those readers who believe that stock markets offer easy money. The EMH generally comes as a rather disappointing but readily acceptable surprise to MBA students, third year undergraduates, and corporate managers. Surely, the competitive activities of a great many traders should generate the equilibrium price where security prices reflect all available information. It is not until we introduce the implications of the EMH that our audience becomes alarmed, even hostile. In efficient markets investors pay the market price for acquisitions. There are no bargains. Share price movements cannot be predicted from past price movements — even with computerised forecasting methods. Company earnings and dividend announcements are generally anticipated and should not result in wild share price movements. Only the shocks cause movements in security prices. There are no mechanical systems for making money. The net present value of any aquisition is zero, because investors must pay the market price of risk. Naturally, the efficient market hypothesis is very unpopular, particularly with stock market professionals and investment advisers. The bad news is that a vast quantity of research supports the hypothesis. The good news is that the investor can beat the EMH with luck, inside information or forecasting ability. For the rest of us, we should expect to be rewarded on average only for the amount of market risk we accept.

Implications for Capital Budgeting

Just as *a portfolio is a collection of investments*, so *a firm can be viewed as a collection or portfolio of individul projects. We can use portfolio theory to estimate the required rates of return on individual projects by estimating the project beta.* The efficient market hypothesis suggests that share prices fully reflect all information, any new or shock information being immediately incorporated into the share price. A financial manager can use movements in market prices to estimate the corporate beta—the extent to which returns on the company's shares move with unanticipated movements in the economy. The corporate beta for a company financed entirely by equity is the weighted average beta of all projects. For example, a company has two projects. Project A is a low-risk investment expected to earn 10 per cent, while project B is a higher risk project with a required rate of return of 20 per cent. Both projects are of equal value, having a present value of £1,000. Figure 8.8 shows both projects and the weighted average required rate of return for the portfolio at 15 per cent. Project A is expected to earn £100 on its £1,000 invested, and project B is expected to earn £200 on £1,000 invested. The expected weighted average is £300 on a £2,000 investment, i.e. 15 per cent. If the company invests only in projects similar to A and B, then the weighted average required rate of return of 15 per cent is arithmetically interesting but cannot be used as the discount rate on the company's project. It is simply the weighted average. Each individual project must be assessed by its market risk, i.e. by its own beta, not the corporate weighted average. In our example, 15 per cent is not the required rate of return on any of the company's projects. If a financial manager uses the weighted average cost of capital to assess individual projects, then that manager is ignoring risk.

Figure 8.9 illustrates the errors which could be made if risk is ignored. The securities market line (SML) is our best estimate of the trade-off between risk and return. Our financial manager discounts the anticipated cash flows on all

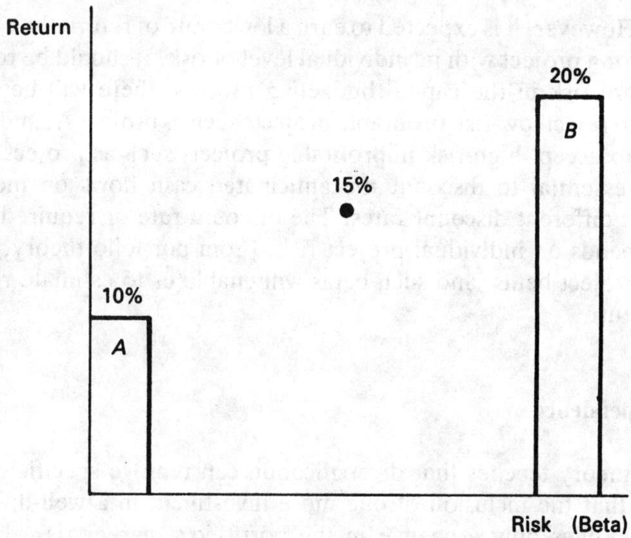

Figure 8.8 The Weighted Average Required Rate of Return

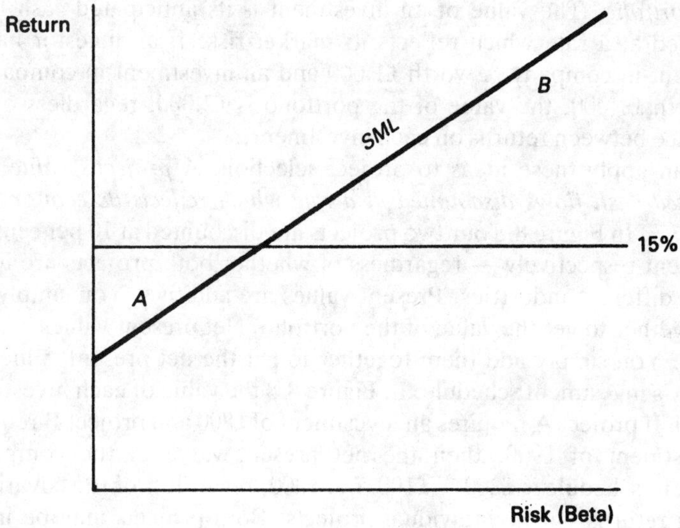

Figure 8.9 The Trade-off Between Risk and Return

projects at 15 per cent. Project A would be rejected because it earns less than 15 per cent. However, if the SML illustrates the true trade-off between risk and return, then project A should be accepted because it earns a higher rate of return than the required rate of return. It has a positive net present value. Project B earns more than 15 per cent. Our financial manager might accept it. However, it is expected to earn a lower rate of return than the rate of return for a project with its individual level of risk. It should be rejected. If we ignore risk in the capital budgeting process, there will be a slight tendency to reject low-risk profitable projects such as project A, and a slight tendency to accept high-risk unprofitable projects such as project B. It is therefore essential to discount the anticipated cash flows on individual projects at different discount rates. The discount rate or required rate of return depends on individual project risk. From portfolio theory, we can estimate project betas, and such betas will enable us to estimate required rates of return.

Risk Independence

Portfolio theory teaches that diversification can remove specific risk and therefore that the inclusion of one more investment in a well-diversified portfolio implies only a change in the portfolio's market risk. Efficient markets offer rewards for unavoidable market risk, not for specific risk which can be avoided at zero cost. *The value of an investment is therefore independent of the way its returns move with the returns on other investments in the portfolio.* The value of an investment is its anticipated cash flows discounted at a rate which reflects its market risk. If an investor has an investment in company A worth £1,000 and an investment in company B also worth £1,000, the value of the portfolio is £2,000, regardless of the covariance between returns on each investment.

We can apply these ideas to project selection. *A project's value is its anticipated cash flows discounted at a rate which reflects its economic or market risk.* In Figure 8.8 our two projects are discounted at 10 per cent and 20 per cent respectively — regardless of whether both projects are in the same or different industries. Present values are additive. You simply add them together to get the value of the portfolio. Net present values are also additive. You simply add them together to get the net present value of a company's investment schedule. In Figure 8.8 the value of each investment is £1,000. If project A requires an investment of £800 and project B requires an investment of £900, then the net present value of the company's investment schedule is £200 + £100, i.e. £300, regardless of the covariance between returns on the individual projects. Both projects may be in the engineering industry with a high positive covariance between returns on the two projects. Alternatively, the two investments may be in ice cream and sausages, with a much lower covariance between returns. Regardless of the covariance, the net value of the investment schedule is £300.

The risk independence idea is important because it implies that *all projects should be assessed independently of the firm's existing projects*. This is the general rule, but we must add that the anticipated cash flows from one investment may be greater for firm A than for firm B, where firm A can achieve *economies of scale* or where *synergy* exists. Economies of scale can be achieved if firm A has spare capacity for a given type of output or is already incurring the fixed costs associated with a particular project. Synergy can be achieved when the whole is greater than the sum of the individual parts: the 2 + 2 = 5 situation, where the firm with excellent products merges with the firm with excellent marketing.

Assessing Individual Project Risk

As the sceptical reader has probably already guessed, it is extremely difficult to establish the beta for an individual project. One very practical approach to risk classification for individual projects is sketched in Figure 8.10. The securities market line (SML) is the best description we have of the trade-off between risk and return in efficient markets. *Although it is very difficult to state where individual projects lie along the SML, at least we can try to classify projects into at least three categories*. Class A projects are low-risk, requiring a rate of return of 10 per cent; average-risk projects are classified as B on which the required rate of return is 20 per cent; and the firm's high-risk projects are classified as class C, requiring a rate of return of 30 per cent. Individual project classification depends on the extent to which the cash flows anticipated on the project are expected to move with unanticipated changes in the economy. We know from our studies of efficient capital

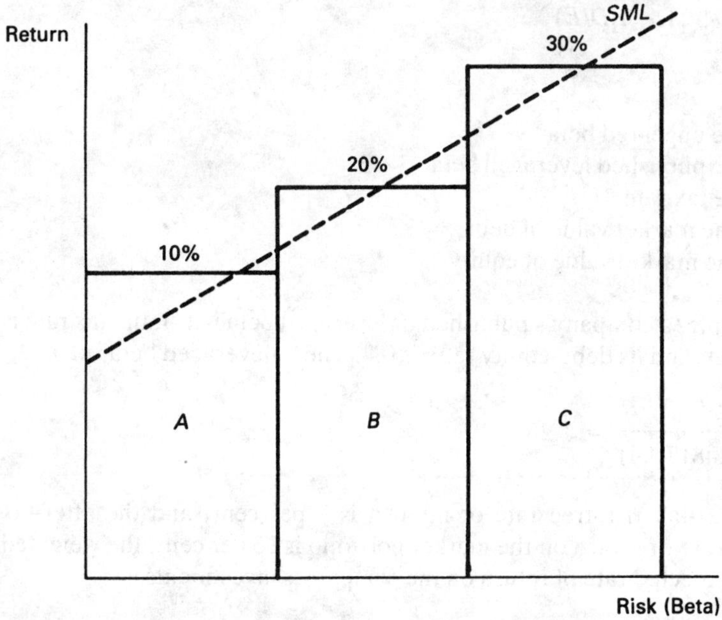

Figure 8.10 Assessing Individual Project Risk

markets that it is the shocks which cause movements in share prices. Returns on individual companies are measured against returns on the total market to estimate corporate betas. In the same way, we can estimate the market sensitivity of an individual project. If the net cash flows on a project are expected to move with unanticipated changes in the economy, its beta will be close to 1 and such a project might be classified as a category B project. Where the cash flows are highly sensitive to unanticipated movements in the economy, such a high-risk project would be regarded as a class C investment. Those projects with cash flows which are expected to be insensitive to economic movements would be regarded as low-risk class A projects. Although this approach is rather subjective, it is a practical method for estimating individual project risk.

An alternative approach, which should lead to roughly the same results, is to use the corporate beta, adjusted for leverage, and then relate individual project betas to the ungeared corporate beta. The inclusion of debt in a company's capital structure increases the risk to shareholders. It adds financial risk to business risk. With a view to obtaining the ungeared corporate beta, it is necessary to adjust the published beta for gearing. The ungeared beta is a measure of the company's economic or business risk. It is the beta the company would have if there were no debt in the firm's capital structure. A published beta can be reduced to an ungeared beta as follows:

$$\beta_u = \frac{\beta_l}{(1 + [1 - t]D/E)}$$

where

β_u is the ungeared beta
β_l is the published leveraged beta
t is the tax rate
D is the market value of debt
E is the market value of equity

For example, a company's published or leveraged beta is 1.5, the tax rate is 52 per cent, and its debt–equity ratio is 0.4. The unleveraged beta is:

$$\frac{1.5}{1 + (0.48)\,(0.4)} = 1.26$$

If the after-tax risk-free rate of interest is 7 per cent, and the after-tax required rate of return on the market portfolio is 16 per cent, the weighted average expected rate of return on the company's investments is:

$$\begin{aligned} E(R) &= R_f + (R_M - R_t) \\ &= 7\% + 1.26(16\% - 7\%) = 18.34\,\% \end{aligned}$$

Using the capital asset pricing model, it is possible to estimate the average required rate of return on a company's investments. The weighted average, of course, does not give the beta for individual projects, products or divisions. These would have to be estimated by relating individual project betas to the firm's average project beta or by relating anticipated cash flows from individual projects to unanticipated changes in the economy. Estimating betas for individual projects is therefore not easy. Corporate betas do change all the time. They are subject to a range of error, and historic betas are generally used as proxies for future betas. Nevertheless, this approach to adjusting required rates of return for market risk is probably the most theoretically acceptable method available for assessing the risk of individual projects.

Calculating Project Betas[1]

Pricing capital investments is conceptually little different from pricing the security which such assets collectively comprise. It is the application of theory that poses the major difficulties. In the first place, it should be understood that the CAPM is a static one-period model. Capital projects, by definition, have cash flows over a number of years. The model therefore requires adjustment to handle the problems of varying interest rates and risk differences in cash flows. Such adjustments are complex and beyond the scope of this book. We will simply assume a single risk-free interest rate and a risk premium which applies to all cash flows. One possible refinement would be to relate the market rate of interest on government bonds to each yearly cash flow.

Secondly, we must consider how a project's beta (or sensitivity to unanticipated changes in the economy) is determined. Much research has been conducted to discover the determinants of security betas. Myers and Pogue (1973) identify the main variables as financial leverage, cyclicality and volatility of operating earnings and, possibly, growth. Many approaches to determining a project's beta have been suggested. We shall illustrate just one approach using probability analysis based on *ex-ante* estimates. A beta for any project is the ratio of the covariance between project and stock market returns to the variance of the market return. Mathematically, it is stated as:

$$\beta_j = \frac{Cov(r_j r_m)}{\sigma_m^2}$$

$Cov(r_j r_m)$ is the covariance of returns on project j with the returns on the stock market, M. With this measure of market risk it becomes a relatively straightforward matter to determine the required rate of return for project j:

$$\bar{r}_j = R_F + (\bar{R}_m - R_F)\beta_j$$

i.e. the expected rate of return (r) on project j is comprised of the two components R_F the risk-free rate of return obtainable on, for example, Treasury bills, and the market risk premium $(\bar{R}_m - R_F)$ multiplied by the project's sensitivity to market returns β_j. As the risk-free return (R_F) and the market return ($\bar{R}_m$) are market constants, it follows that only the beta value is related to the project.

Using probability analysis it is possible to estimate a project's beta by forecasting returns on the market and the project for each economic state-of-the-world. Let us assume that under the four states-of-the-world ranging from 'severe recession' to 'strong recovery' the probabilities and returns are as in Table 8.1.

Table 8.1

State s	*Probability* P_s	*Market return*	*Return on project A*	*Return on project B*
1. Severe recession	0.2	−0.20	−0.05	−0.20
2. Mild recession	0.3	0.10	0.15	0
3. Recovery	0.4	0.30	0.20	0.35
4. Strong recovery	0.1	0.50	0.30	0.60

Table 8.2 illustrates the expected returns and covariances of the two projects with market returns. Applying the above formula for beta we obtain:

$$\beta_A = 0.0223/0.0464 = 0.48$$

$$\beta_B = 0.0544/0.0464 = 1.17$$

Project A has a low beta coefficient, its returns increasing on average by only 4.8 per cent, with 10 per cent increase in stock market returns. Project B has a higher degree of market risk, with a 10 per cent increase in stock market returns producing, on average, an 11.7 per cent increase in project returns. If we further assume that a riskfree return of 10 per cent after personal taxes can be obtained, the market premium for risk is 6 per cent (i.e. 0.16 −0.10) and the required rate of return on the two projects can be estimated:

$$\bar{r}_A = 0.10 + (0.06)\ (0.48) = 12.88\%$$

$$\bar{r}_B = 0.10 + (0.06)\ (1.17) = 17.02\%$$

As the expected return for Project A according to Table 8.2 is 14.5 per cent, the project exceeds the hurdle rate of 12.88 per cent and is acceptable. Project B is economically unacceptable as its expected return of 16 per cent

Table 8.2 Calculation of Expected Returns and Covariance with the Market for Two Projects

Market Returns and Variance

S	P_s	r_M	$P_s r_M$	$(r_M - \bar{r}_M)$	$(r_M - \bar{r}_M)^2$	$P_s(r_M - \bar{r}_M)^2$
1	0.2	−0.20	−0.04	−0.36	0.1296	0.02592
2	0.3	0.10	0.03	−0.06	0.0036	0.00108
3	0.4	0.30	0.12	0.14	0.0196	0.00784
4	0.1	0.50	0.05	0.34	0.1156	0.01156
		$\bar{r}_M = 0.16$			$\text{Var}(r_M)$	= 0.04640

Project A

S	P_s	r_j	$P_s r_j$	$(r_j - \bar{r}_j)$	$(r_M - \bar{r}_M)$	$P_s(r_j - \bar{r}_j)(r_M - \bar{r}_M)$
1	0.2	−0.05	−0.010	(−0.195)	(−0.36)	0.01404
2	0.3	0.15	0.045	(0.005)	(−0.06)	−0.00009
3	0.4	0.20	0.080	(0.055)	(0.14)	0.00308
4	0.1	0.30	0.030	(0.155)	(0.34)	0.00527
	$\bar{r}_A$	= 0.145			$\text{Cov}(r_A r_M)$	= 0.0223

Project B

S	P_s	r_j	$P_s r_j$	$(r_j - \bar{r}_j)$	$(r_M - \bar{r}_M)$	$P_s(r_j - \bar{r}_j)(r_M - \bar{r}_M)$
1	0.2	−0.20	−0.040	(−0.36)	(−0.36)	0.02592
2	0.3	0	0	(−0.16)	(−0.06)	0.00288
3	0.4	0.35	0.140	(0.19)	(0.14)	0.01064
4	0.1	0.60	0.060	(0.44)	(0.34)	0.01496
	$\bar{r}_B$	= 0.16			$\text{Cov}(r_B r_M)$	= 0.0544

fails to meet its hurdle rate requirement of 17.02 per cent. This example shows how a project's hurdle rate is heavily dependent upon the relationship between its cash flows and stock market returns. If possible this approach should use *ex-ante* estimates for the market and project returns for each possible state-of-the-world and attach probabilities to each state. Although project cash flows will be estimated for normal capital budgeting purposes the one-year return requires an estimate of a project's year-end market values. This is possible only if there is a reasonable secondary market for such assets.

Reservations

We have attempted to show how the CAPM can be extended to capital budgeting by adjustments being made to the observed beta for the firm's security. The model itself, however, is not above criticism and we must now consider whether it can be regarded as sufficiently robust to be of practical use in investment decisions. As with any model, the basic assumptions need to be stated before attempting to account for reality by relaxing some of them. Jensen (1972) has summarised the critical assumptions embedded in the CAPM as:

(i) all investors are single-period, expected-utility-of-terminal-wealth maximisers, who choose among alternative portfolios on the basis of the mean and variance of portfolio returns;
(ii) all investors can borrow and lend an unlimited amount at an exogenously given riskfree rate of interest;
(iii) all investors have identical subjective estimates of the means, variances, and covariances of returns among assets; that is, investors have homogeneous expectations;
(iv) all assets are perfectly divisible and perfectly liquid with no restrictions on short sales of any asset;
(v) there are no transaction costs;
(vi) there are no taxes;
(vii) all investors are price takers;
(viii) the quantities of all assets are given.

No one would doubt that the above assumptions do not accord with business reality. Some of the assumptions such as the taxation assumption can be relaxed to make the model more relevant to the real world. Other assumptions are more fundamental. Take, for example, the assumption that investors have homogeneous expectations. The observed facts are somewhat different. Blume and Friend (1975), in an analysis of investors' portfolios of securities, assets and liabilities, concluded that a large proportion of portfolios were highly undiversified. The justification for an investor carrying specific risk in his portfolio is that he knows or thinks he knows something the market does not know. Clearly, some investors are prepared to accept specific risk. They do not accept the EMH. They have heterogeneous expectations of risks and returns and are aware of gains arising from insider trading. To many investors market risk is not the only consideration. In another survey by the same authors 1,000 investors were questioned as to how they measured risk in evaluating the purchase of securities (1978). The results clearly indicated that few either explicitly or implicitly examined the relationship of asset returns with those of the market.

When we attempt to relate the model to fixed investments, which are by definition held for a period of more than one year, we are faced with the issues of whether and to what extent project betas change with time. The evidence for stationarity of betas for securities is at present inconclusive. If we accept the findings of Gonedes (1973) we can conclude that while such betas may not be constant through time, they do not change dramatically over five to ten years. What change there is could arise from changes in the firms' project mix or financial gearing. It is therefore conceivable that individual project betas fluctuate less than security betas over time.

We have seen that empirical studies have in many cases revealed discrepancies between theory and observation. Even if theory and fact differ, the CAPM may still be valuable as a normative theory prescribing what investors *should* do rather than describing what they actually do. The apparent variance between theory and practice leads one to query whether in fact beta is or should be the complete or only measure of risk. Do investors in fact prefer positive skewness in their portfolios and individual assets, as Kraus and Litzenberger (1976) suggest? If so, a measure of co-skewness should be introduced to complement beta. There are, however, more fundamental questions still to be resolved. Firstly, is the objective to maximise shareholder wealth the over-riding corporate objective? In pursuing wholeheartedly such an objective there is a strong possibility that this will create conflict with management and employee goals. Secondly, it is clear from analyses of company shareholdings that some investors deliberately hold undiversified portfolios, preferring to have some degree of control over the running of a company. Although difficult to quantify, few would doubt that real benefits can be derived by investors having a strong voice in corporate decisions. Such investors would then seek to reduce their portfolio risk by encouraging diversification within the company over which they have some influence. For such investors beta would not be a complete measure of risk. Total risk measuring the covariance between new investments and the existing business would also be important.

Summary

The capital asset pricing model states that in market equilibrium the expected return on a security or portfolio is the riskfree rate of interest plus a risk premium determined by the level of market risk. As the market value of the firm is the present value of its investment schedule, there is no reason why the model should not be extended to capital budgeting. A project's required rate of return will depend upon its degree of market risk, thereby evaluating future expected cash flows. The present value of an investment project is the sum of the expected cash flows discounted at risk-adjusted rates for each period. Ross (1978) has concluded that 'in attempting to extend (the CAPM) beyond its original framework it has proven to be somewhat less robust than might have been hoped'. This certainly applies to the area of capital budgeting, where intertemporal extensions to the static one-period model and other attempts to relax critical assumptions have encountered numerous difficulties. We have suggested in this chapter how in practice managers can resolve many of these difficulties. At the same time we recognise the need for further improvement before hurdle rates can be determined with the precision they deserve.

Questions

1. Illustrate and explain the securities market line.
2. What do you understand by the following:

   (i) market risk
   (ii) specific risk
   (iii) market portfolio
   (iv) lending portfolio
   (v) beta
   (vi) efficient market hypothesis
   (vii) ungeared beta

3. The directors of Rancho Inc. usually undertake high-risk contracts (beta = 2.0) in the demolition industry. They have been offered a housing clearance contract which they consider to be about 40 per cent as risky as the company's other contracts. The contract under consideration offers about £750,000 per annum for 4 years, incremental costs associated with the project being about £600,000 per annum. An initial outlay for plant and setting-up costs will be required amounting to £175,000 (which we shall assume will qualify for a 100 per cent first-year tax allowance).The directors expect the company to be paying corporation tax at 52 per cent for the foreseeable future, about 1 year after earning its cash flows. In the financial accounts depreciation at 30 per cent straight-line will be charged on the new plant. The project will be charged with a proportion of the firm's fixed costs. At the end of the contract the acquired plant will probably be sold for about £60,000. After-tax interest rates stand at 8 per cent and the after-tax return on the market is estimated at 15 per cent. As financial director, draft a report to your board outlining the theory of wealth creation, and make a recommendation on the above project using traditional and modern techniques of investment appraisal.
4. Your company undertakes a variety of high- and low-risk contracts in the off-shore oil industry. The company's average beta is 2.4. You are offered a maintenance contract considered to be about 25 per cent more risky than average. The contract offers about £800,000 per annum for 5 years, incremental costs associated with the project being about £625,000 per annum. The initial outlay for plant will be about £200,000 (which you assume will qualify for a 100 per cent first-year tax allowance). You anticipate that the company will pay corporation tax at 52% for the foreseeable future, about 1 year after earning its cash flow. The financial accountant proposes to depreciate at 20 per cent per annum on a straight-line basis. He also seizes upon the opportunity to load the contract with about £100,000 per annum in fixed costs, not directly attributable to the project. You estimate that at the end of the

contract plant can be sold for approximately £100,000. After-tax interest rates stand at 10 per cent, and the after-tax return on the economy is estimated at 16 per cent. As financial director, draft a report to your board making a firm recommendation on the above project, using traditional and modern techniques of investment appraisal. At the end of your report state briefly how the project might be affected by a government grant, a cheap bank loan or partial financing by debt.

5. Zerlina Ltd is considering investing in a risky new project which will have a life of one year only. Since the capital asset pricing model is a single-period model capable of handling risk, the manager of Zerlina, Masetto, is keen to use it to evaluate the project. To this end, he has estimated the returns on existing operations, the new project, the market portfolio and the risk-free security in three future 'states of the world' and these are contained in Table 1.

Table 1

		Return On			
State of the world	*Probability of occurrence*	*Existing projects*	*New project*	*Market portfolio*	*Riskfree security*
1	0.25	0.12	0.10	0.12	0.03
2	0.50	0.10	0.17	0.10	0.03
3	0.25	0.16	0.16	0.16	0.03

Acceptance of the new project will have a negligible impact upon the returns from the market portfolio; it will, however, comprise 10% of the modified total operations of Zerlina if accepted.

You are required to:

(a) calculate the beta factor of the new project;

(b) advise Masetto whether the new project is worthwhile, using the capital asset pricing model;

(c) calculate the minimum required rate of return for Zerlina assuming all future projects will have the same risk, on average, as

(i) existing operations

(ii) existing operations plus the new project;

(d) discuss the usefulness and limitations of the capital asset pricing model for capital budgeting decisions.

Ignore taxation. (ICA, PE II, July 1982)

6. (a) Arbace Ltd is an equity financed company with a beta factor of 1.0. The company's management is contemplating an investment in a project which, if accepted, would increase the beta factor to 1.2. The project would be financed by an issue of equity shares and, on acceptance, would comprise 10% of the total market value of Arbace Ltd. The project has an expected return over its one-year life

of 30%. No economies of scale would accrue to Arbace Ltd if the project were accepted. A riskfree security exists which currently yields 5% per annum, and the return on the market portfolio for the coming year is expected to remain at 15%, its current level.

You are required, stating clearly any assumptions which you believe to be necessary, to indicate whether investment in the project is worthwhile on the basis of a comparison between the project's expected return and:

(i) the existing weighted average cost of capital (WACC) of Arbace Ltd;
(ii) the expected WACC if the project is accepted;
(iii) the required return based on the project's own risk characteristics.

Ignore taxation.

(b) You are required to discuss the problems in raising equity finance encountered by small firms, which are not, and do not intend to become, listed companies.

(ICA, PE II, December 1982)

Note

1. Chapter 18, program 3 gives the computer output for calculating a project's beta.

References

Blume, M. and Friend, I. (1975) 'The asset structure of individual portfolios and some implications for utility functions', *Journal of Finance*, vol. 30, no. 2, May.

Blume, M. and Friend, I. (1978) *The Changing Role of the Individual Investor*, John Wiley.

Gonedes, N. (1973) 'Evidence on the information content of accounting numbers based on market-based estimates of systematic risk', *Journal of Financial and Quantitative Analysis*, no. 8, June.

Jensen, M. C. (1972) 'Capital markets: theory and evidence', *Bell Journal of Economics and Management Science*, Autumn.

Kraus, A. and Litzenberger, R. (1976) 'Skewness preference and the valuation of risk assets', *Journal of Finance*, vol. 31, no. 4, September.

Lintner, J. (1965) 'The valuation of risky assets and the selection of risky investments in stock portfolios and capital budgets', *Review of Economics and Statistics*, February.

London Business School, *Risk Measurement Service* (quarterly).

Markowitz, H. M. (1952) 'Portfolio selection', *Journal of Finance*, March.

Myers, S. and Pogue, G. (1973) 'An evaluation of the risk of consat common stock', Prepared Testimony, Federal Communication Commission.

Ross, S. (1978) 'The current status of the capital asset pricing model (CAPM)', *Journal of Finance*, vol. 33, no. 3, June.

Sharpe, W. F. (1963) 'A simplified model for portfolio analysis', *Management Science*, January.

Tobin, J. (1958) 'Liquidity preference as behaviour towards risk', *Review of Economic Studies*, February.

9

Investment Evaluation and Capital Rationing

In Chapter 2 we saw that, under the somewhat limiting assumptions specified, the wealth of a firm's shareholders is maximised if the firm accepts all investment proposals that have positive net present values. Alternatively, the NPV decision rule may be restated as: accept investments which offer rates of return in excess of their opportunity cost of capital. The opportunity cost of capital is the return shareholders could obtain for the same level of risk by investing their capital elsewhere. Implicit in the NPV decision rule is the notion that capital is always available to finance investment opportunities, at a cost.

In this chapter we relax another assumption of perfect capital markets by considering the practical issue where, for a variety of reasons, firms are restricted from undertaking all the investments offering positive net present values. Although individual projects cannot be accepted/rejected on the basis of the NPV rule, the essential problem remains, namely, to determine the package of investment projects which offers the highest total net present value to the shareholders.

The Nature of Constraints on Investment

In imperfect markets the capital budgeting problem may involve the allocation of scarce resources among competing, economically desirable projects, not all of which can be undertaken. 'Capital rationing', as this is commonly termed, therefore applies equally to non-capital, as well as capital, constraints. For example, the resource constraint may be the availability of skilled labour, management time, or working capital requirements. Investment constraints may even arise from the insistence that top management appraise and approve all capital projects, thus creating a backlog of investment proposals.

Hard and Soft Rationing

Capital rationing may arise (1) because a firm cannot obtain funds at market rates of return or (2) because of internally-imposed financial constraints by management. Externally-imposed constraints are referred to as *hard* rationing, and internally-imposed constraints as *soft* rationing. To what extent do these constraints exist among firms? One of the findings of the Wilson Report (1980) was that there was no evidence of any general shortage of finance for industry at prevailing rates of interest and levels of demand.

A recent survey conducted by Pike (1983) found:

1. The problem of low investment derives essentially not from a shortage of finance but from an inadequate demand for funds.
2. Capital constraints, where they exist, tend to be internally imposed rather than externally imposed by the capital market.
3. Capital constraints are more acutely experienced by smaller, less profitable and higher-risk firms.

The first two findings will be observed in Table 9.1.

Table 9.1 Constraints on a Company's Investment Programme that are 'Very Important' (%)

Lack of profitable investment opportunities	19.8
General economic uncertainty	18.7
Unwillingness to increase level of borrowings	19.0
Lack of capital available	8.7
Lack of trained managers to implement investment opportunities	7.4
Total number of firms: 126	

Source: Pike (1983)

The lack of profitable investment opportunities and the general economic uncertainty surrounding decision making were major factors for the low level of investment in the early 1980s. Soft rationing (partly indicated by the unwillingness to increase borrowings) is also an important constraint; but hard rationing (shortage of capital) is not seen as a particularly important constraint. As it is by no means certain that for the few firms experiencing difficulty in gaining access to financial markets the capital constraint was *binding*, the empirical existence of the hard form of capital rationing must be questioned.

Soft Rationing

We now turn our attention to why the internal management of a company should wish to impose a capital expenditure constraint which may actually result in the sacrifice of wealth-creating projects. Soft rationing may arise because:

1. Management sets maximum limits on borrowing and is unable or unwilling to raise additional equity capital in the short term. In effect, therefore, investment is restricted to internally-generated funds.
2. Management pursues a policy of stable growth rather than a fluctuating growth pattern with its attendant problems.
3. Management imposes divisional ceilings by way of annual capital budgets.

The capital budget forms an essential element of the company's complex planning and control process. It may sometimes be expedient for projects to be restricted — in the short term — to permit the proper planning and control of the organisation. Institution of divisional investment ceilings also provides a simple, if somewhat crude, method of dealing with biased cash flow forecasts. Where, for example, a division is in the habit of 'creating' numbers to justify the projects it wishes to implement, the institution of capital budget ceilings forces divisional management to set its own priorities and to select those offering highest returns.

One-Period Capital Rationing

The simplest form of capital rationing arises when financial limits are imposed for only a single period. This is illustrated in the example below. The manufacturing division of Mantech plc has been set an upper limit on capital spending for the coming year of £20 million. It is not normal practice for the group to set investment ceilings and it is anticipated that the capital constraint will not extend into future years. Assuming a cost of capital of 10 per cent, which of the following investment opportunities set out in Table 9.2 should divisional management select?

In the absence of any financial constraint, projects *A–D*, each with positive net present values, would be selected. Once this information has been communicated to investors, the total stock market value would, in theory at least, increase by £44 million — the sum of their net present values.

Table 9.2 Investment Opportunities (£ million)

Project	*Initial cost*	*Cash flows Year 1*	*Year 2*	*Present value*	*NPV*
A	−15	+17	+17	30	15
B	−5	+5	+10	13	8
C	−12	+12	+12	21	9
D	−8	+12	+11	20	12
E	−20	+10	+10	17	−3

However, the financial constraint prevents the selection of all profitable projects. It is now necessary to select the investment package which offers the highest net present value within the £20 million expenditure limit. A simple method of selecting projects under these circumstances is found in the profitability index, sometimes referred to as the benefit–cost ratio. It will be recalled that this measure was defined in Chapter 4 as:

$$\text{Profitability index} = \frac{\text{Present value}}{\text{Investment outlay}}$$

Project selection is made on the basis of the highest ratio of present value to investment outlay. This method is valuable under conditions of capital rationing because it focuses attention on the net present value of each project *relative* to the scarce resource required to undertake it. Appraising projects according to the NPV per £1 of investment outlay can give different rankings to application of the NPV rule. For example, while in the absence of capital rationing project *A* ranks highest (using the NPV rule), project *B* ranks highest when funds are limited, as shown in Table 9.3. Assuming project independence and infinite divisibility, divisional management will obtain the maximum net present value from its £20 million investment expenditure permitted by accepting projects *B* and *D* in total and 7/15 of project *A*.

Table 9.3

Project	*Profitability index*	*Outlay (£m)*		*NPV (£m)*
B	2.6	5	accept	8
D	2.5	8	accept	12
A	2.0	15	accept 7/15	7
C	1.7	12	reject	–
E	0.8	20	reject	–
				27

However, the profitability index rarely offers optimal solutions in practice. In the first place, few investment projects possess the attractive quality of divisibility. Where it is possible for projects to be scaled down to meet expenditure limits, this is frequently at the expense of profitability. Let us suppose that projects are *not* capable of division. How would this affect the selection problem? The best combination of projects now becomes *A* and *B*, giving a total net present value of £23 million. Project *D*, which ranked above *A* using the profitability index, is now excluded. Even more fundamental than this, however, is the limitation that the profitability index is only appropriate when capital rationing is restricted to a single period. This is not usually the case. Firms experiencing either forms of capital rationing ('hard' or 'soft') tend to experience them over a number of periods.

In summary, the profitability index provides a convenient method of selecting projects under conditions of capital rationing when investment projects are divisible and independent, and when only one period is subject to a resource constraint. Where, as is more commonly the case, these assumptions do not hold, investment selections should be made after examining the total net present values of all the feasible alternative combinations of investment opportunities falling within the capital outlay constraints.

Multi-Period Capital Rationing

Many business problems have similar characteristics to those exhibited in the capital rationing problem, namely:

1. scarce resources required to be allocated between competing alternatives;
2. an overriding objective which the decision maker is seeking to attain;
3. constraints, in one form or another, imposed on the decision maker.

As the number of alternatives and constraints increases, so the decision-making process becomes more complex. In such cases *mathematical programming models* are particularly valuable in the evaluation of decision alternatives for two reasons:

(i) They provide descriptive representation of a real problem using mathematical equations. Because they capture the critical elements and relationships existing in the real system, they provide insights about a problem without having to experiment directly on the actual system.

(ii) They provide optimal solutions, that is, the best solution for a given problem representation.

Many mathematical programming techniques have been developed. We shall concentrate our discussion on the most commonly found technique of linear programming. The assumptions and limitations underlying the LP approach will be discussed in a subsequent section. Problem-solving using the LP approach involves four basic steps:

1. Formulate the problem

This requires specification of the objective function, input parameters, decision variables and all relevant constraints. Take, for example, a firm which produces two products, A and B, with contributions of £5 and £10 respectively. The firm wishes to determine the product mix which will maximise its total contribution. The *objective function* may be expressed as follows:

$$\text{maximise contribution : } £5A + £10B$$

A and B are the *decision variables* representing the number of units of products A and B that should be produced. The *input values* £5 and £10 specify the unit profit values for products A and B respectively. Constraint equations may also be determined to describe any limitations on resources whether imposed by managerial policies or the external environment.

2. Solve the LP problem

Simple problems can be solved using either a graphical approach or simplex method. More complex problems require a computer-based solution algorithm.

3. Interpret the optimal solution

Examine the effect on the total value of the objective function if a binding constraint were marginally slackened or tightened.

4. Conduct sensitivity analysis

Assess for each input parameter the range of values for which the optimal solution remains valid.

These four stages in the LP process are illustrated in the following example:

Example

A particularly awkward problem has emerged for Castle plc following the five-year planning exercise: the cost of its six major projects forming the basis of the firm's investment programme exceeds the planned finance available. Castle plc is already highly-geared and control is in the hands of a few shareholders who are reluctant to introduce more equity funds. Accordingly, the main source of funds is through cash generated from existing operations, estimated to be £300,000 per annum over the next five years. The six projects are independent and cannot be delayed or brought forward. Each project has a similar risk complexion to that of the existing business. If necessary, projects are capable of division. The planned investment shedule and associated cash flows are given in Table 9.4.

Table 9.4 Planned Investment Schedule (£000)

	Project						
Year	*A*	*B*	*C*	*D*	*E*	*F*	*Outlay*
0	−200	–	−220	−110	−24	–	−554
1	−220	−220	−100	−150	−48	–	−738
2		−66	−50			−500	−616
3					−200		−200
NPV	130	184	35	42	186	280	
Total NPV = £857,000							

The six projects, if implemented, are forecast to produce a total NPV of £857,000. However, the annual capital constraint of £300,000 means that for the next three years the required investment expenditure exceeds available investment finance, i.e. there is a capital rationing problem.[1]

Solution

1. Specify the problem

Max: $130A + 184B + 35C + 42D + 186E + 280F$

Subject to constraints:

Year 0 $200A + 220C + 110D + 24E \leqslant 300$
Year 1 $220A + 220B + 100C + 150D + 48E \leqslant 300$
Year 2 $66B + 50C + 500F \leqslant 300$
Year 3 $200E \leqslant 300$
$A, B, C, D, E, F \geqslant 0, \leqslant 1$

This LP formulation tells us to find the mix of projects producing the highest total net present value, given the constraint that only £300,000 can be spent in any year and that not more than one of each project is permitted.

2. Solve the problem

Using a typical linear programme on the computer gives the solution in Table 9.5. Castle plc should accept investment proposals *B* and *E* in full plus

Table 9.5

Project	*Proportion accepted*	*NPV (£000)*	*Year 0*	*Capital Outlay (£000)* *Year 1*	*Year 2*	*Year 3*
A	0.145	19	−29	32	–	–
B	1	184	–	−220	−66	–
C	0	–				
D	0	–				
E	1	186	−24	−48	–	−200
F	0.468	131	–	–	−234	–
		520	−53	−300	−300	−200

14.5 per cent of project *A* and 46.8 per cent of project *F*. This will produce the highest possible total net present value available of £520,000. Notice that this is significantly less than the £857,000 total NPV if no constraints are imposed.

3. Interpret the optimal solution

It will be seen from Table 9.5 that only in years 1 and 2 are the full £300,000 utilised. These years then are *binding* constraints — their existence limits the company's freedom to pursue its objective of NPV maximisation because it restricts the investment finance available to the firm in those years. Conversely, years 0 and 3 are *non-binding*: they do not constrain the firm in its efforts to achieve its objective. Hence while there is no *additional* opportunity cost (in addition to that already incorporated in the discount rate) for non-binding periods, there is an additional opportunity cost attached to the use of investment finance in the two years where constraints are binding. These additional opportunity costs are termed *shadow prices* (or dual values). Shadow prices show how much the decision maker would be willing to pay to acquire one additional unit of each resource that is constrained in the problem. In our particular problem, the computer analysis reveals that the shadow prices are:

Year	*Shadow price*	*Constraint*
0	0	non-binding
1	0.59	binding
2	0.56	binding
3	0	non-binding

This may be interpreted as follows: A £1 increase (reduction) in capital spending in year 1 would produce an increase (reduction) in total NPV of £0.59. Similarly for year 2, a £1 change investment expenditure would result in a £0.56 change in total NPV. Because the capital constraints in years 0 and 3 are non-binding, their shadow prices are zero and a marginal change in capital spending in those years will have no impact on the NPV objective function. Shadow prices, while of value in indicating the additional opportunity cost, can only be used within a specific range. In addition, it is desirable to ascertain the effect of changes in input parameters on the optimal solution. These issues require some form of sensitivity analysis.

4. Perform Sensitivity Analysis

The computer output provides two additional pieces of information. First, it tells the decision maker the maximum variation for each binding constraint. In our example, the shadow price for the year 1 constraint has a range of −36 to +188. In other words, the shadow price of £0.59 would hold up to an increase in capital expenditure for that year of £188,000, or a reduction of £36,000.

The programme also indicates the margin of error permitted for input parameters before the optimal solution differs. Thus, in our example, the actual NPV for the optimal investment mix could fall as indicated below and still not change the optimal solution:

Project	Maximum permitted fall in NPV (£000)
A	−68
B	−17
E	−158
F	−280

This facility is particularly appropriate as a means of assessing the margin of error permitted for risky projects under conditions of capital rationing.

LP Assumptions

In order to assess the value of the basic linear programming approach for solving the problem of project selection under conditions of capital rationing we must consider the assumptions underlying its application. The main assumptions are:

(i) all input parameters to the LP model are certain;
(ii) there is a single objective to be optimised;
(iii) the objective function and all constraint equations are linear;
(iv) decision variables are continuous (i.e. divisible);
(v) there is independence among decision variables and resources available.

Most, if not all, of these limiting assumptions can be relaxed by utilising the more complex mathematical programming models summarised below:

Requirement	*Technique*
Uncertainty	Stochastic LP
	Chance constrained programming
	LP under uncertainty
Multiple goals	Goal programming
Non-linearity	Non-linear programming
	Quadratic programming
Non-divisibility	Integer programming

Discussion of these developments is beyond the scope of this book.

Summary

Two forms of capital rationing were examined in this chapter. *Hard rationing* — where a firm cannot obtain investment funds at the prevailing market rate of interest for the risks involved — is rarely encountered in efficient capital markets. *Soft rationing* — where management voluntarily imposes investment ceilings in the short-term — is more commonly encountered. Essentially, the objective is the same regardless of the existence or otherwise of capital rationing: a firm should find that package of investment projects within its available resources yielding the greatest possible total net present value. Only the means of achieving this goal change. The net present value rule applied to each project is no longer wholly appropriate because the assumption that capital is always available to finance investment opportunities no longer holds.

Single-period capital rationing, in its simplest form, is resolved by ranking projects on the basis of their ratios of present value to investment outlay (profitability index). More complex multi-period capital rationing problems are solved by applying a mathematical programming approach. However, empirical evidence (Pike 1983) suggests that, rather than employing such sophisticated methods, financially constrained firms tend to ration capital by reducing investment search activities, emphasising payback and increasing hurdle rates.

Questions

1. What do you understand by 'soft' and 'hard' forms of capital rationing?
2. Which approaches are available to investment decision makers to resolve capital rationing problems? Discuss their merits and drawbacks.
3. Why do you think that relatively few firms adopt a mathematical programming approach to capital rationing?
4. How realistic are the assumptions underlying the linear programming capital rationing approach?
5. Mace Ltd is planning its capital budget for 1987 and 1988. The company's directors have reduced their initial list of projects to five, the expected cash flows of which are set out below:

Project	*1987*	*1988*	*1989*	*1990*	*NPV*
1	−60,000	+30,000	+25,000	+25,000	+ 1,600
2	−30,000	−20,000	+25,000	+45,000	+ 1,300
3	−40,000	−50,000	+60,000	+70,000	+ 8,300
4	0	−80,000	+45,000	+55,000	+ 900
5	−50,000	+10,000	+30,000	+40,000	+ 7,900

None of the five projects can be delayed and all are divisible. Cash flows arise on the first day of the year. The minimum return required by shareholders of Mace Ltd is 10% per annum. Which projects should Mace Ltd accept if the capital available for investment is limited to £100,000 on 1st January 1987, but readily available at 10% p.a. on 1st January 1988 and subsequently?

6. Macro plc is preparing its investment schedules for 1985. The following projects are available:

Project	*A*	*B*	*C*	*D*
Cash flow	£	£	£	£
1985	−12,000	−30,000	−30,000	−30,000
1986	−12,000	−60,000	−90,000	−90,000
1987	+20,000	+180,000	+120,000	+120,000
1988	+20,000	+20,000	+70,000	+70,000

Macro plc has a cost of capital of 15%. All projects have similar risk complexions, are divisible and cannot be delayed.

Which projects should Macro plc undertake, assuming that:

(i) capital is freely available;
(ii) capital is limited to £70,000 in 1987.

Provide a mathematical programming formulation to assist the directors of Macro plc to select the optimal investment programme, assuming capital is limited to £70,000 for each of the next four years.

7. Raiders Ltd is a private limited company which is financed entirely by ordinary shares. Its effective cost of capital, net of tax, is 10% per annum. The directors of Raiders Ltd are considering the company's capital investment programme for the next two years, and have reduced their initial list of projects to four. Details of the projects' cash flows (net of tax) are as follows (in £000):

Project	*Imme-diately*	*After 1 year*	*After 2 years*	*After 3 years*	*Net present value (at 10%)*	*Internal rate of return (to nearest 1%)*
A	−400	+50	+300	+350	+157.0	26%
B	−300	−200	+400	+400	+150.0	25%
C	−300	+150	+150	+150	+73.5	23%
D	0	−300	+250	+300	+159.5	50%

None of the projects can be delayed. All projects are divisible; outlays may be reduced by any proportion and net inflows will then be reduced in the same proportion. No project can be undertaken more than once. Raiders Ltd is able to invest surplus funds in a bank deposit account yielding a return of 7% per annum, net of tax.

You are required to:

(a) prepare calculations showing which projects Raiders Ltd should undertake if capital for immediate investment is limited to £500,000, but is expected to be available without limit at a cost of 10% per annum thereafter;

(b) provide a mathematical programming formulation to assist the directors of Raiders Ltd in choosing investment projects if capital available immediately is limited to £500,000, capital available after one year is limited to £300,000, and capital is available thereafter without limit at a cost of 10% per annum;

(c) outline the limitations of the formulation you have provided in (b);

(d) comment briefly on the view that in practice capital is rarely limited absolutely, provided that the borrower is willing to pay a sufficiently high price, and in consequence a technique for selecting investment projects which assumes that capital is limited absolutely is of no use.

(ICA, PE II, July 1983)

Notes

1. Strictly speaking, we should have included the expected cash flows from

projects. If this were done, the positive cash flows in early years would increase the cash available for investment.

References

Wilson (1980) *Report of the Committee to Review the Functioning of Financial Institutions*, HMSO.

Pike, R. H. (1983) 'The capital budgeting behaviour and corporate characteristics of capital-constrained firms', *Journal of Business Finance and Accounting*, Winter.

Further Reading

Arditti, F. D., Grinold, R. C. and Levy, H. (1973) 'The investment-consumption decision under capital rationing: an efficient analysis', *Review of Economic Studies*, July.

Baumol, W. and Quant, R. (1965) 'Investment and discount rates under capital rationing — a programming approach', *Economic Journal*, June.

Bernard, R. H. (1969) 'Mathematical programming models for capital budgeting — a survey, generalisation and critique', *Journal of Financial and Quantitative Analysis*, June.

Bhaskar, K. N. (1976) 'Linear programming and capital budgeting: a reappraisal', *Journal of Business Finance and Accounting*, Autumn.

Ederington, L. H. and Henry, W. R (1979) 'On costs of capital in programming approaches to capital budgeting, *Journal of Finance and Quantitative Analysis*, December.

Elton, E. J. (1970) 'Capital rationing and external discount rates', *Journal of Finance*, June.

Hirshleifer, J. (1958) 'On the theory of optimal investment', *Journal of Political Economy*, August.

Lorie, J. H. and Savage, L. J. (1955) 'Three problems in capital rationing', *Journal of Business*, October.

Myers, S. C. (1972) 'A note on linear programming and capital budgeting', *Journal of Finance*, March.

Weingartner, H. M. (1963) *Mathematical Programming and the Analysis of Capital Budgeting Problems*, Prentice-Hall.

Weingartner, H. M. (1977) 'Capital rationing: *n* authors in search of a plot', *Journal of Finance*, December.

10

The Merger Investment Decision

The merger or acquisition decision is an *investment decision*. The objective of the firm is to create wealth, making money satisfying consumer wants in competitive markets. The acquisition decision can therefore be evaluated in terms of the *net present value rule*. Mergers and acquisitions are a good idea when the value of the combined enterprise is greater than the value of the two independent companies. *Genuine economic benefits* can be derived from a merger. For example economies of scale may arise whereby two companies can share fixed costs; they can incur the costs of one research and development department rather than two; share computing costs, achieve economies in production, marketing, and personnel. Benefits may also arise by synergy, whereby the whole is greater than the sum of the individual parts. *Synergy* is usually illustrated as the 2 + 2 = 5 situation. An example is the merging of an ice cream company with a sausage company. The company is in the frozen food industry. It uses the same refrigerated vehicles to deliver 70 per cent ice cream and 30 per cent sausages in summer, and 70 per cent sausages and 30 per cent ice cream in winter.

Benefits can also arise by vertical integration, whereby a manufacturing company may buy forwards into retailing, or backwards into production of primary materials. Horizontal mergers should increase a company's market share, possibly encouraging the introduction of more innovations. A merger may result in the acquired company receiving the benefit of superior managerial skills, whereby more cash flow is generated from the company's existing business. It may even be that the new management will strip the company of its assets when the market value of the acquired company is less than the disposal value of its investments. Another reason sometimes put forward for mergers is to exploit the acquired company's unused debt capacity, where the managers of the acquired firm have failed to take advantage of the tax savings on borrowings.

We are already familiar with the usual techniques for assessing capital expenditure opportunities and, since the merger decision is an investment decision, we can use the same techniques for evaluation:

1. The net present value rule
2. Internal rate of return
3. Profitability index or cost–benefit ratio
4. Payback period
5. Discounted payback period
6. Effect of return on capital employed
7. Effect on earnings per share

In addition to the above techniques for evaluating acquisitions, we must also discuss the following objectives which are often emphasised by managers examining merger and acquisition opportunities:

8. An increase in sales or market share
9. An increase in the firm's total assets
10. An increase in diversification

The Net Present Value Rule

Mergers make economic sense when the combined enterprise has a higher market value than the sum of two independent enterprises before merger or acquisition. The economic gain is the present value of the anticipated cash benefits resulting from the merger:

$$V_{AB} = V_A + V_B + X$$

where

V_{AB} = value of combined enterprise
V_A = value of acquiring firm, independent of the merger or acquisition
V_B = value of target company, independent of merger
X = present value of cash benefits resulting from the merger

Where the X factor is positive, the merger makes economic sense. Using the present value rule, wealth is created by bringing the two companies together. We propose that mergers make sense when the value of the firms combined is greater than the two independent firms. Where the target company is a quoted company, the efficient market hypothesis tells us that the share price reflects all available information. If the share price of the target company does not reflect the possibility of an acquisition, then managers should:

1. forecast the post-merger cash flows and required rates of return;
2. use net present value to estimate the value of the enterprise after merger or acquisition;
3. split the positive *X* factor between the shareholders of company A and company B;
4. negotiate the merger.

If the market value of the target company already reflects an anticipated merger, the acquiring company's managers should value the target company independently of its existing share price, i.e. estimate the intrinsic value of the company which we usually regard as being the same as market value when the company is valued as a separate entity. The *X* factor should be split between the shareholders of the acquiring company and the shareholders of the target company before the anticipated merger is reflected in share prices. To the extent that the merger is already reflected in the share price of both companies, this should be taken into account in negotiating an acquisition price.

We recommend the use of net present value in the evaluation of merger opportunities. Clearly, we could use internal rate of return, the profitability index, the payback period, discounted payback period, and effect on return on capital employed. We prefer to use the NPV rule. This indicates whether or not a merger or acquisition is wealth-creating. Since present values are additive, we can add together the market values of companies A and B and compare the sum of the market values with the expected market value after merger. Net present value is easier to handle than internal rate of return or profitability index. Other methods such as payback, discounted payback, and effect on return of capital employed do not necessarily indicate whether or not a merger or acquisition makes economic sense.

Effect on Earnings Per Share

One of the most popular objectives of industrial organisations is to increase earnings per share. Many mergers have been justified in terms of effect on earnings per share, and companies are often valued on the basis of some multiple of profits. The effect on earnings per share does not indicate whether or not a merger is wealth-creating. Furthermore, companies should not be valued on the basis of some multiple of last year's accounting profit. To increase earnings per share is an unsatisfactory objective. Measurement of corporate performance on the basis of earnings per share is also unsatisfactory. Earnings per share ignores cash flow and risk. It is an historic number based on accounting profit, which is subject to accounting policies on stock valuation, asset depreciation, bad debts, profit on long-term contracts, provisions for accrued income and expenditure, etc. Accounting profit is usually taken from last year's profit and loss account, whereas share prices reflect anticipated cash flows, taking into account risk. Price–earnings ratios cannot be used as a basis for decision making. The numerator is the share price which reflects anticipated cash flows. The denominator is last year's earnings per share. If the company broke even last year, the price–earnings ratio is infinite. If the company made a loss last year, the price–earnings ratio is negative. It is not appropriate to use the price–earnings ratio, which is essentially a payback period, as a basis for merger evaluation. Nevertheless, for many years mergers have been justified on the basis of EPS effect.

Question

Firm A is considering the acquisition of firm B. Fill in the spaces below assuming that there are no merger benefits, and that A intends to acquire B by offering shares for shares. Two shares in A will be given for five shares in B.

	Firm A	*Firm B*	*A + B*
EPS (Earnings per share) (£)	1.00	1.00	
PPS (Price per share) (£)	50	20	
P/E ratio	50	20	
Number of shares	100,000	250,000	
Total earnings (historic) (£)	100,000	250,000	
Total market value (£)	5,000,000	5,000,000	

What is the effect on earnings per share?
Has wealth been created?
Do we believe in financial illusions?
Whatever happened to conglomerates?

Answer

If Firm A acquires firm B without merger benefits, the X factor is zero, and the total market value of A + B is £10,000,000. Historic earnings are £350,000, the number of shares increases to 200,000, the price per share becomes £50, the price–earnings ratio becomes 28.57, and earnings per share increase to £1.75. In fact, earnings per share increase by 75 per cent for both companies. If we make decisions on the basis of increasing earnings per share, then this is indeed a very profitable merger. However, wealth has not been created because the market value of A + B is exactly the same after the merger as before the merger. Furthermore, the wealth of each shareholder is unchanged. This is a conglomerate merger, and conglomerates are not popular with financial theorists. Shareholders can achieve diversification without assistance from corporate managers.

	Firm A	*Firm B*	*A + B*
EPS (£)	1.00	1.00	1.75
PPS (£)	50	20	50
P/E ratio	50	20	28.57
Number of shares	100,000	250,000	200,000
Total earnings (historic) (£)	100,000	250,000	350,000
Total market value (£)	5,000,000	5,000,000	10,000,000

The above example illustrates that the merger could be justified in terms of increasing earnings per share, although only an illusion of wealth is created. We do not believe in financial illusions. We believe that wealth is created when managers make money satisfying consumer wants in competitive markets. The following example illustrates that earnings per share can still give the wrong answer, even when the *X* factor is positive.

Question

Firm A is considering the acquisition of firm B. The *X* factor is estimated at £6,000, and in the first instance A offers B shares in A at fourteen times B's historic earnings. Alternatively, a *reverse takeover* could be arranged whereby B would offer A shares in B at twenty-two times A's historic earnings. Examine the earnings per share effect. Which merger makes most sense, A + B or B + A?

	Firm A	*Firm B*	*A + B* (*i*)	*B + A* (*ii*)
EPS (£)	1.0	1.0		
PPS (£)	20	10		
P/E ratio	20	10		
Number of shares	1,000	1,000		
Total earnings (historic) (£)	1,000	1,000		
Total market value (£)	20,000	10,000	36,000	

Answer

If A acquires B, the X factor is split on the basis of £2,000 for A shareholders and £4,000 for B shareholders. After the merger the value of the combined firm to the original shareholders in A will be £22,000, and the price per share £22. The shareholders in B will receive shares in the new company, A + B, valued at £14,000. It will therefore be necessary to issue 636 shares at £22 per share. Clearly, the merger makes economic sense, the shareholders in Firm A and in Firm B being better off after the merger. Furthermore, earnings per share increase by 22 per cent for both companies to £1.22p.

If the reverse takeover is organised, the total market value of B + A will also be £36,000. The split of the X factor remains exactly as before. Company A shareholders will receive £2,000, and company B shareholders will receive £4,000. After the merger the 1,000 shares owned by the B shareholders will be worth £14 each. At £14 it will be necessary to issue 1,571 shares to the shareholders in firm A. Unfortunately, earnings per share in the combined enterprise fall to 78p, a decrease of 22 per cent. If we make economic decisions on the basis of EPS effect, this merger appears not to make economic sense. This is clearly wrong. Shareholders in firm A and in firm B are wealthier. The fact that earnings per share have fallen is of no consequence to shareholders in efficient capital markets. If we did base our decisions on EPS effect, we would have to argue that A + B is a good idea, whereas B + A is a bad idea. Such an argument is clearly inadmissible.

	Firm A	*Firm B*	*A + B (i)*	*B + A (ii)*
EPS (£)	1.0	1.0	1.22	0.78
PPS (£)	20	10	22	14
P/E ratio	20	10	18	18
Number of shares	1,000	1,000	1,636	2,571
Total earnings (historic) (£)	1,000	1,000	2,000	2,000
Total market value (£)	20,000	10,000	36,000	36,000

Acquisitions to Increase Sales

Having rejected growth in earnings per share as a managerial objective, we must now consider a further three objectives often proposed to justify mergers and acquisitions. These are to increase sales or market share; to increase the quantity of the firm's assets; and to increase diversification. With reference to increasing sales, we must immediately reject this as a sensible objective by asserting that all mergers would make sense. The sales of company A and company B combined must be greater than the sales of company A alone. We must add that this will be the case regardless of the price paid for the acquisition. To increase sales is clearly an unacceptable objective since it justifies all mergers, regardless of cost, and regardless of industry differences.

Increasing sales in the same industry to increase market share can make economic sense. Many such horizontal mergers have been successful. The merger or acquisition may result in economies of scale or the combining of good products with good marketing. In the motor industry it is sometimes claimed that market share is of critical importance because the firm with market share can introduce more innovations. However, the merger or acquisition must be evaluated in terms of the NPV rule as outlined earlier.

Acquisitions to Increase the Quantity of the Firm's Assets

Managers prefer to manage larger rather than smaller organisations. Managerial rewards tend to be related to *span of control* which can be measured in various ways including the number of employees, quantity of sales, size of budget or quantity of the firm's assets. Growth in assets and sales is often stated as an acceptable goal for industrial organisations. It is generally regarded as being a managerial objective which does not necessarily result in the creation of additional wealth. We therefore regard the objective of increasing the quantity of the firm's assets as economically undesirable. Clearly, all mergers make sense if the objective is simply to increase the quantity of assets under control of the directors of the acquisitive company. Again, we return to the NPV rule: mergers should be encouraged when the market value of the combined enterprise is greater than the sum of the individual parts.

Acquisitions for Diversification

The *conglomerate merger* is often described as the 'two plus two equals four' proposition. Such a merger is economically pointless, because no additional wealth is created. However, it sometimes appears that boards of directors are trying to turn public companies into widely diversified unit trusts. In the absence of economies of scale or synergy, present values are additive. However, survival of the company is a top managerial priority, and it should be possible to *reduce the probability of liquidation* by corporate diversification. We must stress that individual companies can face financial distress not only because of movements in the market, but also because of factors unique or specific to the individual company. We therefore understand the temptation of managers to diversify. Such conglomerate diversification is not necessary for shareholders, as investors can and do diversify their holdings across a number of companies without any assistance from corporate managers. Shareholders often object to corporate diversification on the grounds that they can achieve such diversification without the aid of management. Corporate diversification does achieve employment diversification for management and employees, but provides no incremental wealth for shareholders. Conglomerate diversification does in fact reduce investor choice by removing individual companies from the market place.

Managers often claim that they can purchase companies at less than their intrinsic value. However, in an efficient capital market there are no bargains and therefore we should not expect to find cheap acquisitions. Diversification into growth industries by acquisition may encourage the survival of top management, but as the acquisitive company must pay the market price to acquire growth companies, there is no reason to suppose that such acquisitions will increase returns to existing shareholders in the acquisitive company. In fact, many studies including those by Newbould (1970) and Franks, Broyles and Hecht (1977) suggest that *the major portion of the net benefit accrues to the shareholders in the acquired company*. It is commonplace for the market value of a target company to increase when a takeover bid is made for its shares. Investors expect the new management to replace the cash flows expected from existing management with a new set of higher net operational cash flows. The benefits of any increase in the value of a company on the announcement of a formal offer generally accrue to existing shareholders in the target company as that firm's market price has long since reflected the anticipation of an offer. In fact, it is often the case that the market value of the acquisitive company falls when shareholders realise that too high a price is being offered for a target company. Again, we return to the NPV rule. Adding companies together makes economic sense if the market value of the combined enterprise is greater than the sum of the market values of the individual firms. The market value of the company after merger will only be greater when the merger achieves economies of scale or synergy.

Some Notes on Mergers

1. Assets or Shares?

The greatest amount of publicity is usually given to takeovers where the acquisitive company makes an offer for the shares of the target company. Ownership of the shares in the target company changes hands, but the company's assets and liabilities are unchanged. There are some circumstances in which the acquisitive company may not wish to acquire control of all assets in the target company, or accept responsibility for all liabilities. For example, the target company may face considerable legal problems, its stock valuation may be suspect, bad debts may be understated, or the actual amount of creditors may be uncertain. The directors of the acquiring company may decide to make an offer for some of the assets of the target company, rather than purchase shares. It may be considered desirable to purchase the target company's brand names and fixed assets, but to allow existing shareholders to collect cash from debtors, dispose of certain items of stock, settle the creditors and outstanding taxation liabilities, and wind up the company.

2. *The Financing Decision*

The merger decision is an *investment decision* which is therefore very important: the value of the firm depends primarily on its investment schedule. *Financing decisions* are less important: once we reject increasing earnings per share as an acceptable objective in the merger decision, the financing decision becomes less important. As already indicated, all mergers would be financed by cash if the objective were to increase earnings per share. One important consideration which does affect cash flows is taxation. Generally, gains arising on shares exchanged for shares are not subject to capital gains tax until the shares exchanged are eventually sold for cash. Gains arising on disposals for cash do attract capital gains tax.

3. *Merger Cycles*

There appear to have been four waves in this century. The early 1900s witnessed mainly horizontal mergers. A wave of vertical mergers took place during the 1920s. A third merger wave during the 1960s has generally been described as the period of conglomerate mergers. Apparently, we are now in the fourth merger wave. It is always more difficult to pin a label on a series of events currently taking place. Recent mergers have been described as 'strategic'. This often means that the merger or acquisition is defensive, which sometimes means that the objective is to acquire key personnel and technology to avoid takeover by a rival company. No doubt with hindsight we shall acquire greater understanding of the present series of mergers.

It has proved very difficult to explain the four merger waves which have occurred. They all appear to have taken place during periods of buoyant stock market prices, and we therefore conclude that, during bull markets, the good prospects for existing shareholders and capital gains for shareholders in target companies enable managers to put together an acceptable merger package. Managers, as agents of the shareholders, are pursuing managerial objectives including increasing sales, increasing the quantity of the firm's assets, increasing diversification, increasing earnings per share, and avoiding acquisition.

4. Merger Tactics

Merger negotiations and disputes can be very complex. We suggest that before entering merger or acquisition negotiations, managers should have a very clear plan. They should acquire an analysis of existing shareholders, set a price limit, decide on a package, make enquiries, enter into talks, and then make an offer. If the acquisition is opposed, then managers must decide whether to continue or withdraw. Speed is important, and an increased offer must only be made on the basis of new information. Increasing the offer without new information will be interpreted as an indication that an even bigger offer will ensue.

If directors wish to protect themselves against takeover, they should seek to maintain good shareholder relations. This can be achieved by maximising share prices by maximising anticipated cash flows. Directors should monitor share price movements, keep files on potential aggressors, consider long-term contracts with the company for themselves and suppliers, be prepared to appeal to government agencies, consider sale and lease-back arrangements to discourage asset strippers and avoid spare debt capacity. We repeat that the best way to avoid takeover is to maximise the market value of the company by developing a successful investment schedule.

During the period that an offer remains open, directors should defend against takeover by causing delays. They should find reasons for additional talking, emphasise the weaknesses of the bidder, set a non-rejectable share price, justify rejection of the existing offer, attack the bidder's record, and continue to provide new information relating to future cash flows, dividends and investment opportunities. This could provide reason for the attacker to increase the offer price, as well as encourage existing shareholders to expect an increased offer.

Questions

1. When do mergers make economic sense?
2. Discuss the objectives of increasing market share, increasing earnings per share, and increasing the quantity of the firm's assets.
3. Assess the value of the conglomerate merger.
4. Your company pursues growth by scale expansion and diversification. A small screw manufacturing company is being evaluated for acquisition. Standard procedure is to make optimistic forecasts for the target company, discount anticipated cash flows at your company's weighted average cost of capital, assume that all debt finance is repaid immedi-

ately, and then make an offer. Acquisitions are usually made for cash. Your directors are concerned about the EPS effect and the contribution of the acquisition to return on capital employed, as well as to the effect on sales and profit growth. As financial director, draft a report to your co-directors, commenting on the acquisition under consideration and outlining a sensible strategy for mergers and acquisitions.

5. Dick is chief executive of the Bradford Emporium Ltd. He believes in growth in earnings per share as the best corporate objective. Indeed, since joining the Emporium as a lad, he has seen the firm expand its sales, profit and earnings per share, largely on the acquisition of other stores in the Bradford area, financed almost always by cash generated from successful trading at the Emporium. Dick is about to pull off the greatest coup of his career by taking over Leeds Photographics Ltd. Use of only one computer centre, head office, credit control and buying department will reduce the joint corporate costs by a considerable amount which should result in an immediate benefit of about £10m. to the market value of the combined enterprise.

	Bradford	*Leeds*
Earnings per share (£)	1	1
Price per share (£)	20	10
P/E ratio	20	10
Number of shares	4,000,000	4,000,000
Historic earnings (£m.)	4	4
Total market value (£m.)	80	40

Dick's financial director suggests that Bradford could make Leeds an offer for shares at 11 times Leeds's historic earnings. Alternatively, a reverse takeover could be considered whereby Leeds could offer to buy Bradford shares at 21.5 times Bradford's historic earnings. Dick is anxious to examine the EPS effect.

(a) Present data and a report on both proposals.
(b) When do mergers make economic sense?
(c) Why do most mergers fail?

6. Scott is CEO of the CMA Corporation. He believes in growth in earnings per share as the best corporate objective. He has seen CMA expand its sales profit and earnings per share, largely by the acquisition of growth companies in Southern California, financed almost always by cash. Scott is about to make an offer for Ingle Mufflers Inc. Use of only one computer centre, head office, credit control and buying department will reduce the joint corporate fixed costs by a considerable amount which should result in an immediate benefit of about $30m. to the market value of the combined enterprise.

	CMA	*INGLE*
Earnings per share ($)	2	3
Price per share ($)	40	30
P/E ratio	20	10
Number of shares	10,000,000	2,000,000
Historic earnings ($m.)	20	6
Total market value ($m.)	400	60

As Scott's financial director you suggest that CMA could make Ingle an offer for shares at 12 times Ingle's historic earnings. Alternatively, a reverse takeover could be considered whereby Ingle could offer to buy CMA shares at 21 times CMA's historic earnings. Scott is anxious to examine the EPS effect. As financial director, draft a report to your CEO outlining the problems and prospects.

7. Two companies, Colts plc and Cowboy plc, have recently merged. The prime mover for the merger was Colts plc with a beta factor of 1.5 and a market capitalisation of £10,000,000 just before the merger. Cowboy plc is smaller, and had a market capitalisation of £5,000,000, and a beta factor of 0.6 just before the merger. Both companies were all equity financed at the time of the merger and were fairly valued by the market. The two companies were in different industrial sectors and displayed very little co-movement in their earnings streams. While no economies of scale or other synergistic benefits were available from the merger, the management of Colts plc strongly favoured proceeding with the merger in order to achieve a lower risk profile for the combined firm. Shares in the combined entity were distributed on the basis of the total market values of the individual companies just before the merger.

   The expected return on the market before and after the merger was 13% per annum and the return on the risk-free security was similarly constant at 8% per annum.

   You are required to:

   (a) calculate the expected return on the securities both before and after the merger using the capital asset pricing model;
   (b) calculate the impact of the merger on a shareholder who held shares in Colts plc and Cowboy plc before the merger in the ratio 2:1 based on the pre-merger market values of the shareholdings, and indicate the implications for shareholders of mergers of this type;
   (c) discuss the possible reasons why the management of Colts plc were in favour of the merger.

   Ignore taxation. (ICA, PE II, July 1983)

8. The directors of Elisa plc are considering the acquisition of the entire share capital of a private limited company, Aminta Ltd, both companies being wholly financed by equity capital. Elisa plc prepares annual accounts to 31st December and the takeover would take place on 1st January 1983. A project analyst, charged with the task of collecting

sufficient relevant information, has discovered that Tamiri plc is the public company most closely resembling Aminta Ltd. It has an equity cost of capital of 19.3% and a price-earnings ratio of 7.9. Tamiri plc is engaged in the same line of business as Aminta Ltd and has very similar business and financial risk characteristics. The following details relating to Elisa and Aminta have been provided by the analyst:

(1) Elisa plc has an equity cost of capital of 15.85%. The analyst estimates that, if Aminta Ltd is acquired, the cash flow of Elisa plc for the year to 31st December 1983 will be increased by an amount equal to 105% of the 1982 net profit of Aminta Ltd before deducting directors' emoluments. These additional cash flows will amount to 30% of the combined cash flows of the enlarged Elisa plc for 1983. The analyst does not expect any economies of scale from the takeover and predicts that the cash flows of Elisa plc will increase by 5% per annum compound in 1984 and subsequent years whether or not Aminta is acquired.

(2) Aminta Ltd produces annual accounts to 31st December which show the following net profit figures (after deduction of directors' emoluments):

1977	£619,000
1978	£600,000
1979	£524,000
1980	£604,000
1981	£628,000
1982	£790,000 (estimated)

The draft 1982 annual accounts also show that the net assets of Aminta Ltd are £3,618,000 on an historic cost basis and £6,375,000 on a replacment cost basis. The analyst estimates that the assets of Aminta Ltd would realise approximately £4,000,000 on liquidation. The two directors and only shareholders are Mr. and Mrs. Alessandro, whose emoluments appear to average 10% of the net profit figures, after deducting those emoluments.

You are required, explaining the underlying principles, to calculate:

(a) the maximum sum that the directors of Elisa plc should be willing to pay for the share capital of Aminta Ltd;

(b) the minimum sum that Mr. and Mrs. Alessandro should be willing to accept for their shareholding in Aminta Ltd.

Ignore taxation. (ICA, PE II, December 1982)

References

Franks, J. R., Broyles, J. E. and Hecht, M. J. (1977) 'An industry study of the profitability of mergers in the UK', *Journal of Finance*, vol. 32, no. 5, December.

Newbould, G. D. (1970) *Management and Merger Activity*, Guthstead.

Further Reading

Buckley, A. (1979) 'A blueprint for acquisition strategy', *Accountancy*, September–October.

Franks, J. R., Miles, R. and Bagwell, J. (1974) 'A critique of merger valuation methods', *Journal of Business Finance and Accounting*, Spring.

Mandelker, G. (1974) 'Risk and return: the case of merging firms', *Journal of Financial Economics*, December.

Myers, S. C. (1976) 'A framework for evaluating mergers' in S. C. Myers (ed.) *Modern Developments in Financial Management*, Praeger.

Shad, S. R. (1969) 'The financial realities of mergers', *Harvard Business Review*, November–December.

Section B

Financial Decisions and Strategies

11

Financial Strategy (1) The Capital Structure Decision

Once there was a successful hotel chain. The company generated lots of cash from its successful investment schedule. Quite naturally, the company's directors wished to expand the scale of operations, and therefore required additional financing. The financial director recommended borrowing in Swiss francs because the interest rate was lower than interest rates on other currencies. Unfortunately, when the company came to repay these Swiss francs, exchange rates had moved in such a way that the company had to raise far more pounds than it could possibly raise to repay the Swiss francs. The company went into liquidation. We tell this sad but true tale to make three points:

1. Investment decisions are far *more important than financing decisions*.
2. It is possible to cause the firm considerable harm by bad financing decisions.
3. Although financing decisions are not as important as investment decisions, you might as well get it approximately right.

The capital structure decision determines the balance of debt and equity. The decision is only a financing decision, not an investment decision. Firms create wealth by making sensible wealth-creating investment decisions, financing decisions being far less important, although in fact rather complex. Our answer to the capital structure decision is that firms should borrow the amount of debt which they can sustain. Firms should borrow to finance their investment schedules because interest payable on borrowings is tax deductible. However, firms should not borrow beyond the point where bankruptcy becomes a distinct possibility. Firms do not go into liquidation every once in a while. It only happens once. When a firm's investment schedule collapses by failing to generate adequate cash to make compulsory interest payments, shareholders may be forced to suffer the costs and delays of financial distress. To ensure the survival of the firm, even during periods of financial distress, corporate managers should have a strategy for financial emergencies.

Introduction

When discussing capital structure with managers, we usually introduce the subject by discussing the manager's private mortgage. The amount of mortgage a manager will accept depends on both the level and the volatility of his incoming cash flows. The higher the level of cash flows, the more one is prepared to borrow. The greater the volatility of one's annual income, the less one is prepared to borrow. There are several incentives to taking on a mortgage. Firstly, the price of the house is expected to increase, and the whole of the capital gain accrues to the manager. The leverage or gearing is expected to work in favour of the home owner who owns the equity in the property. Secondly, the interest on the mortgage is allowed as a tax deduction. Thirdly, although financial theorists pay little attention to cash shortages, it is very often the case that the manager does not have the equity to purchase his home one hundred per cent. Cash shortages force managers into borrowing money to buy their own homes. If the value of the manager's home falls below the level of the mortgage, the manager may like to exercise his option to declare himself bankrupt. However, lenders usually protect themselves by making the manager personally liable for the loan, regardless of movements in house prices. Very few managers borrow in Swiss francs to finance home purchases, because they wish to avoid the currency exposure.

The objective of the firm is to maximise the current wealth of shareholders. Market value is determined by the firm's investment schedule. Ignoring taxation and the cost of financial distress, the method of financing the investment schedule is, in the first instance, a separate and rather unimportant decision. Financing decisions are rather complex, and we recommend that financial managers get it approximately correct. Leverage, or gearing, is the extent to which the firm is financed by borrowing. As equity is more risky than debt, rational investors will expect a higher rate of return on equity. Leverage can also be defined as *the use of low-cost debt*, although we shall see later that the hidden cost of the debt is the increasing required rate of return on equity.

In a world without taxation and costs of financial distress, there is probably no optimal capital structure. However, as interest is tax deductible, firms can increase after-tax cash flows by borrowing. Taxation favours the use of low-cost debt. The problem with increasing total borrowing is that it increases the volatility of residual cash flows for shareholders. It adds *financial risk* to the *business risk* which all firms must accept. Shareholders do not like risk, and will expect higher returns for taking on this financial risk in addition to the business risk they have accepted by purchasing a stake in the firm's future volatile operational cash flows. In fact, there is a risk of the firm being forced into liquidation should the investment schedule not produce adequate cash flows to pay interest on debt, and make the necessary debt repayments. There are considerable costs of financial distress and, if the company is eventually forced into liquidation, heavy transaction costs and delays will be borne by shareholders. There is therefore a trade-off between the tax benefit of borrowing and the cost of financial distress/bankruptcy. We can devise the following rule of thumb: *firms should borrow to get the tax benefit on interest paid but not so much as to incur the costs of financial distress*, the optimal capital structure being where the incremental tax saving is equal to the incremental cost of anticipated liquidation.

The Firm's Optimal Capital Structure

If there is an optimal capital structure, it is worth finding. At the optimal level of borrowing, the firm's weighted cost of capital is minimised, and the market value of any given level of cash flows is maximised, assuming that cash flows are capitalised at the firm's weighted average cost of capital. For example, a constant £10,000 per annum in perpetuity discounted at a weighted average cost of capital of 20 per cent has a present value of £50,000. If the discount rate is reduced to 10 per cent, the same constant level of cash flows has a present value of £100,000. Lowering the required rate of return increases the present value of anticipated cash flows. Furthermore, there are more wealth-creating projects available to a firm which can lower its required rate of return for a given set of cash flows. Is it possible for firms to lower the average required rate of return by varying the mix of debt and equity? In a world without taxes and costs of financial distress, the answer is almost certainly in the negative.

How does leverage affect financial risk? Table 11.1 illustrates the volatility of cash flow per share for firms with the same investment schedule but different financing policies. It must be emphasised that all three firms have exactly the same investment schedule, generating exactly the same level of cash flow from trading. A is a highly-geared company. It has borrowed a lot. B is low-geared and C has no gearing, being all-equity financed. Having the same investment schedule all three companies generate £200 from successful trading. A has to pay interest at 10 per cent on £800 and B 10 per cent on £200. Cash flow for equity is therefore £120

Table 11.1 The Leverage (Gearing) Effect fo Companies A, B and C

	A	*B*	*C*
Balance sheet data			
Equity (£1 shares)	200	800	1,000
Debt (10% interest payable) (£)	800	200	–
Total financing (and total investment)	£1,000	1,000	1,000
A Cash flow from trading (£)	200	200	200
Less interest on debt (£)	80	20	–
Cash flow for equity	120	180	200
Return on equity (%)	60	22.5	20
Cash flow per share (£)	0.60	0.225	0.20
Cash flow on total investment (%)	20	20	20
B Assume fall in cash flow on total investment of 20%			
Cash flow from trading	160	160	160
Less interest on debt	80	20	–
	80	140	160
Return on equity (%)	40	17.5	16
Cash flow per share (£)	0.40	0.175	0.16
Cash flow on total investment (%)	16	16	16
Fall in cash flow on total investment (%)	20	20	20
Fall in cash flow per share (%)	33.3	22.2	20
C Assume an increase in cash flow on investment of 20%			
Increase in cash flow on total investment (%)	20	20	20
Increase in cash flow per share (%)	33.3	22.2	20

for A, £180 for B, and £200 for C. Returns on equity are 60 per cent, 22.5 per cent and 20 per cent, and cash flow per share 60p, 22.5p and 20p for company C. Marketing and production efforts have generated a 20 per cent return on book investment but the financial arrangements in B have geared up the return on equity to 22.5 per cent, and to 60 per cent in company A. Is wealth being created by financial policy? Can financial managers create successful investment schedules where marketing and production men have failed? Is life all about chartered accountancy or wealth creation by taking on projects with positive net present values? We appear to be witnessing a financial illusion and modern financial thinking asserts that there are no financial illusions. Wealth is created by successful investment policies, not financing policies. Marketing and production efforts create successful investment schedules, and financing decisions are rather complex but usually not very important. As in the example of our hotel chain, financial managers usually have to work very hard to generate financial distress by bad financing decisions.

The B section of Table 11.1 illustrates the consequences of a fall in cash flow of 20 per cent from £200 to £160 for all three companies. Interest has to be paid exactly as before. This is important! The return on equity falls to 40 per cent for company A, 17.5 per cent for B, and 16 per cent for C. Again, the investment schedules of all three companies are the same, only financial policies being different. At last, we reach the punchlines. The fall in cash flows is 20 per cent for all three companies, but the fall in cash flow per share is 33.3 per cent for the highly geared company A, 22.2 per cent for B, and only 20 per cent for C, the company with no borrowings. It is apparent that the greater the gearing, the greater is the volatility of cash flow per share. Another word for volatility is 'risk' and shareholders do not like it! The greater the risk, the greater the reward expected by shareholders. This is the hidden cost of debt. As companies add financial risk to business risk, the required rate of return by shareholders increases. The trade-off between risk and return ensures that three companies with the same investment schedules, ignoring taxation and costs of financial distress, must have the same market value regardless of different financing policies.

Section C of Table 11.1 shows that an increase in operational cash flows of 20 per cent gives increases in cash flow per share of 33.3 per cent for A, 22.2 per cent for B, and 20 per cent for C. Again, the punchlines are important: the business risk is the same for all three firms. They are all in the same business. Their investment schedules exist in the same economic environment. Only the financial risk changes with leverage. Increased leverage increases the volatility (financial risk) of cash flow per share. Investors do not like risk and they require increasing returns with increasing leverage. We no longer believe that different capital structures on the left hand side of the balance sheet can turn an unsuccessful investment schedule into a successful one. Successful investment schedules are created by marketing and production efforts. Marketing and production people make money satisfying consumer wants in competitive markets.

The key issue in the financial structure debate is: *what happens to the required rate of return on equity as leverage is increased*? Let us return to Table 11.1, where cash flows from trading amount to £200 for companies A, B and C. Assuming that the market risk associated with each firm's investment schedule dictates that the cash flows are capitalised at 15 per cent (i.e. multiplied by 6.7) for a perpetual income stream, the value of each firm is:

$$V = \frac{\bar{x}}{pk} = \frac{\pounds 200}{0.15} = \pounds 1{,}333$$

If the firm's investment schedule is valued at £1,333 and the debt is valued at par, the market value of the equity must be the balancing figure, i.e. £533 for A, £1,133 for B, and £1,333 for C. For this to happen, the cost of equity, *Ke*, must increase with the increased financial risk associated with increased

Table 11.2

	A	*B*	*C*
Market value of debt (£)	800	200	–
Market value of equity (£)	533	1,133	1,333
Value of investment schedule	£1,333	1,333	1,333
Cost of equity (*Ke*)	$\frac{120}{533} = 22.5\%$	$\frac{180}{1{,}133} = 15.9\%$	$\frac{200}{1{,}333} = 15\%$

leverage, even though the business, economic, operational, or market risk associated with the firm's investment schedule does not change. The increase in the cost of equity is just enough to offset the increased expected return generated by increased leverage.

The calculations appear in Table 11.2. Note that we are now using market values, which is correct. We used balance sheet values in Table 11.1 as an introductory example. The objective of the firm is to create wealth, to make money satisfying consumer wants by matching the resources of the organisation to the needs of the market place. It is not a balance sheet/profit and loss account game. It is a wealth creation game. The market values of the firm's shares and loan capital are more important than the financial accountant's numbers. Such numbers are not based on net present values and are subject to all the vagaries of accounting policies. Balance sheet numbers are often used for measuring leverage because they are readily available. The usual measure is either debt to debt plus equity or debt to equity. There are also various profit and loss account numbers for examining leverage. For example financial analysts often look at the number of times the interest is covered by cash flows generated from successful trading, the amount of interest paid usually including lease payments as well as loan interest. In Table 11.2 we use, quite correctly, the market value of shares and the market value of debt which, added together, give the market value of the firm's investment schedule. As company C has no debt, the cost of equity reflects only business risk at 15 per cent. Company B has some financial risk as well as business risk, and the cost of equity therefore rises to 15.9 per cent. In company A the cost of equity rises to 22.5 per cent. Ignoring taxation and the cost of financial distress, the market value of each company is the same, and is determined by anticipated cash flows and market risk. The value of the firm is clearly determined by the value of the firm's investment schedule, and not the financing arrangements.

This modern view of leverage is often illustrated graphically as in Figure 11.1. The cost of equity, *Ke*, is higher than the cost of debt, *Ki*, because the equity is subject to greater volatility of returns. The equity is the *risk capital*. In our example the cost of debt is 10 per cent and the cost of equity with no

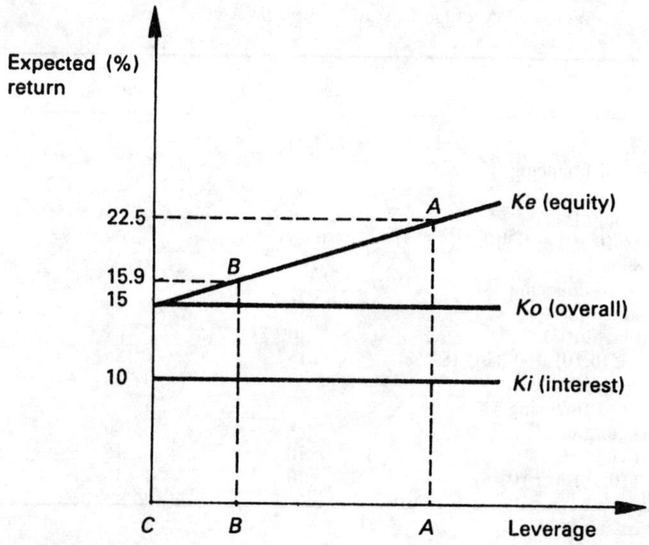

Figure 11.1 The Modern View (Ignoring Taxation and Liquidation Costs)

leverage is 15 per cent. As the amount of borrowing increases, *Ke* must rise to reflect the increased volatility of returns to equity caused by increased financial risk. With some borrowings *Ke* rises to 15.9 per cent for company B, and with more leverage, *Ke* rises to 22.5 per cent for company A. The result is that the weighted average of the two sources of funds, *Ko*, the *overall cost of capital, remains constant for all levels of leverage.*

The calculations of the weighted average cost of capital, WACC, are given in Table 11.3. The market value of the investment schedule for each company is £1,333. In company A this is reflected in the market value of debt at £800 and the market value of equity at £533. The market value of debt is 60 per cent of total market capitalisation and equity is 40 per cent. Given expected levels of 10 per cent and 22.5 per cent the WACC = 0.6(0.10) + 0.4(0.225) = 0.15. For all levels of leverage the weighted average cost of capital, *Ko*, is 15 per cent. The market value of the firm is equal to the market value of the debt plus the market value of the equity, and the market value of the firm depends on the firm's investment schedule, which generates cash flows from successful trading discounted at the rate of return which reflects the market price of risk. Ignoring taxation and the costs of financial distress, the market value of the firm's investment schedule is:

$$V = \frac{\bar{x}}{pk} = \frac{200}{0.15} = £1{,}333$$

This modern view of leverage has proved to be very controversial. The *traditional view* of financing policy is that the market value of the firm's

Table 11.3 The Weighted Average Cost of Capital (WACC)

	Debt		*Equity*		*Total*
A Market value (£)	800	+	533	=	1,333
Proportion of financing at market value (%)	60	+	40	=	100
Expected yield (%)	10		22.5		–
WACC 0.6 (0.10) + 0.4(0.225) (%)	0.06	+	0.09	=	0.15
B Market value (£)	200	+	1,133	=	1,333
Proportion of financing at market value (%)	15	+	85	=	100
Expected yield (%)	10		15.9		–
WACC 0.15(0.10) + 0.85(0.159)%	0.015	+	0.135	=	0.15
C Market value (£)	–	+	1,333	=	1,333
Proportion of financing at market value (%)	–	+	100	=	100
Expected yield (%)	10		15		
WACC 0 (0.10) + 1 (0.15) (%)	0	+	0.15	=	0.15

Table 11.4 No Change in *Ke* with Increasing Leverage (£)

	A	*B*	*C*
Market value of debt	800	200	–
Market value of equity:			
A 120/0.15	800		
B 180/0.15		1,200	
C 200/0.15			1,333
Market value of investment schedule	1,600	1,400	1,333

investment schedule can in fact be increased by the judicious use of debt finance, whereas we have shown that, ignoring taxes and the cost of financial distress, it is the firm's investment schedule which determines market value, not the sources of funds. Table 11.4 illustrates an extreme view of the traditional approach in that the cost of equity remains constant for all levels of leverage at 15 per cent. If this is the case, it is possible for managers to manipulate the market value of the company by manipulating the capital structure. In company B, if *Ke* remains constant at 15 per cent, the market value of equity is £1,200, and the total market value of the firm is increased from £1,333 for the all-equity financed company to £1,400. Company A has an even cleverer chartered accountant. (Apologies to any chartered accountants reading this chapter. Some of our best friends are chartered accountants!) By borrowing a lot he has increased the market value of the firm's investment schedule to £1,600. Do we believe this? The answer is surely no. We must reject this naive view of the world because rational investors will expect higher rewards for the increased financial risk they must bear as leverage is increased.

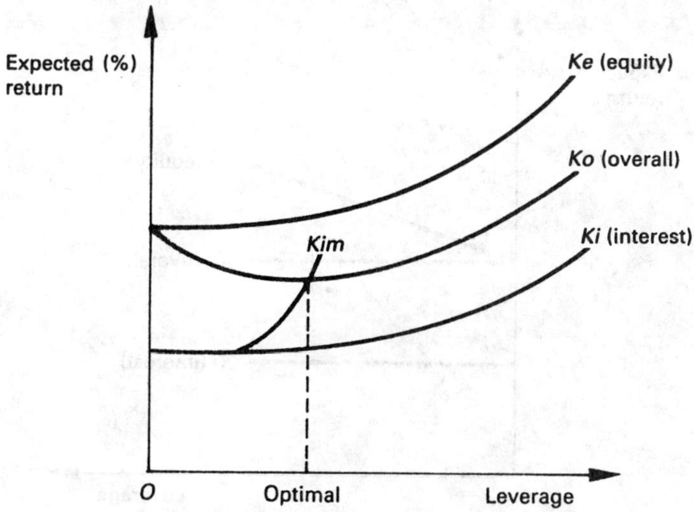

Figure 11.2 The Traditional View

Although we can reject this extreme approach, a less extreme interpretation of the traditional view demands closer examination. Figure 11.2 shows that the cost of debt is lower than the cost of equity. Firms can borrow at some low rate of interest until lenders begin to worry about the security of interest payments and repayments of loans. The interest rate will be higher on additional loans. Therefore, *Ki*, the average cost of all loans, will begin to rise. The ordinary shareholders will ignore small amounts of debt completely but will eventually become concerned about the level of interest payments affecting the volatility of the cash flow for equity. They will demand higher rates of return for taking on additional risk. A combination of both sources of finance, *Ko*, the weighted average cost of capital, will therefore start at *Ke* with no borrowings, fall as low-cost debt is introduced into the capital structure, and then rise as both *Ki* and *Ke* are rising. The optimal level of borrowing is the lowest point on *Ko*, the point where the marginal cost of borrowing, *Kim*, equals *Ko*. If the traditionalists are right, then there is an optimal capital structure which financial managers should seek. If we believe this less extreme version of the traditional view, we probably feel that the required rate of a project depends on its economic risk, but that there is also a little bit of extra wealth to be created by finding the optimal capital structure.

This traditional view is rejected by the modern view, which was originally rigorously expounded by Modigliani and Miller (1958). They assert that the rationality of investors prevails. In a rational world, the traditional view must be rejected because ordinary shareholders will not ignore small amounts of debt. They will demand increasing expected returns for every incremental increase in financial risk. The *MM* view has been illustrated in Figure 11.1 and appears again in Figure 11.3. Again, debt is less expensive than equity, but has

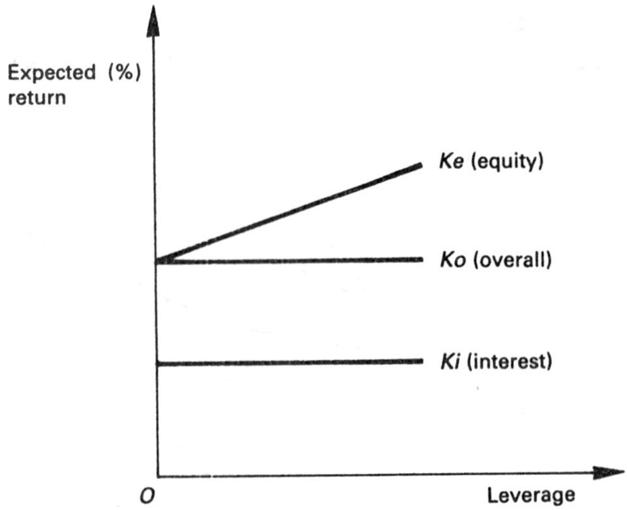

Figure 11.3 The Modern View

a hidden cost which is the increasing rate of return on equity as borrowing is increased. The increase in *Ke* is just enough to offset the benefit of low-cost debt. Consequently, *Ko* is constant for all levels of leverage. The value of the firm depends on anticipated cash flows and volatility, i.e. the firm's investment schedule. The value of the firm is independent of the method of financing. Leverage determines the split of cash flows between the providers of debt and the providers of equity. It does not determine the level of cash flows arising from successful trading, or the volatility of total operational cash flows. In a world in which cash flows are capitalised at a rate reflecting their market risk, financing arrangements have no bearing on firm valuation. The firm valuation is the market value of shares plus the market value of debt.

The basic *MM* proposition is that in a rational world identical commodities — such as the cash flows generated by the investment schedules of companies A, B and C in Table 11.1 — cannot sell in highly competitive and efficient markets at different prices. Any tendency for the anticipated cash flows of A, B or C to sell at different prices will be eliminated by a process akin to arbitrage. Arbitrage is the buying and selling of the same commodity in different markets. Table 11.5 is based on the same assumption as Table 11.4 that, regardless of different levels of leverage, cash flows for equity will be capitalised at 15 per cent. This is the extreme traditional view. Assuming this to be reasonable, the market value of company A would be £1.6m., company B £1.4m., and company C £1.333m. In a rational world the shares of A Ltd and B Ltd are clearly overvalued. The income streams of £0.2m., ignoring taxation and the cost of financial distress, being of the equivalent risk class must have the same market value. In a rational world, one per cent

Table 11.5 Overvaluation of Companies A and B (£000)

	A	*B*	*C*
Equity (£1 shares)	200	800	1,000
Debt (10% interest payable)	800	200	–
	1,000	1,000	1,000
Cash flow from trading	200	200	200
Less interest on debt	80	20	–
Cash flow for equity	120	180	200
Equity market capitalisation rate 15%			
Market value of shares	800	1,200	1,333
Market value of debt (par)	800	200	–
Market values (as in Table 10.4)	1,600	1,400	1,333

of the cash flows of companies A, B and C cannot be valued at £16,000 for A, £14,000 for B, and £13,333 for C. If such irrationality were to occur, investors could indulge in home-made leverage and restore equilibrium.

Table 11.6 shows how a shareholder can use home-made leverage to exploit any irrationality, thereby very quickly restoring market equilibrium. For example, a shareholder owns 1,000 shares in A Ltd. His present income is £600. He can indulge in home-made leverage by selling his shares for £4,000 and borrowing £16,000 giving a total investment capability of £20,000. The important point is that he has borrowed in the same proportion and at the same rate as company A. By investing in company C, he increases his income by £800. In effect, he has turned himself into company A, and increased his income. The modern view is that a sufficient number of investors would do this to equate the market values of all three companies. As a second example, a shareholder with 1,000 shares in company B, with an income of £225, can sell for £1,500 and borrow in the same proportion and at the same rate as company B. The result is an increase in income of £18.75. Surely, in a rational world, investors would exploit such wealth creating opportunities until market equilibrium is restored and the market values of companies A, B and C are equated.

As one would expect, this modern view of rationality has been the subject of rigorous criticism and questioning from supporters of the traditional view.

(1) Are securities markets perfectly competitive?
(2) Is it possible to classify firms into equivalent risk categories?
(3) Can individuals borrow at the same rate as companies?
(4) Is personal leverage equivalent to corporate leverage?
(5) Can individuals get the tax benefit on interest?
(6) Is the arbitrage process likely to occur in the real world?

Table 11.6 Arbitrage

	£
Present income (all cash flows paid in dividends) 1,000 (0.6)	600
Shareholder can sell for 1,000 $\left(\frac{800}{200}\right)$	4,000
and borrow in the same proportion and at the same rate as *A Ltd*. (1:4)	16,000
	20,000
He buys shares in *C Ltd*. $\frac{20,000}{1,3333}$ = 15,000 shares	
New income 15,000 (0.20)	3,000
Less interest at 10% on £16,000	1,600
	1,400
He has increased his income by 1,400 − 600	800
A second shareholder owns 1,000 shares in *B Ltd*	
Present income (all cash flows paid in dividend), 1,000 (0.225)	225
He can sell for 1,000 $\left(\frac{1,200}{800}\right)$	1,500
and borrow in the same proportion and at the same rate as *B Ltd*. (4:1)	375
	1,875
He buys shares in *C Ltd*. $\frac{1,875}{1.3333}$ = 1,406 shares	
New income 1,406 (0.20)	281.25
Less interest at 10% on £375	37.50
	243.75
He has increased his income by 243.75 − 225	18.75

Without dwelling on the many arguments for and against, let us simply conclude that, given their assumptions, the *MM* arguments are very sound. Surely, in a rational world, identical commodities must sell at the same price. If we wish to criticise the modern view, we must examine the assumptions. There are two very important aspects of the leverage controversy which we have so far ignored and which were assumed away in the argument. Firstly, interest payments are allowed as a tax deduction, whereas dividends are not. Secondly, when firms have very high levels of borrowing they are more likely to run into the costs of financial distress.

Table 11.7 The Gain from Taxation

	A	*B*	*C*
Cash flow from trading	400	400	400
Less interest on debt	80	20	–
Cash flow after interest	320	380	400
Taxation at 50%	160	190	200
Cash flow from trading after tax	160	190	200
Market value of debt	800	200	–
Market value of equity:			
A $\frac{160}{0.225}$	711		
B $\frac{190}{0.159}$		1,195	
C $\frac{210}{0.15}$			1,333
Market value of firm	1,511	1,395	1,333
Less:			
Value of firm without tax shield	1,333	1,333	1,333
Market value of tax shield	178	62	–
Capitalised value of tax savings	$\frac{40}{0.225} = 178$	$\frac{10}{0.159} = 62$	

The Tax Shield on Interest Payments

Table 11.7 presents data relating to our three companies with a corporation tax rate of 50 per cent. Cash flows from successful trading are £400 with companies A and B deducting interest to arrive at taxable profits. After-tax cash flows from successful trading for equity amount to £160 for A, £190 for B, and £200 for C. If debt is valued at par and after-tax cash flows are capitalised at 22.5 per cent for A, 15.9 per cent for B, and 15 per cent for C, the market values of the companies are £1,511, £1,395 and £1,333 respectively. Company C, with no tax shield, is valued exactly as in previous examples. Companies A and B have increased their market values by the capitalised value of the tax savings. For modest levels of leverage the market value of the firm is increased by the capitalised value of such tax savings. In our example the tax savings are capitalised at the same rates as cash flows for shareholders. It is maintained by many authors, including Myers (1974), that the tax savings should be capitalised at *Ki* rather than *Ke*, because the tax savings are based entirely on the interest payments and must therefore be of the same risk. If we accept this argument, the tax savings are worth:

$$\frac{40}{0.1} = £400 \text{ for A, and } \frac{10}{0.1} = £100 \text{ for B}$$

and the market values of companies A and B become £1,733 and £1,433. The value of the leveraged firm is its capitalised after-tax operational cash flows plus the present value of the tax savings which is the market value of debt multiplied by the tax rate for a company with tax savings on interest in perpetuity:

$$V = \frac{\bar{X}}{pk} + DT$$

where

$\bar{X}$ = anticipated operational cash flows
pk = capitalisation rate
D = market value of debt
T = the corporation tax rate

$$\text{for company A, } V = \frac{200}{0.15} + 800(0.5) = £1,733$$

$$\text{for company B, } V = \frac{200}{0.15} + 200(0.5) = £1,433$$

The tax benefit derived from borrowing is an incentive to use debt, and this point is acknowledged by Modigliani and Miller (1963). However, this benefit should not be overstated (as it probably is in the above formula):

(1) The firm may not be paying corporation tax at the present time or perhaps even for the foreseeable future. The tax benefit may be delayed for several years or lost completely.
(2) If the tax benefit from debt is real, the strong demand for borrowed funds may push up interest rates, thereby reducing, to some extent, the benefit of low-cost debt. It is argued by Miller (1977) that the tax benefit of debt has been overstated generally. He argues that the cost of debt after taxes is the same as the cost of equity. In a world without taxes debt may even be more expensive than equity. The Miller arguments have attracted a good deal of attention in recent years. Researchers have had great difficulty trying to explain why higher rates of tax have not been accompanied by higher levels of borrowing, and why firms in the same industry with similar risk characteristics have a wide range of debt–equity ratios.

(3) In highly competitive markets, the tax benefit may be passed on to consumers.

In calculating the market values of A and B to be £1,733 and £1,433 respectively, we have used the equation:

$$V_D = V_o + DT$$

Expressed in words: the value of the firm with debt is equal to the value of the firm without debt *plus the present value of the tax savings*. This formula may hold for moderate levels of debt, but cannot hold for high levels of debt because it ignores the cost of financial distress. Including the anticipated costs we arrive at the formula:

$$V_D = V_o + DT - BC$$

Expressed in words: the value of the firm with debt is equal to the value of the firm without debt, plus the present value of the tax savings, *minus the present value of the anticipated costs of bankruptcy* or other financial distress. We can see from the equation that optimal capital structure exists where there is an equal trade-off between the benefit of increased tax savings and the costs of anticipated financial distress. In the real world, the equation may be of no great value but it does emphasise that the capital structure decision is a financial policy decision for the present time, any increase in debt being associated with increased tax savings and an increased probability of running into the costs of financial distress.

The Costs of Financial Distress

The gain from taxation suggests that firms should borrow a lot. However, because of the increase in the probability of bankruptcy, it is an observable fact in the real world that firms do not finance 99 per cent of their investment schedules by borrowing. Even if they did, at 99 per cent, the loan creditors would very likely become the shareholders. When firms finance by 99 per cent debt, it is very likely that at some stage they will not be able to make annual interest payments and loan repayments. The debt holders would then take control of the firm as shareholders. Company law dictates that at least two shares must be issued but companies appear to pursue target debt-equity ratios much lower than 99 per cent. The best explanation for this at the present time is that firms wish to avoid the costs of financial distress and ultimately the costs and delays of liquidation. A firm may be forced into liquidation when it becomes impossible to pay interest on loans together with loan repayments. Dividends for shareholders can be bypassed, but failure to pay interest on loans often gives the lender the right to claim the company's operating assets, thereby preventing the continuation of trading.

Professional managers want to avoid this. This makes sense for both managers and employees who wish to protect their employment, and for investors who wish to avoid the costs and delays of liquidation. We would point out at this stage that managers and employees are concerned with total risk, not simply market risk. Shareholders can and do diversify, and are therefore concerned only with the market risk of their investment. The financial wellbeing of the company is endangered by total risk, i.e. market and specific risk. Managers and employees suffer from total risk. Directors in private companies are especially concerned with the wellbeing of the firms since it is very common for loan creditors to lift the veil of incorporation and demand that directors personally guarantee loans made to the company. The costs of financial distress can therefore be very high for managers as well as shareholders. These costs are not only the costs and delays of liquidation, but may include the making of suboptimal investment decisions as well as suboptimal financing decisions as the company experiences financial distress.

Suboptimal investment decisions would include: the sale of the successful investments and products at bargain prices; disinvestment in successful areas; abandonment of promising new projects; emphasis on short-term projects to generate cash; avoidance of highly profitable projects which do not promise immediate positive cash flows; reduced investment in training, promotion, research and development, as well as reductions in stock levels which may lose sales; reduction in credit periods which may lose customers; damage to corporate image by publicity and price reductions; and even the seeking of an unprofitable merger to acquire cash. Suboptimal financing decisions would include: borrowing beyond the level for our target debt–equity ratio; acceptance of higher interest rates; leasing rather than borrowing and buying thereby losing capital allowances; a cut in dividend thereby giving a false signal to the market depressing share prices and making a new issue difficult; and the loss of credit availability from suppliers making it necessary to borrow even more. The considerable costs of financial distress have therefore led academics to suggest that efficient capital markets may penalise firms which are perceived as being overlevered. It may well be that two firms with exactly the same investment schedule can, in a rational world, be priced differently where one firm is running a higher risk of incurring the costs of financial distress. These costs are reflected in market values when firms are facing an increasing probability of financial distress or even eventual liquidation. The acknowledgement of the tax benefit for modest amounts of debt, and the need to avoid the costs of financial distress, suggest that there is probably an optimal capital structure, as illustrated in Figure 11.4.

The value of the firm with debt is the value of the firm without debt, plus the present value of the tax savings, minus the present value of the anticipated costs of financial distress. Figure 11.4 shows that there is an optimal capital structure at the point where the market value of the firm is

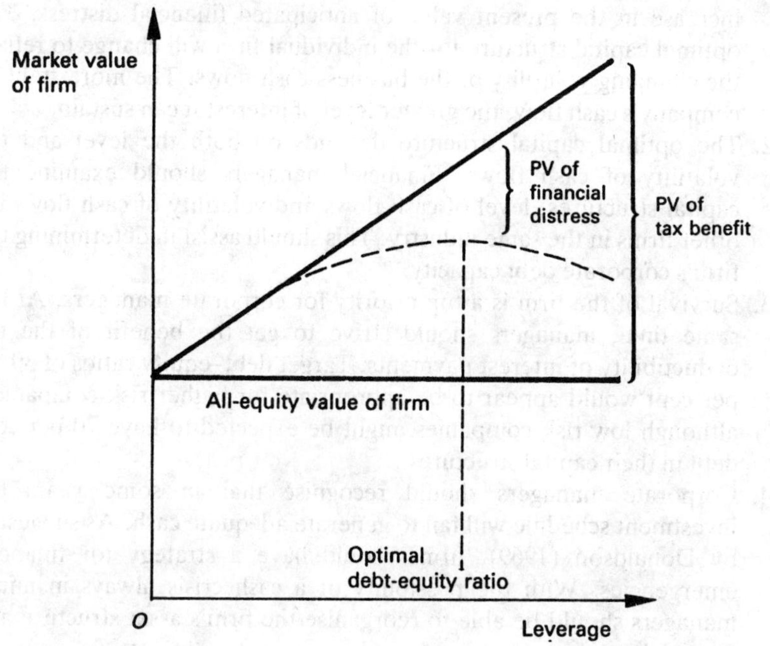

Figure 11.4 Leverage with Corporation Tax and Liquidation Costs

maximised. As interest is tax deductible, after-tax cash flows are increased with borrowing, and therefore the market value of the firm with debt is greater than the all-equity value of the firm. This might appear to suggest that firms should finance with 99 per cent debt. However, corporate managers do not do this, because increasing the amount of debt also increases the financial risk, possibly to the point where liquidation may occur if the firm fails to generate adequate cash to make interest payments and capital repayments. It should be stressed that the reason for the financial distress of the firm lies in unsuccessful investment policies, not financing policy. It is the failure of the firm's investment schedule to generate adequate cash flow which results in corporate collapse. The increasing probability of liquidation can result in costs, delay, and the making of suboptimal investment and financing decisions. There is, therefore, some optimal debt–equity ratio resulting from a trade-off between the tax benefit and the increasing probability of incurring the costs of financial distress. We can now state our conclusions from Figure 11.4:

1. On capital structure, all the protagonists go home happy. The *MM* supporters are perfectly correct given their assumptions, and the traditionalists told us all along that there was an optimal capital structure. Our conclusion is that there is an optimal capital structure where the marginal increase in tax benefit is equal to the marginal

increase in the present value of anticipated financial distress. The optimal capital structure for the individual firm will change to reflect the changing volatility of the business cash flows. The more stable a company's cash flow, the greater level of interest it can sustain.

2. The optimal capital structure depends on both the level and the volatility of cash flows. Financial managers should examine the capital structures, level of cash flows and volatility of cash flows for other firms in the same industry. This should assist in determining the firm's corporate debt capacity.
3. Survival of the firm is a top priority for corporate managers. At the same time, managers should strive to get the benefit of the tax deductibility of interest payments. Target debt–equity ratios of 30–40 per cent would appear to be appropriate for higher risk companies, although low risk companies might be expected to have 70 per cent debt in their capital structures.
4. Corporate managers should recognise that in some years the investment schedule will fail to generate adequate cash. As suggested by Donaldson (1969), firms should have a strategy for financial emergencies. With the possibility of a cash crisis always in mind, managers should be able to reorganise the firm's asset structure and financial structure to generate cash.
5. At each decision point, the debt or equity decision is part of a sequential financing decision. As the firm trades successfully it generates cash flows, some of which are paid in dividends, the balance being reinvested in the company. Increasing equity can be used as the base to justify and sustain more debt.
6. At any decision point, if in doubt, we recommend that companies should issue equity. An increase in equity can always be used as the basis for increasing debt. An increase in debt beyond the optimal debt–equity ratio implies that more equity must be raised in the future. If in doubt, issue more equity which gives more future financing flexibility.

New Insights from Option Pricing Theory

A tramp borrows £100,000 from the bank to gamble at Las Vegas. He puts it all on the red rather than the black. If he wins, the tramp gains £100,000 (less expenses). The bank is repaid its £100,000, and everybody is happy except the shareholders in the casino. If red does not come up, the tramp loses the £100,000 and informs the bank. The tramp is no worse off than before, but the shareholders in the bank are worse off to the tune of £100,000. The bank recognises that you cannot get blood out of a stone and does not sue. In this example, the tramp would be deliriously happy to borrow £100,000 from the bank to finance an investment schedule with a net present value of zero.

There is a real transfer of utility from the shareholders in the bank to the tramp. He either wins £100,000 or loses nothing. The shareholders in the bank win nothing (perhaps interest at 14% for 72 hours) or lose £100,000. Bank managers are rarely foolish enough to lend funds to impoverished gamblers. They tend to lend cash to individuals and companies with substantial assets or substantial cash expectations. Furthermore, they protect bank shareholders against the reckless use of bank funds by restrictive covenants. In our example, if the bank made the mistake of lending money to the tramp then we suggest the loan would be made on condition that the full £100,000 be deposited with the bank at 8%. The tramp would agree to pay 14% on his £100,000 overdraft. No cheques or withdrawal slips would be valid without the prior approval of the bank manager. Under these restricted covenants, neither the tramp nor the bank gains any economic benefit.

We tell this tale because it illustrates the transfer of utility from lenders to borrowers when companies borrow money. If a company is all-equity financed and the company's investment schedule collapses, the total loss is borne by shareholders. However, imagine a company with an investment schedule worth £100 financed £30 by equity and £70 by debt. The firm's investment schedule collapses to £50. The shareholders do not stand all of the loss. They lose their £30 but the bank or the lender loses £20. The shareholders have the option of walking away from the problem and allowing the debt holders to inherit the corporate collapse. This option is worth money. New insights into the value of the corporate liabilities such as debt are emerging with the development of *option pricing theory* and, in particular, the Black/Scholes (1973) option pricing model. The existence of repayable debt in the firm's capital structure gives the ordinary shareholders an option to claim a firm's investment schedule by paying the interest on outstanding debt or defaulting on the payment of the loan, an option which they may exercise should the value of the firm fall below the amount of repayable debt. The Black/Scholes option pricing model demonstrates that this option can result in a transfer of wealth from the holders of debt to the owners of equity. Debt holders can reduce the possibility of default by imposing financial and operational constraints in their loan agreements with borrowing firms. The objective of restrictive covenants is to protect debt holders against the owners of equity. Restrictive covenants come in many forms, such as the ability to appoint a receiver on the failure of a company to make repayments of capital or pay interest, insistence on personal guarantees by officers of the company for corporate loans, restriction on dividend payments, restriction on additional borrowings which increase the risk to original debt holders, restrictions on leases which bond holders quite rightly regard as additional debt, agreement that interest payments must be covered some number of times by earnings or cash flows, maintenance of working capital at agreed levels, and restriction of new investment in fixed assets. Managers should enter into loan agreements which involve restrictive covenants with great caution. It is usually the breaking of the terms of loan agreements which results in bankruptcy proceedings.

Conclusion

We have now come full circle. We began by suggesting that the traditional approach was inappropriate by proving that in a world with no taxes or costs of financial distress the financing decision is irrelevant to firm valuation. The value of the firm depends on its investment schedule. We then saw that, on the introduction of corporation tax, firms should borrow a lot because of the tax deductibility of interest. The optimal structure appeared to be the one which included a large amount of debt. However, as managers seek to avoid liquidation and the costs of other financial distress, the optimal capital structure stops short of 99 per cent debt and in fact appears to depend on the probability of running into financial distress. Firms should borrow only the amount of debt they can sustain, and should devise strategies for financial emergencies for those occasions when the firm's investment schedule fails to generate adequate cash. We suggest that the traditional rules of thumb of 30 per cent debt for manufacturing companies and 70 per cent for property companies appear to make good sense. In Table 11.8 we provide a debt versus equity checklist for financial managers making capital structure decisions.

The fact that we have come full circle suggests that the capital structure decision is still something of a mystery. A recent article (Myers 1984) suggests that capital structure is still a puzzle. Although there is some evidence that high-risk companies have debt ratios lower than low-risk companies, there is still a wide disparity between the debt–equity ratios of firms in the same industry. Many firms are clearly not over-anxious to seize upon the tax savings on interest payments. Higher rates of taxation are not necessarily associated with higher levels of borrowing. We very tentatively suggest that capital structure problems should be examined by the behaviouralists. Perhaps the level of corporate borrowing reflects the attitudes of senior managers. Perhaps these attitudes are not consistent with what we would expect from financial theory.

Questions

1. Illustrate the traditional view of optimal capital structure.
2. Illustrate the MM view with and without taxes.
3. Illustrate the modern view with taxation and financial distress.
4. Discuss the factors involved in choosing an issue of either debt or equity.

Table 11.8 Debt versus Equity Checklist

Debt	*Equity*
Capital repayable	Capital not repayable
Interest compulsory	Dividends not compulsory
Interest tax deductible	Dividends not deductible
Increases financial risk	No increase in financial risk
Increases probability of financial distress	Financial distress less likely
Possible option value to shareholders	No option value
Restrictive covenants	No restrictive covenants
No control dilution, until terms of restrictive covenant broken	New issue may lead to control dilution
Cheaper issuing costs	Higher issuing costs
Often easier to issue to financial institutions	More complex rights issues, or new issue
Less future financing flexibility	Greater future financing flexibility
EPS and return on equity should be higher	Yes, but greater risk (volatility)
Possible adverse effect on supplier credit rating	Less adverse effect

5. The Western Manufacturing Co. Ltd has to raise £3m. immediately as part of its 5-year expansion programme. The company can raise the £3m. by issuing either debt or equity.

   As financial director, draft a report to your board outlining the factors to be considered in identifying an optimal capital structure, and making a firm recommendation for the current year.
6. The Sceptre Corporation must raise £30 million during the coming year by issuing either debt or equity. The company recently made a large loan and plans to raise further additional capital in the next 2–5 years. The company's balance sheet debt–equity ratio is 34 per cent, which is less than the 40–60 per cent ratio of other firms in the same industry. However, both the company's earnings and share price are more volatile than the industry averages.

   As financial director, draft a report to your codirectors outlining the factors for consideration in making this decision. Summarise the theory of optimal capital structure, and suggest the best course of action for the coming year.
7. Rosina Ltd is at the present time an all-equity financed company with a cost of capital of 12½%. The manager, Basilio, is considering whether it might be desirable to issue some debt capital. Debt is currently yielding 5% p.a. and may be assumed to be risk-free for all firms which issue it (or may wish to issue it). To this end, Basilio has collected data on four other companies, each of which falls into one of two industrial sectors (A and B). The data that he has collected are summarised below:

Company	*Industrial sector*	*Debt/ equity ratio*	*Anticipated growth of earnings/ dividends*	*Ex div. market price per share*	*Dividend per share*
X	A	0	0	£1	10p
Y	A	1 : 1	0	£2	30p
T	B	0	0	£2	30p
U	B	1 : 4	0	£2	35p

You are required to:

(a) advise Basilio on the capital structure policy which he should follow, explaining and justifying your figures;
(b) indicate how your advice might be modified if corporate taxes were introduced into the analysis.

Ignore taxation for requirement (a). (ICA, PE II, December 1982)

8. Iowa Ltd and Arizona Ltd are quoted companies. Both earn an annual profit, before charging debenture interest, of £2.5 million and both are expected to continue doing so for the indefinite future. The profits of both companies, before charging debenture interest, are generally regarded as being subject to identical levels of risk. It is the policy of both companies to distribute all available profits as dividends at the end of each year.

Iowa Ltd is financed by 20 million 25p ordinary shares, which have a current market value of 43p *ex div.* and by £3 million 12% irredeemable debentures, which have a current market value of £66⅔ per cent, *ex interest*. It has reserves of £500,000.

Arizona Ltd is financed by 10 million 50p ordinary shares, which have a current market value of £1.16 *ex div.* It has reserves of £1.2 million.

Mr Utah owns 100,000 ordinary shares in Arizona Ltd. He is considering whether to sell these shares and invest the proceeds in the ordinary shares and debentures of Iowa Ltd. He would be willing to do so if he could increase his annual income without incurring any extra risk. Mr Utah is able to borrow money at an annual compound rate of interest of 20%.

You are required to:

(a) prepare calculations to demonstrate to Mr Utah how he might improve his position in the way he has suggested, stating clearly any reservations you have about the scheme;
(b) explain and discuss the hypothesis that a firm should be indifferent as between all possible capital structures.

Ignore taxation for (a) but *not* for (b). (ICA, PE II, December 1981)

9. The Mariners Co Ltd is soon to be incorporated. Its promoters are considering five different possible capital structures for the new company. An analysis of comparable companies with equivalent business risks has

been undertaken. This analysis shows that, if the before-tax cost of debt is a constant 10% irrespective of the capital structure, then the cost of equity capital, after corporation tax, will be as follows:

Gearing ratio (debt capital/total capital) %	*Cost of equity capital* %
0	20.000
20.0	21.250
40.0	23.333
50.0	25.000
60.0	27.500

The above predictions for the equity cost of capital also assume that the earnings of the Mariners Co. Ltd. will be taxed at a rate of 50% and that the debt interest is an allowable expense for tax purposes. The promoters expect that the company will generate a steady annual earnings stream of £12.6 million, before the payment of debt interest, for the foreseeable future.

You are required to:

(a) calculate the effective after-tax weighted average cost of capital and the total market value for each of the five possible capital structures, assuming that the before-tax annual cost of debt will be a constant 10% (irrespective of the capital structure chosen);
(b) interpret the results of your calculations in (a) above and explain their significance in financial management;
(c) discuss the possible consequences to a company of having a capital structure containing a high gearing ratio.

Ignore advance corporation tax. (ICA PE II, December 1983)

References

Black, Fischer and Scholes. Myron (1973) 'The pricing of options and corporate liabilities', *Journal of Political Economy*. vol. 81, May–June.

Donaldson, Gordon (1969) 'Strategy for financial emergencies', *Harvard Business Review*. vol 47, November–December.

Miller, Merton H. (1977) 'Debt and taxes', *Journal of Finance*, vol 32, May.

Modigliani, Franco and Miller, Merton H. (1958) 'The cost of capital corporation finance and the theory of investment', *American Economic Review*, vol 48, June.

Modigliani, Franco and Miller, Merton H. (1963) 'Corporate income taxes and the cost of capital: a correction', *American Economic Review*, vol 53, June.

Myers, Stewart C. (1974) 'Interactions of corporate financing and investment decisions — implications for capital budgeting', *Journal of Finance*, vol. 29, March.

Myers, Stewart C. (1984) 'The capital structure puzzle', *Journal of Finance*, vol. 39, July.

Further Reading

Baron, D. P. (1975) 'Firm valuation, corporate taxes and default risk', *Journal of Finance*, December.

Brearly, R. (1973) 'A note on dividends and debt under the new taxation', *Journal of Business Finance*, Spring.

Dickinson, J. P. and Kyuno, K. (1977) 'Corporate valuation: a reconciliation of the Miller–Modigliani and traditional views', *Journal of Business Finance and Accounting*, Summer.

Stapleton, R. C (1972) 'Taxes, the cost of capital and the theory of investment', *Economic Journal*, December.

Wrightsman, D. (1977) 'Tax shield valuation and the capital structure decision', *Journal of Finance*, May.

12

Financial Strategy (2) The Dividend Decision

Introduction

The objective of the firm is to *create wealth*, maximise the wealth of the firm's shareholders, make money satisfying consumer wants in competitive markets by matching the resources of the organisation to the needs of the market place. Successful investment decisions generate positive net cash flows which can be used to make interest payments, pay dividends, or be retained in the company to finance new investment, thereby generating higher positive net cash flows in the future. *Investment decisions* are far more important than *financing decisions* because it is the investment decisions which decide the level of future cash flows generated from successful trading. Financing decisions relating to capital structure, dividends, and leasing are not as important as investment decisions, but financial managers should seek to make sensible rather than less sensible financial decisions. The *dividend decision* is regarded as a *financing decision* because, given the firm's investment policy, any cash dividend paid which reduces the amount of cash available for investment must be replaced either by a new issue of shares or an issue of debt. If corporate managers can maximise the market value of the firm by manipulating dividend payments, they should do so. The optimal dividend policy, if there is one, is the policy which maximises the wealth of the shareholders. As the value of the firm depends upon anticipated operational cash flows, new investment and risk, it seems improbable that managers can create wealth by distributing the net cash flows generated by successful trading between dividend payments and retentions within the company.

Graham, Dodd and Cottle (1962) once stated that one dollar in dividends is worth about three dollars of retained cash flows. This intuitively sounds reasonable because we assume that the purchaser of a share buys a dividend expectation. However, what happens to cash flows generated from trading which are not paid in dividends? They are reinvested in the company. Which would you rather have: £1 in the bank, £1 in the hand, or £1 reinvested in the company on your behalf? Suppose you deposit £100 in the bank and at the end of a one-year period you receive £10 in interest. Which would you prefer: a £10 cheque in the post, or £10 credited to your account at the bank? Clearly you are indifferent because you can devise your own 'dividend' policy by withdrawing £10 from the bank or reinvesting your £10 'dividend' in the bank deposit. Once we take into account the fact that funds not paid in dividends are reinvested in the company on the shareholder's behalf to create higher dividends or retentions in the future, the assumed preference for dividends is not at all obvious. When we also take into account the taxation of dividends and the costs incurred by shareholders reinvesting cash dividends, it appears that shareholders should prefer retentions. So why do companies pay dividends? An investigation of this question becomes something of a mystery tour. Unfortunately, we have no simple formula similar to the NPV formula for solving the dividend problem. There are many factors in the dividend decision, and it would be necessary to generate a very complex dividend model to determine the level of dividend which ought to be paid. Furthermore, the weightings attached to the various determinants of the level of dividend would be different at different times. Later in this chapter we list sixteen factors influencing the level of dividend payment.

Almost by definition, shareholders prefer shares, not cash. Shareholders who prefer cash can sell their shares. If a shareholder has a need for cash, he or she can devise his or her own dividend policy. If the company has a very low payout ratio, the company's increased investment schedule should generate higher cash expectations in the future, resulting in increased share prices. The shareholder can sell shares to obtain cash and still have the same level of investment as before. An advantage is that capital gains are taxed at a maximum of 30 per cent. The fact that dividend yields are generally around 5 per cent suggests that investors are looking for and anticipating about 10 per cent capital gains in addition to dividends.

Dividend policy determines the distribution of cash flows generated from successful trading between dividend payments and corporate retentions. If companies pursue the objective of wealth maximisation, shareholders might be interested in dividends because they receive their return in two forms — dividends and changes in the value of their shares. The return on an equity investment is:

$$R = \frac{D + P_2 - P_1}{P_1}$$

where

R = the return
D = the dividend
P_2 = the end of period price
P_1 = the beginning price

For example, if a shareholder buys a share for 100 which has a price of 120 at the end of the period, and receives a dividend of 5, then:

$$R = \frac{5 + 120 - 100}{100} = 25 \text{ per cent}$$

The question is: can corporate managers increase total returns to shareholders by manipulating dividend policy? The value of the firm depends on its investment schedule:

$$V = \sum_{t=1}^{n} \frac{1}{[1 + r]^t} [R - W - I]_t$$

where

V = the value of the firm
r = the required rate of return
R = operational cash receipts
W = operational cash expenditures
I = new investment

Having generated positive cash flows from trading, directors might call them retained earnings, depreciation, transfer to revenue reserve, etc., or they may choose to pay a cash dividend. Clearly, the decision relates to the split between dividends and retentions, and Table 12.1 considers both. Which is worth more — the dividend stream or the reinvestment stream? From the present value formula it is clear that both have the same capitalisation rate and are worth exactly the same amount in a rational world. Net cash flows of £6,000 in perpetuity calculated at 20 per cent have a present value of £30,000 regardless of the split between dividends and retentions. Those who believe that dividends are worth more than

Table 12.1

DIVIDENDS		RETENTIONS
Stream (1) £3,000		Stream (2) £3,000
Value $= \dfrac{\bar{X}}{P_k}$	$= \dfrac{£6{,}000}{0.2} =$	$\dfrac{\text{free cash flow}}{\text{capitalisation rate}}$
Value =	£30,000	

retentions do not accept that the NPV of a project is its cash flows discounted at some rate reflecting the project's economic risk. The NPV must be adjusted somehow to reflect the intended allocation of future cash flows between dividends and retentions. To the best of our knowledge no formula has as yet emerged to cope with the implied problem of valuing cash flow allocations to revenue reserve, depreciation and dividends.

'Proof' of Dividend Irrelevance

It is possible to prove both mathematically and graphically that dividends are irrelevant to the current wealth of shareholders given certain assumptions. Modigliani and Miller (1961) offer mathematical proof under certain assumptions:

1. Transaction costs can be ignored.
2. The firm's investment schedule is held constant.
3. Capital gains and dividends are taxed at the same rate.
4. Dividends convey no information to the stock market.
5. Stock markets are perfectly competitive.
6. Investors are rational and expect other investors to behave rationally.

Given these assumptions, it can be shown that an increase in dividend per share results in an equal reduction in price per share, shareholder wealth being unaffected. The current wealth of shareholders will not change with changes in dividend policy. The following formula gives the value of a firm at time t:

$$V_t = \frac{1}{1 + r_{t+1}} [D_{t+1} + n_t v_{t+1}] \tag{1}$$

where

V_t = the value of the firm = $n_t v_t$
D_{t+1} = the dividend at $t + 1 = n_t d_{t+1}$
n_t = the number of existing shares
v_{t+1} = the ex-dividend price per share at $t + 1$

If new shares m are issued at $t + 1$ at the v_{t+1} price, then

$$V_t = \frac{1}{1 + r_{t+1}} [D_{t+1} + V_{t+1} - m_{t+1}v_{t+1}] \qquad (2)$$

$$\therefore V_{t+1} = n_t v_{t+1} + m_{t+1}v_{t+1} = n_{t+1}v_{t+1}$$

Expressed in words: the value of the shares existing at t is equal to the present value of the dividend paid at $t + 1$ plus the present value of all shares existing at $t + 1$ less the present value of new shares issued at $t + 1$ at the $t + 1$ market price.

Since the total sources of funds must always equal the total applications of funds,

$$R_{t+1} + m_{t+1}v_{t+1} = D_{t+1} + W_{t+1} + I_{t+1} \qquad (3)$$

where

R_{t+1} = the year's operational cash receipts
$m_{t+1}v_{t+1}$ = cash raised by the issue of new shares at $t + 1$
D_{t+1} = the dividend paid at $t + 1$
W_{t+1} = the year's wages and other operational expenditures
I_{t+1} = the year's capital investment

$$\therefore R_{t+1} - D_{t+1} - W_{t+1} - I_{t+1} = -m_{t+1}v_{t+1}$$

Substituting $-m_{t+1}v_{t+1}$ in equation (2),

$$V_t = \frac{1}{1 + r_{t+1}} [D_{t+1} + V_{t+1} - R_{t+1} - D_{t+1} - W_{t+1} + I_{t+1}]$$

$$\therefore V_t = \frac{1}{1 + r_{t+1}} [R_{t+1} - W_{t+1} - I_{t+1} + V_{t+1}]$$

As the expression D_{t+1} does not appear in the final equation, the value of the firm is deemed to be independent of the firm's dividend policy. Valuation depends on the required rate of return, operational income, operational expenditures, the level of new investment, and the market value of the company's shares at $t + 1$ which is again determined by the following year's operational income, expenditure, new investment and year-end value. Given the firm's investment policies, the dividend decision does not affect the current wealth of the shareholders. A company's value is independent of the dividend payout. The value of the firm depends on its investment schedule. Given efficient capital markets and ignoring transaction costs and taxation, an increase in the dividend reduces the investment schedule and therefore reduces the ex-dividend price of the equity by the same amount. Given the firm's required level of investment, cash paid in dividends can be replaced by the issue of additional shares. It is the investment policy, not the financing arrangements, which determines the value of the enterprise. A change in dividend policy implies only a change in the distribution of total returns between dividends and capital gains. Dividends can be reinvested by the same shareholders in the company should the company need to issue new shares. Alternatively, where existing shareholders receive dividends and do not take up their proportionate share of new issues, there is a shift in wealth to new shareholders from old shareholders equal to the amount of dividend received by existing shareholders which is also the amount that the new shareholders paid for their shares.

Given their assumptions, the Modigliani/Miller proof is correct. We shall discuss their assumptions later, but at this point would mention that considerable support is given to the irrelevance of dividend policy by Black and Scholes (1974) who conclude that generous dividend payments do not result in higher share prices, and that no effect can be found between a change in dividend policy and returns to shareholders. It appears that there is little evidence to support the notion that shareholders are prepared to pay a premium for either high or low dividends.

Additional support for the Modigliani/Miller proof is given by Fama and Miller (1972) in their *graphical proof* of dividend irrelevance given the assumptions of no transaction costs, perfect capital markets, and dividends conveying no information. The graphical proof appears in Figure 12.1 which further develops the investment–consumption model introduced in Chapter 3. The curve X_1Z in Figure 12.1(a) is the investment opportunities curve. Projects offering very high internal rates of return are close to X_1. As we move to the left, the internal rate of return declines. Projects beyond the point X toward Z and beyond have unacceptable internal rates of return. Alternatively, projects to the left of X have negative net present values, whereas projects to the right have positive net present values. As we move to the left of X_1, more and more funds are invested, and projects are ranked in accordance with internal rates of return, with the most profitable projects being undertaken in the earlier stages. The firm will continue to invest up to point X, where the internal rate of return offered is equal to the required rate of return by shareholders. The horizontal axis represents period 1 resources which must be invested to claim period 2 resources. Period 2 resources K_1X can be claimed if we invest K_1X_1 in period 1. The

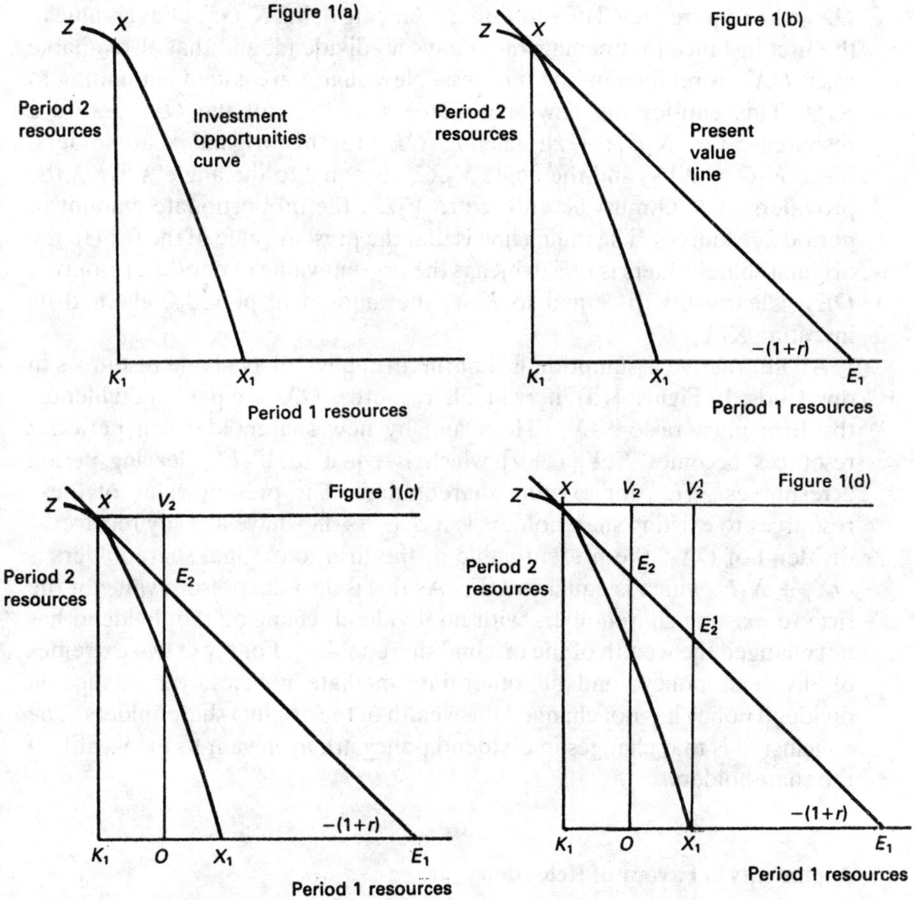

Figure 12.1 Graphical 'Proof' of Dividend Irrelevance

present value of period 2 resources, shown in Figure 12.1(b), must be greater than the present value of period 1 resources K_1X_1. In fact, the present value of period 2 resources K_1X is K_1E_1. This present value is given by the present value line XE_1. The present value line XE_1 transforms K_1X period 2 resources to K_1E_1 period 1 resources by discounting at the required rate of return r. The required rate of return determines the angle marked $-[1 + r]$. The greater the angle, the less period 2 resources are worth in period 1; and the smaller the angle, the greater is the present value of period 2 resources. Clearly, the lower the required rate of return, the greater is the present value of any level of anticipated cash flows. Management invests to point X where the internal rate of return is equal to r, the required rate of return.

In Figure 12.1(c) we observe that available resources in period 1 are

OX_1, the required level of additional financing being K_1O. Let us assume in the first instance that management pays no dividend, and that all available cash, OX_1, is retained in the business. New shares are issued amounting to K_1O. This entitles the new shareholders to V_2E_2 of the OV_2 period 2 resources, i.e. $K_1O[1 + r]$, leaving OE_2 to the original shareholders. Since $K_1O = XV_2$, and the angle V_2XE_2 is equal to the angle XE_1K_1, the providers of K_1O must be entitled to V_2E_2, the proportionate amount of period 2 resources. The punch line is that the present value of the firm to the original shareholders is OE_1 which is the present value of period 2 resources OE_2. Clearly OV_2 is equal to K_1X, the amount of period 2 claimed by investing K_1X_1.

An alternative assumption is that the firm pays all available resources in dividends. In Figure 1(d), if available resources OX_1 are paid in dividends, the firm must raise K_1X_1. The claim by new shareholders on period 2 resources becomes $K_1X_1[1 + r]$ which is equal to $V'_2E'_2$, leaving period 2 resources $X_1E'_2$ for existing shareholders. The present value of these resources to existing shareholders is X_1E_1. As they have already received a dividend of OX_1, the present value of the firm to original shareholders is $OX_1 + X_1E_1$ which is equal to OE_1. As this is also the present value of the firm to existing shareholders with no dividend, changing the dividend has not changed the wealth of the original shareholders. For these two extremes of dividend policy, and all other intermediate policies, the change in dividend policy has not changed the wealth of the original shareholders. The conclusion is that changes in dividend policy are irrelevant to the wealth of the shareholders.

Arguments in Favour of Retentions

When the assumptions of the previous discussions are relaxed, it appears that shareholders should prefer retentions. The rate of taxation on dividends ranges from zero for very low-income shareholders to 60 per cent plus occasional investment surcharges for high-income groups. Many institutional investors such as pension funds do not pay tax at all, and generally express a preference for dividends because they attempt to pay current pensions out of current 'income', i.e. dividends. Many pension fund managers assume that capital gains are not income until those gains are actually turned into cash. The Inland Revenue also has a long-established habit of taxing cash rather than increases in wealth. Taxation on realized (i.e. turned into cash) capital gains is a maximum of 30 per cent. Furthermore, before the introduction of the imputation system in April 1973, shareholders were taxed on dividends and the company received no relief for such tax. Surely the company could do better for the shareholder with £1 than the shareholder could manage with £1 less income tax. Surely high-rate tax payers prefer low-dividend yields. They may even be prepared to pay a premium for the low yields. Pension fund managers prefer high yields, and will tend to ignore the low-yield shares which are in great demand by high-rate tax payers. In general, the taxation of dividends suggests a penalty against high dividend payments. (Our own tentative conclusion is that firms should pay low dividends and increase/decrease the dividend in line with cash flow expectations.)

Further support is given for retentions in that investment in plant and equipment has made available the 100 per cent first-year allowance, a deliberate government incentive to reinvestment rather than dividends. The 100 per cent allowance is being reduced to 75, 50, and eventually 25 per cent, following the 1984 budget. Furthermore, when dividends are paid the amount must be grossed up at the standard rate of taxation and the tax paid over to the Collector of Taxes. This advanced corporation tax can be set off against the company's mainstream corporation tax liability on its taxable trading income — if any. Excesses of advanced corporation tax over the mainstream liability cannot be reclaimed but can be carried forward and used against future mainstream taxation. The encouragement not to pay dividends was greater under the 'classical' system of taxation before the introduction of the imputation system. Under the earlier system, tax deducted from dividends could not be set off against mainstream corporation tax. Corporate profits were taxed, and furthermore dividends paid out of after-tax cash flows were subject to income tax in the hands of shareholders. In summary, our tax system has tended to favour retentions.

With reference to transaction costs, if companies pay dividends and then issue new shares to finance the firm's investment schedule, transaction costs are incurred on the share issue. These can be considerable and are particularly so when measured as a percentage of smaller issues. Retentions do not incur transaction costs. What could be simpler and cheaper than *debit* appropriation account and *credit* revenue reserves?

Arguments in favour of retentions based on taxation and issuing costs are sometimes countered by criticism of the efficiency with which companies use retained cash flows. Directors have been accused of using these sums generated by successful trading to finance new projects which do not generate cash. They may build monuments in the centres of major cities to their own status. They may regard retained cash flows as free money, available for indulgence in excessive diversification to provide job security for top management and employees. Under these circumstances, shareholders may well prefer cash in the form of dividends rather than retentions. However, this is hardly a criticism of dividend policy, but rather a criticism of the investment policies of the firm. We would agree that directors should take on only wealth-creating opportunities, making money by satisfying consumer wants.

Recommended Dividend Policies

(1) A 100 Per Cent Payout Ratio

What should a firm do about dividends? There are several suggestions, including that of having a 100 per cent payout ratio. Rubner (1966) suggests that companies should be legally required to adopt a policy of 100 per cent payout. His idea is based on the notion that shareholders prefer dividends. Futhermore, directors requiring additional finance should have to convince investors that proposed new investments offer positive increases in wealth. This would encourage the rejection of projects which serve mainly to enhance the status and job security of managers and employees. Whatever the merits of these strong socio-economic arguments, companies do not generally pursue a target payout ratio of 100 per cent, and they are not encouraged to do so by either the government or shareholders.

(2) A 100 Per Cent Retention Ratio

Clarkson and Elliot (1969) offer the antidote to Rubner. They argue that given taxation and transaction costs, dividends are a luxury that neither shareholders nor companies can afford. Surely the company can be more successful with £1 than can be the shareholder with £1 less income tax. Again, whatever the merits of this proposal, only a few firms pursue a dividend policy of 100 per cent retention. Where they do, they argue that successful investment opportunities are open to the firm and that there is no point in paying dividends and then raising additional capital. It is rational for shareholders to prefer dividends if reinvested funds are wasted on unprofitable projects. If directors increase dividends rather than wasting cash resources on unprofitable projects, we would expect share prices to rise. We repeat that this is a result of a more successful investment policy, rather than a change in dividend policy.

(3) Dividends as a Residual

The residual theory suggests that firms should take on all investments which increase the wealth of shareholders, i.e. all projects with positive net present values. Any excess cash should be repaid to the shareholders as dividend, or repayment of capital if this is possible. Clearly, this policy is not pursued by companies. Dividends appear to be the active decision variable with retentions being the residual. Figure 12.2 shows a typical dividend policy. Earnings per share (EPS) increase with time but are very volatile. Dividends per share (DPS) are far less volatile than earnings. Dividends increase with a lag after earnings, and appear to signal the directors'

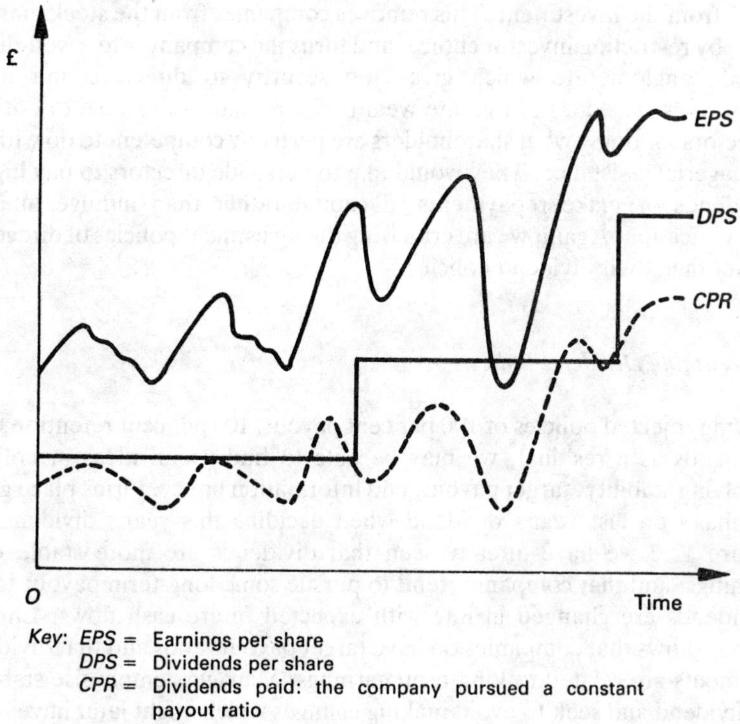

Figure 12.2 A Firm's Typical Dividend Policy

expectations of higher future earnings. The company appears to pursue a long-term payout ratio of approximately 50 per cent. Even in a period when EPS falls below DPS, the directors maintain the dividend in line with long-term expectations. It appears that the dividend is the active decision variable, and that retentions (EPS — DPS) are the residual. The dotted line represents the dividend that would be paid if the company pursued a policy of constant payout ratio (CPR). A policy of constant payout ratio implies that dividends will be some constant percentage of earnings. It is very rare for a company to pursue such a policy.

An additional argument against the residual theory is that firms increase their borrowings and at the same time continue to pay dividends. This is strange behaviour if we assume that directors take on all projects with positive NPVs and then repay any surplus cash to shareholders. The residual theory is interesting from a theoretical viewpoint, because it suggests that directors should take on all projects with positive net present values, and should not use shareholders' funds to turn the company into a unit trust. Directors sometimes do this by pure diversification when they acquire a £1,000,000 company for £1,000,000, there being no synergy or economies of scale from the investment. This removes companies from the stock market, thereby restricting investor choice, and turns the company into a well-diversified conglomerate which gives job security to directors and other employees, but does not create wealth. Shareholders are wise to criticise directors for doing what shareholders are perfectly competent to do without managerial assistance. They would like to persuade directors to pay higher dividends or make repayments of capital rather than indulge in pure diversification. Again, we are criticising the investment policies of directors, rather than their dividend policies.

(4) A Stable Dividend Policy

Having rejected policies of 100 per cent payout, 100 per cent retention, and dividends as a residual, we may be able to find useful ideas in policies involving stability, target payout, and information policy. Firms place great emphasis on last year's dividend when deciding this year's dividend. In Figure 12.2 we have already seen that dividends are more stable than earnings, and that companies tend to pursue some long-term payout ratio. Dividends are changed in line with expected future cash flows. Lintner (1956) shows that companies do have target payout ratios and that dividend payments are related to long-term earnings. Managers emphasise stability of dividend and seek to avoid making changes which might later have to be reversed. Lintner found that managers place great emphasis on the change in dividend from the previous period. This can be reconciled with the notion of the information content of dividends in that directors appear to use dividends as a signal relating to long-run expectations.

(5) Dividends as Information Policy

Changes in dividend policy convey information to the stock market. An increase in dividends is interpreted as good news. A cut in dividend is regarded as bad news. The complete bypassing of a dividend is interpreted as very bad news indeed. Managers should use this information channel to inform investors. In perfectly competitive markets, share prices fully reflect all information. One assumption of the efficient market hypothesis is that traders have access to all information. Many tests of the efficient market hypothesis suggest that stock markets are efficient in that share prices fully reflect all available information. However, shareholders do not have access to all the information relating to the company's future cash flows and risk. Surely corporate managers are better informed about cash flow expectations than the market. The efficiency of the stock market in generating best estimates of intrinsic values depends to some extent on the ability of management to communicate economic information to the market place.

Dividend policy provides a vehicle for conveying such information to shareholders. The common practice of declaring quarterly dividends gives a regular indication to shareholders. Perhaps this is the major role of dividend policy. An increase in dividend is an announcement by the directors that higher average cash flows are expected in the future than in the past.

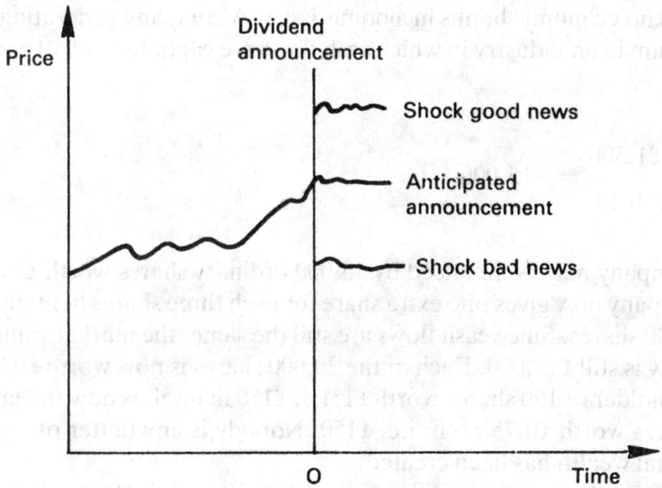

Figure 12.3 The Effect of Dividend Announcements on Share Price

If this information has not already been anticipated by the market, then the 'shock' will result in higher share prices. It is not the dividend which has changed the price but *new information relating to the firm's investment schedule* being immediately incorporated into the share price. Figure 12.3 shows three possible effects of the dividend announcement on share price. In an efficient market shareholders anticipate the dividend announcement. On average they get it right and nothing happens to the share price at the date of the announcement. Sometimes, shareholders get a pleasant surprise, the dividend announcement being greater than expected. This raises their hopes relating to future cash flows, bearing in mind that the firm pursues a target payout ratio, and the share price immediately reflects the shock good news. Alternatively, if the dividend is not increased to the anticipated level, the shock will result in a fall in share price. The target payout ratio is important because directors only increase dividends when they are fairly certain that the new dividend can be maintained. A study by Pettit (1972) suggests that it is possible to fool shareholders for a short period of time by increasing the dividend capriciously. However, the share price soon reflects the subsequent disappointment. Directors are very reluctant to cut dividends until they feel certain that the present level cannot be maintained. A cut in dividend is interpreted by shareholders as being very bad news. Rational shareholders pay careful attention to the *information content* of dividends.

A Note on Stock Dividends, Script Issues, Bonus Issues

There is no economic bonus in a bonus issue. A company generating £1,500 per annum in an industry in which cash flows are capitalised at 10 per cent is worth:

$$V = \frac{£1,500}{0.1} = £15,000$$

The company may be financed by 15,000 ordinary shares worth £1 each. If the company now gives one extra share for each three shares held, there will be 20,000 shares. Since cash flows are still the same, the market value of the company is still £15,000. Each of the 20,000 shares is now worth £0.75. The former holder of 150 shares worth £1, i.e. £150 in total, is now the holder of 200 shares worth £0.75 each, i.e. £150. Nobody is any better off, since no additional wealth has been created.

However, there will be a bonus in a bonus issue if the bonus issue, stock dividend, or script issue conveys new or shock information to the market. For example, the directors may announce their intention to pay the same dividend per share, or the shareholders may assume that this is the intention of the directors. The company has a target payout ratio and the increased dividend implies an increase in anticipated cash flows. A major study of the effect of stock splits by Fama, Fisher, Jensen and Roll (1969) suggests that it is the increased anticipated dividends (and therefore anticipated cash flows) which result in an increase in shareholder wealth.

Although many institutional and private shareholders express a need for dividends, we conclude that it is the information content of dividends that they seek. Some companies have pursued a policy of no cash dividends, and have justified this policy usually in terms of good investment opportunities. Shareholders in these companies can in fact devise their own dividend policies. Increased retentions should result in higher share prices, and the shareholder wishing to generate cash can sell shares. (We assume here that the shares are quoted on a stock exchange.) This is of considerable value to the high-rate taxpayer who avoids high rates of income tax on the dividend, but suffers capital gains tax at a maximum of 30 per cent. Some authors feel that all shareholders would be better off pursuing such policies, but they wish to avoid the chore of dealing in securities. Shareholders are assumed to prefer that directors pay dividends.

Why Do Companies Pay Dividends?

Perhaps we can now attempt to justify the payment of dividends. Companies pay dividends because they have always been expected to pay them. It was a reasonable assumption on the introduction of the joint stock company in a capitalist society that the cash flows (assumed to be the same as profit flows) generated from successful trading should be paid out in dividends. The allegiance of directors tends toward shareholders rather than the providers of debt. It is the shareholders who have the right to remove directors (rarely used), and the ability to decide the outcome of merger battles. If the objective of the firm is to create wealth, directors might be expected to be indifferent as to the distribution of rewards between interest payments, dividends and retentions. In fact, professional managers seek to increase the wealth of shareholders rather than the providers of loan capital.

Furthermore, professional managers prefer to have a large span of control measured by the number of employees, sales or market share, total assets or even total expenditure. In pursuit of the managerial objective of increasing the span of control we should expect directors to prefer retentions rather than distributions. Dividends are, however, still paid for all the reasons discussed in this chapter. The level of interest payments (and other contractual obligations such as lease payments) is determined by the capital structure decision. Dividend policy determines the distribution of after-tax-and-interest cash flows between distributed dividends and retentions. Retentions increase the status, remuneration and security of managers. The conflict between dividends and increases in the firm's investment schedule should result in tax-free growth in the value of shares to the extent that cash flows are reinvested in profitable projects.

It was many years before capital gains became generally taxable in the UK. Many shareholders were content with payout ratios much lower than 100 per cent. Dividends were not reduced to zero because companies have always been expected to pay dividends, and shareholders have learned to rely on the dividend as an expensive way of receiving economic information. Many charities, pension funds, insurance companies and banks were not allowed to invest in companies which did not pay dividends. This 'prudent man' thinking is reflected in the Trustee Investment Act 1961. Taxation favours retentions, but directors continue to pay dividends and continue to borrow money from banks. This being the case, dividend policy is used as an expensive but necessary way of communicating economic information to the stock market and encouraging institutional investment. Firms even continue to pay dividends in the knowledge that on occasion they will need to make new issues of shares to existing or new shareholders.

Finally, we must always remember that only about two per cent of all UK companies enjoy the status of a stock exchange listing. For the remaining companies, the sale of shares by investors is a much more complicated business. For non-quoted companies the importance of dividends is heightened as it becomes the only regular source of cash.

Dividend Policy Considerations

(1) The most important determinants of this year's dividend appear to be last year's dividend, recent earnings and anticipated earnings.
(2) Dividend payments should be legal. The general rule is that the cash dividend payment is restricted to the amount of accounting profit. The rules are devised for the protection of creditors, the general fear of the lawyers being that directors will make very generous dividend payments to shareholders and possibly bankrupt the company. Professional managers do not find it in their interest to behave in this way. They prefer retentions.
(3) We must emphasise that dividends are paid 'out of cash' and not 'out of profits'. The measurement of accounting profit is extremely difficult and the bottom line figure subject to accounting policies relating to stock valuation, depreciation, treatment of bad debts, treatment of goodwill, and the view taken of accrued income and expenditure.
(4) Corporate treasurers should plan for dividend payments just as much as other cash payments.
(5) Attention should be paid to dividend restrictions imposed by lenders.
(6) Corporate managers should be aware of all sources of new funds, including bank borrowings, and not simply look to retained cash flows to finance new investment. Retained earnings are not 'free'. Shareholders expect a return on these funds and prefer that they should not be employed in the erection of monuments to managerial status.
(7) Taxation and the cost of issuing new shares favour retentions as a source of new capital. We feel that the best dividend policy is probably a low cash dividend with small changes to reflect managerial anticipations.
(8) Corporate managers stress stability as an important determinant of dividends. Dividends are the active decision variable and retentions the residual.
(9) There is some evidence of a *clientele effect*. Low and zero rate tax payers appear to prefer high payout ratios, while high taxation groups prefer low dividends and hope for subsequent realised capital gains.
(10) Companies should continue to pay dividends, probably because they have always paid dividends. Such payments are an expensive way of communicating information to the stock market. Corporate

treasurers tend to pursue a target payout ratio over the long term and use changes in dividend to convey new information to the market.

Table 12.2 Factors Influencing The Dividend Decision

1. Information Content
2. Target Payout
3. Stability
4. Clientele Effect
5. Market Expectations
6. Financial Institutions
7. New Investment Opportunities
8. Ability to Make Annual Payment
9. Equity Base for More Debt
10. Debt–Equity Substitution
11. Taxation
12. Restrictive Covenants
13. Legality
14. Cash Flow vs. Profit Flow
15. Control
16. Special Circumstances

Table 12.2 lists the factors influencing the dividend decision. We recommend that boards of directors reviewing dividend policy and the annual dividend change should consider the following questions:

(1) Information Content

What has been our historic dividend policy?
What information about our expectations of future cash flows do we wish to communicate to the market?
What effect will an increase/decrease of X per cent have on our share price?
What dividend payment will have the optimal effect on share price, if any?
Can we sustain any proposed increase?
How can we best convey our intentions to shareholders?

(2) Target Payout

What is our target payout ratio over all time periods?
Have we communicated our target to the market?
Will the market believe it?

(3) Stability

By how much should our dividend increases lag behind earnings/net cash flow increases?

For how many periods should we pay the same dividend?
By how much should earnings/net cash flows fall before we cut the dividend?

(4) Clientele Effect

Who are our shareholders?
Are they high, low, or zero rate tax payers?
Do they prefer dividends or capital gains?
What are the costs involved if shareholders choose to devise their own dividend policy?

(5) Market Expectations

What do the financial pages predict?
What is our dividend yield?
How many times are dividends covered by earnings?

(6) Financial Institutions

Do we wish to encourage share ownership by financial institutions?
Will they support us in merger battles?
Can we use them as a source of loan capital?
Should we ever consider paying no dividend at all?

(7) New Investment Opportunities

What is our proposed investment schedule?
How should we announce it?
Can we really isolate the dividend decision from investment and financing decisions?

(8) Ability to Make Annual Payments

Do we need to convince shareholders of our ability to make annual dividend payments?
Do we need to convince lenders of our ability to make annual payments?
If we increase/decrease the dividend what effect will it have on our credit ratings?

(9) Equity Base for More Debt

Do we need to increase our equity base to justify the issuing of more debt?
At what price could we raise additional equity?
Why should we pay dividends and consider issuing equity?

(10) Debt – Equity Substitution

To what extent have we replaced equity with debt?
Do we wish to continue the trend?
What is our target debt–equity ratio?
How will dividend payout affect our debt–equity ratio?

(11) Taxation

What is the company's tax bill?
Can we reduce it by the amount of tax deducted from dividends?
What is the tax position of our shareholders?
Can we reduce the shareholders' tax bill by justifying to the Inland Revenue a repayment of capital, rather than the payment of dividends?

(12) Restrictive Covenants

Are there any restrictions on the amount of dividends we are allowed to pay?
Should we negotiate any change?

(13) Legality

Is our proposed dividend payout legal?
How will a change in dividend affect the risk to our creditors?

(14) Cash Flow Versus Profit Flow

Are we making a clear distinction between the effect of dividend on cash balance and retained earnings?
How many times will the dividend be covered by earnings?
How many times will the dividend be covered by net cash flow?
What will be the effect of the dividend payment on our cash balance?

(15) Control

If we need to issue more shares, what will be the effect on our controlling shareholders?

(16) Special Circumstances

Is the government asking companies to restrict dividend increases?
Are employees/trade unions critical of our dividend policy?
Will the proposed change in dividend affect our applications for special government grants?
Will our dividend to overseas shareholders cause friction with the Treasury or Inland Revenue?
Is our dividend policy out of step with policies pursued by other firms in the same industry?
Do we wish to encourage/discourage the conversion into equity of outstanding convertible debt?

Conclusion

Our readers are entitled to be puzzled. When we desert the mathematical and graphical world for reality, we are unable to resolve the most important issue in the dividend controversy: what is the policy which maximises shareholder wealth? We must agree with Black (1976) that in the pursuit of the objective of market value maximisation the role of cash payments to shareholders remains something of a 'dividend puzzle'. However, it seems appropriate that we should make a recommendation to managers and students in our textbook relating to financial management.

Firstly, the dividend decision is only a sort of financing decision. Given the firm's investment schedule, finance must come from somewhere. The higher the dividend, the greater the need for additional debt financing or an issue of equity. It must be emphasised that the dividend decision is not an investment decision. Investment decisions are concerned with new projects, increases in working capital, and acquisitions. Financing decisions include the debt–equity decision, the dividend decision, and the lease vs. borrow-and-buy decision. It appears that the three most important ingredients in the dividend decision are information content, target payout and stability. *Our conclusion is that companies should pay low cash dividends, making such changes as are necessary to indicate directors' anticipations of future net operational cash flows*. Payment of a small dividend minimises the need for additional external financing, whilst at the same time allowing ownership of the company's shares by institutional investors. Our consolation to all MBAs, managers, and undergraduates who are about to join a company is that the firm will already have an established dividend policy. *Only the annual change needs to be considered.* If introducing a completely new dividend policy, we recommend low cash dividends with annual changes to convey information to the market, even though dividends can be a very expensive way of communicating information to shareholders.

Questions

1. Present the mathematical proof of dividend irrelevance.
2. Present the graphical proof of dividend irrelevance.
3. Can incremental wealth be created by an effective dividend policy?
4. Discuss the important determinants of a company's payout policy.
5. A major U.S. utility company is considering a change in its dividend policy. Dividends have been paid since 1885. Many shareholders look forward to the quarterly dividend. However, for many years the company's capital expenditure has exceeded its reported net income. A great deal of cash will be needed for the company's proposed capital investment programme and it may be necessary to obtain financial support from the State. Both the need for working capital and energy prices have risen rapidly. For many years a quarterly dividend of 45c has been paid and the present market price of the stock is $18.

   As financial director, draft a report to your board outlining all the factors associated with the establishment of an effective dividend policy and make a recommendation for the current quarter.
6. Washington Ltd is an unquoted company which manufactures motor vehicle components. The company's summarised balance sheet at 30th November 1981 is as follows:

	£	£
Freehold land and buildings at original cost		350,000
Plant and equipment at original cost	2,800,000	
Less Accumulated depreciation	1,680,000	
		1,120,000
Working capital		430,000
		1,900,000
Represented by:		
Issued ordinary shares of £1		1,000,000
Reserves		900,000
		1,900,000

The estimated realisable values of the assets of Washington Ltd at 30th November 1981 are:

	£
Freehold land and buildings	2,200,000
Plant and equipment	1,000,000
Working capital	420,000

Washington Ltd's summarised financial record for the past five years is as follows:

Year ended 30th November	*1977*	*1978*	*1979*	*1980*	*1981*
	£	£	£	£	£
Profit	374,400	402,500	432,700	465,100	500,000
Dividend	262,100	281,800	302,900	325,600	350,000
Added to reserves	112,300	120,700	129,800	139,500	150,000

Washington Ltd currently earns an average annual rate of return of 25% on new investment. The directors are considering whether to increase the percentage of profit retained and reinvested each year to 50%. They estimate that, if they do so, the average annual rate of return on *all* new investment will fall to 22%.

The directors of Washington Ltd have recommended a dividend of £350,000 for the year ended 30th November 1981. This dividend is due to be paid shortly. If the directors decide to increase the proportion of profit retained to 50%, the current dividend will be reduced to £250,000.

Seventy per cent of the issued share capital of Washington Ltd is owned by Mr Missouri. Mrs Ohio, Mr Virginia and Miss Florida each own ten per cent of the issued capital. All four shareholders require a minimum rate of return of 20% per annum from their investment in Washington Ltd.

None of the shareholders is a director of the company.

You are required to:

(a) estimate the *cum div* value per ordinary share—

(i) of the shares held by Mr Missouri, and
(ii) of the shares held by Mrs Ohio,

on the basis of the information given and on the assumption that the new retention and reinvestment policy being considered by the directors is *not* adopted;

(b) discuss any additional information you think would be useful in estimating the values of the shares held by Mr Missouri and Mrs Ohio;

(c) prepare calculations showing whether the new retention and reinvestment policy being considered by the directors is preferable to the existing policy.

Ignore taxation. (ICA, PE II, December 1981)

7. Idomeneo plc is considering whether to invest in a project with a life of two years. The project involves the purchase of machinery for £100,000 on 31st December 1984 on which you are to assume a 100% first-year tax allowance will be available. The machinery will be sold at the end of two years for £30,000. The machinery will be used to manufacture a product, the demand for which will be 200,000 units in 1985 and 250,000 in 1986. The selling price per unit of the product will be £3 during 1985 and £4 during 1986. Fixed costs will be £30,000 in 1985 and are expected to increase by one-third in 1986. Variable costs per unit will be 80% of selling price in both years.

   Idomeneo has an effective after-tax cost of capital of 10%. The company's existing operations generate considerable corporation tax liabilities and are expected to continue doing so. The company's effective corporation tax rate is 52% and you are to assume that this rate will continue in the future. Corporation tax is payable twelve months following the end of each financial year. Idomeneo's accounting reference date is 31st December. All cash flows will arise on the last day of the financial year to which they relate. Advance corporation tax is payable immediately on all dividends paid at the rate of 3/7ths of the dividend paid.

   If the project is accepted, Idomeneo will distribute all available net cash inflows, after making associated taxation payments, immediately as dividends. The initial outlay of £100,000 will be provided by reducing the dividend due on 31st December 1984.

   You are required to:

   (a) calculate the year-by-year changes in dividends payable by Idomeneo plc for 1984, 1985, 1986 and 1987 if the project is undertaken;
   (b) on the basis of the dividend changes calculated in (a) evaluate whether acceptance of the project is worthwhile for:

      (i) a shareholder whose marginal tax rate is 30%,
      (ii) a shareholder whose marginal tax rate is 60%,

      and comment upon your results;

   (c) discuss how personal taxes might influence a company's decision on whether to retain earnings or distribute them as dividends.

(ICA, PE II, July, 1984)

References

Black, Fischer (1976) 'The dividend puzzle', in Stewart C. Myers, *Modern Developments in Financial Management*, The Dryden Press.

Black, Fischer, and Scholes, Myron (1974) 'The effects of dividend yield and dividend policy on common stock prices and returns', *Journal of Financial Economics*, vol. 1.

Clarkson, G. P. E. and Elliott, B. J. (1969) *Managing Money and Finance*, Gower Press.

Fama, Eugene F.; Fisher, Lawrence; Jensen, Michael; and Roll, Richard (1969) 'The adjustment of stock prices to new information, *International Economic Review*, vol. 10, February.

Fama, Eugene F. and Miller, Merton H. (1972) *The Theory of Finance*, Holt, Rinehart and Winston.

Graham, B., Dodd, D. L. and Cottle, S. (1962) *Security Analysis: Principles and Techniques*, McGraw-Hill.

Lintner, John (1956) 'Distribution of incomes of corporations among dividends, retained earnings and taxes', *American Economic Review*, vol. 46, May.

Miller, Merton H. and Modigliani, Franco (1961) 'Dividend policy, growth and the valuation of shares', *Journal of Business*, vol. 34, October.

Pettit, R. R. (1972) 'Dividend announcement, security performance, and capital market efficiency', *Journal of Finance*, December.

Rubner, Alex. (1966) *The Ensnared Shareholder*, Pelican.

Further Reading

Brennan, M. J. (1971) 'A note on dividend irrelevance and the Gordon valuation model', *Journal of Finance*, December.

Elton, E. J. and Gruber, M. J. (1970) 'Marginal stockholder tax rates and the clientele effect', *Review of Economics and Statistics*, February.

Keane, S. (1974) 'Dividends and the resolution of uncertainty', *Journal of Business Finance and Accounting*, Autumn.

Ryan, T. M. (1984) 'Dividend policy and market valuation in British industry', *Journal of Business Finance and Accounting*, Autumn.

Wilkes, F. M. (1977) 'Dividend policy and investment appraisal in imperfect capital markets', *Journal of Business Finance and Accounting*, Summer.

13

Financial Strategy (3) The Leasing Decision

Introduction

Firms generating lots of cash from successful trading need not worry too much about *financing decisions — capital structure decisions*, *dividend decisions* and *leasing decisions*. Successful firms can honour interest payments and loan repayments, they can pay generous or ungenerous dividends, and they need not worry very much about whether they should lease equipment or borrow the money and buy. Firms generating lots of cash from successful trading can borrow if they need funds, they can issue more equity, they have no difficulty in arranging leases on property or plant. As in the cases of capital structure and dividend policy, we recommend that managers might as well get it approximately right. The 'lease or borrow-the-money-and-buy' decision is very unlikely to determine the success or failure of the enterprise, although it is possible if you try very hard. We recall an ex-MBA student of ours who decided to go into the paper bag manufacturing business. (We would like to point out that the majority of MBAs from our institution have a somewhat better story to tell than what follows!) His natural ambition led him to take on a 5,000 square foot factory on a 50-year lease. Failing to achieve his target market share, he could neither pay the lease nor negotiate a smaller floor area. His company went into liquidation, the biggest creditor being the lessor. The company would have faced very similar cash flow problems had the entrepreneur borrowed the funds to finance purchase of the property. The lesson is that both loans and leases increase the company's contractual payments, i.e. the gearing. The lease was badly negotiated because it did not allow cancellation or renegotiation when it proved impossible to continue making the lease payments.

The Leasing Decision

At the outset we must say that we are discussing *financial leases* rather than *operating leases*. Financial leases are a source of long-term finance because to all intents and purposes the lessee assumes all the benefits of ownership and is using the financial lease as an alternative to borrowing the money and buying. An operating lease is usually a short-term lease equivalent to renting for only a few weeks or months. Fortunately, the lease-versus-borrow-and-buy decision can be solved within the framework of the net present value rule. This comes as something of a relief after considering the difficult areas of capital structure and dividend policy. A few notes should prove helpful.

1. *The leasing decision is only a financing decision*, not an investment decision. Once a firm has decided to invest in a computer, a fleet of vehicles, property or plant, a second decision must be made as to the most appropriate method of financing.
2. Short-term operating leases whereby a firm may rent for a few weeks — an exhibition hall, grass-cutting machinery, decorating equipment, etc. — are regarded as expenses to be set against cash inflows rather than as methods of long-term financing. The lease evaluation technique we discuss in this chapter relates to *financial leases* whereby the economic benefit of ownership over the life of the asset generally passes to the lessee, usually a commercial company or local authority, from the lessor, usually a bank subsidiary or large leasing company such as IBM or Xerox.
3. The rapid growth in the leasing industry over the past twenty years is generally attributed to four factors. Firstly, leasing can make economic sense when the lessee is not paying tax, or is paying tax at a lower rate than the lessor. Secondly, it is generally easier and quicker to lease an asset than to arrange a loan to finance its purchase. Thirdly, during periods of rising interest rates, when lease agreements are agreed at interest rates which do not reflect anticipated increases in interest rates, nor allow for changes in lease payments to adjust for increases in interest rates, some leases have turned out to be very cheap sources of finance. Fourthly, for many years all leases, including financial leases, were treated as expenses in the profit and loss account rather than as sources of financing in the balance sheet, and some financial managers felt that this was a valuable source of

'off the balance sheet' financing. (A fifth reason sometimes put forward is that banks can borrow more cheaply than commercial companies.)

The *tax factor* is extremely important because in the United Kingdom a 100 per cent first-year allowance has until recently been available on plant and equipment. When a company does not expect to pay corporation tax for the foreseeable future, the 100 per cent tax deduction is lost. It should be possible to set up a deal with a bank's leasing subsidiary so that the bank buys the equipment, claims the 100 per cent first-year allowance, and then passes on some of the benefit to the lessee in the form of a cheap lease, i.e. a lease which to the commercial company is cheaper than borrowing the money and buying. The commercial company gets the economic benefit of use of the equipment. When the commercial company is paying corporation tax and expects to carry on paying corporation tax, it will want to claim the 100 per cent first-year allowance, and the leasing deal becomes much less attractive. We can establish a general rule of thumb that when a company expects to pay corporation tax it should take the benefit of the available tax allowances and borrow to buy, rather than lease. On the other hand, should the company expect not to get the benefit of the first-year allowances (now reducing to 75 per cent, then 50 per cent, then 25 per cent), the financial manager should explore the leasing alternative.

Our second reason for the growth in leasing relates to the ability of capital markets to provide funds for new investment. This is an uncomfortable area for academics. We teach capital market efficiency in the sense that share prices fully reflect all available information and that share prices react instantaneously to new information. We also like to feel that funds are always readily available to finance projects with positive net present values. However, experience tells us that finance is not always readily available for the acquisition of plant and machinery and motor vehicles, particularly to the smaller company which lacks a track record and does not have a balance sheet asset base to offer as security for loans. Anticipated cash flows are not always enough for bank managers. A lease has often proved easier to arrange than a bank loan to finance purchase by commercial enterprise. Expensive cars for company directors have often been financed by leasing rather than by bank loans for purchase. This has often made good economic sense as well as being easier to arrange. Generally, all the lease payments have been allowed as a tax deduction, whereas only a 25 per cent writing-down allowance has been available on cars subject to a maximum of £2,000 per annum. However, the generosity of the Inland Revenue in its treatment of leasing has been severely curtailed in recent years. Long gone are the days when directors could get all the lease payments allowed as a tax deduction on an expensive car and purchase it for £1 after two or three years without tax penalties.

A third reason offered to explain the growth in leasing is that the fixed-lease payments can turn out to be very cheap if interest rates rise. Clearly, the same benefit is attached to a loan arranged at a fixed rate of interest. Bank lending has for many years been based on points above base rate and interest rates on loans have therefore changed during the life of the loan. In the early years many leases were fixed for the period of the lease. Interest rates were rising and it turned out that many leases were very inexpensive. Lessors soon learned to adjust lease payments during the life of the lease for changes in interest rates. Furthermore, interest rates do tend to reflect anticipated rates of inflation. We therefore suggest that financial managers should not enter into leasing deals in the expectation that rising interest rates will result in the lease being inexpensive. Interest rates move downwards as well as upwards, and lessors can and do link lease payments to changes in base rate.

Our fourth reason offered for the growth in leasing is that leasing is 'off the balance sheet' financing. We recommend that financial managers should not be fooled by this aspect of leasing, and suggest that they should not expect others to be fooled. Leasing involves making contractual payments in the same way as does borrowing. For most practical purposes the financial lease is a method of purchase because the lessee has the full economic use of the asset. Lease payments reduce net cash flows as do payments of interest and repayments of capital. They are all contractual, risk-free payments which the lessee fully intends to honour, and the lessor fully expects to receive. For practical purposes both leasing and borrowing increase the amount of leverage on a £1-for-£1 basis. We should not expect investors and bank managers to be fooled by balance sheet numbers. Wealth creation is not a balance sheet game. The key ingredients are cash flow and risk. Debt–equity ratios are often calculated from balance sheet numbers because such numbers are readily available. We should use the market values of debt and equity, not balance sheet numbers.

Furthermore, the amount of leverage can be and is ascertained by examining the extent to which contractual payments, including lease and interest payments, are covered by net cash flows. Accounting bodies around the world are recognising that the use of balance sheet numbers to measure gearing leads to some distortion. Many are introducing accounting standards which require accountants to include the capitalised amount of outstanding leases in their balance sheets. Financial managers should understand that the taking on of leases and loans increases the gearing. This increases the risk or volatility of return to shareholders who expect increasing rewards for taking on additional financial risk. Increased gearing is an economic fact which financial managers should not expect to be hidden for very long 'off the balance sheet'.

The opportunity cost of leasing is to borrow the money and buy. Both a lease and a loan increase the gearing of the firm, more or less on a £1-for-£1 basis. It is generally true that if a financial manager can borrow the funds to purchase, he can also find a lessor. It might not be anything like as generally true the other way round, but to develop a workable rule we assume that the opportunity cost of leasing is borrowing to finance purchase. If we accept the generalisation, we can advise the financial manager how to evaluate a leasing opportunity. The rule is: *discount all after-tax cash flows for both the lease and the loan at the after-tax cost of borrowing*, and accept whichever method of financing is cheaper. We assume that the allegiance of directors is to the shareholders rather than to the providers of loan capital, and therefore we assume that directors prefer cheaper loans to more expensive loans. All that is required is for the financial manager to identify the cheaper source of financing — the lease or the loan. The rate of interest on the loan is usually readily available. If we discount the after-tax cash flows on the lease at the after-tax cost of borrowing and find that the present value of the lease is cheaper than the present value of the loan, we should advise leasing. If leasing is more expensive, we should borrow the funds and purchase.

A Leasing Example

A company can purchase a machine for £10,000 or make four annual lease prepayments of £3,000. The machine's life is four years with no residual value. The company pays corporation tax at 52 per cent, approximately one year after earning its cash flows. A bank loan is available to finance the purchase at an interest rate of 21 per cent. Should the company lease or borrow and buy, assuming that:

(a) the company does not expect to pay corporation tax for the foreseeable future;
(b) the company expects to pay corporation tax at 52 per cent?

In the answer to the (a) part of the question we are evaluating the lease in terms of the loan. In Table 13.1, column (2) shows the lease payments as negative numbers because they are cash outflows. If we make these cash payments we save £10,000 immediately which is the present value of the loan we would accept if we borrowed. This appears in column (4). This is also the

Table 13.1 No Corporation Tax Payable: Lease versus 'Borrow and Buy' (£)

(1) *Period*	(2) *Lease payments*	(3) *Tax savings*	(4) *Loan (cost)*	(5) *FYA*	(6) *Cash flow*	(7) *21%*	(8) *Present value*
0	(3,000)		10,000		7.000	1.000	7,000
1	(3,000)				(3,000)	0.826	(2,478)
2	(3,000)				(3,000)	0.683	(2,049)
3	(3,000)				(3,000)	0.564	(1,692)
NPV of lease is positive, therefore lease.							781

Note: FYA = first-year allowance

price of the machine, but we emphasise that the £10,000 is the present value of a loan repayment schedule of £10,000. Students always wonder why we do not spell out the interest and capital repayments. It is not necessary. The present value of the loan repayment schedule must be £10,000. The after-tax cost of borrowing, in column (7), is 21 per cent because in a world without taxation the tax shield on interest is lost. Multiplying the annual cash flows by the after-tax cost of borrowing gives the present value of each year's cash flow in column (8). The sum of the cash flows is positive at £781, which means that the lease is cheaper than the loan, and we should recommend that the firm lease rather than borrow and buy. Textbooks usually lay out the lease versus borrow-and-buy cash flows as above. In fact, we find that managers and students prefer to examine each source of finance separately. The present value of the loan repayment is £10,000, whereas the present value of the lease payments is £3,000 immediately, plus £3,000 (2.073) which equals £9,219. Since the present value of the lease payments is £781 less than the present value of the loan repayments, we recommend that the lease be accepted because it is the cheaper source of financing.

Table 13.2 Corporation Tax Payable: Lease versus 'Borrow and Buy' (£)

(1) *Period*	(2) *Lease payments*	(3) *Tax savings*	(4) *Loan (cost)*	(5) *FYA*	(6) *Cash flow*	(7) *10.08%*	(8) *Present value*
0	(3,000)		10,000		7,000	1.000	7,000
1	(3,000)	1,560		(5,200)	(6,640)	0.908	(6,029)
2	(3,000)	1,560			(1,440)	0.825	(1,188)
3	(3,000)	1,560			(1,440)	0.750	(1,080)
4		1,560			1,560	0.681	1,062
NPV of lease is negative, therefore buy.							(235)

If the company does expect to pay corporation tax, Table 13.2 shows that columns (2) and (4) remain exactly as before. The company can still make the lease payments and save the cost or present value of the loan. In column (3) the lease payments save tax at 52 per cent approximately one year later, and in column (5) the first-year allowance (FYA) of 100 per cent is lost approximately one year later if the company leases. (The old capital allowance rate is used here to simplify the illustration. New rates are discussed in Chapter 5.) Remember that we are evaluating the lease in terms of its opportunity cost which is borrowing the money and buying. If we lease, we lose the first-year allowance which is claimed by the lessor, usually a bank subsidiary. The net cash flows in column (6) are now discounted at 10.08 per cent which is the after-tax cost of borrowing in a world with taxes, i.e. 21 per cent less 52 per cent. After-tax costs of borrowing are not at all obvious, but all we are saying is that a loan of £10,000 has a present value of £10,000. If you work out the repayment schedule in a world without taxes and then discount at 21 per cent you will find that the present value of the loan is £10,000. Similarly, if you work out the repayment schedule in a world with taxes, reducing the income payments by the tax savings on interest, and then discount at 10.08 per cent, you will find that the present value of a £10,000 loan in a world with taxes is still £10,000 (see Table 13.2). Discounting the cash flows at 10.08 per cent, we find that the net present value of the lease is now negative and we therefore recommend that the company should buy. As we said earlier, we should expect the company to buy rather than lease when the company can get the benefit of the 100 per cent first-year allowance.

Again, we can calculate the present value of the lease opportunity and the present value of the loan alternative. The present value of the lease is £3,000 (1.000) + 1,440 (0.808) + 1,440 (0.825) + 1,440 (0.750) – 1,560 (0.681) = £5,513. The present value of the loan opportunity is £10,000 – 5,200 (0.908) = £5,278. Since the present value of borrowing and buying is £235 less than the present value of leasing, we should recommend acquisition rather than the lease.

We repeat that the decision being made is a financing decision, not an investment decision. The acquisition of the machine has been incorporated into a net present value calculation whereby the anticipated cash flows are discounted at some rate reflecting their economic risk. The project presumably has a high and positive net present value, or an internal rate of return of 160 per cent, 86 per cent, 45 per cent, or some other number. This investment has been made on the basis of net present value which has been found to be positive, or on the basis of internal rate of return which has been found to be greater than the required rate of return. Our decision now relates to the financing of the project — a lease or a loan to finance acquisition.

Residual Values

When we established the rule: discount the after-tax cash flows at the after-tax cost of borrowing — we did not mention residual values. Lease payments, interest, and capital repayments are all contractual obligations fixed in advance. They are almost risk-free payments which the company expects to honour. We assume that the lease payments and loan repayments are of equal risk. Residual values are not risk-free amounts. The residual value of our £10,000 machine is a very uncertain amount which must be the exception to the rule that it should be discounted at the risk-free rate. Theoretically, we should establish the beta of the residual value and derive the discount rate from the capital asset pricing model. This is very difficult. We suggest that the residual value should be discounted at the same rate of return as was required on the investment decision. If all else fails, we may even simply 'double' the discount rate for residual values.

Let us assume that the estimated residual value of our £10,000 machine is £2,000 at the end of its four-year life. If we own the machine, we claim the full £2,000 which is taxed approximately one year later. If we lease, let us assume that the lessors will refund the company 80 per cent of the residual value. In a tax world, should the company lease, or borrow and buy?

In Table 13.3 we see that the introduction of a residual value increases our resolve to purchase. This must be the case because we receive 100 per cent of the residual value rather than only 80 per cent. We have assumed that the required rate of return on the investment opportunity which requires use of the machine is 20.16 per cent, or alternatively we have simply doubled the after-tax required rate of return because the residual value is a more risky amount than the contractual payment (we apologise for the very strange rate of 20.16 per cent which is clearly only for demonstration purposes). Again, we could have simplified the calculations. Our previous negative net present value of the lease was £235. If we lease, we lose £400 on the sale but suffer a balancing charge (BC) for tax purposes of £208 less than would have been the case if we had purchased. The new net present value of the lease is (235) + (400) (0.480) – 208 (0.399) = (344).

Leasing Example II

Factorybright Limited offers industrial cleaning services to companies in Southern England. Rapid growth in demand for such services has led the directors to accept many profitable contracts, in fact more than can possibly be managed with existing machinery. The time has come either to lease or to buy £500,000 worth of additional equipment. The bank is prepared to lend £500,000 at 18 per cent repayable over two or three years. Alternatively, the machinery distributors offer a leasing deal whereby the company can pay £150,000 immediately, plus three additional annual payments of £150,000. At the end of the lease period the lessor would refund Factorybright 90 per cent of the market value, which is expected to be about £120,000. For ease of calculation, assume that the equipment can be written off for tax purposes at 100 per cent in the first year. Your chief executive asks you as Financial Director to work out which is the cheaper source of finance, assuming firstly that the company pays no corporation tax for the foreseeable future, and secondly that corporation tax is payable throughout the period at 48 per cent.

Table 13.4 shows that, on purely financial grounds, in a no-tax world, the company should lease. The residual value of £120,000 on sale is lost if the company leases, but the company would receive £108,000, the net loss being £12,000. This is discounted at a higher rate than the other contractual payments. We could use the required rate of return on the investment opportunity, but as this is not known we have simply doubled the borrowing rate and discounted at 36 per cent.

Table 13.3 Lease versus 'Borrow and Buy', with Taxes and Residual Values (£)

(1) *Period*	(2) *Lease payments*	(3) *Tax savings*	(4) *Loan (cost)*	(5) *FYA*	(6) *Residual value*	(7) *BC*	(8) *Cash flow*	(9) *10.08%*	(10) *20.16%*	(11) *Present value*
0	(3,000)		10,000				7,000	1.000		7,000
1	(3,000)	1,560		(5,200)			(6,640)	0.908		(6,029)
2	(3,000)	1,560					(1,440)	0.825		(1,188)
3	(3,000)	1,560					(1,440)	0.750		(1,080)
{4		1,560					1,560	0.681		1,062
{4					(400)				0.480	(192)
5						208			0.399	83
NPV of lease is negative, therefore buy.										(344)

Notes: BC = balancing charge
FYA = first-year allowance

Table 13.4 No Corporation Tax Payable: Factorybright Limited — Lease versus Buy (£)

(1) *Period*	(2) *Lease payments*	(3) *Tax savings*	(4) *Loan (cost)*	(5) *FYA*	(6) *Residual value*	(7) *BC*	(8) *Cash flow*	(9) *18%*	(10) *36%*	(11) *Present value*
0	(150)		500				350	1.000		350
1	(150)						(150)	0.847		(127)
2	(150)						(150)	0.718		(108)
3	(150)						(150)	0.609		(91)
4					(12)				0.292	(4)
NPV of lease is positive, therefore lease.										20

Table 13.5 Corporation Tax Payable: Factorybright Limited — Lease versus Buy (£)

(1) *Period*	(2) *Lease payments*	(3) *Tax savings*	(4) *Loan (cost)*	(5) *FYA*	(6) *Residual value*	(7) *BC*	(8) *Cash flow*	(9) *9.36%*	(10) *18.72%*	(11) *Present value*
0	(150)		500				350	1.000		350
1	(150)	72		(240)			(318)	0.914		(291)
2	(150)	72					(78)	0.836		(65)
3	(150)	72					(78)	0.765		(60)
4		72			(12)		60		0.503	30
5						6	6		0.424	3
NPV of lease is negative, therefore buy.										(33)

The position in a tax world is summarised in Table 13.5. Tax at 48 per cent is saved on the lease payments as shown in column (2). A first-year allowance (FYA) of £240,000 is lost if the company leases. Column (6) shows the net loss of £12,000 on the residual value if the equipment is leased, but this saves tax of approximately £6,000 one year later because the balancing charge (BC) is smaller than would have been the case if the company received 100 per cent of the residual value. Again, this after-tax discount rate of 9.36 per cent is doubled to 18.72 per cent for both the net residual value lost and the tax saved. Our recommendation is that the company should buy because the net present value of the lease is negative. Clearly, the 100 per cent first-year allowance on £500,000, worth £240,000 one year later, is a big incentive to purchase if the company expects to pay corporation tax.

The Leasing Decision: Other Factors

1. Obsolescence

A firm concerned about possible obsolescence of high technology equipment may not want to own. A cancellable lease may be arranged whereby the lessee has the option to terminate the lease during the lease period. The lessor may not be quite as concerned about obsolescence as the lessee because the lessor is familiar with the leasing industry and is aware of the existence of alternative lessees. Outright ownership gives the commercial company the flexibility of instant disposal but some flexibility can be negotiated under a lease.

2. Restrictive Covenants

Restrictions on managerial behaviour are often attached to loans but are less common and less rigorous under leases. Loan creditors may impose restrictions on dividend payments, additional loans, working capital movements, and acquisition and disposal of assets. Financial managers who are concerned about restrictive covenants on additional loans may be encouraged to lease.

3. Effect on Reported Earnings

Accounting profit should be higher under lease financing than under loan financing. Only the lease payments are charged in the profit and loss account, whereas when a company borrows and buys, both the interest payments and depreciation charges on the asset acquired will be charged as an expense. We should therefore expect that, particularly in the earlier years of a loan, accounting profit will be higher under a lease arrangement.

4. Balance Sheet Numbers

The level of total assets appearing in the balance sheet is generally lower under a lease arrangement than a loan. All loans appear in the balance sheet as sources of finance and all purchased assets appear as part of total assets employed. Traditionally, with leased assets no lease obligation has appeared in the balance sheet. It therefore follows that reported return on capital employed is generally higher under a lease. If accounting profits are higher and total assets (or sources of finance) are lower, return on capital employed can be much higher under a lease. We emphasise that wealth creation is not a balance sheet and profit and loss account game. Wealth is created by taking on projects with positive net present values, trading anticipated cash flows against risk. We must also add that many countries, including the UK, now have an accounting standard relating to financial leases. The effect is to treat lease financing in a similar way to hire purchase financing. Leased assets appear in the balance sheet, and depreciation is charged in the profit and loss account. The beneficial effect on ROCE has therefore been largely eroded.

5. Maintenance and Insurance

Both leasing and ownership usually impose upon the lessee the costs of maintenance and insurance so that the lease versus borrow-and-buy decision can ignore such costs. If, however, the leasing arrangement imposes costs on the lessor rather than the lessee, the savings to the lessee must appear in the cash flows when evaluating the lease opportunity.

6. The Capital–Revenue Myth

Many local authorities and companies are fooled by the capital–revenue myth. Both leasing and acquisition involve lessees in the making of contractual payments — cash outflows. Such payments are cash outflows regardless of whether they are charged against the revenue budget or the capital budget. Leasing has been encouraged in some areas because leasing is generally regarded as a revenue item rather than a capital item. In periods of financial distress organisations often impose restrictions on capital expenditure. Managers avoid these restrictions on acquisition of capital items by acquiring the same assets under a financial lease. We exhort all not to be fooled by the nonsense of capital–revenue budgeting systems.

7. Secondary Leases

The period of a lease is often referred to as the primary period. It may well be the case that the asset is not exhausted at the end of the primary period, and leasing agreements sometimes offer the lessee the right to continue using the asset for a secondary period for a purely nominal lease rental. Financial managers should try to secure such arrangements as an additional option against outright purchase. Lessors should be fairly flexible on this point because the primary lease usually recovers the full cost of the asset to the lessor.

8. *Flexibility of Lease Payments*

Many leases now provide for changes in interest rates, changes in taxation, and inflation. We suggest that financial managers should not enter into leases in the expectation that interest rates will rise and make the fixed lease payments a cheap source of finance. Interest rates tend to reflect anticipated inflation. Interest rates can move downwards and forecasting changes in taxation is a hazardous business.

9. *Cash Flow Advantage*

There is no cash flow advantage to leasing if leasing replaces loan financing on a pound-for-pound basis. However, it is often the case that companies lease because they cannot borrow. The cash flow advantage does sometimes exist because the allocation of scarce resources throughout industry is not perfectly efficient. We encourage managers not to overstate the advantage by assuming that leasing does not increase the extent to which the company is financed by borrowing. Lease payments are contractual payments which increase the financial risk to shareholders who demand a higher rate of return to reflect the additional financial risk. The hidden cost of additional lease and interest payments is the increasing required rate of return by shareholders.

10. *The Lessor's Year-End*

A potential lessee should ideally seek a lessor just before the lessor's year-end. If the lessor buys an asset just before a year-end, the benefit of the first-year allowance is received at the earliest time. This is an inducement to the lessor to arrange a deal.

11. *Lessor and Lessee Borrowing Rates*

One of the advantages of bank leasing is that banks can generally borrow at lower rates than companies. This accounts for only a small portion of the leasing benefit. Far more important is the 100 per cent first-year allowance which the bank subsidiary can claim when the lessee cannot because insufficient taxable profits are being earned. Both the commercial enterprise and the bank can benefit at the expense of the Inland Revenue.

12. Temporary Non-Taxpaying Lessee

A company may not expect to pay tax for two or three years but may expect to resume paying corporation tax thereafter. When this is the case the financial manager must forecast the periods when taxation is expected to be paid and introduce the anticipated tax savings lost into the lease evaluation.

13. Loss of 100 per cent First-Year Allowance

At first sight it would appear that one of the biggest incentives to leasing is the loss of the first-year allowance (FYA) when a company is not paying corporation tax. This allowance has been reduced by the 1984 budget and falls to 75 per cent for expenditure incurred from 14.3.84 to 31.3.85, and then to 50 per cent for expenditure incurred from 1.4.85 to 31.3.86. This is expected to lower the financial manager's enthusiasm for leasing. It remains to be seen whether the alleged 'cash flow advantage' proves sufficient to maintain the growth in lease financing.

When the commercial company does not expect to pay tax, the financial manager may be less enthusiastic about leasing because the lease could well become more expensive. Since the leasing company will lose the 100 per cent first-year allowance, one of the alleged advantages of leasing will be gradually eroded. Referring back to Table 13.1, the financial manager's position remains unchanged in a world without taxes. He can either make four annual lease prepayments of £3,000 or borrow £10,000. Since the commercial company does not expect to pay tax, the NPV of the lease remains the same at £781 when the first-year allowance is reduced. However, the bank as lessor loses the 100 per cent first-year allowance and must be expected to increase the lease payments above £3,000 per annum, thereby making the lease more expensive.

In a world in which the commercial company does expect to pay tax, we can see from Table 13.6 that the reduction of the FYA appears to encourage corporate leasing. From Table 13.2 we may recall that the NPV of the lease is negative at £235, with a 100 per cent first-year allowance. Table 13.6 suggests that with a 75 per cent FYA the net present value of the lease is negative at £3, and that with a 50 per cent FYA the net present value of the lease is positive, suggesting a switch to leasing as the first-year allowance reduces. This is not expected to be the case because the bank subsidiary as lessor will lose the benefit of the 100 per cent first-year allowance. This must

Table 13.6 (a) 75 Per Cent First-Year Allowance: Lease versus Borrow and Buy (£)

(1) *Period*	(2) *Lease payments*	(3) *Tax savings*	(4) *Loan (cost)*	(5) *Tax*	(6) *Cash flow*	(7) *10.08%*	(8) *Present value*
0	(3,000)		10,000		7,000	1.000	7,000
1	(3,000)	1,560		(3,900)	(5,340)	0.908	(4,849)
2	(3,000)	1,560		(325)	(1,765)	0.825	(1,456)
3	(3,000)	1,560		(244)	(1,684)	0.750	(1,263)
4		1,560		(731)	830	0.687	565
NPV of lease is negative (just), therefore buy.							(3)

Table 13.6 (b) 50 Per Cent First-Year Allowance: Lease versus Borrow and Buy (£)

(1) *Period*	(2) *Lease payments*	(3) *Tax savings*	(4) *Loan (cost)*	(5) *Tax*	(6) *Cash flow*	(7) *10.08%*	(8) *Present value*
0	(3,000)		10,000		7,000	1.000	7,000
1	(3,000)	1,560		(2,600)	(4,040)	0.908	(3,668)
2	(3,000)	1,560		(650)	(2,090)	0.825	(1,724)
3	(3,000)	1,560		(488)	(1,928)	0.750	(1,446)
4		1,560		(1,462)	98	0.681	67
NPV of lease is positive, therefore lease.							229

be expected to encourage the lessor to increase the lease payments, thereby cancelling out any expected benefit to the lessee.

The Leveraged Lease

In the early 1970's the Anaconda Corporation decided to invest in an aluminium reduction mill at Sebree in Kentucky, USA. The company then had to decide on the method of financing. It was expected that the corporation would not be paying tax for many years and the leasing possibility was therefore examined. A leverage lease was arranged whereby part of the total cost of the new plant was financed by borrowing. The deal is illustrated in a widely-used case study (Butters *et al.* 1981). Figure 13.1 shows the Anaconda Corporation at the summit as lessee. The company makes lease payments to the First Kentucky Trust Company as lessor. This company is financed by $72 million of loan capital provided by three insurance companies and $38 million of equity provided by six banks and Chrysler. The First Kentucky Trust Company pays the Aluminium Company of America $138 million to build the aluminium reduction mill, $38 million being provided by the banks and Chrysler, $72 million being provided by the three insurance companies, and the final $28 million

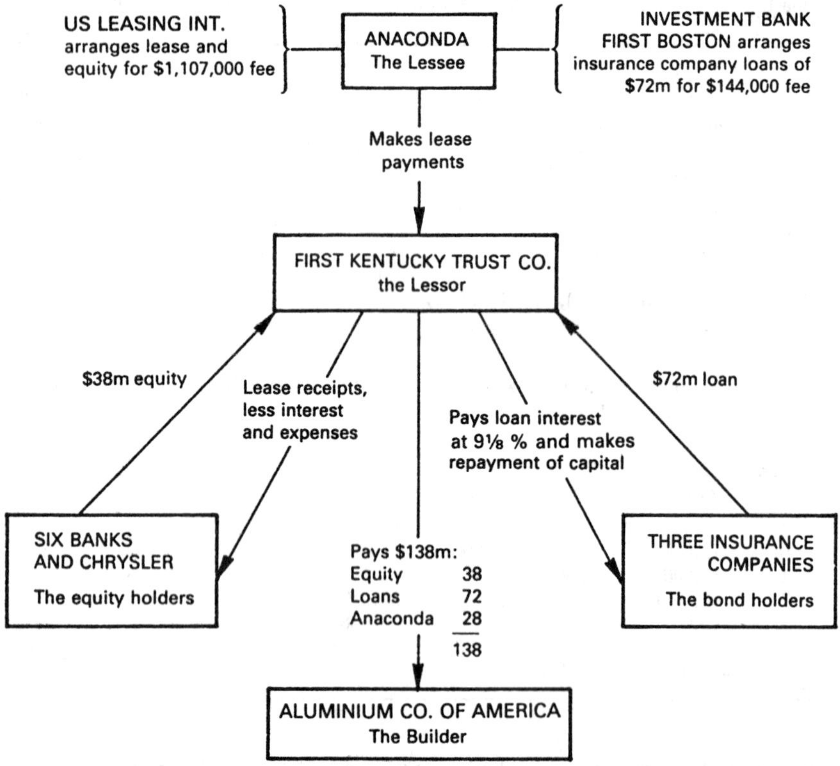

Figure 13.1 The Anaconda Leveraged Lease (see Butters *et al.* 1981)

being provided by Anaconda. The First Kentucky Trust Company collects lease payments from Anaconda. Interest at 9⅛ per cent is paid to the three insurance companies together with repayments of capital. The six banks and Chrysler receive the balance of lease payments after deducting interest and expenses incurred by the First Kentucky Trust Company, together with the tax benefits foregone by Anaconda (readers will now be familiar with the basic idea in leasing, which is, the switching of tax allowances from companies which do not expect to pay tax to companies which do expect to pay tax). Anaconda estimates that the leasing arrangement will be cheaper by $74 million over the cost of borrowing and buying over the 20-year lease period, if the company does not pay corporation tax. Aspiring bankers and financial consultants should note the fees paid to the investment bank for arranging the insurance company loans ($144,000) and to the leasing broker for arranging the lease and equity ($1,107,000).

Summary

The leasing decision is a financing decision, not an investment decision. The opportunity cost of leasing is 'borrow the money and buy'. A lease should be accepted when it is cheaper than borrowing and buying, after considering all additional factors. The leasing rule is: discount the after-tax cash flows at the after-tax cost of borrowing — apart from the residual value, which should be discounted at a higher rate. We should expect companies to borrow and buy rather than lease when it is expected that corporation tax will be paid, although many financial managers emphasise the value of leasing as a source of immediate financing.

Questions

1. Explain the growth of leasing.
2. When does leasing make economic sense?
3. List all the known factors involved in considering a financial lease.
4. As financial director of Manningham Engineering Ltd you are asked to draft a report to your board on the most appropriate method of financing plant for a scale expansion. The purchase price of the plant is £900,000 and the required rate of return on the investment is 28 per cent. The decision has been made to finance the new plant by either a loan or a lease. The bank has offered to lend the company £900,000 at 5 per cent above base rate (base rate being 10 per cent). The bank manager has offered either a three or five-year loan. He suggests that you approach the bank's leasing subsidiary. Your enquiry results in an offer of a financial lease whereby Manningham Engineering Ltd can make four annual lease prepayments of £260,000. At the end of the lease period, 85 per cent of the residual value (estimated at £180,000) would be refunded to the company by the bank's leasing subsidiary. You are not sure as to whether your company will be paying tax in the foreseeable future, but any corporation tax payable will be at the rate of 40 per cent.

   Draft a report to your board making a firm recommendation, and outline all the factors involved in the leasing decision.
5. Extravert Ltd offers grass-cutting services to companies, local authorities, and country estates in West Yorkshire. Rapid growth in demand for such services has led the directors to accept many profitable contracts, in fact more than can possibly be managed with existing machinery. The time has come to either lease or buy £100,000 worth of additional equipment. The bank is prepared to lend £100,000 at 15 per cent repayable over three years. Alternatively, the machinery distributors offer a leasing deal whereby Extravert can pay £30,000 immediately and three additional annual payments of £30,000. At the end of the lease period the lessors would refund Extravert 95 per cent of the market value, which is expected to be about £20,000.

   Your chief executive asks you as financial director to draft a brief report assuming firstly that the company pays no corporation tax for the foreseeable future, and secondly that corporation tax is paid throughout the period at 40 per cent. Your report should cover (a), (b) and (c) below.

(a) Distinguish between investment and financing decisions.
(b) When does leasing make sense?
(c) Should Extravert lease or buy-borrow?

6. As financial director of West Yorkshire Engineering Ltd you are asked in February 1984 to draft a report to your board on the most appropriate method of financing plant for a new division. The purchase price of the plant is £800,000. The required rate of return on the total investment in the new division is 30 per cent, and the decision has been made to finance the new plant from an external source. The bank has offered to lend the company £800,000 at 3 per cent above base rate (base rate is 11 per cent). The bank loan can either be repaid over 3–5 years or a loan can be so structured as to have the same characteristics as a lease. Alternatively, West Yorkshire Leasing Ltd, a subsidiary of the company offering to sell the plant, has offered a financial lease whereby West Yorkshire Engineering Ltd can make four annual prepayments of £240,000. At the end of the lease period 90 per cent of the residual value (estimated at £150,000) would be refunded to W.Y.E. Ltd by W.Y.L Ltd. You are not sure as to whether or not your company will be paying tax in the foreseeable future. If corporation tax is paid, it will be at the rate of 30 per cent.

   Draft your report to the board making a firm recommendation and outline all the factors involved.

7. (a) Annio Ltd is considering whether to invest in a new machine costing £60,000. The machine is expected to have a five-year life, at the end of which time it will have a zero scrap value. Use of the machine will allow Annio Ltd to lay off immediately one supervisor currently earning £10,000 per annum, and to reduce its other overheads by £6,000 per annum at current prices. Annio Ltd expects to pay salary increases to all supervisory labour in the future at an annual compound rate of 5%, and estimates that its bill for overheads will rise at an annual compound rate of 10%.

   Annio Ltd's financing policy is to maintain a constant debt/equity ratio, and as part of this overall policy the directors have decided to finance the cost of the machine either by negotiating a loan of £60,000, or by obtaining a lease for the life of the machine. The loan would run for five years and would incur annual interest payments of £9,258, which represent an effective after-tax interest rate of 8%. The lease would cost £15,000 per annum payable in advance.

   Annio Ltd obtains corporation tax relief at 52% on its costs one year after they arise and expects such relief to continue indefinitely. A 100% first year tax allowance is available on this type of machine. Annio Ltd has a weighted average cost of capital, net of corporation tax, of 15% per annum.

Unless stated, you may assume that all cash flows arise on the last day of the year to which they relate. You are required, as chief accountant, to prepare a report for the directors of Annio Ltd showing:

(i) whether the investment in the machine is worthwhile and
(ii) which financing alternative is to be preferred.

(b) You are required to explain the reasons for the recent growth in leasing as a method of financial new investment.

Ignore advance corporation tax. (ICA, PE II, July, 1982)

8. The directors of Expos plc are currently deciding whether to lease or buy a new machine. The machine, which would attract a 100% first-year allowance, costs £70,000 and has a life of five years, after which time it will have zero scrap and resale values. If the machine were to be leased, the lease agreement would specify five annual payments of £16,300, payable annually in advance. Lease payments would start on 1st January 1984, the same day on which purchase of the machine would take place. The company's accounting reference date is 31st December.

The company's tax advisers are unsure whether or not the company will have to pay any corporation tax on the profits of the next five years, as they are currently awaiting judgment on a tax reduction scheme that they have devised. Consequently, the directors of Expos plc would like to know whether to lease or buy the machine, both if the company has to pay corporation tax on the profits of the next five years, and if the company has no corporation tax liability over that period. Expos plc pays tax twelve months following the end of its accounting year. If the company has a corporation tax liability, the effective corporation tax rate will be 52%.

You may assume for simplicity that the company's effective cost of capital will be 10% per annum if no corporation tax liability arises during the next five years and 5% per annum if the company is liable to pay corporation tax.

You are required to:

(a) prepare calculations showing whether the machine should be bought or leased, assuming that

(i) Expos plc will have no corporation tax liability during the next five years;
(ii) Expos plc will have to pay corporation tax on its profits for the next five years;

(b) explain the difference between a finance lease and an operating lease, and discuss the importance of the distinction for corporate financing.

Ignore advance corporation tax. (ICA, PE II, December 1983)

Reference

Butters, J. K., Fruhan, W. E., Mullins, D. W. and Piper, T. R. (1981) 'Midwest Communications Inc.', *Case Problems in Finance*, Irwin. (The case is reprinted from *Stanford Business Cases 1974* and the source of the data stated as *Fortune*, November 1973.)

Further Reading

Bower, R. S. (1973) 'Issues in lease financing', *Financial Management*, Winter.

Fawthrop, R. A. and Terry, B. (1976) 'The evaluation of an integrated investment and lease-financing decision', *Journal of Business Finance and Accounting*, Summer.

Franks, J. R. and Hodges, S. D. (1978) 'Valuation of financial lease contracts: a note', *Journal of Finance*, May.

Gordon, M. J. (1974) 'A general solution to the lease-or-buy decision: a pedagogical note', *Journal of Finance*, March.

Johnson, R. W. and Lewellen, G. (1972) 'Analysis of the lease-or-buy decision', *Journal of Finance*, September.

Myers, S. C., Dill, D. A. and Bautista, A. J. (1976) 'Valuation of financial lease contracts', *Journal of Finance*, June.

Schall, L. D. (1974) 'The lease-or-buy and asset acquisition decisions', *Journal of Finance*, September.

Vancil, R. F. (1961) 'Lease or borrow—new method of analysis', *Harvard Business Review*, September.

14

Adjusted Present Value

Making Investment and Financing Decisions Simultaneously

So far, we have kept *investment* and *financing* decisions almost completely separate. Project decisions have been based on *anticipated cash flows*, the *initial outlay* and the *discount rate*. Merger and acquisition decisions are also based on incremental cash flows — the x factor being the present value of anticipated incremental cash flows arising from the merger. Working capital increases are also justified in terms of increased incremental cash flows, although working capital decisions do not slot as easily into the net present value equation as project and merger decisions. Financing decisions involving capital structure, dividends and leasing are considered to some extent independently of investment decisions. The capital structure decision is based largely on tax savings and anticipated financial distress. Dividends are something of a mystery and should probably be based on the three most important factors: information content, target payout, and stability. A leasing opportunity can be compared with its opportunity cost which is 'borrow the money and buy', managers accepting whichever is the cheaper source of financing.

Managers are often reluctant to accept the complete separation of investment and financing decisions. As sensible, practical individuals they know that one must solve investment and financing decisions at the same time. It is not possible to take on a £1m investment schedule unless you have £1m to invest. There is no point in raising £1m in finance unless you have a good idea as to its destination. Investment and financing decisions must be solved simultaneously and we can now turn our attention to this problem.

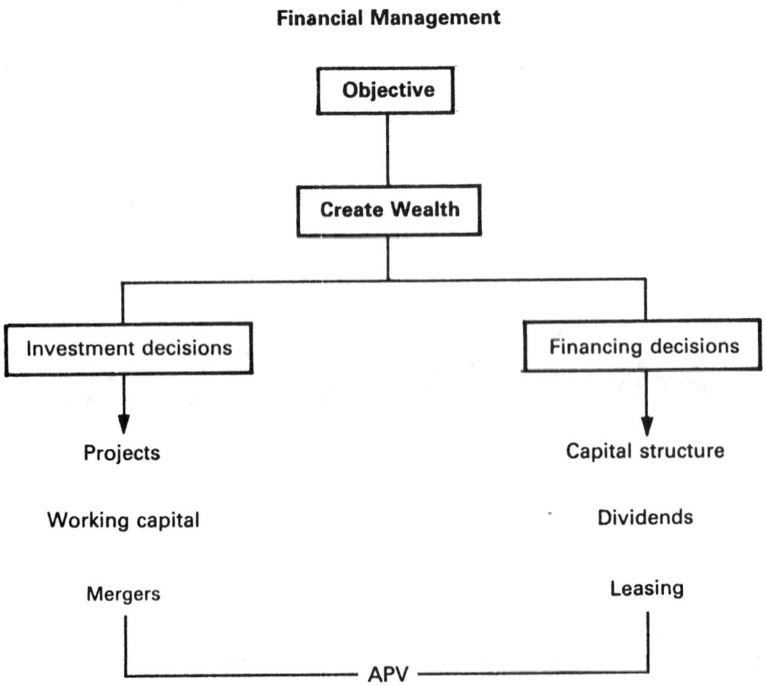

Figure 14.1 Simultaneous Solution of Investment and Financing Problems

Fortunately, there is a fairly straightforward answer to it: the answer is *adjusted present value*.

Figure 14.1 outlines a financial management programme. The objective of the firm is to create wealth or make money satisfying consumer wants in competitive markets by matching the resources of the organisation to the needs of the market place. Financial management relates to the making of wealth-creating investment decisions and devising a sensible financing strategy. Investment decisions can be made within the framework of the net present value formula which attempts to measure the present value of wealth created by taking on an investment opportunity. Financing decisions are more complex than investment decisions but not as important, although it is possible to cause the firm considerable financial distress by making bad financing decisions. We therefore recommend that corporate financial managers get their financing decisions approximately right. At the foot of Figure 14.1 we show APV, adjusted present value, the technique for solving investment and financing problems at the same time.

The APV of a project is the project NPV calculated in the usual way plus any benefit, or minus any cost, of the financing decision. Net present value is simply adjusted for anything special about the financing decision which affects NPV. Examples include government grants, special tax allowances, cheap loans, issuing costs, and the ability to sustain additional debt. We can use the following equation to calculate adjusted present value:

$$APV = NPV \left. \begin{matrix} + \, benefits \\ - \, costs \end{matrix} \right\} \text{ of financing.}$$

Example 1

A project has a net present value of £100 million. The project cash flows have been discounted at a rate reflecting the economic risk of the project. Net present values calculated in the usual way are calculated on the assumption that the project is financed entirely with *equity*. It now transpires that the government decides that our project is socially and environmentally worthy, and offers a *tax-free grant* of £10 million. This is a special financing arrangement which affects the net present value of the project. The adjusted present value is 100 + 10 = £110 million.

Example 2

A second project also has a net present value of £100 million. With a view to raising capital to finance the project it is necessary to incur *issuing costs* amounting to £5 million (assume not tax-deductible). The issuing costs relate entirely to the financing decision, but they are an incremental cost of accepting the project. The adjusted present value is therefore 100 − 5 = £95 million.

Readers should realise that at the margin such costs can be important. If our project has a positive NPV of £3 million but it is necessary to incur financing costs of £5 million, the adjusted present value is negative, and the project would not be undertaken. It should be noted that issuing costs should only be related to a project if they would not otherwise be incurred in the foreseeable future.

Example 3

A third project also has a positive NPV of £100 million. The project will sustain *perpetual debt* of £4 million per annum at 10 per cent interest with a tax rate at 50 per cent. From our knowledge of capital structure, we know that the value of the firm with debt is equal to the value of the firm without debt plus the present value of the tax savings, ignoring any incremental anticipated costs of financial distress. The equation $V_D = V_o + TD$ can be applied not only to the firm in its entirety but also to individual projects. A project which will sustain debt has a higher present value than a project which will not sustain debt, because the tax shield on debt has a positive present value. In our example, the project has a positive net present value of

£100 million, ignoring the present value of the tax shield. The anticipated perpetual interest payments amount to £400,000 per annum, the resulting tax shield being £200,000 per annum. The present value of that tax shield discounting at 10 per cent is £2 million. The adjusted present value of the project is therefore 100 + 2 = £102 million.

We have probably overstated the present value of the tax shield because we have ignored any incremental costs of anticipated financial distress. We have also ignored the possibility of firms in the same industry passing on to their customers the benefit of the tax shield. For simplification, we assume perpetual debt. For debt which is not perpetual, it is necessary to work out the interest repayment schedule and calculate the annual tax savings. These are discounted at the going rate of interest to give the present value of the tax shield, which is then added to the net present value to give adjusted present value. We should also note that the present value of a project tends to fall with time, as the project nears the end of its life. The amount of debt which a project will support should be expected to fall. As it happens, it is normal for a loan to be paid off over the life of a project, and financial managers should examine the extent to which the falling value of a project is matched by reductions in sustainable debt.

Example 4

A fourth project has a net present value of £100 million. A specialist financial institution offers a cheap loan of £12 million at 5 per cent interest rather than the market rate of 10 per cent. There is clearly an *element of gift* in the financing arrangements. A perpetual loan of £12 million offered at half the going rate of interest includes a gift element of £6 million. Annual interest payments of £600,000 discounted at 10 per cent have a present value of £6 million. The adjusted present value of the project so far is therefore 100 + 6 = £106 million. If the project can sustain this amount of debt without any increase in the anticipated costs of financial distress, we should also increase the adjusted present value by the present value of the tax shield. Assuming a 50 per cent tax rate, annual interest payments of £600,000 entitle us to a tax shield of £300,000 per annum which, discounted at 10 per cent, has a present value of £3 million. The final adjusted present value of the project is therefore 100 + 6 + 3 = £109 million. As in example 3, the loan is assumed to be perpetual for simplicity of illustration. For loans which are not perpetual, it is necessary to work out the actual tax shield for each year and calculate the present value of that stream of savings. Financial managers should be careful not to overstate the present value of the tax shield. It may be passed on to customers, or the tax shield may be lost when the company is not in a tax-paying position. Furthermore, as the firm takes on more debt, the probability of incurring the costs of financial distress increases. We should remember that the value of the firm with debt is equal to the value of the firm without debt plus the present value of the tax savings minus the present value of the costs of financial distress:

$$V_D = V_o + TD - BC$$

We do not know how to put a value on BC, but the costs of financial distress must be considered when making decisions on the firm's capital structure as well as the amount of debt an individual project can sustain.

Adjusted present value is a useful technique for making investment and financing decisions at the same time. Managers are often disappointed in the lack of complexity of APV. Some argue that the technique is pointless because any sensible decision maker would take the additional costs of financing etc. into account when making the investment decision. In defence of APV we would say that it does enable us to keep investment and financing decisions completely separate until the end of a financial management programme, by which time course participants have a reasonable grasp of the ideas supporting the modern approach to making sensible investment and financing decisions.

Questions

1. Distinguish between investment and financing decisions.
2. List the factors which could change NPV to APV.
3. A company has decided to increase output by acquiring a plant costing £5 million immediately. After-tax incremental cash inflows are expected to amount to £2 million per annum for five years, and the required rate of return on scale expansion programmes is 20 per cent. The project will be financed partly by an issue of equity amounting to £3 million, plus £200,000 issuing costs. A government grant of £½ million is available, and the remaining £1½ million will be made available by Barclays Bank at 6 per cent, rather than the market rate of 12 per cent, repayable in five instalments at the end of each of the five years. The company pays tax at 30 per cent. Calculate the NPV and APV.

Further Reading

Bar-Yosef, S. (1977) 'Interactions of corporate financing and investment decisions — implications for capital budgeting: comment', *Journal of Finance*, March.

Myers, Stewart C. (1974) 'Interactions of corporate financing and investment decisions — implications for capital budgeting', *Journal of Finance*, March.

Myers, Stewart C. (1977) 'Reply', *Journal of Finance*, March.

Section C

Investment Practices and Processes

15

Investment Appraisal in Practice

Introduction

An organisation's ability to survive and prosper in the hostile environment within which it frequently operates depends to a great extent on its ability to regenerate itself through astute and strategically-compatible capital investment decisions. In recent years over half of the combined internal and external funds generated by UK firms has been committed to fixed capital investment. Committing such resources to long-term capital projects in anticipation of an adequate return — although a hazardous step — is essential for the vitality and wellbeing of the company.

So far, we have discussed the mechanics of appraising investment projects under both the simple condition of certainty and the more complex condition of uncertainty. It is the purpose of this chapter to consider the historical development of capital budgeting, and the extent to which the principles of project appraisal have been *applied* in practice. Attention will focus on the disparities arising between investment theory and practice and the role of traditional measures of investment worth in the modern capital budgeting system.

Historical Perspective

It is a common misconception that the discounted cash flow approach, involving the forecasting of relevant cash flows and the time value of money, is a relatively recent phenomenon. Historical records, however, reveal an understanding of compound interest (upon which discounted cash flow techniques are based) as far back as the Old Babylonian period (c. 1,800–1,600 B.C.) in Mesopotamia.[1] The earliest manuscripts setting out compound interest tables date back to the fourteenth century, while the first recorded reference to the net present value rule is found in a book by Stevin published in 1582. Simon Stevin, a Dutch mathematician, accountant and engineer, describes 'a general rule for finding which is the most profitable of two or more conditions, and by how much it is more profitable than the other'. Thus the net present value rule for choosing between options was established.

In these early days, the application of discounted cash flow methods was restricted to financial investments such as loans and life assurance, where the cash flows are either known or their probabilities can be determined based on actuarial evidence. It was not until the nineteenth century that, with the industrial revolution well established, the scale of capital investments led engineering economists to apply discounted cash flow concepts to capital assets. One of the first was the American civil engineer A. M. Wellington (1887) who advocated the use of present value in his book on the location of railways. In considering the difficulties of forecasting relevant cash flows based on the probable volume of rail traffic, he concludes:

> ... the rate of this growth of traffic is excessively variable and uncertain — liable to cease altogether at any time for many years.
>
> For this cause alone it is in general inexpedient to look forward more than at most five years for traffic to justify an increase in immediate expenditure.

During the early part of the present century a number of writers from engineering and economics disciplines developed capital budgeting theory,[2] but little of this work found its way into actual practice. From the surveys conducted it is clear that, with very few exceptions, discounted cash flow concepts were largely ignored in reaching investment decisions until as late as the early 1950s in America and the early 1960s in the United Kingdom.

It is difficult to explain why the now universally accepted benefits of discounted cash flow techniques were denied to businessmen for so long. Parker (1980) attributes much of this delay to a reluctance within the accounting profession to accept innovation. Accountants — with their expertise in evaluating financial investments, and their special role in advising management on capital investment matters — seemed to prefer the traditional methods, despite an excellent series of articles on the subject by Coase, published in the *Accountant* as early as 1938.

Recent DCF Trends

Interest in discounted cash flow methods began to quicken in the 1950s following a number of useful theoretical contributions to the literature by

Lutz and Lutz (1951), Hirshleifer (1958) and Solomon (1959). In particular, the writings of Joel Dean (1951) in the US and, subsequently, Merret and Sykes (1963) in the UK had a profound influence in popularizing the internal rate of return method.

Table 15.1 DCF Usage Rates Obtained in Prior UK Surveys

Year	*Author*	*Number of respondents*	*Response rate %*	*DCF usage %*
1966	Rockley	69	29	59
1973	Carsberg and Hope	103	32	85
1974/75	Westwick and Shohet	81	n.a.	80
1980	Scapens and Sale[1]	211	45	52
1980	Pike	150	76	69

Notes: [1]The DCF usage rate refers to the 211 divisionalised companies responding.
n.a. = not available

For more than thirty years, academics have espoused the adoption of ever more advanced and sophisticated methods for evaluating investment options. A number of surveys conducted over this period[3] indicate that while businessmen have been somewhat more hesitant, there has been a gradual but unmistakable trend towards the use of sophisticated investment techniques in general and DCF methods in particular. Extreme care, however, is called for before making generalisations based on survey comparisons. In the first place, the surveys upon which trends are based are so dissimilar as to invalidate proper comparison. Furthermore, the low response rates typically found in postal surveys give rise to considerable potential for non-response bias, where respondents have a far higher DCF usage rate than non-respondents.[4] This may explain the anomalous situation in Table 15.1 which suggests that, since the early 1970s, DCF usage has fallen considerably. Such an allegation is questioned by our survey (Pike 1983a) which examined investment practices in both 1975 and 1980 (Table 15.2). The results show that for the 150 companies sampled DCF usage actually *increased* from 57 per cent to 69 per cent.

Although the use of DCF methods has continued to grow, there are clear signs in many organisations that excutives are becoming increasingly disenchanted with the discounted cash flow approach, along with other 'sophisticated' capital budgeting methods. Many are placing greater reliance on traditional measures, such as payback period, and on non-quantitative aspects such as judgement, 'feel' and intuition.

Much of the discussion that follows draws upon a recent survey of 150 major UK manufacturing and retailing companies. Of particular interest in

Table 15.2 Evaluation Techniques Used by 150 Firms

	1980 %	*1975* %
Discounted cash flow (IRR or NPV)	69	57
Internal rate of return (IRR)	54	42
Net present value (NPV)	38	32
Payback period	79	71
Accounting rate of return	51	51
Other	7	5

Source: Pike (1983a)

this chapter is Table 15.2 giving the main investment evaluation techniques employed in 1980 and 1975. Further analysis revealed that companies with larger capital budgets have been more ready to employ DCF methods. For instance, 87 per cent of firms with annual capital budgets in excess of £50 million employed the internal rate of return method in 1980, while only 30 per cent of firms investing below £5 million a year used this method.

Table 15.3 Project Evaluation Methods used by 150 large Firms, 1980

Primary[1] *method* %		*One method* %		*Two methods* %		*Three methods* %		*Four methods* %	
a	32	a	11	ab	12	abc	10	abcd	10
b	32	b	8	ac	12	abd	6		
c	41	c	4	ad	6	acd	10		
d	17	d	3	bc	3	bcd	1		
				bd	1				
				cd	3				
	122[1]		26		37		27		10

Notes: [1] This adds to more than 100 per cent because some methods ranked 'equal first'.
a = payback
b = average rate of return
c = IRR
d = NPV

It is interesting to note that, while the popularity of discounting approaches has grown, it has not come at the expense of traditional methods such as payback period and accounting rate of return. Payback period is still the most widely used evaluation technique among major firms — employed by 79 per cent of those surveyed. It would appear that DCF methods supplement, rather than substitute, traditional approaches. In fact, Table 15.3 shows that only 26 per cent of firms surveyed used a single evaluation method — a combination of methods being preferred to appraise the wide range of projects encountered. At least two interpretations can be given for this. First, it may indicate that no single appraisal technique is sufficiently simple for managers to understand, yet sufficiently complicated to embody the important relationships holding in the real world. Second, if the formal evaluation stages seek to develop a case to justify the form of project chosen, as King (1975) suggests, managements will select that technique which reflects the project in the best possible light.

Respondents were asked to discuss the value of advanced investment techniques and how they envisaged their firm's investment practices would develop in the 1980s. Almost half indicated that no change was contemplated, many stating that they could see no benefit from further development. Approximately one-third of respondents were particularly concerned with devising criteria for rationing limited funds among competing projects in times of high economic uncertainty. Whereas theory would advocate employment of sophisticated techniques such as mathematical programming and probability analysis to solve such problems, the clear approach adopted in practice was to resort to the payback period. One financial director summed it up succinctly:

> Concentration will be on short payback periods. The techniques will become simpler, getting back to basics rather than sophisticated mathematical formulae.

This and many similar comments received echo the observation of the Wilson Committee (1980) that 'high inflation has greatly increased the uncertainty of business forecasts and has led some companies to abandon the orthodox DCF technique and place more emphasis on payback period and cash flow'. Can the rejection of more sophisticated investment methods really be justified in the present economic climate? In the remainder of this chapter we shall examine the disparity existing between investment theory and practice and assess how the two may be reconciled.

Disillusionment with Discounting

Formal evaluation techniques based on discounted cash flow analysis now dominate the capital budgeting literature. Unfortunately, much of the discussion concerning its merits bears little relation to the financial goals and economic conditions applicable to most investment decisions. In the application of investment theory, it is appropriate to question DCF methods in terms of their importance, relevance to sound investments and acceptability to managers.

From the emphasis devoted by most textbooks to advanced capital budgeting methods one might be forgiven for assuming that successful investment is exclusively attributable to the correct evaluation method. Only a handful of businessmen and academics have suggested that the emphasis on sophistication is misplaced (Adelson 1970; Vandel and Stonich 1973; Hastie 1974; King 1975). The art of capital investment involves asking the appropriate strategic questions, operating thorough search and screening procedures, and generally providing a framework which permits managers to make better decisions. Sophisticated methods often create an illusion of exactness which the underlying assumptions do not warrant. The experience in many firms has been that greater reliance on such methods has come at the expense of the human element in decision making. As top management places more weight on the quantifiable element, there is a danger that the unquantifiable aspects of the decision, which frequently have a critical bearing on a project's success or failure, will be devalued. The human element is particularly important with regard to project sponsoring. It is not uncommon to find that the margin between a project's success or failure hinges on the enthusiasm and commitment of the person sponsoring it.

Table 15.4 Importance of Systematic Procedures and Qualitative Factors

Importance Scale	*Systematic procedures*		*Qualitative factors*	
	Number of firms	*%*	*Number of firms*	*%*
Very important	30	23	28	22
Important	42	32	54	41
Average importance	37	29	41	32
Below average importance	15	11	4	3
Relatively unimportant	6	5	3	2
	130	100	130	100

Our survey supports the importance of unquantified aspects in capital budgeting. Table 15.4 shows that sixty-three per cent of respondents ranked 'qualitative' factors as 'important' or 'very important' in investment decisions, while only fifty-five per cent gave such ratings to sophisticated investment methods and systematic procedures. The message is clear: formal evaluation such as DCF is just one of many factors in the investment decision process.

Discounting approaches may also be questioned in terms of relevance. Managers cannot afford to treat investment decisions in a vacuum, ignoring the complexities of the business environment. Any attempt to incorporate such complexities, however, will, at best, consist of abstractions from reality predicated on generalised and simplified assumptions concerning business relationships and environments. A fundamental assumption underlying DCF methods is that decision makers pursue the primary goal of maximising shareholders' wealth. Empirically, this assumption must be questioned. As reported in Chapter 1, our survey found that a return-on-assets financial goal was the most commonly used investment objective; shareholder goals were given a low priority.

The literature generally assumes that DCF methods are appropriate for all organisations, regardless of context. Such distancing of the technical from the organisational is increasingly coming under question. Employment of sophisticated tools and formal approaches to decision making does not suit all organisations — the process will vary with a firm's external environment and internal characteristics. A number of studies have developed contingency frameworks which highlight the significance of such characteristics in the design of accounting systems (Waterhouse and Tiessen 1978; Gordon and Miller 1976). Extending this notion to capital budgeting, effective and efficient allocation of resources depends to a great extent on how well the investment process fits the corporate context. For example, DCF methods and formal risk analysis may well be appropriate in larger, capital-intensive, decentralised organisations operating in high-technology industries and with a management which feels comfortable with analytical decision methods. But smaller organisations, preferring a more interpersonal managerial approach, may find sophisticated techniques distinctly unhelpful. A director in a major brewing company admitted that his firm's sophisticated investment process left 'little room for entrepreneurs to manoeuvre. Perhaps a new breed of manager has to develop who is prepared to live with such systems.' Alternatively it could be argued that the price of investment sophistication is too great if it stifles the intuitively-minded manager.

The relevance of the DCF methods is also questioned on pragmatic grounds. Executives remain sceptical that adoption of such techniques actually results in a discernible improvement in performance. Indeed, a major reason for the slow acceptance of DCF methods may be the apparent lack of evidence that it improves performance. As one executive explained:

> Over-sophisticated financial tools will be avoided since there is no guarantee whatsoever that they will achieve more accurate forecasts than the methods currently used.

Empirical studies examining the association between investment sophistication and performance offer little support either (Klammer 1973; Pike 1983b). The associations found between the use/non-use of various techniques and the profitability for each firm suggest that the *more* profitable firms tend to operate *less* sophisticated investment techniques. It would, of course, be unwise to suggest a causal relationship based on cross-sectional data. The relationship between sophisticated methods and performance is undoubtedly complex, requiring more thorough analysis. Nonetheless, managers have every right to be sceptical of advanced techniques which neither they nor academics have been able to demonstrate to be cost effective in practice.

The final reason for disenchantment with DCF methods arises more from *errors in application* than from the model itself. Time and again one observes critical errors in the way theory is applied by managers. Usually these errors are biased against investment. To illustrate this point, a few of the more common examples of errors are summarised below.

1. Cash flows are specified in today's money (excluding inflation), while hurdle rates are based on the money cost of capital, including inflation.
2. Hurdle rates are based on a pre-tax basis while operating cash flows are calculated after tax.
3. Hurdle rates are adjusted upwards to compensate for non-economic statutory and welfare investments.
4. Managerial aversion to uncertainty and obsolescence frequently results in unrealistically short project lives or conservative terminal values.
5. Use of a single cut-off rate instead of a risk-adjusted rate: this leads to deferral of low-risk/low-return replacement projects, sometimes indefinitely. Yet such projects tend to carry far lower degrees of uncertainty. A recent survey of 87 investment failures was unable to find a single replacement investment failure (Honko 1982).

The shortcomings of DCF methods have led to the allegation by Hayes and Garvin (1982) that —

> The discounting approach has contributed to a decrease in the willingness to invest. Is it pure coincidence that in the period of most rapid growth in the use of sophisticated techniques we have seen a slowing up or decline in capital investment?

Preference for IRR

Table 15.3 shows that in 41 per cent of the firms surveyed the internal rate of return is the *primary* appraisal method employed. This is in stark contrast to the theoretically more acceptable net present value approach, which is the primary method in only 17 per cent of firms surveyed. Why does management have such a clear preference for the IRR method? It is surely not on theoretical grounds for, as outlined in Chapter 4, the IRR has a number of technical shortcomings compared with the NPV method. Nor is the preference based on ease of computation — it is actually more complicated to compute, if only because it involves repeated application of the same calculation. Discussions with financial managers suggest that there are three main reasons for their preference for the internal rate of return.

Project Ranking

The first reason given is that the IRR is a convenient method for choosing from mutually exclusive projects or in selecting projects when capital rationing prevails. Comparison between alternatives, it is argued, is simplified by ranking projects according to their rate of return. Although such an approach possesses a certain intuitive appeal, it is exactly in this area that the IRR is most suspect. Its use in the evaluation of mutually exclusive investment options cannot be condoned unless very careful steps are taken to modify the model. One such modification would be to calculate the IRR for the differential cash flows of the options under evaluation. Consider the following mutually exclusive investment options, *X* and *Y*:

	Cash Flows						
Year	*0*	*1*	*2*	*3*	*4*	*IRR*	*NPV @ 10%*
Option *X*	−18,896	8,000	8,000	8,000	8,000	25%	6,463
Option *Y*	−18,896	0	4,000	8,000	26,164	22%	8,290
Y − *X*	0	−8,000	−4,000	0	18,164	16.7%	

Project rankings reveal that *X* has the higher internal rate of return, but the lower net present value. The correct approach to calculating the internal rate of return for investment alternatives is:

1. Calculate the incremental cash flows between the two options.
2. If the internal rate of return on the incremental cash flows is above the opportunity cost of capital, accept the option with the *smaller* IRR.[5].

Applying this to our example, the internal rate of return on the differential cash flows for option *Y* over option *X* is 16.7 per cent. As this exceeds the cost of capital estimate of 10 per cent, project *Y* should be accepted in preference to project *X*, thus concurring with the net present value decision outcome.

Timing

Another reason why management prefers the internal rate of return is that it permits separation of the IRR *calculation* from its *application* as a decision rule. The analyst can concentrate on the data collection and cash flow estimates which combine to produce a proposal's internal rate of return estimate. Management then receives the proposal and decides where to place the cut-off rate.

This approach has obvious practical advantages, particularly in large divisionalised firms where project preparation, evaluation and approval are conducted at different stages and at different levels in the organisational hierarchy. It permits the decision maker to apply the most current cost of capital estimate without necessitating further computation, as in the case of net present value. As we saw in Chapter 8, the cost of capital estimate should reflect the degree of risk for the particular project under consideration. This risk assessment is generally difficult to quantify and may alter during the decision process. Such changes are far easier to accommodate using the IRR method.

A further practical advantage of distancing the DCF calculation from the cut-off rate concerns the 'numbers game' commonly played within divisionalised organisations, particularly when top management imposes annual capital budget ceilings. Under such competition for a limited available amount of finance, divisional management may feel obliged to submit proposals based on somewhat over-optimistic forecasts to ensure that the 'essential' elements of its investment programme are approved. (It must be said that this is sometimes encouraged by top management setting unrealistically high target cut-off rates.) A cut-off rate is, therefore, seen as a number to beat rather than the criterion for assessment. When such behaviour is prevalent, it may not be appropriate to communicate the cut-off level to divisional management. Central management would then adjust the required rate of return, not simply for the degree of underlying project risk, but also for the perceived degree of optimism in the underlying forecasts.

Psychology

The popularity of the IRR is in part psychological: managers simply prefer a measure of investment worth which is expressed in percentage terms. From the following comments by executives, it is clear that they feel far more comfortable with a discounting approach based on a rate of return than on value:

> 'People are familiar with rates of return.'
> 'Percentages are more readily understood by authorising bodies.'
> 'I can't see the net present value meaning much to a non-accountant — or even an accountant for that matter!'

In the final analysis, it seems that managers much prefer the internal rate of return to the net present value method. If so, we suggest that, rather than impose a slightly more theoretically sound method on a reluctant management team, the IRR method should be *properly* applied. However, the simple rule we recommend is: when in doubt — use net present value.

The Role of Traditional Measurement of Investment Worth

Over the years managers have developed and come to rely upon a number of simple rule-of-thumb approaches to analyse investment worth. Two of the most popular of these traditional methods are the payback period and the undiscounted accounting rate of return, both of which are described in greater detail in Chapter 4. We are here interested in examining whether they have a valuable role to play in the modern capital budgeting process. Do they in fact offer anything to the decision maker that cannot be found in the DCF approaches?

Accounting Rate of Return (ARR)

The use of the rate of return on capital employed as a tool for evaluating an organisation's past performance and as a criterion for assessing the acceptability of planned operating activities is well established. As Table 15.2 reports, a little over half the companies surveyed employ the accounting rate of return approach in assessing investment decisions. This is not altogether surprising, seeing that the rate of return on capital remains the single most important financial goal in practice. Despite the theoretical shortcomings referred to in Chapter 4, there has been a certain amount of support for the ARR in the literature.[6] Part of the case in favour of retaining the ARR lies in the fact that its absence leads to an inconsistency between methods commonly used to *report* a firm's operating results and the techniques most frequently employed to *appraise* investment decisions. This inconsistency is most acutely experienced where the manager of an investment centre is expected to use a DCF approach in reaching investment decisions while his short-term performance is being judged on a return on investment basis. Little wonder then that the divisional manager generally shows a marked reluctance to enter into these profitable long-term investment decisions producing low returns in the early years.

An assumption commonly held by managers is that the accounting rate of return and the internal rate of return produce much the same solutions. While there is a relationship between a project's discounted returns and the ARR, the relationship is not a simple one. Consider an investment costing £10,000 and generating an annual stream of net cash flows of £3,000. Assuming a straight-line depreciation policy, the relationship between the internal rate of return and the accounting rate of return calculated on both the total investment and the average investment is as shown below:

Project duration (years)	5	10	20	40
IRR (%)	15.2	27.3	29.8	30
ARR on total investment (%)	10	20	25	27.5
Deviation from IRR	−5.2	−7.3	−4.8	−2.5
ARR on average investment (%)	20	40	50	55
Deviation from IRR	+4.8	+12.7	+20.2	+25

From this example the following general observations may be drawn: the accounting rate of return on total investment consistently *understates*, and the accounting rate of return on average investment *overstates*, investment proposals' internal rates of return. The case for retaining the accounting rate of return is, in our view, only valid when applied as a secondary criterion to highlight the likely impact on the organisation's profitability upon which the divisional manager is judged.

Charm of Payback

While academic writers have almost unanimously condemned the use of the payback period as misleading and worthless in reaching investment decisions, Table 15.2 shows that it continues to flourish as the most widely applied formal technique, being employed in 79 per cent of firms surveyed. In this section we attempt to explain this phenomenon and to ascertain whether the payback period does possess certain qualities not so apparent in more sophisticated approaches.

The two main objections to payback are well known: it ignores all cash flows beyond the payback period and it does not consider the time-shape of the project's cash flows within the payback period. Although such theoretical shortcomings could fundamentally alter a project's ranking and selection, it would seem that the payback criterion possesses more internal theoretical strength than it is sometimes credited with; for the majority of investment proposals it provides a reasonable approximation to the current decision obtained in applying the net present value rule. As Hoskins and Mumey (1979) point out, one reason for this is that the two fundamental objections referred to above counteract each other to some extent. Consider the following example: two mutually exclusive projects each have an investment outlay of £20,000 and an estimated life of eight years. Only the annual net cash flows differ: over the first four years project *A* has a uniform annual series of £5,000, while project *B* has first-year cash flows of £8,100 declining thereafter at the rate of one-third of the previous year's cash flow.

Project	*Year* 1	2	3	4	*Total*	*Present value @ 15%*
A	5,000	5,000	5,000	5,000	20,000	14,275
B	8,100	5,400	3,600	2,400	19,500	14,867

Ranking these proposals according to their payback would lead to project *A* (with a four-year payback) being accepted; but, applying a discounted payback approach which considers the time-shape of cash flows within the payback period, project *B* offers a higher present value over the first four years.

In many cases, however, the time-shape of cash flows in the early years has an informational content with regard to the later years. Data collection in the later years is a difficult and costly business, and the estimates so obtained are often subject to a considerable degree of uncertainty. In the absence of specific information to the contrary, it is not unreasonable to assume that for most projects the time-shape of the cash flows within the payback calculation is a fair predictor of post-payback cash flows. This gives rise to the following:

Project	*Year* 5	6	7	8	*Present value 1–8 @ 15%*
A	5,000	5,000	5,000	5,000	22,436
B	1,600	1,067	711	474	16,555

When all cash flows are included in the computation, project *A* is seen to be the better option and the only project with a positive net present value, after deducting the £20,000 investment outlay. It will be recalled that this accords with the payback ranking. This example illustrates that in ranking projects using a simple payback method, the error from ignoring post-payback cash flows is, to some extent, compensated by the error arising from failure to consider the time value of money in the payback calculation. It should be noted that these 'compensating errors' only arise where the early cash flows are a reasonable predictor of later cash flows.

Having discussed the two main theoretical objections to payback, we can now proceed to examine some of its practical merits.

1. Profitability

The payback period provides a measure of investment profitability (see Weingartner 1969; Sarnat and Levy 1969). When the annual cash receipts from a project are uniform, the payback reciprocal is the internal rate of return for a project of infinite life, or a good approximation to this rate for long-lived projects.

Chapter 4 defined the internal rate of return as that rate which equates the present value of cash receipts with the initial investment outlay:

$$\frac{A_1}{(1+R)} + \frac{A_2}{(1+R)^2} + \ldots\ldots \frac{A_n}{(1+R)^n} - C = 0$$

where

A = the net cash flow receipts
R = the internal rate of return
C = the present value of the investment outlay

Applying the simplifying assumptions that the net cash flow receipts, A, are constant, this formula can be rewritten as:

$$\frac{A}{1 + R}\left[1 + \frac{1}{(1+ R)} + \frac{1}{(1 + R)^2} + \ldots\ldots + \frac{1}{(1 + R)^{n-1}}\right] - C = 0$$

After summing the geometric progression within the square brackets and rearranging we obtain:

$$R = \frac{A}{C} - \frac{A}{C}\left(\frac{1}{1 + R}\right)^n$$

As the investment life approaches infinity the last term tends towards zero, leaving

$$R = \frac{A}{C}$$

It will be seen that this expression is also the payback reciprocal. Thus, in the case of long-lived projects where the cash inflows are, on average, spread evenly over the life of the project, the payback reciprocal is a reasonable proxy for the internal rate of return.

Executives generally show a definite preference for a rate of return measure rather than an absolute measure such as net present value. A project offering a four-year payback period with relatively stable annual cash returns can conveniently be converted into a 25 per cent internal rate of return (i.e. the reciprocal of payback period). However, if the project life is only ten years, the IRR would fall to 21 per cent — some four points below the payback reciprocal. In fact, the payback reciprocal consistently overstates the true rate of return for finite project lives. Here, perhaps, is the key: whereas it was noted earlier that the application of discounting approaches tends to be biased *against* investment, payback period — when used as a profitability criterion — is biased in *favour* of investment. The one tends to counteract the other, leaving the decision maker to exercise judgement and consider the non-quantitative aspects.

2. Constraint

Payback period provides a simple, reasonably efficient measure for ranking projects when constraints prevail. The most obvious constraint is the time managers can devote to initial project screening. Only a handful of the investment ideas originally generated may stand up to serious and thorough financial investigation. Payback period serves as a simple, first-level screening device which, in the case of marginal projects, tends to operate in their favour and permits them to go forward for more thorough investigation.

Many firms resort to payback period when experiencing liquidity constraints (see Pass and Pike 1983). Ranking projects according to their ability to repay quickly, although possessing certain intuitive logic, can lead to sub-optimal solutions. Such a policy may make sense when funds are constrained and better investment ideas are in the pipeline. This could arise, for example, where a major strategic investment is to be made two years hence, and when capital rationing conditions prevail. The attractiveness of investment proposals considered during the interim period will be more a function of their ability to pay back rapidly than their overall profitability.

3. *Uncertainty*

Payback period is seen as a useful tool in times of high levels of uncertainty and inflation. Whereas more sophisticated techniques attempt to model the uncertainty surrounding project returns, payback period assumes that risk is time related; the longer the period, the greater the chance of failure. The high levels of inflation and worldwide recession experienced in recent years have rendered the task of forecasting cash flows highly speculative; but for the most part cash flows are correlated over time. If the operating returns are below the expected level in the early years they will tend to influence later years adversely — the greater the degree of correlation, the greater the dispersion. Discounted cash flow, as practised in most firms, ignores this increase in uncertainty over time. Early cash flows, therefore, have an important information content on the degree of accuracy of subsequent cash flows. By concentrating on the early cash flows, payback chooses to base its evaluation on data in which managers have greater confidence. Should such evaluation provide a different signal from DCF methods, it highlights the need for a more careful consideration of the project's risk characteristics.

The final quality of payback period discussed here concerns general acceptability at all management levels. Why do managers feel more 'comfortable' with payback period than with DCF? In the first place, its acceptability is a function of its simplicity. The non-quantitative manager is reluctant to rely on the recommendations of sophisticated models when he lacks both the time and expertise to verify such outcomes. Confidence in and commitment to a proposal depend to some degree on how thoroughly the evaluation model is comprehended. Another useful role for payback period is as a communication device. It offers a convenient shorthand for the desirability of each investment that is acceptable at all levels of the organisation, namely: how quickly will the project recover its initial outlay? Some firms use a project classification system in which the payback period indicates how rapidly proposals should be processed and put into operation.

Ultimately, it is the manager — not the method — who makes investment decisions and is appraised on their outcome. An evaluation method, therefore, has to be assessed in terms of its value both *ex ante* and *ex post*. In the latter case, payback is particularly attractive to managers not only because it is convenient to calculate and communicate, but also because it signals good investment decisions at the earliest opportunity.

As the above discussion has sought to convey, while the payback concept may lack the refinements of its more sophisticated evaluation counterparts, it possesses many endearing qualities which make it irresistible to most managers. Herein lies the secret of its resilience. One finance executive summed up the situation:

> Certain managers have been campaigning to use payback but I have argued that to have two appraisal techniques would be misleading.

Time will tell whether similar campaigns by managers to retain or return to payback period are successful.

Summary

This chapter has provided an empirical overview of the capital investment appraisal practices adopted within organisations from earliest times up to the present day. The trend over the past thirty years or so has shown an unmistakable growth in the application of discounted cash flow methods, of which the primary method in use is the internal rate of return. Three general observations may be made:

1. Investment appraisal methods employed in many firms are simpler but theoretically less satisfactory than those recommended in earlier chapters. In many cases, however, their theoretical shortcomings are compensated for by their practical advantages.
2. There are growing signs of disillusionment with discounted cash flow approaches. Although this may in part be reduced by greater management awareness of the concepts involved and the errors in its application, it is unlikely that DCF will ever become a panacea for every investment problem.
3. Most firms employ some combination of appraisal methods in which payback is almost universally a part. Each method has its own particular advantage; for some this may simply be that it is easy to understand and communicate.

It is the task of the financial manager in industry to identify those criteria which are most useful in the capital investment decision process of the particular firm. Where some combination of methods is selected, it is also necessary to establish the procedure to be followed when methods offer conflicting rankings or acceptance advice. Finally, we would again remind the reader that none of the methods considered can produce a definite decision, but they can act as a decision *guide*. Most investment projects are sufficiently complex that only a part of them can be assessed quantitatively. The decision maker must ultimately *decide*.

Questions

1. Your boss tells you, 'All this *new* stuff they teach at business schools on capital budgeting may be OK in theory — but it's of no use to me!' Try to explain to him that DCF is not as new as he thinks.
2. Discuss the validity of the following comments made by finance executives:

   'We use payback in support of other methods. It is not sufficiently reliable a tool to be used in isolation.'

   'When liquidity is under pressure payback is particularly relevant.'

   'It helps to give some idea of the riskiness of the project — a long time to get one's money back is obviously more risky than a short time.'
3. A project costing £20,000 offers an annual cash flow of £5,000 over its life.

   (i) Calculate the internal rate using the payback reciprocal assuming an infinite life.
   (ii) Use tables to test your answer assuming the project life is (a) 20 years (b) 8 years.
   (iii) What conclusions can be drawn as to the suitability of payback reciprocal in measuring investment profitability?

4. State whether the following rule-of-thumb approaches under- or over-state the internal rate of return.

   (i) Payback period
   (ii) Accounting rate of return on total investment
   (iii) Accounting rate of return on average investment

5. Payback is a much maligned method which is useful in both project ranking and selection. Discuss.
6. 'At present the methods which are most commonly used to report a firm's operating results are inconsistent with those appraisal techniques which are most frequently advocated as being necessary for sound investment decisions.' Discuss.
7. 'If the trend towards DCF methods continues there will soon be only a handful of organisations not employing this technique.' Discuss this statement in the light of recent UK experience.

8. Most capital budgeting textbooks strongly recommend NPV, but most firms prefer IRR. Explain.
9. Your firm uses the IRR method and asks you to evaluate the following mutually exclusive projects:

	Cash flows				
	0	*1*	2	3	4
Proposal *L*	−47,232	20,000	20,000	20,000	20,000
Proposal *M*	−47,232	0	10,000	20,000	65,350

   Using the appropriate IRR method, evaluate these proposals assuming a required rate of return of 10%. Compare your answer with the net present value method.
10. The evidence of many recent studies suggests that there are major differences between current theories of investment appraisal and the methods by which firms actually evaluate long-term investments. For example, the Wilson Committee on the Financing of Industry and Trade reported in 1980 that 'high inflation has greatly increased the uncertainty of business forecasts and has led some companies to abandon the orthodox DCF technique and place more emphasis on payback period and cash flow.'
    You are required to:
    (a) present the theoretical arguments for the choice of Net Present Value as the best method of investment appraisal;
    (b) explain why, in practice, the Internal Rate of Return method has proved to be consistently more popular with decision makers than the Net Present Value method;
    (c) explain the continued popularity among decision makers of non-discounting methods of investment appraisal.

    (ICA, PE II, December 1982)

Notes:

1. An excellent discussion of the history of investment decisions may be found in Parker (1968).
2. Two of the earliest writers are Boulding (1935) and Samuelson (1935).
3. A list of some of the main surveys conducted on both sides of the Atlantic is provided at the end of the chapter.
4. A critique of the methodologies used in comparing capital budgeting surveys is found in Rosenblatt and Jucker (1979), Rappaport (1979) and Agarwal (1980).
5. This was developed by Weingartner (1963).
6. See, for example, Lerner and Rappaport (1968), Searbey (1975), Longbottom and Wiper (1977) and Mepham (1978).

References

Adelson, R. M. (1970) 'Discounted cash flow — can we discount it?' *Journal of Business Finance*, Summer.

Agarwal, R. (1980) 'Corporate use of sophisticated capital budgeting techniques: a strategic perspective and a critique of survey results', *Interfaces*, April.

Boulding, K. (1935) 'The theory of a single investment', *Quarterly Journal of Economics*, May.

Coase, R. H. (1938), 'Business organisation and the accountant', *Accountant*, October 1–December 17.

Dean, J. (1951) *Capital Budgeting*, Columbia University Press.

Gordon, L. A. and Miller, D. (1976) 'A contingency framework for the design of accounting information systems', *Accounting, Organisations and Society*.

Hastie, K. L. (1974) 'One businessman's view of capital budgeting', *Financial Management*, Winter.

Hayes, R. H. and Garvin, D. A. (1982) 'Managing as if tomorrow mattered', *Harvard Business Review*, May–June.

Hirshleifer, J. H. (1958) 'On the theory of optimal investment decisions', *Journal of Political Economy*, August.

Honko, J. (1982) *Critical Areas of the Capital Investment Process of Enterprises*, Helsinki School of Economics.

Hoskins, C. G. and Mumey, G. A (1979) 'Payback: a maligned method of asset ranking?' *Engineering Economist*, Fall.

King, P. (1975) 'Is the emphasis of capital budgeting theory misplaced?' *Journal of Business Finance and Accounting*, Spring.

Klammer, T. D. (1973) 'The association of capital budgeting techniques with firm performance', *Accounting Review*, April.

Lerner, E. M. and Rappaport, A. (1968) 'Limit D.C.F. in capital budgeting', *Harvard Business Review*, September–October.

Longbottom, D. A. and Wiper, L. (1977) 'Capital appraisal and the case for average rate of return', *Journal of Business Finance and Accounting*, vol. 4, No. 4.

Lutz, F. and Lutz, V. (1951) *The Theory of Investment of the Firm*, Princeton University Press.

Mepham, M. J. (1978) 'A reinstatement of the accounting rate of return', *Accounting and Business Research*, Summer.

Merret, A. J. and Sykes, A. (1963) *The Finance and Analysis of Capital Projects*, Longmans.

Parker, R. H. (1968) 'Discounted cash flow in historical perspective', *Journal of Accounting Research*, Spring.

Parker, R. H. (1980) 'History of accounting decisions', in J. Arnold, B. Carsberg, and R. Scapens (eds) *Topics in Management Accounting*, Philip Allan.

Pass, C. L. and Pike, R. H. (1983) 'Investment constraints in British industry: a managerial perspective', *Journal of General Management*, Summer.

Pike, R. H. (1982) *Capital Budgeting in the 1980s*, Institute of Cost and Management Accountants.

Pike, R. H. (1983a) 'A review of recent trends in formal capital budgeting processes', *Accounting and Business Research*, Summer.

Pike, R. H. (1983b) 'Sophisticated capital budgeting systems and their association with corporate performance', *Managerial Decision Economics*.

Pike, R. H. (1984) 'DCF trends and the problem of nonresponse bias' *Managerial Finance*, Vol. 10, No. 3.

Rappaport, A. (1979) 'A critique of capital budgeting questionnaires', *Interfaces*, May.

Rosenblatt, M. and Jucker, J. (1979) 'Capital expenditure decision-making: some tools and trends', *Interfaces*, February.

Samuelson, P. A. (1937) 'Some aspects of the pure theory of capital', *Quarterly Journal of Economics*, May.
Sarnat, M. and Levy, H. (1969) 'The relationship of rules of thumb to the internal rates of return: a restatement and generalisation', *Journal of Finance*, June.
Searbey, F. W. (1975) 'Return to return on investment', *Harvard Business Review*, March–April.
Solomon, E. (1959) *The Management of Corporate Capital*, The Free Press.
Stevin, S. (1582) 'Tafalen van interest', in D. J. Struik (ed.) (1958) *The Principal Works of Simon Stevin*, Swets and Zeitlinger.
Vandel, R. F. and Stonich, P. J. (1973) 'Capital budgeting: theory or results?' *Financial Executive*, Autumn.
Waterhouse, J. H. and Tiessen, P. (1978) 'A contingency framework for management accounting systems research', *Accounting, Organisations and Society*.
Weingartner, H. M. (1963) 'The excess present value index: a theoretical basis and critique', *Journal of Accounting Research*, August.
Weingartner, H. M. (1969) 'Some new views on the payback period and capital budgeting decisions', *Management Science*, Autumn.
Wellington, A. M. (1887) *The Economic Theory of the Location of Railways*, Wiley.
Wilson Committee (1980) *Report of the Committee to Review the Functioning of Financial Institutions*, HMSO.

Further Reading: Surveys

The reader wishing to delve more deeply into the practical aspects of capital budgeting may find the following references covering some of the surveys conducted in the United Kingdom and America of interest.

UK Surveys

Carsberg, B. and Hope, A. (1976) *Business Investment Decisions under Inflation: Theory and Practice*, Institute of Chartered Accountants in England and Wales.
Pike, R. H. (1982) *Capital Budgeting in the 1980s*, Institute of Cost and Management Accountants.
Rockley, L. E. (1973) *Investment and Profitability*, Business Books.
Scapens, R. W. and Sale, J. J. (1981) 'Performance measurement and formal capital expenditure controls in divisionalised companies', *Journal of Business Finance and Accounting*, Autumn.
Westwick, C. A. and Shohet, P. S. D. (1976) *Investment Appraisal and Inflation*, Research Committee Paper No. 7, Institute of Chartered Accountants in England and Wales.

American Surveys

Boersema, J. M. (1978) *Capital Budgeting Practices Including the Impact of Inflation*, The Canadian Institute of Chartered Accountants.
Fremgen, N, J. (1973) 'Capital budgeting practices: a survey', *Management Accounting*, May
Gitman, L. J. and Forrester, J. R. Jr. (1977) 'A survey of capital budgeting techniques used by major U.S. firms', *Financial Management*, Fall.

Gort, M. (1951) 'The planning of investment: A study of capital budgeting in the electrical power industry', *Journal of Business*, April and July.

Heller, W. W. (1951) 'The anatomy of investment decisions', *Harvard Business Review*, March.

Hoskins, C. and Dunn, M. (1974) 'The economic evaluation of capital expenditure proposals under uncertainty', *Journal of Business Administration*, Fall

Istvan, D. F. (1961) *Capital Expenditure Decisions: How They Are Made in Large Corporations*, Indiana University.

Kim, S. H. (1979) 'Capital budgeting practices in large corporations and their impact on overall profitability', *Baylor Business Studies*, November–December.

Klammer, T. (1972) 'Empirical evidence of the adoption of sophisticated capital budgeting techniques', *Journal of Business*, July.

Mao, J. C. T. (1970) 'Survey of capital budgeting: theory and practice', *Journal of Finance*, May.

Neuhauser, J. J. and Viscione, J. A. (1973) 'How managers feel about advanced capital budgeting methods', *Management Review*, November.

Petty, J. W., Scott, D. F. Jr., and Bird, M. M. (1975) 'The capital expenditure decision-making process of large corporations', *The Engineering Economist*, Spring.

Rosenblatt, M. J. (1980) 'A survey and analysis of capital budgeting decision processes in multi-division firms', *The Engineering Economist*, Summer.

Schall, L. D., Sundem, G. L. and Geijsbeek, W. R. Jr (1978) 'Survey and analysis of capital budgeting methods', *Journal of Finance*, March.

16

The Capital Investment Process

The focus of attention so far in this book has been directed towards the appraisal of investment options. Similar emphasis is found in much of the capital budgeting literature, the assumption being that application of theoretically correct methods leads directly to optimal investment selection and, hence, maximises shareholders' wealth. The decision maker is viewed as having a passive role — acting more as a technician than as an entrepreneur. Somehow investment ideas come to the surface; assumptions and cash flow estimates are made; risk is incorporated within the discount formula to produce the project's net present value. If positive, the proposal becomes part of the admissible set of investment possibilities. This set is then further refined by the evaluation of mutually exclusive projects and the appraisal of projects under capital rationing, where appropriate. Inherent in this approach to capital budgeting are the following assumptions:

1. Investment ideas simply emerge.
2. Projects can be viewed in isolation, i.e. projects are not interdependent.
3. Risk can be fully incorporated within the net present value framework.
4. Non-quantifiable investment considerations are unimportant.
5. Cash flow estimates are free from bias.

Increasingly, it has become apparent that the emphasis on investment appraisal rather than on the whole capital investment process is misplaced and will not necessarily produce the most desirable investment programme (see Haynes and Solomon 1962; Bromwich 1970; Adelson 1970; Cooper 1975; Bower 1970; King 1975). The important question raised in this chapter is: how can an organisation develop a framework within which sound and successful investment programmes can operate? This does not necessarily imply the use of sophisticated methods or procedures. K. L. Hastie (1974) writes:

> I am continually amazed at the academic community's preoccupation with refining capital expenditure analysis rather than with improving investment decisions... Investment decision making could be improved significantly if the emphasis were placed on asking the appropriate strategic questions rather than on increasing the sophistication of measurement techniques.
>
> 'One businessman's view of capital budgeting', *Financial Management*, Winter, p. 36.

Managers need to re-evaluate the investment procedures within their organisation, not to determine whether they are aesthetically and theoretically correct, but to determine whether they allow managers to make better decisions. The capital investment process may be subdivided into four main areas.

Project Generation

(a) Search for investment opportunities which tie in with corporate strategy.
(b) Screen proposals to see if they are worth investigating in more detail.
(c) Define the project.
(d) Determine the alternative investments available.
(e) Collect data and develop assumptions.

Project Evaluation

(a) Calculate the incremental cash flow benefits.
(b) Measure the net benefits.
(c) Assess the effect that different assumptions have on the project's measured results.
(d) Analyse the risks of the project.
(e) Weigh the benefits and strategic purpose of the project against its risk and the constraints of the organisation.

Project Authorisation

(a) Prepare and approve the total planned capital expenditure within the annual capital budget.

(b) Communicate the capital appropriation requests for each proposal together with the back-up material to the appropriate authorisation level.
(c) Investment decision made (accept, reject, modify).

Project Implementation

(a) Monitor and control implementation stage.
(b) Evaluate the progress and expected outcome of the investment decision.

This process is also illustrated in Figure 16.1 and discussed in greater detail in subsequent sections.

Investment Opportunities

Economic theory views investment as the interaction of the supply of capital and the flow of investment opportunities. It would be a mistake to assume from this that there is a continuous flow of investment opportunities presenting themselves for evaluation. Only investment 'problems' give themselves up, such as the machine that breaks down beyond repair during a job for a valued customer. In general, the earlier an investment opportunity is identified, the greater is the scope for reward.

For any organisation there exists a potential set of investment opportunities which match the prescribed corporate objectives and strategy. It is management's task to conduct a creative search to identify this set. Many larger companies are aware of this and place heavy emphasis on innovation and development, but even the smaller firms can, at little additional expense, place a higher priority throughout the organisation on encouraging early identification of investment opportunities. It is difficult to know quite how much attention should be given to project generation. The costs of ignoring opportunities do not show up directly in the income statement while the costs of searching (research and development, management time, etc.) do.

Capital Budget

Most firms prepare an annual capital budget which lists the planned investment projects for each operating unit (bottom-up proposals) together with the strategic projects planned by senior management. Our survey (Pike 1983) found that 65 per cent of firms surveyed prepared a capital budget for more than two years ahead. Many companies require rough estimates of

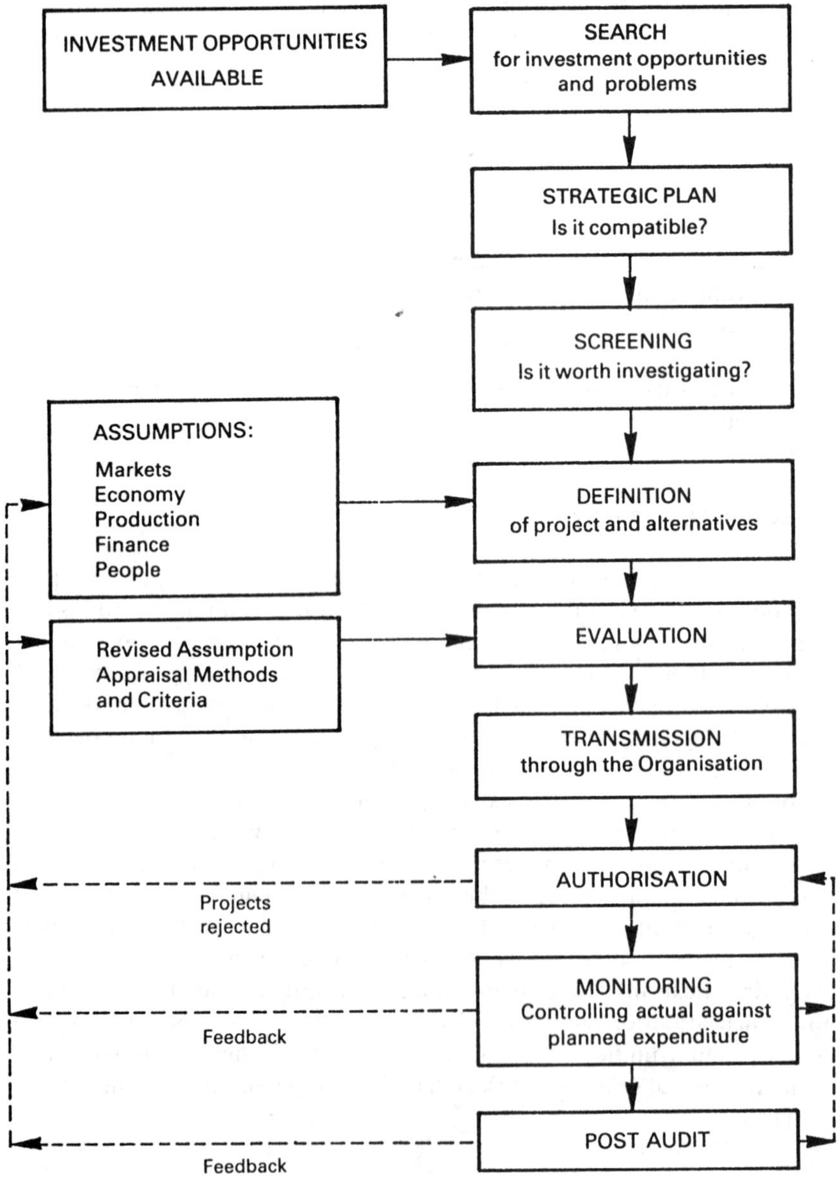

Figure 16.1 Capital Investment Process

capital expenditures over a five or even a ten-year period. Once prepared, the capital budget is reviewed by senior management and corporate financial staff and finally approved as the basis for planning over the coming year. This does not normally imply specific approval of each project within the capital budget. This must be submitted at the appropriate time via capital appropriation requests and usually requires considerably greater analysis than is given in the capital budget.

Management must decide on the extent to which the investment process is to be decentralised. This implies determining which investments are to be delegated to subordinate managers subject only to scrutiny in total (within the capital budget). One simple method is to delegate all investment proposals falling below a given amount. Other methods delegate according to the nature of the project, e.g. 'strategic' proposals, 'high risk' projects or projects not incorporated in the capital budget may require authorisation at a higher level. Most large companies (74 per cent in our survey) have capital budget manuals containing instructions and checklists covering the important procedures in the investment process.

Strategic Considerations

The capital budgeting system should not view projects in isolation — accepting those offering positive net present values and rejecting all else. It forms an integral part of the firm's corporate planning process and must, therefore, be consistent with business goals and strategies. The investment process, or resource-allocation process as it is sometimes referred to, is the main vehicle by which strategy is implemented. Hall (1979) quotes one chief planning officer: 'Allocating resources to investments without a sound concept of divisional and corporate strategy is a lot like throwing darts in a darkened room.'

The attractiveness of investment proposals coming from different sectors of the firm's business portfolio depends not only on the rate of return offered, but also on the strategic importance of the sector. By way of example we will discuss the Boston Consulting Group approach which describes the business portfolio in terms of relative market share and rate of growth as shown in Figure 16.2. This two-by-two matrix identifies four product markets within which a firm may operate: 'stars' (high market share, high market growth), 'cash cows' (high market share, low market growth), 'question marks' (low market share, high market growth) and 'dogs' (low market share, low market growth). The normal progression of a product over time, as shown in Figure 16.2, starts with the potentially successful product ('question mark') and moves in an anti-clockwise direction, eventually to be withdrawn (divested). From this strategic analysis of the firm's business portfolio we suggest the pattern of resource allocation outlined in Figure 16.2.

Figure 16.3 shows how this analysis aids resource allocation strategy. Businesses offering high growth and the possibility of acquiring market dominance are the main areas for investment ('stars' and 'question marks'). Once such dominance is achieved the growth rate declines and investment is only necessary to maintain market share. These 'cash cows' become funds

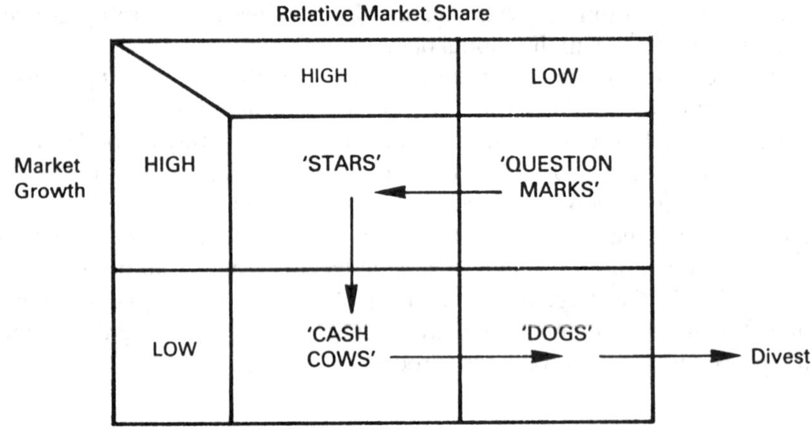

Figure 16.2 Normal Progression of Product over Time

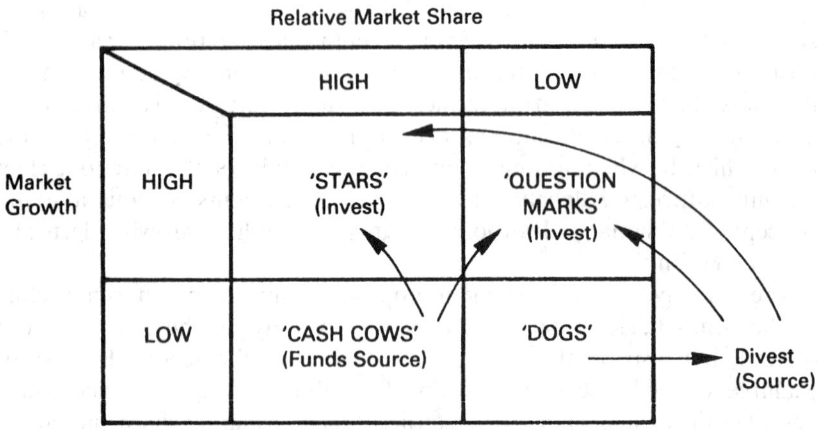

Figure 16.3 Investment Strategy

generators for other growth areas. Business areas which have failed to achieve a sizeable share of the market during their growth phase ('dogs') become candidates for divestment and should be evaluated accordingly. Any cash so generated should be applied to high-growth sectors.

The above method is one of many approaches available to the firm in determining the impact of strategy on resource allocation. Having developed its investment strategy, it can then assess individual projects in terms of where they fit into the firm's long-term strategic plan. It will be recognised from this that project appraisal or, in the case of capital shortage, project ranking, is not simply judged according to the rates of return. Many companies will reject projects offering high returns because they fall outside strategic thinking. Ultimately, the capital budget must tie up with corporate strategy so that each project contributes to the implementation of some element of that strategy.

Screening Proposals

It is neither feasible nor desirable to conduct a full-scale evaluation of investment opportunities until they are properly defined. The screening process is an important means of filtering out projects which, for one reason or another, are not worth investigating further. The screening stage should consider the following:

1. Is the investment opportunity compatible with corporate strategy? Does it fall within a section of the business designated for growth, maintenance, or divestment?
2. Are the resources required by the project available? (e.g. expertise, finance, etc.)
3. Is the idea technically feasible?
4. What evidence is there to suggest that it is likely to provide an acceptable return?
5. Are the risks involved acceptable?

As the quality of data used at the screening stage is generally poor, it makes little sense to apply sophisticated financial analysis. Accordingly, the simple payback method is frequently used at this stage because it offers a crude assessment of project profitability and risk.

Definition

An investment proposal is vague and shapeless until it has been properly defined. At the definition stage of the capital investment process detailed specification of the investment proposal is made involving the collection of data describing its technical and economic characteristics. For each *proposal* a number of alternative *options* should be generated, defined, and subsequently appraised in order to create the project offering the most attractive financial characteristics.

Even at this early stage proposals are gaining commitment. The very act of collecting information necessitates communicating with managers who may either lend support or seek to undermine the proposal. In this process Aharoni (1966) found that commitments are accumulated until a situation is created which leads almost inevitably to investment. The amount of information gathered for evaluation is largely determined by the data perceived as desirable to gain a favourable decision, by the ease of its development, and by the extent to which the proposer will be held responsible for later performance related to the data (Carter 1971).

Classification of Investments

The information required and method of analysis will vary according to the nature of the project. A suggested investment proposal classification is given below:

1. Replacement
2. Cost reduction
3. Expansion or improvement
4. New products
5. Strategic
6. Statutory and welfare

Replacement proposals are justified primarily by the need to replace assets that are nearly exhausted or have excessively high maintenance costs. Little or no improvement is expected from the replacement, but the expenditure is essential to maintain the existing level of capacity or service (e.g. replacement of vehicles). Engineering analysis plays an important role in these proposals.

Cost reduction proposals are intended to reduce costs through addition of new equipment or through modification to existing equipment. Line managers and specialists (such as industrial engineers and work study groups) should conduct a continuous review of production operations for profit improvement opportunities.

Expansion or improvement proposals relate to existing products, and are intended to increase production, service and distribution capacity; to improve product quality, or to maintain and improve the firm's competitive position.

New products proposals refer to all capital expenditure pertaining to new products.

Strategic proposals are generated at senior management level and involve expenditure in new areas, or where benefits go beyond the investment itself. A project may offer a negative net present value and yet, in a wider sense, create wealth. Three examples demonstrate this point:

(i) Diversification projects may have the effect of bringing the company into a lower risk category (this assumes that specific risk is important, as may be the case for a family-controlled company).

(ii) A patent may be acquired not for use within the firm, but to prevent its use by competitors.
(iii) Where information is difficult to obtain, such as in overseas markets, it may make sense to set up a small plant at a loss because it places the firm in a good position to build up information and to be ready for major investment at the appropriate time.

Statutory and welfare proposals do not usually offer a financial return, although they may contribute in other ways. The main consideration is whether standards are met at minimum cost.

Each proposal should be ranked within each category in terms of its effect on profits, its degree of urgency, and whether or not it can be postponed.

Critical proposals are capital projects which must be carried out in the current year to avoid some emergency or significant cost penalty.

Desirable proposals are projects which are highly profitable or otherwise important to the firm.

Necessary proposals are similar to critical proposals except that the timescale is longer — that is, they can be postponed for one or more years if insufficient finance is available.

Evaluation

The evaluation stage involves the assembly of information in terms of inputs and outputs and the application of specified investment criteria to produce the optimum capital project mix. A firm must decide whether to apply rigorous, sophisticated evaluation models or use models sufficiently simple to understand yet sufficiently complicated to embody the most important relationships holding in the real world. We saw in Chapter 15 that most firms operate a number of investment criteria. An investment evaluation is only as good as the assumptions upon which it rests. Careful consideration is required regarding the influence on the investment of such key factors as markets, the economy, production, finance and people. In the following section a brief check-list of questions outlines the most important considerations.

Marketing Factors

1. To which segment of the market does the investment proposal relate?
2. How critical is the proposal to the marketing strategy?
3. Does the asset life exceed the economic life of the product?
4. What market research has been conducted to support the marketing assumptions within the proposal?

5. In the case of an expansion proposal:

   (a) has the market reached or passed its peak?
   (b) can projected volume increases be sold?
   (c) how will such increases affect market size, prices and margins?
   (d) could a price war result from a reduction in price to achieve higher volumes?

6. In the case of a new product, has the product been fully tested?

Production Factors

1. What stage has the product specified in the investment proposal reached in its life cycle (gestation, development, maturity, decline)? How does this relate to the assumptions concerning volume, unit cost and selling price?
2. Is there any known experience of the use of the proposed investment

   (a) within the organisation?
   (b) outside the organisation?

   If so, how can such experience be drawn upon?
3. Can the production facilities adequately achieve the quality, timing and cost specifications assumed by the proposal?
4. How will the investment affect capacity utilisation in the short and medium term?

Financial Factors

1. How is the discount rate applied to this proposal justified?
2. Does the project give rise to any special financing opportunities (e.g. low-cost loans linked specifically to the project)?
3. Have 'at best' and 'at worst' scenarios been quantified in addition to the actual assumptions?
4. Has sensitivity analysis been conducted? What percentage fall in key assumptions is required for the project to become unacceptable?
5. To what extent does the riskiness of the project arise from microeconomic factors (i.e. *specific* risk, such as changes in competition) or from macroeconomic factors (i.e. *market* risk, such as government economic policies)?

External Economic Factors

1. To what extent is the project's success sensitive to fluctuations in the following external economic factors?

(a) foreign exchange movements
(b) commodity prices
(c) inflation rates
(d) interest rates
(e) government economic and fiscal policies

2. To what extent is the project's viability dependent upon government grants and other inducements? What costs (economic and social) are incurred? (For example, relocation of a factory induced by generous government incentives may result in the transfer of staff who will be dependent on the continuation of the project.)

'People' Factors

A major reason why projects do not live up to their original expectations is because 'people problems' are ignored. Major projects create structural changes and affect managerial motivation.

1. Will the proposal require additional manning or further training?
2. Is management able to cope with the proposal?
3. Is the individual/team sponsoring the proposal best suited to implementing it?
4. Are existing management structures and procedures adequate for the new investment?
5. What effect will the new investment have on management and the existing work force?
6. Have the work force and trade unions been properly consulted?

Authorisation

Following evaluation, the proposal is transmitted through the various authorisation levels of the organisational hierarchy until it is finally approved or rejected. Bower (1970) suggests that the central force in the decision process is the willingness of the manager to commit himself to sponsor a proposal. This he decides not so much on the grounds of the proposal itself as on whether or not it will enhance his reputation as a manager and his career prospects. Bower cites several examples where those involved in the preliminary investigation and appraisal of major projects were promoted into head office decision-making positions in time to support and speed the approval of the same projects.

In larger organisations the authorisation of major projects is usually a formal endorsement of commitments already given. Complete rejection of proposals is rare but proposals are, on occasions, referred back. The approval stage would appear to have a two-fold purpose:

1. Quality control function. As long as the proposals have satisfied the requirements of all previous stages there is no reason for their rejection other than on political grounds. Only where the rest of the investment planning process is inadequate will the approval stage take on greater significance in determining the destiny of projects.
2. Motivational function. An investment project and its proposer are inseparable. The decision maker, in effect, forms a judgement on the proposal and the person or team submitting the proposal at the same time. As one decision maker put it to us:

> 'Obviously if we think Joe (divisional sponsor) has performed wonderfully well in the past it will have an important bearing on how we evaluate doubtful projects. We would normally back his judgement the first two or three times, but eventually it comes down to whether Joe is the right person for running the business.'

Sometimes the costs associated with rejection of capital projects, in terms of managerial motivation, far exceed the costs associated with accepting a marginally unprofitable project. The degree of commitment, enthusiasm and drive of the management team implementing the project is a major factor in determining the success or failure of marginal projects.

Project Control

Thus far in this chapter we have dealt with the various steps leading up to the investment decision. This is by no means the end of the process. Once a firm commits itself to a particular project, it must regularly and systematically evaluate the assumptions and other factors upon which the decision was made and monitor the progress of the project through its various stages of implementation. When changes to those assumptions and planned cash flows are significant, management must then ask what changes are necessary regarding either the particular investment or the decision-making process. A full discussion of the control aspects is beyond the scope of this book. Attention is directed to the control of projects in progress and the role of post audits.

Controlling Projects in Progress

The capital appropriation request approved at the decision stage will stipulate the total amount and timing of capital spending, but the real control of expenditure commences with the placing of orders. Ordering involves:

1. precise specification of requirements in terms of delivery and erection time scales, performance and performance proving time;

2. selection of suppliers to submit quotations;
3. selection of the best quotation.

Major investment projects may justify determining the *critical path* in the delivery and installation schedule. The critical path is defined as the longest

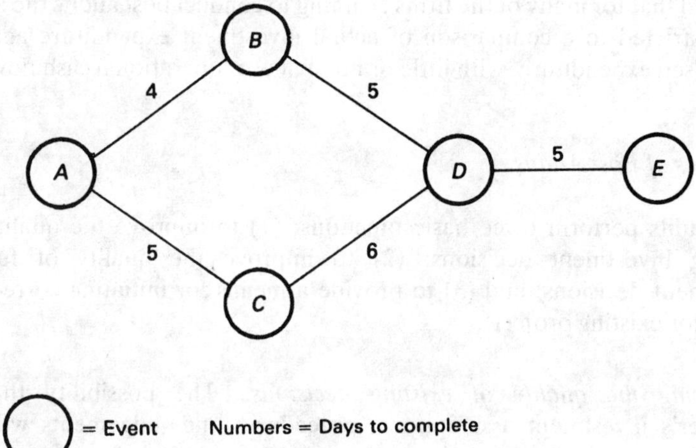

Figure 16.4 Critical Path

path through a network. Figure 16.4 illustrates the point. In practice, determining the critical path is frequently more complex. Control is established by accounting procedures for recording expenditures. Progress reports usually include actual expenditure; amounts authorised to date; amounts committed against authorisations; amounts authorised but not yet spent; and estimate of further cost to completion. It is common to find that firms allow projects to be overrun by up to 10 per cent before supplementary appropriation requests have to be submitted. Our survey (Pike 1983) found that 81 per cent of firms review major projects if cost overruns are likely.

Post Audit

Any control system requires a feedback loop indicating how well the system is operating. Post audits can usefully be employed to fulfil this role within the investment performance process. A post — or project — audit is defined as:

> ... an objective and independent appraisal of the measure of success of a capital expenditure project in progressing the business as planned. The appraisal should

> cover the implementation of the project from authorisation to commissioning and its technical and commercial performance after commissioning.
>
> ICMA 1984

Our survey revealed that post audits were regularly employed on major projects in 48 per cent of responding firms. Closer examination, however, revealed that for many of the firms claiming to conduct post audits the audit was restricted to a comparison of actual investment expenditure against authorised expenditure, with little or no review of operational cash flows.

Purposes of Post Audits

Post audits perform three basic functions: (1) to improve the quality of existing investment decisions; (2) to improve the quality of future investment decisions; and (3) to provide a means for initiating corrective action for existing projects.

Improving the quality of existing decisions. The possibility that a manager's investment assumptions, procedures and judgements will be audited at a later date may endanger further effort on his part to improve the quality and accuracy of input data and curb the natural tendency for undue levels of optimism. Over-optimistic investment performance projections are often encouraged by senior management setting unrealistically high investment hurdle rates. The possibility that such bias in forecasting will be detected at the audit review may discourage or reduce the bias.

Of course, post audits may be counterproductive if they lead managers to adopt unduly conservative projections or if the rewards for success appear less attractive than the penalties for failure. This may result in fewer projects being generated, particularly of the high-risk, high-return variety. It is important, therefore, that post audits are not viewed as recriminatory post mortems, but rather as means of encouraging accurate and thorough project analysis.

Improving the quality of future decisions. Post audits perform an extremely useful role in allowing managers to profit in the future by avoiding the mistakes of the past. Unlike most other managerial decisions, it takes many years before the success or failure of capital investment decisions is fully realised. This is further complicated by the lack of investment performance data generated through the normal accounting process, and the likelihood that managers do not expect to remain with the firm for the whole of the project's life. A post audit, conducted within one or two years of a project's implementation, provides important feedback to managers responsible for the quality of decision inputs. This should enable managers to learn from experience and avoid the same mistakes on future investment proposals. Post audits should produce timely feedback information on why a project failed to live up to its promise and reduce the chance of failure for future projects. For example:

Was sufficient data gathered to support the estimates?
What specific errors were made in assumptions and forecasts?
Were the risks adequately assessed?
What improvements should be made to the decision process?

Post audits are not merely concerned with financial analysis. An investment project should be designed to answer specific strategic questions. The audit should help determine how well the investment outcome fits the strategic question asked of it. If a project is essentially aimed at increasing market share it will be audited very differently from one whose purpose is to improve employee morale.

One of the problems in using post audits as a means of estimating the degree of systematic bias in analysts' forecasts arises from the fact that post audit samples are themselves biased. Brown (1974) points out that the total set of proposals generated by a manager must be examined to assess any bias in forecasting. Assume a manager generates a set of four proposals in a year with planned net present values of −£2,000, −£1,000, +£1,000 and +£2,000. The expected net present value of these projects is zero. Assume also that the *actual* net present value for each project is zero, i.e. any differences arise from random forecasting errors. Senior management, applying the NPV criterion, would only accept the two projects with positive net present values, totalling £3,000. When the post audits on these projects reveal that the actual net present values total to zero, they might naturally conclude that the manager making such forecasts was systematically biased in his forecasting. In fact it is the post audit sampling frame that is biased because it excludes rejected proposals (which never see the light of day). Senior management should take care not to jump to erroneous conclusions in estimating systematic bias in forecasts and would do well to encourage managers to make more reliable forecasts than to attempt to adjust managers' forecasts for anticipated systematic bias. This problem is particularly acute in risky projects where the variability surrounding unbiased estimates is high.

Basis for corrective action. A third purpose of post audits is to review the project with a view to its future prospects. Where variations from actuals are significant, or where key assumptions are no longer valid, the future of the investment in its originally-intended form should be questioned. It may be that a project appears to be far more profitable than planned, and this could lead to an expansion of the investment or bring the next phase of development on stream earlier. Where the variances are adverse, it may lead to a more thorough review with the possibility of the contraction or abandonment of the project.

Post Audit Programme

Prior to the investment decision being taken, a programme for post audit should be designed covering such questions as whether an audit is required, when it is to be conducted, the procedures involved, and the person(s) responsible for conducting it.

Audits can be expensive and time consuming and it is therefore unlikely that all projects will be reviewed. Among those selected for audit the scale of investigation may differ. Selection of projects for audit will depend on the potential benefits available. In terms of the benefits from existing projects this will usually include large, high-risk projects where significant adverse variances are critical to overall profitability. Greatest potential for control arises in projects where heavy cash outflows arise in the later stages of the project's life. In terms of improving the quality of future decisions, a reasonable cross-section of projects is desirable in order to assess the forecasting ability of various management teams and individuals. Post audits should not be restricted only to poorly performing projects, as this gives rise to the idea that their purpose is primarily to apportion blame. One reason for deciding on the projects to be reviewed at the selection stage is that this will ensure that both good and poor projects are examined.

It is common to exclude from review, projects where the availability of information is excessively difficult or costly to collect. For example it is well-nigh impossible to evaluate the wisdom of investment decisions for mutually exclusive projects or when capital rationing conditions prevail as there is no available information on rejected projects. An audit programme should be designed for each project where a post audit is required. Preferably, the programme should be designed at the evaluation stage of the decision process and should form part of the proposal submitted for approval.

To avoid unnecessary cost and time in the conduct of audits the programme should concentrate on those assumptions and events that are critical to the net present value estimate. Sensitivity analysis will identify those assumptions and variables having greatest impact on a project, and the programme should detail how they are to be reviewed. Attainment of the expected net present value may hinge on certain critical events taking place. Will competitors react to a new product by reducing prices or introducing better products themselves? Will legislation be introduced that might prejudice the projects? For instance, new pollution or safety control requirements might be introduced in a country to which we intend to export. Will the planned reduction in manning levels assumed in the proposal be accepted by the workforce and trade unions? Such critical events may have a major impact on project profitability and, if so, the audit should concentrate on them. They will also influence the timing of the audit. If, for example, the major critical event is the number of repeated orders placed by customers following the initial launch of a new product, this may be known within six months of the investment, and thus an early post audit may be appropriate.

Proper design of the audit programme in terms of critical assumptions and events and timing will assist the auditor in explaining variance from the planned cash flow estimates. These variances should then be further analysed into *controllable* or *non-controllable* events and *predictable* or *non-predictable* assumptions. Such an analysis assists in evaluating whether forecasting errors arose largely from biased estimating and inadequate project control.

The timing of the post audit review is an important consideration. While many firms adopt a specific time span (e.g. one year following completion), it is preferable to set review dates prior to critical decision points. This may fall, for example, prior to the second phase of development. A policy of reviewing projects when, say, 10 per cent of capital expenditure is committed is a useful guide when the purpose of audit is primarily as a basis for corrective action.

The procedures involved in a post audit programme must vary according to purpose and project. Most audits should consider the following:

1. *Background to the investment project.* It is easy to forget the original purpose of the investment and to judge it according to the wrong criteria. If, for example, the main motivation behind a capital outlay is to improve the organisation's image it would be foolish to assess it purely on economic grounds.

2. *Comparison of actual and currently projected performance with originally anticipated performance*. Emphasis should be placed on those factors which have deviated significantly from original projections, particularly those which may have caused delay in completion, changes in investment, or may have affected the profit-generating potential of the project.

3. *Economic indicator comparison.* Using the information generated above, the economic indicator (such as net present value) can be calculated and compared with the original project projection. Deviations in excess of a prescribed range for acceptable forecasting errors would require additional analysis and comment. Where significant adverse deviations arise, sufficient information should be prepared to enable a judgement to be formed on the need for a full reappraisal before abandonment.

4. *Audit recommendations and conclusions*. Audit reviews are costly exercises which can only be justified if specific proposals are made on ways in which the investment process in general and project projections in

particular can be improved, or if action plans are proposed to improve the profitability of the current project. In particular the conclusions should specify the lessons learned from the investment project; these could suggest improvements in future investment appraisals. It is also relevant to include in this section non-economic aspects, such as the impact of the investment on employee morale, corporate image, and environmental aspects. Such social costs and benefits commonly have a longer-term profit impact on the organisation.

5. *Feedback*. Finally, it is imperative that relevant parts of the audit review are communicated to the appropriate personnel so that investment procedures and practices improve as a result of the audit. Ultimately, the cost of conducting post audits must be weighed against overall corporate benefits to be derived from their use. These benefits are a dynamic multiple of the sum of specific project benefits.

Summary

The resource allocation process is the main vehicle by which business strategy can be implemented. We have seen that investment decisions are not simply the result of applying some evaluation criterion. The investment decision process is essentially one of search: search for ideas, search for information, search for alternatives, and search for decision criteria. The prosperity of a firm depends more on its ability to create profitable investment opportunities than on its ability to appraise them.

Once a firm commits itself to a particular project, it must regularly and systematically monitor and control the project through its various stages of implementation. Post audit reviews — if properly designed — fulfil a useful role in improving the quality of existing and future investment analysis and provide a means of initiating corrective action for existing projects.

Questions

1. 'Capital budgeting is simply a matter of selecting the right decision rule.' How true is this statement?
2. Outline the important stages in the capital budgeting process.
3. Why might allocating resources to investments without a sound concept of divisional and corporate strategy be linked to 'throwing darts in a darkened room'?
4. What are the aims of post audits?
5. Discuss the value of post audits. Who should conduct them? When should they be carried out? What should they entail?

6. Discuss how bias and forecasting errors may creep into the investment process. What steps can be taken to reduce them?
7. Investment evaluation is as much an appraisal of the proposer as the proposal. Do you agree?

References

Adelson, R. M. (1970) 'Discounted cash flow — can we discount it?', *Journal of Business Finance*, Summer, pp. 50–66.

Aharoni, Y. (1966) *The Foreign Investment Decision Process*, Harvard Graduate School of Business.

Bower, J. L. (1970) *Managing the Resource Allocation Process: A Study of Corporate Planning and Investment*, Harvard University.

Bromwich, M. (1970) 'Capital budgeting — a review', *Journal of Business Finance*, Autumn, pp. 3–26.

Brown, K. C. (1974) 'A note on the apparent bias of net revenue estimates for capital investment projects', *Journal of Finance*, September.

Carter, E. E. (1971) 'The behavioural theory of the firm and top-level corporate decisions', *Administrative Science Quarterly*, December, pp. 413–427.

Cooper, D. J. (1975) 'Rationality and investment appraisal', *Accounting and Business Research*, Summer, pp. 198–202.

Hall, W. K. (1979) 'Changing perspectives on the capital investment process', *Long Range Planning*, February, pp. 37–40.

Hastie, K. L. (1974) 'One businessman's view of capital budgeting', *Financial Management*, Winter, pp. 36–44.

Haynes, W. and Solomon, M. (1962) 'A misplaced emphasis in capital budgeting', *Quarterly Review of Economics and Business*, February, pp. 39–46.

ICMA (1984) *Capital Expenditure Control*, Management Accounting Guide.

King, P. (1975) 'Is the emphasis of capital budgeting theory misplaced?', *Journal of Business Finance and Accounting*, Spring, pp. 69–82.

Pike, R. H. (1983) 'A review of recent trends in formal capital budgeting processes', *Accounting and Business Research*, Summer, pp. 201–208.

Further Reading

Boersema, J. M. (1978) *Capital Budgeting Practices Including the Impact of Inflation*, Canadian Institute of Chartered Accountants.

Johnson, R. W. (1981) 'Theory and policy of public audit', in F. Derkinderen and R. Crum (eds) *Readings in Strategy for Corporate Investment*, Pitman.

Piper, J. (1980) 'Classifying capital projects for top management decision-making', *Long-Range Planning*, June, pp. 45–55.

Sandberg, M. L. (1976) *The Capital Budgeting Process of a Large Rapidly-Growing Franchising Corporation*, Ph.D thesis, Iowa University.

Scapens, R. W. (1980) 'Overview of current trends and directions for the future' in J. Arnold *et al. (eds) Topics in Management Accounting*, Philip Allan, pp. 277–295.

Scapens, R. W. and Sale J. T. (1981) 'Performance measurement and formal capital expenditure controls in divisionalised companies', *Journal of Business Finance and Accounting*, October, pp. 389–419.

Smidt, S. (1979) 'A Bayesian analysis of project selection and post audit evaluations', *Journal of Finance*, June, pp. 675–688.

Vandel, R. F. and Stonich, P. J. (1973) 'Capital budgeting: theory or results?', *Financial Executive*, August, pp. 46–56.

Weaver, J. B. (1974) 'Organizing and maintaining a capital expenditure program', *Engineering Economist*, Spring, pp. 1–35.

17

The Foreign Investment Decision

Thus far discussion of the literature on capital budgeting has been restricted to domestic investment. Many investment decisions have wider implications than the domestic economy, and it is therefore appropriate to devote a chapter to international capital project appraisal.

What is Foreign Investment?

Foreign investment may be divided into *direct* and *portfolio* investment. Portfolio investment refers to the participation in overseas investment without any control over the running of the business. It involves the purchase of loan stock or shares in an overseas organisation. Direct investment refers to a lasting interest in an enterprise in an economy other than that of the investor, where the investor's purpose is to have an effective voice in the management of the enterprise. Such direct investment usually arises from the acquisition of an overseas business or the setting up of an overseas branch or subsidiary.

Foreign investments are different in degree rather than kind. They should not be regarded as fundamentally different from domestic investment although, as will be discussed more fully later, the political structures, economic policies and value systems are more variable. It is therefore not unreasonable to assume that broadly the same capital budgeting approach should be applied to foreign investments as to domestic investments. This is substantiated in a survey by Robbins and Stobaugh (1973), which concluded that 95 per cent of multinational enterprises use precisely the same basis for evaluating domestic subsidiaries as for overseas subsidiaries. Piper (1971) suggests that the foreign investment decision is actually subject to less rigorous analysis: in general, many US firms' overall approach to foreign decision making is much less sophisticated than their domestic approach.

Why Invest Abroad?

Both international and domestic trade are founded on the principle that economic units (whether firms or nations) should specialise where they have some comparative economic advantage. However, no comprehensive economic rationale has yet been satisfactorily developed to explain why and when a company should cease exporting goods to a country and invest directly.

Brooke and Remmers (1977) categorise the reasons for direct foreign investment into economic and defensive. Economic justification covers:

(1) Comparative cost advantages
(2) Scale economies to preserve or improve profit margins
(3) Diversification to secure against over-exposure in any single market
(4) Strategic reasons

Strategic reasons for companies investing abroad are primarily the desire for new markets, production efficiency and new sources of raw materials. Defensive justification is mainly concerned with fear.

Aharoni (1966), in a survey of 38 primary 'market-seeking' US companies which had considered direct investment in Israel, identified four main exogenous reasons for direct investment, as follows:

(i) An outside proposal, provided it comes from a source that cannot easily be ignored. The most frequent sources of such proposals are foreign governments, the distributors of the company's products, and its clients;
(ii) Fear of losing a market;
(iii) The 'band wagon' effect: very successful activities abroad of a competing firm in the same line of business, or a general belief that investment in some area is 'a must';
(iv) Strong competition from abroad in the home market.

Aharoni also found that although the final decision to commit funds was made at the board-of-directors level, this was typically only a formal ratification of the organisational commitments accumulated during the investigation. Financial evaluation and analysis have traditionally then been applied as a screening device to eliminate unacceptable investment proposals, to test the validity of marketing assumptions, and to determine the amount and method of financing the investment.

Evaluation

Corporations increase shareholders' wealth by selecting investments with positive net present values. The evaluation of foreign investments can be viewed from two levels. Firstly, a project can be considered in terms of its viability in its country of operation. The cash-flow analysis will be expressed in local currency and includes:

(a) initial investment outlays in fixed and working capital;
(b) incremental operational cash flows after local taxes and realistically determined transfer charges;
(c) net terminal value based on the estimated market value of the investment at the end of the evaluation time horizon.

The second approach to evaluation is to consider the investment from the parent company viewpoint. Cash flows will be actual receipts and disbursements in parent company currency. These cash flows will include the equity and loans provided, dividends remitted after taxes and other intra-company cash flows, plus the net terminal value

It will be appreciated that the two approaches could give very different cash-flow patterns. This is particularly the case where an overseas operation is expected to be very profitable but unable, because of exchange control regulations, to remit dividends to the parent company. The following illustrates the difference between the two evaluation levels.

Example

Tintinnabulation plc manufactures musical instruments for sale in the domestic market and export abroad. It is currently investigating the possibility of setting up a manufacturing plant in Bongo-Bongo Land (BBL). Initial discussions with the BBL Minister of Economic Development have met with favourable response, providing the project can generate the 10 per cent pre-tax return currently obtained by other firms in that country. The Company requires a project of this kind to earn at least 15 per cent.

The planned investment will be partly import substituting, and partly export based, selling to neighbouring countries. Additionally the local consumption element has been classified as of strategic military and special cultural significance. The project has been offered a tax holiday exempting it from all corporate and income taxes for the first ten years, except to the extent that profits are remitted abroad, in which case a 12½ per cent withholding tax will be deducted. A modern factory on a well-serviced industrial estate has also been proffered at a reasonable rent.

The initial investment by the Company will be £100,000, mostly plant, machinery and commissioning costs, all payable in hard currency by the parent company. Additional finance will come from a bank loan of 200,000 Bongs (note 4฿ = £1 stg.) which has been negotiated with a local bank, and which carries interest at 10 per cent per annum. This will be used to finance working capital. Operating cash flows (upon which tax is assumed to be calculated) are estimated to be ฿100,000 in Year 1 and ฿220,000 thereafter until Year 5. It is proposed that the whole of each year's profit be declared as dividend and repatriated to the UK. In the UK these dividends will be treated as a gross dividend (before BBL withholding tax) subject to corporation tax at the full rate (which is currently 50 per cent). The BBL withholding tax will be allowable as a deduction in calculating the tax paid over to the UK revenue. All such transfers may be treated as arising on the last day of the accounting period to which they relate, at which time all tax becomes due and payable.

It is expected that the new venture will have a small, but significant, effect on the exports which the Company would otherwise have made. This can be expressed as equivalent to £5,000 loss of profit, in after tax terms, for each of Years 2 through to 5.

In order to simplify the evaluation, it is considered that Year 5 will be a cut-off year. At that time the realisable value of the plant and equipment may be taken as ฿240,000. The working capital will be realised, subject to losses on stocks of ฿20,000 and debtors of ฿20,000. These funds will be used firstly to pay off the local bank loan. Any balance remaining will be transferred to the UK without suffering any further tax or restriction. The exchange rate is forecast to remain at ฿4 = £1 until Year 2 when it will change to ฿5 = £1.

Solution

Evaluation of such an overseas project can be viewed from a number of different perspectives. We shall consider three:

(1) Is the project acceptable as far as the BBL economy is concerned?
(2) Is it a wealth-creating project from the foreign subsidiary company's viewpoint?
(3) Is it wealth-creating for the shareholders of the parent company?

Table 17.1 summarises the cash flows for the three levels. Net present values for the three levels are given in Table 17.2. It will be seen that the project meets the country requirement to achieve a 10 per cent return. Discounting the country-level cash flows produces an NPV of £373,100. It

Table 17.1 Project Cash Flows (B000)

	Year 0	1	2	3	4	5
Plant	(400)					
Working capital	(200)					
Operating cash flows		100	220	220	220	220
Realisation of plant						240
Realisation of working capital						160
Country cash flow	(600)	100	220	220	220	620
Loan and interest	200	(20)	(20)	(20)	(20)	(220)
Project cash flow	(400)	80	200	200	200	400
Withholding tax		10	25	25	25	25
Remitted to UK	(400)	70	175	175	175	375
Exchange rate	4	4	5	5	5	5
Sterling equivalent (£000)	(100)	17.5	35	35	35	75
UK tax (50% on profit less withholding tax)		(7.5)	(15)	(15)	(15)	(15)
	(100)	10	20	20	20	60
Loss in exports (after tax)			(5)	(5)	(5)	(5)
Parent company cash flow (£000)	(100)	10	15	15	15	55

Table 17.2

Year	*Country (B000)*	*PV (10%)*	*Project (B000)*	*PV (15%)*	*Parent Co. (£000)*	*PV (15%)*
0	(600)	(600)	(400)	(400)	(100)	(100)
1	100	90.9	80	69.6	10	8.7
2	220	181.7	200	151.2	15	11.3
3	220	165.2	200	131.6	15	9.9
4	220	150.3	200	114.4	15	8.6
5	620	385.0	400	198.8	55	27.3
	NPV	373.1	NPV	265.6	NPV	(34.2)

also achieves a satisfactory £265,650 NPV at the project level in BBL after local financing costs and discounted at the appropriate cost of capital. Alas, however, the project fails to offer an acceptable net present value for the parent company. Why is there such a contrast? You will recall that three additional elements were introduced at this last stage:

(1) deteriorating exchange rates;
(2) UK taxation and withholding taxes; and
(4) effects on the whole business in terms of lost exports.

In our example, all three work against the project to produce a negative NPV of £34,200. The foreign investment proposal, in its present form, does not make economic sense for the shareholders.

Required Rates of Return

Modern capital market theory leads us to conclude that the rate to be applied in discounting project cash flows is the required rate of return for the project's degree of market risk. The problem with this approach is in its practical implementation. The problem is further complicated in the case of overseas investments by the different monetary interest rates and market returns obtainable in various countries and the lack of efficient capital markets in certain countries.

One practical approach towards estimating the cost of capital for foreign investments is to base it on the local opportunity cost of capital. This is the return currently achieved or required for comparable investments in the same country of operation. If the multinational enterprise (MNE) is prepared to operate at a level of return below the opportunity cost of capital, it would mean that the nation's scarce resources are not being utilised efficiently. In the longer term this would hinder good relations with the host government and possibly give rise to government interference. This logic does not apply to short-lived investments where there is currently an underemployment of national resources.

One reason often cited for investing overseas is that by diversifying corporate assets across a number of different countries, the overall business risk is reduced. Domestic investments are all subject to the same underlying economic circumstances. Foreign investments are subject to different economic circumstances, although most countries are to some extent positively correlated with each other economically.

This has been more clearly demonstrated with portfolio investment. Watson (1978) has calculated the correlation coefficients between the monthly rates of return on industrial stock-market indices for seven countries. His findings were that, on average, the inter-country correlation coefficients were approximately +0.55. As this is substantially less than +1 (perfect correlation), it lends support to the belief that international diversification can offer significant benefits beyond those offered by diversification within a single country.

The question which logically follows is whether the obvious diversification benefits can legitimately be extended to foreign direct investment. The answer lies, firstly, in the ability of companies to diversify efficiently direct investments and, secondly, in whether it is desirable. To eliminate most of diversifiable risk requires a portfolio of approximately fifteen randomly selected investments. Although some diversification may be achievable, it cannot be as effective as portfolio diversification as only the large MNEs will invest in fifteen or more countries. Furthermore, most foreign investments are in the same product market as the domestic market and therefore cannot be well diversified. It can also be argued that corporate diversification is not a thing of value. It does nothing that the company's shareholders could not better do themselves by holding a well-diversified world portfolio in bonds and stocks. International diversification of direct investments is not, therefore, a valid means of reducing risk.

Currency Risk

Businessmen do not need to be reminded that currency risk is one of the major problems of overseas investments. We have witnessed in recent years, under the present so-called 'dirty float' system of exchange rates, sterling depreciation against the dollar of up to 5 per cent in a single day. Such movements could effectively wipe out much of the profit on a project. Before discussing how currency risk can be managed, we must first consider exactly what we mean by foreign exchange risk in relation to overseas investments.

The overriding concern in the appraisal of foreign investment is with economic (cash-flow) exposure rather than balance-sheet (translation) exposure. Balance-sheet exposure depends on the asset/liability structure of the investment and on the method used in translating foreign balance-sheet items (closing rate, monetary/non-monetary, current/non-current, etc). Economic exposure considers how the net present value of the investment expressed in parent company currency is affected by exchange-rate movements. The value of an overseas investment is expressed mathematically as:

$$NPV_0 = \sum_{t=0}^{n} \frac{X_t E_t}{(1+r)^t}$$

where

NPV = net present value in parent currency
X_t = after tax net cash flows at time t in local currency
E_t = exchange rate for period t
r = required rate of return required by parent for degree of risk
n = project life

Foreign exchange markets permit the trading of currencies for most of the major importing and exporting countries. Foreign currency can be purchased immediately in the *spot market*, or it can be purchased in the *forward market* for delivery at a specified future time.

Exchange-rate movements are inextricably related to relative movements in inflation and interest rates. We shall consider two explanations of exchange-rate movements.

Purchasing Power Parity Theorem

The purchasing power parity (PPP) theorem states that the rate of change in the spot exchange rate is proportional to the difference between the rates of inflation in the two countries. Purchasing power parity rests on the assumption that in a world where assets can be traded freely, identical assets in different places will only differ in price because of transport costs. Thus, in the longer term the impact of exchange-rate movements or cash flows tends to be offset by countervailing changes in prices. The following formula can be used as a basis for making long-term forecasts of future spot rates of exchange:

$$S_t = S_o \left(\frac{1 + I_D}{1 + I_F} \right)^t$$

where S is measured in units of currency D per unit of currency F and I_D and I_F are the rates of inflation in the domestic and foreign currencies respectively.

Calculation of the net present value for overseas projects should be on the basis of the commercial merits without distortion by the effects of possible exchange gains or losses. Any exposure to exchange-rate movements can, if required, be hedged and should be treated as a separate issue. The PPP proposition provides us with a reasonable longer-term estimate of future exchange rates.

Consider a Manchester-based company which is currently appraising setting up a sales subsidiary in Ohio. Expected incremental cash flows for the project are shown in Table 17.3. The US dollar is currently quoted at 75 pence (direct quote) or \$1.33/£1 (indirect quote). Inflation rates in the United States and the United Kingdom are 4 per cent and 8 per cent respectively. Assuming the PPP proposition holds, the expected future spot dollar rate in, say, two years' time will be:

$$£0.75 \times \left(\frac{1.08}{1.04} \right)^2 = £0.809$$

Table 17.3 gives the forecast exchange rate for Years 1 to 3 based on this calculation. The remittances received in the United Kingdom are then discounted to obtain the project's net present value. If the real discount rate

Table 17.3 Value of an Overseas Project given Purchasing Power Parity

	Year end			
	0	*1*	*2*	*3*
US $ (thousands)				
Project cash flow (all remitted to parent company)	−200	100	200	200
US exchange rate	× 0.75	× 0.779	× 0.809	× 0.839
£ (thousands)				
Remittances received in UK	−150	77.9	161.8	167.8
Discount rate 20%	1.0	0.833	0.694	0.579
Present value	− 150	64.89	112.29	97.16
Net present value £124,340				

for a project with this level of risk is, say, 11 per cent, and given an 8 per cent domestic rate of inflation, the nominal discount rate is computed:

$$(1.11 \times 1.08) - 1 = 0.199$$

or approximately 20 per cent. Applying this rate produces a positive net present value for the project of £124,340.

From the above we can observe that if the domestic rate of inflation exceeds the foreign rate of inflation, the foreign currency will strengthen and more pounds will be required to purchase each unit of the foreign currency. If the PPP theorem holds in the longer term, assets and liabilities denominated in foreign currencies are self-adjusting in value and not exposed to foreign-exchange risk. Exchange risk therefore exists mainly in the shorter term because of unexpected changes in currency values from the anticipated longer-term path.

Interest-Rate Parity Theorem

A second explanation of the difference between the forward and spot rates of exchange is provided by the differences in nominal interest rates in two countries. *Interest-rate parity* (Aliber 1978) implies that in efficient international capital markets, an investor will obtain much the same rate of interest on risk-free investments in different countries once the proceeds have been converted into the domestic currency and currency risks covered. In other words, it assumes that there are no easy profits to be made from lending in currencies where interest rates are higher than in one's own country, or by borrowing in currencies where interest rates are lower. This is because any apparent gain is offset by the cost of covering for the risk of changes in exchange rates in the forward exchange market.

Example

Global plc has just raised £100,000 to finance an investment. As these funds will not be required for twelve months, two options are being considered for its short-term employment.

Option A Invest in a one-year United Kingdom 10 per cent government bond issued and redeemable at par.
Option B Invest in a similar United States bond offering 13 per cent.

On the face of it, the US bond, offering a higher interest rate, looks more attractive. Table 17.4 compares the sterling equivalent of the two investments. The current spot rate of exchange of \$1.25/£1 means that Global's treasurer can raise \$125,000 (ignoring transactions costs) which in one year's time will have a value of \$141,250. To cover the exchange risk, the treasurer will wish to contract to sell the proceeds of the US bond one year hence at the current one-year forward exchange rate of 1.296. This would then yield £108,989, which is very close to the future value of the UK bond.

Table 17.4 Comparison of UK Bond with Covered US Bond under Interest Rate Parity

	UK bond	*US bond*
Spot rate of exchange \$/£		1.25
Cost of bond	£100,000	\$125,000
Interest rate	9%	13%
Interest	£9,000	\$16,250
Future value of bond	£109,000	\$141,250
One-year forward rate of exchange		1.296
Future value of bond in sterling		£108,989

In this example, interest-rate parity is seen to hold. Comparable risk-free transactions in different currencies will yield the same rate of interest when expressed in the same currency and covered for exchange risk. This is because any differences in nominal interest rates are reflected already in differences in the spot and forward exchange rates. What would happen if this were not the case? Assume that the US interest rate falls below 13 per cent but the forward exchange rate is unchanged. Clearly, the UK bond is now more attractive than its US counterpart. Speculators would exploit the situation by selling US bonds and buying UK bonds at the spot rate. At the same time they would 'hedge' their currency exposure by selling sterling in the forward market. In such a manner, the arbitrage process would eventually bring the forward exchange rate into line with the new interest-rate levels and interest-rate parity would return.

What action can be taken to manage investment currency risk? Companies can adopt either a *profit-maximising* strategy or a *risk-minimisation* strategy. The former approach assumes that it is possible to forecast exchange-rate movements. This will lead firms to finance their operations in currencies with minimum expected effective interest costs (i.e. interest plus or minus exchange losses/gains). If a depreciation of local currency were expected, positive net cash flows would be exposed as the company would benefit from such a currency movement.

Unfortunately, it is virtually impossible to forecast consistently short-term currency movements without superior knowledge to that of others in the market. This leads most UK companies to adopt a risk-minimising strategy involving the following steps:

(i) determine how currency movements affect net operating cash flows; and
(ii) select a finance structure, for the subsidiary or within the group, to offset as far as possible the adverse effects of currency movements.

Dufey and Walker (1978) have summarised this:

> Ideally then, the portfolio of assets and liabilities which represents the firm should be structured in such a way that the cost of the liabilities and the cost of servicing these liabilities is affected in a countervailing direction by the same economic event, i.e. the currency movement. In this way, the cash-flow variability resulting from the deviations of an exchange rate from its expected path can be minimised.

Other ways by which economic exposure can be reduced are to:

(i) minimise cash balances and receivables;
(ii) accelerate debt repayments or remittances to the parent company (though this will obviously conflict with the desire to reinvest cash flows in the overseas business); and
(iii) invest surplus funds in assets that will move in line with inflation.

Political Risk

It is hardly surprising that foreign investment by multinational corporations should involve a strong element of political and social risk. Their very size and strength in relation to host nations create the possibility of political action, whether favourable (such as granting generous incentives) or adverse (such as expropriation of assets).

Where the objectives of the host nation and the MNE are clearly at odds with each other, the political risk is heightened. It is not at all easy sometimes for corporations to be clear as to their own objectives, but it is considerably more difficult to ascertain the objectives of various countries.

Political risk is heightened where political and social instability prevails. How can instabilities be defined, identified and predicted? Political and social instability is the result of internal pressures or civil strife which may be caused by such factors as inequalities between various internal factions (whether racial, religious, tribal, etc.), extreme political programmes, recent or forthcoming independence or impending elections. Gurr (1948) argues that *relative deprivation* is the root cause of civil strife and political instability. This perceived deprivation is strong when there exists a sizeable gap between what people believe they are entitled to (value expectations) and what they can obtain (value capabilities). Whether such pressures will lead to outright civil strife, such as recently witnessed in Iran, depends on a number of factors, not least of which is the ability of the government to repress such pressure.

An MNE considering foreign investment may observe the signals of political instability, but to measure the extent is more complex.

A major cause of political and social instability is attributable to economic influences. This has become very apparent for many industrialised as well as developing nations in the 1970s, with two oil crises and their resulting price increases in oil and related imports, deterioration in balance of payments, rampant inflation and a sluggish world economic growth rate.

Economic instability often gives rise to heavy overseas borrowings. The risk of default can be gauged by such factors as the overseas debt service ratio (debt services payments to exports of goods and services), debt age profile, the extent to which such overseas borrowing will finance exports, and the likelihood that domestic savings will eventually replace overseas borrowings. The political risks of such economic pressures will lead to any of the following actions:

(i) exchange controls and currency regulations;
(ii) restrictions on registration of foreign companies (e.g. there must be local equity participation);
(iii) restrictions on local borrowing;
(iv) expropriation or nationalisation;
(v) tax discrimination;
(vi) import controls;
(vii) limitations on access to strategic sectors of industry.

Expropriation (confiscation of corporate assets with or without compensation), asset freezing (loss of control over the management of assets) and nationalisation represent the greatest political threat to foreign investors. The risk is not so much the expropriation itself as the risk that compensation will be inadequate and deferred.

Full-scale, or 'creeping' expropriation (where there are increasing restrictions on prices, issuing work permits, transfer of shares, imports and dividends) is more likely to occur where a nation feels threatened by the size and dominance of multinationals. Thus, before deciding to operate in a new country, a pertinent question to ask is whether the company, individually or collectively with other multinationals, will dominate the industry. If this is a strong possibility, then political risk is greater than when penetration is low.

Managing Political Risk

Managing political risk does not imply that a company can control risk, for risk is by definition an uncontrollable factor. What is possible, to a certain extent, is that such risk can be identified, appraised and sometimes reduced. Lloyd (1976) suggests that political risk management is best applied on a project basis, but it is essentially an overall company approach that involves:

(a) dispassionate analysis of the project and its likely results;
(b) identification of all community groups and organisations that will be affected by, and will possibly react in a significant way to, the project;
(c) comparison of objectives and consequences of the project with the aims of local and national government;
(d) a carefully organised programme of information and involvement using the whole company, which is reflected in the way the total organisation operates and is therefore much more than just another public relations exercise.

The risk-averse company will want either to *avoid* any clear political risk, simply by not investing in such countries, or to *fully insure* against such risks materialising. A number of governments have introduced insurance guarantee programmes such as the Exports Credit Guarantee Department (ECGD) in the UK, and in addition private insurance schemes are often available. Most of these guarantee programmes cover risks for direct investments of:

(i) nationalisation, expropriation and confiscation;
(ii) war, revolution and insurrection;
(iii) restrictions or delays in repatriation of profits and capital.

Generally, it would be uneconomic to cover such risks in all situations. Premiums on government schemes are usually levied on a uniform basis over a wide spread of countries. (It would be politically unwise for governments to reveal their perception of the political risk of other nations by operating a premium risk scale!) It follows, therefore, that relatively risky investments are worth insuring but less risky projects are likely to prove expensive. This third approach to risk management, then, is to accept some degree of political risk after full consideration of the probability and effect of losses being sustained.

A firm is very largely a hostage to future events with no power to influence the future. However, it can so position itself that should adverse events materialise, it will sustain the minimum of discomfort. This requires the prior agreement of risk-minimising policies and contingency plans. Take, for example, an MNE that believes it is economically viable to invest in a developing nation which has recently gained independence, or where there is known tribal conflict and severe economic pressures in terms of inflation and currency value. How can the company manage the high-perceived political risk? A suggested risk-management programme is outlined in Table 17.5.

Table 17.5 Risk Management Programme and Contingency Plan for Major Overseas Direct Investment in Politically Unstable Nations

A. *Reduce probability of political interference*

DO

- Keep informed of social, political and economic developments within the country and of its neighbours and partners
- Monitor government attitude towards overseas investment
- Understand the role and workings of government
- Develop links and skills in dealing with government officials
- Identify with national aspirations and objectives and be a model citizen
- Develop allies with local employees, suppliers and customers
- Use local materials and labour wherever possible
- Train local labour force for technical and managerial positions
- Co-operate in joint ventures or provide local equity participation (if political benefits outweigh economic drawbacks)

DON'T

Antagonise host government by:

(i) major repatriation of capital or profits
(ii) unfair competition with local traders, e.g. price subsidies
(iii) ignoring local customs and cultures
(iv) maintaining foreign or colonial image
(v) over-partisan involvement

B. *Reduce financial consequences of political interference*

- Borrow locally
- Insure risks with insurance guarantee scheme
- Share risks through participation of international agencies in financing
- Pledge corporate assets as collateral

C. *Contingency plan in the event of expropriation, etc.*

- Seek meeting with government for rational negotiation
- Decide on whether voluntary divestiture of ownership is best policy
- Explore legal remedies (locally, overseas or internationally)
- If all else fails, surrender ownership and seek only salvage value

Incentives

One way by which a country can improve its investment climate is through the lure of generous government incentives. These incentives may take many forms including cash grants, tax reliefs or exemptions, low-rate financing cost, financial guarantees, rent-free factories and many more. Incentives are mainly given on a regional basis to reduce unemployment. Companies should therefore first ask why firms are generally reluctant to invest there without the aid of such incentives: perhaps skilled labour is not readily available or there is a strong tradition of poor labour relations and labour productivity.

For some multinationals the incentives offered often determine the investment location. A good example recently lies in the car industry. Ford Europe was seeking to expand its car production capacity at an estimated cost of $5 billion over a three-year period, but because its American parent had to replace its whole model range to meet American government fuel economy regulations, it intended to keep its borrowing to a minimum. In September 1978 it asked Spain, Belgium, Britain, France and West Germany what aid would be offered to set up a plant to produce 750 cars a day. As the Economist (1979) points out: 'Governments which offer ever-higher bribes to get big firms to bring them jobs have no grounds for complaint when the companies play one off against another...' Ford's approach 'shows how one big company's careful gamesmanship shows up the structure of grants, loans, tax holidays, interest subsidies and other promises and caresses that underlie so much of Western Europe's big investment schemes these days.'

Summary

Specific consideration has been given in this chapter to the foreign investment decision. Such decisions involve a number of further complexities rarely found in domestic investments on anything like the same scale. Three such issues discussed in the chapter are the exposures to foreign currency risks and political risks, and the opportunities for generous government-funded investment incentives. Although a more complex problem, the essential approach to evaluating foreign investments in financial terms is little different from that for domestic investments.

Questions

1. Give reasons why a company may decide to make foreign direct investment. To what extent are those reasons purely financial?

2. How does a foreign investment differ from a domestic investment in terms of its appraisal?
3. Does international diversification reduce risk (a) to the firm, and (b) to the shareholders?
4. What action can firms take to 'manage' investment currency risk?
5. Discuss the various forms of political risk to which an overseas investment might be exposed.
6. Dolphins plc is a large UK company which manufactures and sells a range of household goods. It currently has no overseas manufacturing or selling operations. The marketing director has recently returned from an overseas tour and is enthusiastic about the potential market for the products of Dolphins plc in a number of third world countries. The marketing director's enthusiasm is shared by the other directors.

   The company's project analyst has been instructed to prepare a report for consideration by the board of directors on the possibility of meeting this potential demand by setting up a subsidiary company in a third world country to manufacture and distribute Dolphins plc's range of products.

   You are required to discuss the factors to be considered by the project analyst in making recommendations for dealing with the following:

   (a) the financing of the initial investment involved in setting up the overseas subsidiary company
   (b) the remittance of funds from the subsidiary to the UK;
   (c) the variability of exchange rate movements between sterling and the currency of the overseas country in which the subsidiary company would be set up.

   Ignore taxation. (ICA PE II, December 1983)

References

Aharoni, Y. (1966) *The Foreign Investment Decision Process*, Harvard Graduate School of Business Administration, Division of Research.

Aliber, R. (1978) *Exchange Risk and Corporate International Finance*, Macmillan pp. 26–37.

Brooke, M. and Remmers, H. (1977) *The International Firm*, Pitman.

The Conference Board (1966) *US Production and the Balance of Payments*, New York, p. 63.

Dufey, G. and Walker, D. (1978) 'Alternative strategies for managing foreign risk', *Managerial Finance*, Vol. 4, No. 2, pp. 119–130.

Economist, 20 January 1979, p. 72.

Gurr, E. (1948) 'A causal model of civil strife: a comparative analysis', *American Political Science Review*, Vol. LXII, No. 4, pp. 1104–1124.

Lloyd, B. (1976) *Political Risk Management*, Keith Shipment Developments.

Piper, J. (1971) 'How US firms evaluate foreign investment opportunities', *MSU Business Topics*, Summer, pp. 11–20.

Robbins, S. and Stobaugh, R. (1973) 'The bent measuring stick for foreign subsidiaries', *Harvard Business Review*, September/October, pp. 80–88.

School, R. D. (1975) 'The determinants of foreign opportunity attractiveness', referred to in *The Accountant*, 19 June, p. 787.

Watson, J. (1978) 'A study of possible gains from international investment', *Journal of Business Finance and Accounting*, Vol. 5, No. 2, pp. 195–205.

18

Practical Computer Programs for Capital Budgeting

In previous chapters we have discussed many of the theoretical and practical issues surrounding capital budgeting and financial strategies. Some of these issues lend themselves to fairly straightforward but useful computer-based applications. In this chapter we discuss four such applications based on programs developed and listed in the appendices. These programs, written in BASIC[1] are self-documenting and easy to run. The purpose of this chapter is to demonstrate their use in tackling investment problems solved manually in earlier chapters or elsewhere. The four programs discussed are:

Program 1	*Purpose*
Investment Evaluation	Evaluates and ranks projects and conducts sensitivity analysis.
Program 2	
Probability Analysis	Calculates the mean and standard deviation of a project's NPV and performs probability analysis (assumes a normal distribution).
Program 3	
Evaluation of Risky Investments	Evaluates risky investments using weighted average cost of capital and capital asset pricing model approaches.
Program 4	
Simulation Model	Performs risk analysis using the Monte Carlo simulation method.

The relevance of the computer applications in this chapter can be summarized by the flow chart in Figure 18.1.

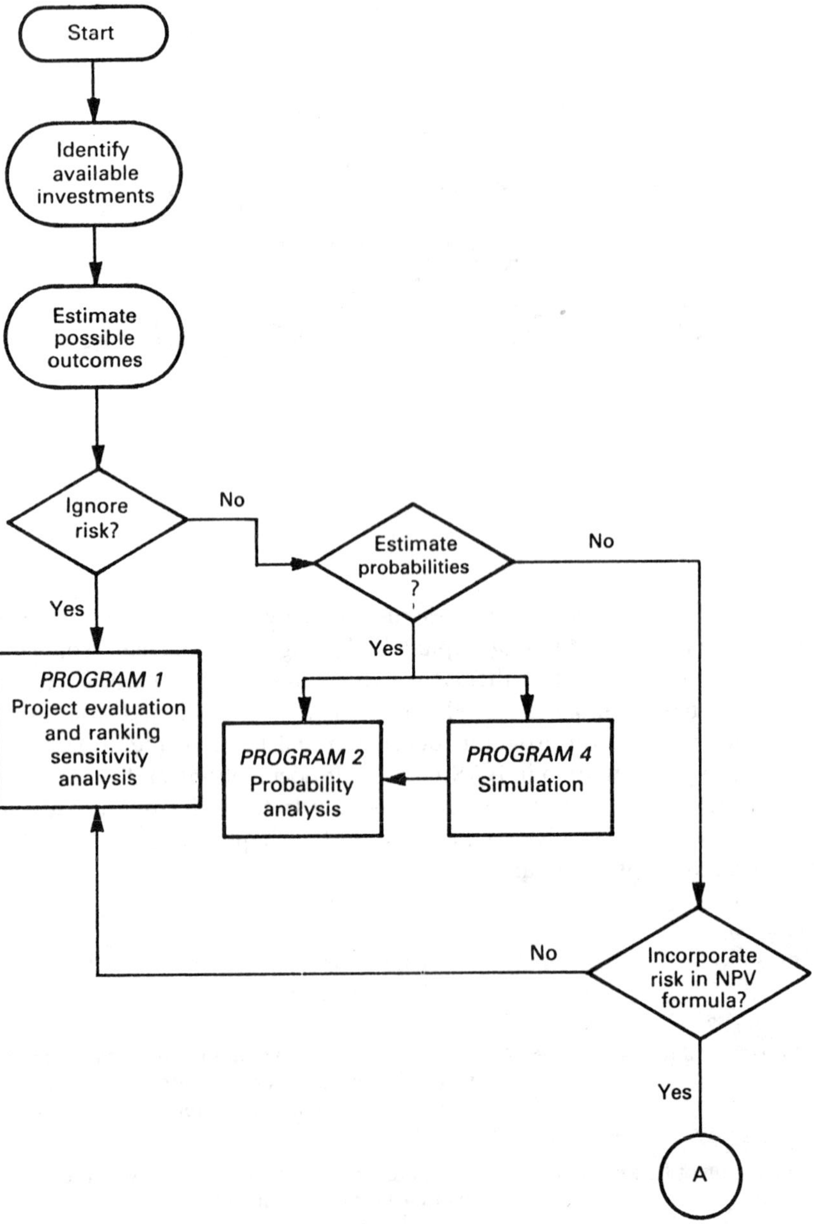

Figure 18.1 Flow Chart for Investment Evaluation Process

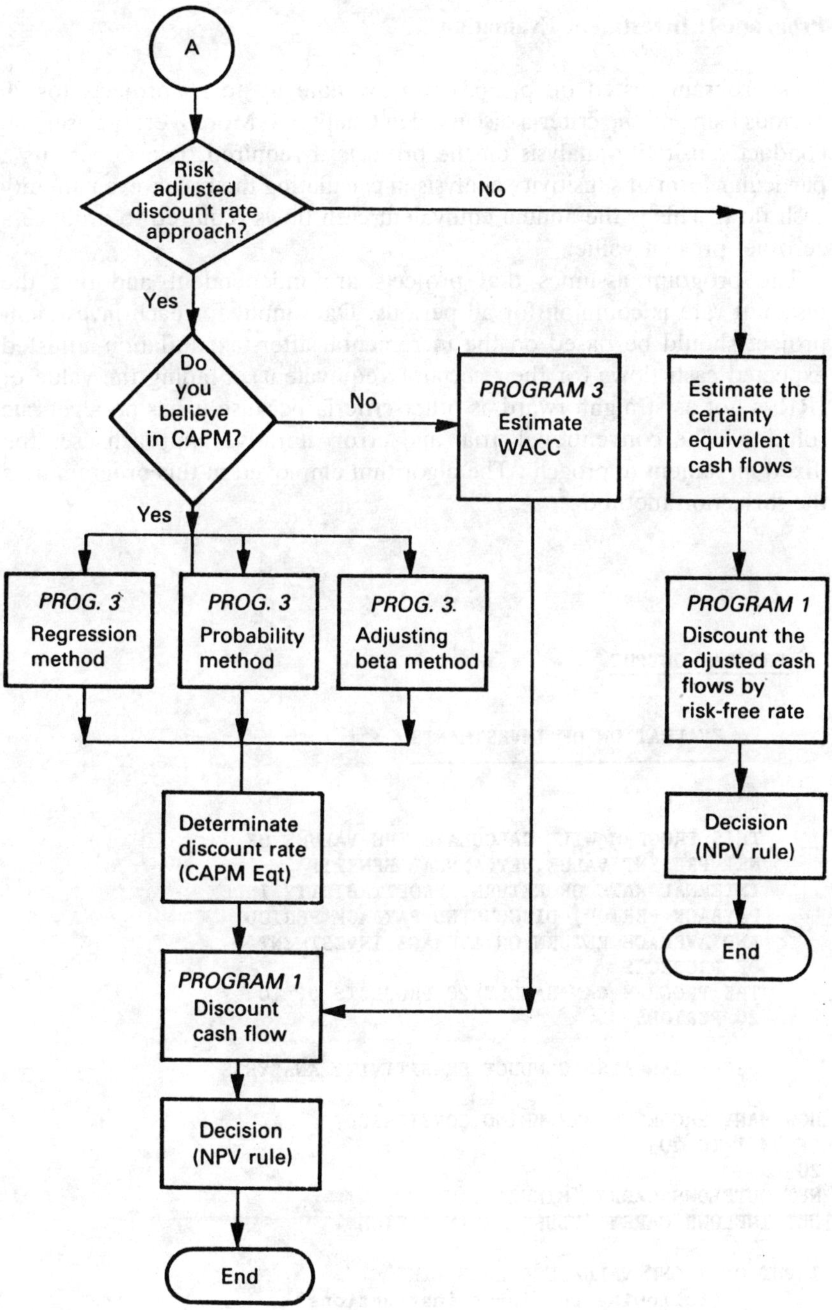
A
Risk adjusted discount rate approach?
No
Yes
Do you believe in CAPM?
No
Yes
PROGRAM 3
Estimate WACC
Estimate the certainty equivalent cash flows
PROG. 3
Regression method
PROG. 3
Probability method
PROG. 3.
Adjusting beta method
PROGRAM 1
Discount the adjusted cash flows by risk-free rate
Decision
(NPV rule)
End
Determinate discount rate (CAPM Eqt)
PROGRAM 1
Discount cash flow
Decision
(NPV rule)
End

Program 1: Investment Evaluation

This program (listed on p. 363) can evaluate up to 20 projects for 20 periods using all the criteria discussed in Chapter 4. Moreover, the user can conduct sensitivity analysis on the projects if required. It also permits a particular form of sensitivity analysis in calculating the break-even annuity cash flow. This is the annual equivalent cash flows required to produce a zero net present value.

The program assumes that projects are independent and that the discount rate is common for all periods. Data input for each investment project should be based on the incremental after-tax, inflation-adjusted expected cash flows (or their certainty equivalent). Finding the value of IRR is not as straighforward as other criteria because it has no algebraic solution. The conventional 'trial and error' iterative approach uses the 'fixed increment approach'. The algorithm employed in this program uses the 'bisection method'.[2]

```
  PROGRAM OUTPUT
  --------------

         EVALUATION OF INVESTMENTS
         -------------------------


      THIS PROGRAM WILL CALCULATE THE VALUES OF
      NET PRESENT VALUE,NET ANNUAL BENEFIT
      INTERNAL RATE OF RETURN, PROFITABILITY INDEX
      PAYBACK PERIOD, DISCOUNTED PAYBACK PERIOD
      AND AVERAGE RETURN ON AVERAGE INVESTMENT
      OF PROJECTS
      THE PROGRAM CAN HANDLE 20 PROJECTS UP TO
      20 PERIODS

      USERS CAN ALSO CONDUCT SENSITIVITY ANALYSIS

HOW MANY PROJECTS ARE BEING CONSIDERED?
(FROM 1 TO 20)
20
NET OUTFLOWS CARRY 'MINUS' SIGN
NET INFLOWS CARRY 'PLUS' OR 'NO' SIGN

INPUT ONLY ONE VALUE FOR EACH LINE
        (following the input instructions)

CASH FLOWS ARE STORED IN COMPUTER
DO YOU WANT TO PRINT OUT THE DATA ?
PLEASE INPUT '1' FOR 'YES','0' FOR 'NO'
1
```

```
                YEAR 0   YEAR 1   YEAR 2   YEAR 3   YEAR 4

PROJECT 1  :  -10000    8000     8000     1000     500
PROJECT 2  :  -10000    500      500      3000     17500
PROJECT 3  :  -1000     800      200      500      500
PROJECT 4  :  -1000     200      800
PROJECT 5  :  -1000     300      300      200      200
PROJECT 6  :  -1000     200      200      200      200
PROJECT 7  :  -1000     600      600      400      200
PROJECT 8  :  -10000    5000     4000     2000     2000
PROJECT 9  :   1000    -3000     2500
PROJECT 10 :  -3000     1000     1000     1000     1000


PLEASE ENTER THE DISCOUNT RATE
FOR EXAMPLE, 10% IS ENTERED AS '10'
10
PLEASE ENTER THE ACCURACY FOR IRR
FOR EXAMPLE, 0.01 MEANS CORRECT TO 2 SIG. FIGURES
0.01

DISCOUNT RATE= 10 %
IRR IS CORRECTED TO .01


PROJECT  NPV       NAB      IRR(%)   PI    PB     DPB    ARAI(%) LIFE

 1       4977.12   1570.14  42.7     1.5   1.25   1.41   88      4
 2       5074.45   1600.84  22.98    1.51  3.34   3.58   107     4
 3       609.73    192.35   38.94    1.61  2      2.29   100     4
 4      -157.02   -90.47    0        .84   2      NEVER  100     2
 5      -192.47   -60.72    0        .81   4      NEVER  50      4
 6      -366.03   -115.47  -8.37     .63   NEVER  NEVER  40      4
 7       478.45    150.94   34.74    1.48  1.67   1.92   90      4
 8       719.9     227.11   13.99    1.07  2.5    3.47   65      4
 9       338.84    195.24   UNFOUND  1.34  NEVER  NEVER -50      2
 10      169.87    53.59    12.58    1.06  3      3.75   67      4

DO YOU WANT TO CONDUCT SENSITIVITY ANALYSIS ?
PLEASE ENTER '1' FOR 'YES', '0' FOR 'NO'
1


            SENSITIVITY ANALYSIS
            --------------------

DO YOU WANT TO ADJUST CASH FLOWS ? (YES OR NO)
YES
YOU GIVE THE PERCENTAGE CHANGES IN CASH FLOWS
THEN THE COMPUTER WILL CALCULATE THEIR EFFECTS ON NPV
```

```
INPUT NUMBER OF CHANGES IN CASH FLOWS
(MAX. IS 10)
6
PLEASE INPUT THE % CHANGE IN CASH FLOW
 E.G. 10% DECREASE IN CASH FLOW IS ENTERED AS  -10
      10% INCREASE IN CASH FLOW IS ENTERED AS   10
-20
-10
-5
5
10
20


     NOTE : DISCOUNT RATE IS  10 %


     TABLE OF NPV FOR DIFFERENT CHANGES OF CASH FLOWS
     ------------------------------------------------
```

% CHANGE IN CASH FLOW

PROJECT	-20 %	-10 %	-5 %	5 %	10 %	20 %
1	1981.7	3479.41	4228.26	5725.98	6474.83	7972.54
2	2059.56	3567	4320.73	5828.17	6581.89	8089.34
3	287.78	448.75	529.24	690.21	770.7	931.67
4	-325.62	-241.32	-199.17	-114.88	-72.73	11.57
5	-353.98	-273.23	-232.85	-152.1	-111.72	-30.97
6	-492.82	-429.42	-397.73	-334.33	-302.63	-239.23
7	182.76	330.61	404.53	552.37	626.3	774.14
8	-1424.08	-352.09	183.9	1255.89	1791.89	2863.88
9	471.07	404.96	371.9	305.79	272.73	206.61
10	-464.11	-147.12	11.37	328.36	486.85	803.84

```
THE FOLLOWING TABLE WILL GIVE THE ANNUAL EQUIVALENT
CASH FLOW WHICH WHEN DISCOUNTED AT 10 % OVER
PROJECT LIFE WILL GIVE      ZERO     NPV
                            ------


     NOTE : DISCOUNT RATE IS  10 %
```

	BREAK-EVEN ANNUITY	PROJECT LIFE
PROJECT 1 :	3154.71	4
PROJECT 2 :	3154.71	4
PROJECT 3 :	315.47	4

```
PROJECT 4  :   576.19      2

PROJECT 5  :   315.47      4

PROJECT 6  :   315.47      4

PROJECT 7  :   315.47      4

PROJECT 8  :   3154.71     4

PROJECT 9  :   576.19      2

PROJECT 10  :  946.41      4

DO YOU WANT TO TRY DIFFERENT DISCOUNT RATES ?

PLEASE INPUT '1' FOR 'YES', '0' FOR 'NO'
1
HOW MANY DISCOUNT RATES YOU WANT TO TRY ?
5
PLEASE ENTER THE DISCOUNT RATES
5
10
15
30
50


TABLE OF NPV FOR DIFFERENT DISCOUNT RATES
-----------------------------------------

PROJECT    5 %        10 %       15 %       30 %       50 %
           ----------------------------------------------------

 1         6150.47    4977.12    3949.06    1517.8     -716.049
 2         7918.51    5074.45    2791.08   -1826.79   -5098.77
 3         786.581    609.726    461.516    136.375   -130.864
 4        -83.9002   -157.025   -221.172   -372.781   -511.111
 5        -104.869   -192.473   -266.433   -430.657   -567.901
 6        -290.81    -366.027   -429.004   -566.752   -679.012
 7         625.722    478.451    352.782    68.6601   -175.309
 8         1763.1     719.896   -169.06    -2176.39   -3901.23
 9         410.431    338.843    281.664    171.598    111.111
 10        545.951    169.865   -145.022   -833.759   -1395.06


PROGRAM ENDED

YOU CAN RE-RUN THE PROGRAM FOR NEW SET OF INPUT
```

When only one project is considered, the output format is as follows:

```
HOW MANY PROJECTS ARE BEING CONSIDERED?
(FROM 1 TO 20)
1
HOW MANY VARIABLES(E.G. SALES,COST,OVERHEAD)
ARE CONSIDERED? (FROM 1 TO 20)
7
HOW MANY PERIODS FOR THE VARIABLES ? (MAX. IS 20)
6

        (Following the input instructions)

CASH FLOWS ARE STORED IN COMPUTER
DO YOU WANT TO PRINT OUT THE DATA ?
PLEASE INPUT '1' FOR 'YES','0' FOR 'NO'
1

YEAR     0        1        2        3        4        5

REVENUE  0        160      259      437      615      690
DIR.MAT  0       -21      -31      -49      -72      -80
LABOUR   0       -30      -59      -82      -93      -100
SELLING  0       -50      -87      -53      -22      -25
ADMIN    0       -6       -9       -10      -12      -14
TAX      0        100     -53      -83      -104     -202
INVEST  -400      0        0        0        0        0
        ------   ------   ------   ------   ------   ------
NCF     -400      153      20       160      312      269

PLEASE ENTER THE DISCOUNT RATE
FOR EXAMPLE, 10% IS ENTERED AS '10'
10
PLEASE ENTER THE ACCURACY FOR IRR
FOR EXAMPLE, 0.01 MEANS CORRECT TO 2 SIG. FIGURES
0.05

DISCOUNT RATE= 10 %
IRR IS CORRECTED TO .05


PROJECT  NPV      NAB     IRR(%)  PI      PB     DPB    ARAI(%)  LIFE

 1       255.96   67.52   28.23   1.64    3.21   3.58   91       5


DO YOU WANT TO CONDUCT SENSITIVITY ANALYSIS ?
PLEASE ENTER '1' FOR 'YES', '0' FOR 'NO'
1

              SENSITIVITY ANALYSIS
              --------------------

DO YOU WANT TO ADJUST CASH FLOWS ? (YES OR NO)
YES

                   (Following the input instructions)
```

```
    NOTE : DISCOUNT RATE IS  10 %

    TABLE OF NPV FOR DIFFERENT CHANGES OF CASH FLOWS
    ------------------------------------------------


                        % CHANGE IN CASH FLOW

PROJECT  -20 %       -10 %       0 %        10 %        20 %
         ---------------------------------------------------

 1        124.77      190.36      255.96     321.55      387.15


THE FOLLOWING TABLE WILL GIVE THE ANNUAL EQUIVALENT
CASH FLOW WHICH WHEN DISCOUNTED AT 10 % OVER
PROJECT LIFE WILL GIVE       ZERO      NPV
                             ------

    NOTE : DISCOUNT RATE IS  10 %


                BREAK-EVEN
                ANNUITY       PROJECT LIFE

PROJECT 1  :    105.52           5

DO YOU WANT TO TRY DIFFERENT DISCOUNT RATES ?
PLEASE INPUT '1' FOR 'YES', '0' FOR 'NO'
1

TABLE OF NPV FOR DIFFERENT DISCOUNT RATES
-----------------------------------------


PROJECT   5 %         10 %        15 %        20 %        30 %
          ----------------------------------------------------

 1        369.521     255.958     165.497     92.5495    -15.9574



PROGRAM ENDED

YOU CAN RE-RUN THE PROGRAM FOR NEW SET OF INPUT
```

Program 2: Probability Analysis

This program (listed on p.375) is based on the discussion in Chapter 6. Two input formats are allowed. Users can either input the probability distribution of project cash flows for each period, or input the 'most likely', 'maximum deviations' and the 'probabilities of the maximum deviations' of project cash flows for each period. The program then computes the expected value and standard deviation of project cash flows for each period. Users are asked whether the cash flows in different periods are independent or perfectly correlated. Having specified this assumption, the program will calculate the expected values and SD of the project's NPV over its life. By assuming that the probability distribution of the project NPV is normally distributed, it is possible to construct a confidence interval of the project NPV or determine the probabilities of a project with an NPV less than (or greater than) a specified amount.

Problem

A project with initial outlay of £500 has the following possible returns:

	Probability	*Net cash flow*
Period 1	0.1	100
	0.2	200
	0.4	300
	0.2	400
	0.1	500
Period 2	0.1	200
	0.2	400
	0.4	600
	0.2	800
	0.1	1,000

Calculate:

a) The expected return and SD of cash flow for each period
b) The probability of having negative NPV
c) The probability of NPV < 100

assuming the cash flows in different periods are independent and then assuming they are perfectly correlated.

OUTPUT OF PROBABILITY ANALYSIS

```
HOW MANY PERIODS ARE CONSIDERED ?
(INCLUDING INITIAL PERIOD)
(MAX. IS 10)
3
ARE THE DATA THE SAME FOR ALL PERIODS ?
(EXCEPT INITIAL PERIOD)
PLEASE INPUT 'YES' OR 'NO'
NO
```

```
WHICH INPUT FORMAT YOU WANT ?
INPUT '1' FOR 'PROB. DIST.' OF CASH FLOW
      '2' FOR 'MOST LIKELY AND DEVIATON OF CASH FLOW
1
NET CASH OUTFLOWS CARRY 'MINUS' SIGN
         INFLOWS  CARRY 'PLUS' OR 'NO' SIGN

HOW MANY 'STATES OF WORLD' FOR THE DISTRIBUTION ?
(MAX. IS 10)
5

           NOW INPUT THE PROB. DIST.

FOR EACH LINE,FIRST INPUT THE PROBABILITY
AND THEN THE CORRESPONDING CASH FLOWS

REMARK  :  NEED A COMMA(,) BETWEEN EACH DATA
                ---------

PERIOD '0' IS THE STARTING PERIOD (INITIAL INVESTMENT)
IF INITIAL INVESTMENT IS CERTAIN, SAY, -1000
THEN INPUT AS
               1,-1000
AND PUT        0,0       TO THE OTHER STATE OF WORLD

PLEASE INPUT THE PROB. DIST. OF PERIOD    0
PLEASE INPUT THE PROB. DIST. OF PERIOD    1
PLEASE INPUT THE PROB. DIST. OF PERIOD    2
DO YOU WANT TO PRINT OUT THE DATA ?
INPUT 'YES' OR 'NO'
YES


         PROBABILITY  NET CASH FLOW

PERIOD 0       1           -500
               0            0
               0            0
               0            0
               0            0
          ----------------------

PERIOD 1      .1            100
              .2            200
              .4            300
              .2            400
              .1            500
          ----------------------

PERIOD 2      .1            200
              .2            400
              .4            600
              .2            800
              .1            1000
          ----------------------
```

```
THE EXPECTED RETURN AND S.D. FOR EACH PERIOD ARE

PERIOD            EXP. RETURN      S.D.

   0             -500              0
   1              300              109.545
   2              600              219.089


PLEASE INPUT THE RISK-FREE INTEREST RATE
(IN DECIMAL FORM)
0.1
ARE THE CASH FLOWS IN DIFFERENT PERIODS
INDEPENDENT   OR PERFECTLY CORRELATED ?
-----------      --------------------

PLEASE INPUT  '1'  FOR INDEPENDENT
              '2'  FOR PERFECTLY CORRELATED
1

       (ASSUMING PERIOD CASH FLOWS ARE INDEPENDENT)


THE RISK-FREE INTEREST RATE IS   10 (%)

THE EXPECTED VALUE OF THE PROJECT NPV IS   268.595
                                           -------

THE   S.D.          OF THE PROJECT NPV IS   206.645
                                            -------


68% CONFIDENT THAT THE PROJECT NPV IS BETWEEN    61.95 AND  475.24

95% CONDIDENT THAT THE PROJECT NPV IS BETWEEN -144.7   AND  681.88

99% CONFIDENT THAT THE PROJECT NPV IS BETWEEN -351.34 AND  888.53

DO YOU WANT TO CONDUCT PROBABILITY ANALYSIS ?
INPUT 'YES' OR 'NO'
YES

              PROBABILITY ANALYSIS
              --------------------


PLEASE ENTER THE '<' OR '>' SIGN FIRST
FOLLOWED BY COMMA(,) THEN THE FIGURES
            --------

E.G.  IF YOU WANT TO KNOW THE PROBABILITY OF
      NPV<1000, SAY, THEN INPUT AS
                                        <,1000
<,0

PROB. OF NPV < 0 = .0968
                   --------
```

```
MORE PROBABILITY ANALYSIS ?
PLEASE INPUT 'YES' OR 'NO'
NO
DO YOU WANT TO RECONSIDER THE RISK FREE
INTEREST RATE AND THE DEPENDENCE OF CASH FLOWS?
PLEASE INPUT 'YES' OR 'NO'
YES
PLEASE INPUT THE RISK-FREE INTEREST RATE
(IN DECIMAL FORM)


0.1
ARE THE CASH FLOWS IN DIFFERENT PERIODS
INDEPENDENT  OR PERFECTLY CORRELATED ?
-----------     --------------------

PLEASE INPUT  '1'  FOR INDEPENDENT
              '2'  FOR PERFECTLY CORRELATED
1

 (ASSUMING PERIOD CASH FLOWS ARE PERFECTLY CORRELATED)

THE RISK-FREE INTEREST RATE IS   10 (%)

THE EXPECTED VALUE OF THE PROJECT NPV IS  268.595
                                          -------

THE    S.D.        OF THE PROJECT NPV IS  280.651
                                          -------


68% CONFIDENT THAT THE PROJECT NPV IS BETWEEN   -12.06 AND  549.25

95% CONFIDENT THAT THE PROJECT NPV IS BETWEEN  -292.7  AND  829.9

99% CONFIDENT THAT THE PROJECT NPV IS BETWEEN  -573.36 AND 1110.55

DO YOU WANT TO CONDUCT PROBABILITY ANALYSIS ?
INPUT 'YES' OR 'NO'
'NO'
```

Suppose that managers have no idea of the probability distribution of the project NPV, but they have estimated the 'most likely' outcomes and the 'maximum deviations' from the most likely outcomes. Then the second input format is useful. An example of the second input format is listed below:

```
HOW MANY PERIODS ARE CONSIDERED ?
(INCLUDING INITIAL PERIOD)
(MAX. IS 10)
4
ARE THE DATA THE SAME FOR ALL PERIODS ?
```

```
(EXCEPT INITIAL PERIOD)
PLEASE INPUT 'YES' OR 'NO'
NO
WHICH INPUT FORMAT YOU WANT ?
INPUT '1' FOR 'PROB. DIST.' OF CASH FLOW
      '2' FOR 'MOST LIKELY AND DEVIATON OF CASH FLOW
2
NET CASH OUTFLOWS CARRY 'MINUS' SIGN
         INFLOWS  CARRY 'PLUS' OR 'NO' SIGN


FOR EACH LINE, FIRST INPUT THE MOST LIKELY
CASH FLOW,FOLLOWED BY MAX. DEVIATION AND
PROBABILTY OF DIVIATION AT LAST

REMARK: COMMA(,) IS NEEDED BETWEEN INPUT OF EACH LINE


         --------


PERIOD '0' IS THE PERIOD OF INITIAL INVESTMENT
IF INITIAL INVESTMENT IS CERTAIN WITHOUT DEV.
SAY, -1000, THEN INPUT AS
                               -1000,0,0

 PLEASE INPUT DATA OF PERIOD 0
 PLEASE INPUT DATA OF PERIOD 1
 PLEASE INPUT DATA OF PERIOD 2
 PLEASE INPUT DATA OF PERIOD 3
DO YOU WANT TO PRINT OUT THE DATA ?
INPUT 'YES' OR 'NO'
YES

              MOST LIKELY    MAX. DEV. PROB.

PERIOD 0      -10000          0         0
PERIOD 1       5000          2000       .1
PERIOD 2       6000          2500       .15
PERIOD 3       5000          3000       .2


THE EXPECTED RETURN AND S.D. FOR EACH PERIOD ARE


PERIOD         EXP. RETURN     S.D.

  0           -10000          0
  1            5000          1600
  2            6000          2500
  3            5000          3750.


PLEASE INPUT THE RISK-FREE INTEREST RATE
(IN DECIMAL FORM)
0.04
```

```
ARE THE CASH FLOWS IN DIFFERENT PERIODS
INDEPENDENT  OR PERFECTLY CORRELATED ?
-----------  --------------------

PLEASE INPUT  '1'  FOR INDEPENDENT
              '2'  FOR PERFECTLY CORRELATED
1

      (ASSUMING PERIOD CASH FLOWS ARE INDEPENDENT)


THE RISK-FREE INTEREST RATE IS   4 (%)

THE EXPECTED VALUE OF THE PROJECT NPV IS   4800.01
                                           -------

THE   S.D.        OF THE PROJECT NPV IS   4338.57
                                           -------

68% CONFIDENT THAT THE PROJECT NPV IS BETWEEN   461.4  AND  9138.6

95% CONDIDENT THAT THE PROJECT NPV IS BETWEEN -3877.1  AND 13477.2

99% CONFIDENT THAT THE PROJECT NPV IS BETWEEN -8215.7  AND 17815.7

DO YOU WANT TO CONDUCT PROBABILITY ANALYSIS ?
INPUT 'YES' OR 'NO'
 NO
```

Program 3: CAPM and Cost of Capital

This program (listed on p. 387) demonstrates the applications of traditional approach and CAPM approaches to evaluate a risky project, the calculations being based on discussion in Chapters 5 and 8. Users are first requested to input a project's cash flows. Then they must choose a hurdle rate to discount the cash flows. The traditional method uses the company's weighted average cost of capital. However, the CAPM states that only the project's systematic risk (measured by beta) is a relevant measure of project risk. The required rate of return of project is given by

$$R_j = R_f + (R_m - R_f)\beta_j$$

The project cash flows should be discounted by R_j instead of WACC. To apply CAPM we need to know the value of the project's beta. This program provides three methods to calculate a project's beta:

(a) regression of a project's excess return on the market's excess return;
(b) probability distribution of a project's return;

(c) adjusting observed beta for the company's share to a specific capital project.

Program Output (CAPM and Cost of Capital)

The output solved the following problems:

Problem 1 (WACC)

The directors of Osmin plc are considering opening a factory to manufacture a new product. Detailed forecasts of the product's expected cash flows have been made, and it is estimated that an initial capital investment of £2.5 million is required. The company's current (31 December 1981) authorised share capital consists of 4 million ordinary shares, each with a nominal value of 25p. During the last five years the number of shares in issue has remained constant at 3 million, and the market price per share at 31 December 1981 is 135p ex div. The company pays only one dividend each year (on 31st December) and dividends for the last five years have been as follows:

Year	*1977*	*1978*	*1979*	*1980*	*1981*
Dividend per share (pence)	10.0	10.8	11.6	13.6	13.6

Osmin plc currently has in issue 800,000 8% debentures redeemable on 31st December 1985. The current market price of these debentures is 82.5 ex interest, and the interest is payable in one amount each year on 31st December. The company also has outstanding a £900,000 bank loan repayable on 31st December 1989. The rate of interest on this loan is variable, being fixed at 1.5% above the bank base rate which is currently 15%.

You are required to:

(a) calculate the weighted average cost of capital (WACC) for Osmin plc as at 31 December 1981.

Ignore taxation.

Source of Question

Question 1, Financial Management
Professional Examination II, July 1982
The Institute of Chartered Accountants in England and Wales.
(start running the program)

```
          EVALUATION OF RISKY INVESTMENT
          ------------------------------

      THIS PROGRAM WILL EVALUATE A RISKY PROJECT
      BY USING COMPANY'S AVERAGE COST OF CAPITAL
      OR CAPITAL ASSETS PRICING MODEL APPROACH
      FINALLY, AN ACCEPT/REJECT DECISION IS MADE


WHICH METHOD TO CALCULATE THE DISCOUNT RATE ?
PLEASE INPUT
              '1' FOR COMPANY'S AVERAGE COST OF CAPITAL
              '2' FOR CAPITAL ASSETS PRICING MODEL
1

      EVALUATE A RISKY PROJECT BY USING  'WACC'
      -----------------------------------------

WHAT IS THE NUMBER OF SHARES FOR THE COMPANY ?
3000000
WHAT IS THE CURRENT PRICE PER SHARE ( IN POUNDS) ?
1.35
WHAT IS THE REQUIRED RETURN OF EQUITY ?
PLEASE INPUT   '1' IF INPUT BY USERS
               '2' IF USING CONSTANT GROWTH FORMULA
2
WHAT IS THE TREND OF DIVIDEND GROWTH ?
FOR EXAMPLE, IF DIVIDEND GROW FROM 6P TO 14P
IN 10 YEARS' TIME, THEN INPUT AS
     0.06,0.14,10
0.1,0.136,4
ANY DEBENTURE ISSUED ? (YES OR NO)
YES
PLEASE INPUT TOTAL AMOUNT (IN POUNDS) OF
DEBENTURE ISSUED
800000
WHAT IS THE INTEREST RATE OF THE DEBENTURES (%) ?
8
PLEASE INPUT THE CURRENT PRICE OF THE DEBENTURES
(BASE ISSUE PRICE IS ASSUMED TO BE 100)
82.5
HOW MANY YEARS LATER THE DEBENTURES BE REDEEMED ?
4
ANY BANK LOAN IN THE CAPITAL STRUCTURE ? (YES OR NO)
YES
PLEASE INPUT THE AMOUNT (IN POUNDS) OF BANK LOAN
900000
WHAT IS THE INTEREST RATE OF THE LOAN (%) ?
16.5
ANY NEW ISSUE OF SHARES ? (YES OR NO)
NO
PLEASE INPUT TAX RATE
E.G. IF TAX RATE IS 40% THEN INPUT   '40'
    IF NO TAX CONSIDERED THEN INPUT '0'
0
*****************************************************
```

```
MARKET VALUE OF SHARES                    = 4.05000E+6
REQUIRED RETURN OF EQUITY                 = 19 %

MARKET VALUE OF DEBT                      = 660000
REQUIRED RETURN OF DEBT AFTER TAX         = 14 %

MARKET VALUE OF BANK LOAN                 = 900000
REQUIRED RETURN OF BANK LOAN AFTER TAX = 16.5 %

MARKET VALUE OF NEW ISSUE OF SHARES       = 0
REQUIRE RETURN OF NEW ISSUE               = 0 %
                                          ---------

WEIGHTED AVERAGE COST OF CAPITAL          = 18.01 %

DO YOU WANT TO APPLY THE INFORMATION INTO A
RISKY PROJECT (YES OR NO) ?
YES
HOW MANY PERIODS OF CASH FLOW CONSIDERED ?
(INCLUDING INITIAL PERIOD,MAX. IS 20)
5
PLEASE INPUT THE PROJECT'S CASH FLOWS

NET OUTFLOWS CARRY 'MINUS' SIGN
NET INFLOWS  CARRY  'PLUS' OR 'NO' SIGN

EACH LINE ONLY INPUT 'ONE' CASH FLOW


THE PROJECT CASH FLOWS ARE

-1000     400     400     400     300

THE DISCOUNT RATE IS  18.01 %

THE NET PRESENT VALUE OF THE PROJECT IS          24.2541

NPV>0, SO THE PROJECT IS ACCEPTABLE

****************************************************
```

Problem 2 (Probability Analysis)

Zerlina Ltd is considering investing in a risky new project which will have a life of one year only. Since the capital asset pricing model is a single-period model capable of handling risk, the manager of Zerlina, Masetto, is keen to use it to evaluate the project. To this end, he has estimated the returns on existing operations, the new project, the market portfolio and the risk-free security in three future 'states of the world' and these are contained in the table below:

State of the world	*Probability of occurrence*	*Existing projects*	*New project*	*Market portfolio*	*Risk-free security*
1	0.25	0.12	0.10	0.12	0.03
2	0.50	0.10	0.17	0.10	0.03
3	0.25	0.16	0.16	0.16	0.03

Acceptance of the new project will have a negligible impact upon the returns from the market portfolio: it will, however, comprise 10% of the modified total of operations of Zerlina if accepted.

You are required to:

(a) calculate the beta factor of the new project;
(b) advise Masetto whether the new project is worthwhile, using the capital asset pricing model;
(c) calculate the minimum required rate of return for Zerlina assuming all future projects will have the same risk, on average, as
    (1) existing operations
    (2) existing operations plus the new project;
(d) discuss the usefulness and limitations of the capital asset pricing model for capital budgeting decision.

Ignore taxation.

Source of Problem

Question 5, Financial Management
Professional Examination II, July 1982
The Institute of Chartered Accountants in England and Wales.

```
DO YOU WANT TO RE-RUN THE PROGRAM ? (YES OR NO)
YES
WHICH METHOD TO CALCULATE THE DISCOUNT RATE ?
PLEASE INPUT

             '1' FOR COMPANY'S AVERAGE COST OF CAPITAL
             '2' FOR CAPITAL ASSETS PRICING MODEL
2

WHICH METHOD YOU WANT TO CALCULATE PROJECT BETA ?
INPUT.       '1' FOR PROBABILITY ANALYSIS METHOD
             '2' FOR ADJUSTING OBSERVED BETA METHOD
1

 PROBABILITY ANALYSIS TO CAL. PROJECT BETA (CAPM)
 ------------------------------------------------
HOW MANY STATES OF THE WORLD ARE CONSIDERED ?
(MAX. IS 10)
3
FOR EACH LINE, INPUT
```

```
PROBABILITY,RETURN OF EXISTING PROJECT(%)
RETURN OF NEW PROJECT(%),RETURN OF MARKET PORTFOLIO(%),
RETURN OF RISK-FREE SECURITY (%)

0.25,12,10,12,3
0.50,10,17,10,3
0.25,16,16,16,3


*****************************************************

EXPECTED RISK-FREE RATE OF RETURN = 3 %
EXPECTED MARKET RETURN            = 12 %
S. D. OF MARKET RETURN            = 2.44949 %

EXISTING PROJECT
----------------

EXPECTED RETURN                                  = 12 %
S.D. OF RETURN                                   = 2.44949 %
COVARIANCE WITH MARKET RETURN                    = 6
CORRELATION COEFF. WITH MARKET RETURN            = 1.
BETA VALUE                                       = 1.
REQUIRED RATE OF RETURN                          = 12. %


NEW PROJECT
-----------

EXPECTED RETURN                                  = 15 %
S.D. OF RETURN                                   = 2.91548 %
COVARIANCE WITH MARKET RETURN                    =-1
CORRELATION COEFF. WITH MARKET RETURN            =-.140028
BETA VALUE                                       =-.166667
REQUIRED RATE OF RETURN                          = 1.5 %

PROJECT IS ACCEPTABLE

DO YOU WANT TO KNOW THE IMPACT OF THE NEW PROJECT
ON THE COMPANY'S SYSTEMATIC RISK (TOTAL) ?
       ---------
PLEASE INPUT 'YES' OR 'NO'
YES
WHAT IS THE PROPORTION OF THE NEW PROJECT TO
THE OVERALL COMPANY OPERATIONS ?
(IN DECIMAL FORM)
0.1

AFTER ACCEPTED THE PROJECT, COMPANY BETA BECOMES       .883333
COMPANY'S AVERAGE REQUIRED RETURN (CAPM) BECOMES      10.95 %


DO YOU WANT TO APPLY THE INFORMATION INTO A
RISKY PROJECT (YES OR NO) ?
YES
```

```
HOW MANY PERIODS OF CASH FLOW CONSIDERED ?
(INCLUDING INITIAL PERIOD,MAX. IS 20)
5
PLEASE INPUT THE PROJECT'S CASH FLOWS

NET OUTFLOWS CARRY 'MINUS' SIGN
NET INFLOWS  CARRY  'PLUS' OR 'NO' SIGN

EACH LINE ONLY INPUT 'ONE' CASH FLOW


THE PROJECT CASH FLOWS ARE

-1000    400    400    400    300

THE DISCOUNT RATE IS  1.5 %

THE NET PRESENT VALUE OF THE PROJECT IS           447.535

NPV>0, SO THE PROJECT IS ACCEPTABLE

**************************************************
```

Problem 3 (Adjusting Observed Beta)

A company has a security beta of 1.2 which is typical for the industry. Its financial gearing level as measured by the ratio of debt to equity is 40% based on market values. Corporation tax is 52%. The company is believed to have growth opportunities valued at one-quarter of the total market value. Such opportunities are estimated to have a beta value 20% above that for net tangible assets. The risk free interest rate is 10% and the market premium 7%, both after personal taxes.

A study of the likely revenue sensitivity suggests that the division-to-company sensitivity is 1.2. Similarly, it is estimated that the sensitivity of the project revenues relative to its division is 1.5.

The division in which the investment project would operate has a similar cost structure to the company as a whole. The Contribution Margin Ratio is 30% for the division compared with 40% for the project.

Source of Problem

Pike, R. H. (1981) 'Calculating a project's hurdle rate', in G. H. Lawson and R. H. Pike (eds), *Capital Investment: Theory and Practice*, MCB Publications, p. 84.

```
DO YOU WANT TO RE-RUN THE PROGRAM ? (YES OR NO)
YES
WHICH METHOD TO CALCULATE THE DISCOUNT RATE ?
PLEASE INPUT
```

```
              '1' FOR COMPANY'S AVERAGE COST OF CAPITAL
              '2' FOR CAPITAL ASSETS PRICING MODEL
 2

WHICH METHOD YOU WANT TO CALCULATE PROJECT BETA ?
INPUT        '1' FOR PROBABILITY ANALYSIS METHOD
             '2' FOR ADJUSTING OBSERVED BETA METHOD
2

   ADJUSTING OBSERVED BETA METHOD (CAPM APPROACH)
  -----------------------------------------------

PLEASE INPUT THE OBSERVED COMPANY BETA
1.2
PLEASE INPUT THE DEBT/EQUITY RATIO
0.4
PLEASE INPUT THE TAX RATE(%)
52
PLEASE INPUT THE % OF GROWTH OPPORTUNITIES
TO THE COMPANYS' TOTAL MARKET VALUE
25
PLEASE INPUT THE % OF GROWTH OPPORTUNITIES
BETA 'ABOVE' THE BETA OF TANGIBLE ASSETS
20
PLEASE INPUT THE PROJECT REVENUE SENSITIVITY
 (RELATIVE TO THE COMPANY)
1.8
PLEASE INPUT THE PROJECT OPERATIONAL GEARING FACTOR
 (RELATIVE TO THE COMPANY)
1.33
PLEASE INPUT THE AVERAGE RISK-FREE RATE IN %
10
PLEASE INPUT THE AVERAGE MARKET RETURN IN %
17


*****************************************************

THE PROJECT BETA VALUE IS                               2.2953
THE REQUIRED RETURN OR THE PROJECT IS                   26.0671 %

DO YOU WANT TO APPLY THE INFORMATION INTO A
RISKY PROJECT (YES OR NO) ?
YES
HOW MANY PERIODS OF CASH FLOW CONSIDERED ?
(INCLUDING INITIAL PERIOD,MAX. IS 20)
5
PLEASE INPUT THE PROJECT'S CASH FLOWS

NET OUTFLOWS CARRY 'MINUS' SIGN
NET INFLOWS  CARRY  'PLUS' OR 'NO' SIGN

EACH LINE ONLY INPUT 'ONE' CASH FLOW


THE PROJECT CASH FLOWS ARE
```

```
-1000    400    400    400    300

THE DISCOUNT RATE IS  26.0671 %

THE NET PRESENT VALUE OF THE PROJECT IS          -112.609

NPV<=0, SO REJECT THE PROJCET

**********************************************************

DO YOU WANT TO RE-RUN THE PROGRAM ? (YES OR NO)
NO
```

Program 4: Monte Carlo Simulation Method

This program (listed on p. 395) is based on the Hertz risk analysis approach outlined in Chapter 6.

Problem

A company has prepared an investment evaluation for a proposed major project based on the probability distributions of 9 economic variables. The probability distributions of the variables are:

	Project life						
Possible values	7	9	12	15	18		
Probability	0	0.2	0.4	0.3	0.1		
	Market size						
Possible values	100000	150000	200000	250000	340000		
Probability	0	0.2	0.2	0.4	0.2		
	Market growth rate						
Possible values	0	0.01	0.02	0.03	0.04	0.05	0.06
Probability	0	0.05	0.10	0.35	0.30	0.15	0.05
	Share of market						
Possible values	0.03	0.06	0.09	0.12	0.15	0.17	
Probability	0	0.10	0.40	0.40	0.30	0.05	
	Selling price						
Possible values	300	330	370	400	450		
Probability	0	0.10	0.45	0.35	0.10		
	Operating costs						
Possible values	250	270	300	310	330	350	
Probability	0	0.15	0.35	0.35	0.10	0.05	
	Investment						
Possible values (000)	7000	8000	9000	9500	10000	10500	
Probability	0	0.05	0.15	0.35	0.35	0.10	
	Residual values						
Possible values (000)	3500	4000	4500	5000			
Probability	0	0.2	0.4	0.4			
	Fixed costs						
Possible values (000)	250	275	300	325	350	375	
Probability	0	0.1	0.3	0.3	0.2	0.1	

Assess the risk of the above project.

Procedure

Overwrite the above given values to the data statement in line 04080 to line 04340 and then run the program.

```
OUTPUT OF SIMULATION MODEL

***** DISCOUNT RATE (Z9) IS ALREADY SET TO 10%   *****
***** IF REQUIRE NEW DISCOUNT RATE, CHANGE LINE 00440

***** IF USERS DO NOT WANT TO INPUT FROM TERMINAL
***** CHANGE SAMPLE DATA 'BEFORE' RUNNING PROGRAM
DO YOU WANT TO USE 'SAMPLE DATA '? (YES OR NO)      YES

FLOWS FOR THE FIRST ITERATION FOR 10  PERIODS

PERIOD          FLOW

 0              -9.60787E+6
 1               489126.
 2               226555.
 3               137332.
 4               594199.
 5               1.40105E+6
 6               455588.
 7               2.47342E+6
 8              -123857.
 9               4.30292E+6

RATES OF RETURN FOR 100 SAMPLES

-.0268     TO      .0112        *****                     5
 .0112     TO      .0492        *********                 9
 .0492     TO      .0872        *************             13
 .0872     TO      .1252        ********************      20
 .1252     TO      .1632        *************             13
 .1632     TO      .2012        **************            14
 .2012     TO      .2392        ***********               11
 .2392     TO      .2772        ****                      4
 .2772     TO      .3152        *****                     5
 .3152     TO      .3532        **                        2
 .3532     TO      .3912        *                         1
 .3912     TO      .4292        *                         1
 .4292     TO      .4672        *                         1
 .4672     TO      .5052                                  0
 .5052     TO      .5432        *                         1

MEAN .1511

STANDARD DEVIATION .0998
```

```
NET PRESENT VALUES FOR 100 SAMPLES

FOR ACTUAL VALUE MULTIPLY BY 1000

-5086     TO     -3569     *********            9
-3569     TO     -2053     ********             8
-2053     TO     -536      ************         12
-536      TO     980       *************        13
 980      TO     2496      ********             8
 2496     TO     4013      ************         12
 4013     TO     5529      *********            9
 5529     TO     7046      ************         12
 7046     TO     8562      ***                  3
 8562     TO     10078     ****                 4
 10078    TO     11595     ****                 4
 11595    TO     13111     ****                 4
 13111    TO     14628     *                    1
 14628    TO     16144                          0
 16144    TO     17660     *                    1

MEAN 2.74573E+6

STANDARD DEVIATION 4.86053E+6

PROFITABILITY INDEX FOR  100 SAMPLES

 ,5115    TO     .6935     ************         12
 .6935    TO     .8755     *********            9
 .8755    TO     1.0575    ******************   18
 1.0575   TO     1.2395    ***********          11
 1.2395   TO     1.4215    ***********          11
 1.4215   TO     1.6035    **********           10
 1.6035   TO     1.7855    ***********          11
 1.7855   TO     1.9675    ****                 4
 1.9675   TO     2.1495    ******               6
 2.1495   TO     2.3315    **                   2
 2.3315   TO     2.5135    ***                  3
 2.5135   TO     2.6955    *                    1
 2.6955   TO     2.8775    *                    1
 2.8775   TO     3.0595                         0
 3.0595   TO     3.2415    *                    1


MEAN 1.3109

STANDARD DEVIATION .5474
```

Explanation of the program

Lines 14040 to 04340 already contain a set of sample data and hence the program is ready to run. To input a new set of data, two methods can be used:

1. *Use 'DATA STATEMENT'*

Before executing the program, users should overwrite the sample data and answer YES to the first question:

'DO YOU WANT TO USE SAMPLE DATA (YES OR NO)?'

when program starts execution.
The program data is defined as follows:

Line 04040 : Number of iterations to be used to generate the cash flows
Line 04050 : Number of discrete increments wanted in histogram
Line 04060 : Number of constant variables in the model (No constant variables in the sample data)
Line 04070 : Number of random variables in the model (sample data contains 9 random variables)
Line 04080 : Number of the first variable factor, number of possible outcomes for this factor (never more than 8)
Line 04100 : Probabilities of possible outcomes. The first number must always be 'zero' and the sum of probabilities should be equal to 1. Total number of values must be equal to the number of possible outcomes entered in line 04080. The figures in the sample data mean:

0% chance of project life being less than 7
20% chance of project life between 9 and 12
40% chance of project life between 12 and 15
30% chance of project life between 15 and 18
10% chance of project life over 18

Data of other random variables are input from line 04110 to 04340 similarly.
Note: If line 04060 is not equal to zero, the constant 'name' and 'value' must be inserted between lines 04060 and 04070. e.g. if 2 constants called 'month' and 'tax' having values 12 and 40 respectively are in the model, then insert

```
4060 DATA 2
4061 DATA MONTH, 12
4062 DATA TAX, 40
```

2. *Enter data interactively*

Users can input data from terminals by answering NO to the question —

'DO YOU WANT TO USE SAMPLE DATA (YES OR NO)?'

— and follow the instructions of the program. Users are strongly advised to use 'DATA STATEMENT' to input data because it can save executing time and, more importantly, users can re-run the program for as many times as they want without inputing again (since the program is 'RANDOMISED', each run will produce different answers).

Lines 01080 to 01370 are reserved for the simulation model. Hertz specified 9 random variables in his simulation model. In this program the relationships between the 9 random variables are described as below:

Line 01090 : Random draw for 'Project Life'
Line 01110 : Random draw for 'Market Size'
Line 01130 : Random draw (negative) for 'Initial Cost'
Line 01140 : Set Market Growth Rate = 1 in period 0
Lines 01160–01350 : Loop to compute cash flows for each period
Line 01180 : Set
Market Growth Rate = (growth rate in previous period) × (1 + market growth rate)
where market growth rate is randomly drawn
Line 01200 : Set
Total Market Size = (market size in previous period) × (market growth rate)
Line 01220 : Set
Quantity Sold = Total Market Size × Market Share
where market share is randomly drawn
Line 01240 : Let
Sales = Quantity Sold × Selling Price
where selling price is randomly drawn
Line 01260 : Random draw of operating cost per unit
Lines 01280–01300 : If Total Sales >= Total Operating Costs then produce the product otherwise stop production
Line 01320 : Let
Total Costs = Fixed Costs + Total Operating Costs
where fixed costs is randomly drawn
Line 01340 : Period Cash Flow = Period Sales − Period Total Costs
Line 01370 : Cash Flow in last period = Period Cash Flow + Residual Value
where residual value is randomly drawn.

Users can modify the model so that it can compute the distribution of internal rate of return, profitability index and net annual benefit, etc. Moreover, users can also specify the interrelationships between the random variables in the model. All they need to do is to delete lines 01080 to 01370 and insert their own model within the lines reserved for that model.

It must be pointed out that the random numbers generated by computer are not 'real' random numbers, but form a 'predefined' sequence of random numbers uniformly distributed over the range of 0 and 1 (called PSEUDO random numbers). Each time the program is run it will call the same set of 'random' numbers. However, the 'RANDOMISE' statement in line 00370 causes a new initial or seed value to be placed in the random number generator. Each time the program containing the RND function is run, a different sequence of pseudo random numbers will be generated.

To ensure that the pseudo random numbers thus generated give a closer representation of the random numbers, users are recommended to run the program several times, say 10, and calculate the mean of the results. (Since the pseudo random numbers are being randomised, each run will produce different values for the mean and SD or project NPV.)

Notes

1. The programs are written in BASIC version 3 for CYBER computer systems, but can easily be adapted to other versions of BASIC. We are grateful to Y. H. Lee who wrote these programs as part of his MBA dissertation.
2. See Day, B. (1982) 'A basic program for DCF rate of return', *Management Accounting*, vol. 60, no. 11.

Computer Program 1:

Investment Evaluation

```
00100 REM ***********************************************
00110 PRINT
00120 PRINT "         EVALUATION OF INVESTMENTS"
00130 PRINT "         -------------------------"
00140 PRINT
00150 PRINT
00160 PRINT "      THIS PROGRAM WILL CALCULATE THE VALUES OF"
00170 PRINT "      NET PRESENT VALUE,NET ANNUAL BENEFIT"
00180 PRINT "      INTERNAL RATE OF RETURN, PROFITABILITY INDEX"
00190 PRINT "      PAYBACK PERIOD, DISCOUNTED PAYBACK PERIOD"
00200 PRINT "      AND AVERAGE RETURN ON AVERAGE INVESTMENT"
00210 PRINT "      OF PROJECTS"
00220 PRINT "      THE PROGRAM CAN HANDLE 20 PROJECTS UP TO"
00230 PRINT "      20 PERIODS"
00240 PRINT
00250 PRINT "      USERS CAN ALSO CONDUCT SENSITIVITY ANALYSIS"
00260 PRINT
00270 REM ************************************************
00280 REM *                                              *
00290 REM *       THE VARIABLES ARE DEFINED AS FOLLOWS : *
00300 REM *                                              *
00310 REM *   ARRAY D=DATA MATRIX STORE THE NET CASH FLOW *
00320 REM *   ARRAY A=DATA OF ACCOUNTING VARIABLES       *
00330 REM *   ARRAY S=RESULTS OF DIFF. EVALUATION METHODS *
00340 REM *   ARRAY R=DATA OF DIFFERENT DISCOUNT RATES   *
00350 REM *   ARRAY C=AMOUNT CHANGE IN CASH FLOW         *
00360 REM *   K1=NO. OF INVESTMENTS                      *
00370 REM *   R9=NO. OF CHANGE IN CASH FLOW              *
00380 REM *   R1=NO. OF DISCOUNT RATES                   *
00390 REM *   N$=NAME OF ACCOUNTING VARIABLES            *
00400 REM *                                              *
00410 REM ************************************************

00420 REM
00430 REM                      MAIN PROGRAM
00440 REM                      ------------
00450 DIM D(20,22),R(10),S(20,16),N$(20),A(21,20),C(10)
00460 PRINT "HOW MANY PROJECTS ARE BEING CONSIDERED?"
00470 PRINT "(FROM 1 TO 20)"
00480 INPUT K1
00490 LET K1=INT(K1)
00500 IF K1<=20 AND K1>0 THEN 00540
```

```
00510 PRINT "NO. OF PROJECT CONSIDERED IS BETWEEN 1 AND 20"
00520 PRINT "PLEASE TRY AGAIN"
00530 GOTO 00480
00540 IF K1=1 THEN GOSUB 01180
00550 IF K1<>1 THEN GOSUB 01620
00560 PRINT
00570 PRINT "CASH FLOWS ARE STORED IN COMPUTER"
00580 PRINT "DO YOU WANT TO PRINT OUT THE DATA ?"
00590 PRINT "PLEASE INPUT '1' FOR 'YES','0' FOR 'NO'"
00600 INPUT W1
00610 IF W1<>1 THEN 00650
00620 IF K1=1 THEN GOSUB 01870
00630 IF K1<>1 THEN GOSUB 02160
00640 PRINT
00650 PRINT "PLEASE ENTER THE DISCOUNT RATE"
00660 PRINT "FOR EXAMPLE, 10% IS ENTERED AS '10'"
00670 INPUT R
00680 GOSUB 02380
00690 GOSUB 04740
00700 GOSUB 02760
00710 GOSUB 03080
00720 GOSUB 02510
00730 GOSUB 04850
00740 GOSUB 03190
00750 GOSUB 03320
00760 IF K1=1 THEN 00790
00770 PRINT
00780 PRINT
00790 PRINT
00800 PRINT
00810 PRINT "DO YOU WANT TO CONDUCT SENSITIVITY ANALYSIS ?"
00820 PRINT "PLEASE ENTER '1' FOR 'YES', '0' FOR 'NO'"
00830 INPUT W4
00840 IF W4<>1 THEN 01030
00850 GOSUB 03900
00860 PRINT "DO YOU WANT TO TRY DIFFERENT DISCOUNT RATES ?"
00870 PRINT "PLEASE INPUT '1' FOR 'YES', '0' FOR 'NO'"
00880 INPUT W2
00890 IF W2<>1 THEN 01040
00900 PRINT "HOW MANY DISCOUNT RATES YOU WANT TO TRY ?"
00910 INPUT R1
00920 LET R1=INT(R1)
00930 IF R1>0 AND R1<11 THEN 00970
00940 PRINT "NUMBER OF DISCOUNT RATE SHOULD BE FROM 1 TO 10"
00950 PRINT "PLEASE TRY AGAIN"
00960 GOTO 00910
00970 PRINT "PLEASE ENTER THE DISCOUNT RATES"
00980 FOR I=1 TO R1
00990 INPUT R(I)
01000 NEXT I
01010 PRINT
01020 GOSUB 03620
01030 PRINT
01040 PRINT
01050 PRINT
01060 PRINT "PROGRAM ENDED"
```

```
01070 PRINT
01080 PRINT "YOU CAN RE-RUN THE PROGRAM FOR NEW SET OF INPUT"
01090 PRINT
01100 GOTO 05080
01110 REM
01120 REM ***************************************************
01130 REM *                                                 *
01140 REM *            SUBROUTINES OF THE PROGRAM           *
01150 REM *                                                 *
01160 REM ***************************************************
01170 REM
01180 REM   SUBROUTINE FOR INPUT DATA (ONE PROJECT)
01190 REM   ---------------------------------------
01200 PRINT "HOW MANY VARIABLES(E.G. SALES,COST,OVERHEAD)"
01210 PRINT "ARE CONSIDER ? (FROM 1 TO 20)"
01220 INPUT V
01230 LET V=INT(V)
01240 IF V>0 AND V<21 THEN 01280
01250 PRINT "INPUT SHOULD BE FROM 1 TO 20"
01260 PRINT "PLEASE TRY AGAIN"
01270 GOTO 01220
01280 PRINT "HOW MANY PERIODS FOR THE VARIABLES ? (MAX. IS 20)"
01290 INPUT P
01300 LET P=INT(P)
01310 IF P>0 AND P<21 THEN 01350
01320 PRINT "INPUT SHOULD BE FROM 1 TO 20"
01330 PRINT "PLEASE TRY AGAIN"
01340 GOTO 01290
01350 PRINT
01360 PRINT "OUTFLOWS CARRY 'MINUS' SIGN"
01370 PRINT "INFLOWS  CARRY 'PLUS' OR 'NO' SIGN"
01380 PRINT
01390 FOR I=1 TO V
01400 PRINT "PLEASE ENTER THE ROW";I;"VARIABLE NAME"
01410 PRINT "(MAX. IS 7 CHARACTERS)"
01420 INPUT N$(I)
01430 PRINT "PLEASE ENTER THE CASH FLOWS OF VARIABLE ";I
01440 FOR J=1 TO P
01450 INPUT A(I,J)
01460 NEXT J
01470 NEXT I
01480 FOR I=1 TO P
01490 LET S9=0
01500 FOR J=1 TO V
01510 LET S9=S9+A(J,I)
01520 NEXT J
01530 LET A(21,I)=S9
01540 NEXT I
01550 LET D(1,21)=P
01560 FOR I=1 TO P
01570 LET D(1,I)=A(21,I)
01580 NEXT I
01590 RETURN
01600 REM
01610 REM ***************************************************
```

```
01620 REM        SUBROUTINE FOR INPUT DATA
01630 REM        ------------------------
01640 PRINT
01650 PRINT "NET OUTFLOWS CARRY 'MINUS' SIGN"
01660 PRINT "NET INFLOWS CARRY 'PLUS' OR 'NO' SIGN"
01670 PRINT
01680 PRINT "INPUT ONLY ONE VALUE FOR EACH LINE"
01690 PRINT
01700 FOR I=1 TO K1
01710 PRINT "HOW MANY PERIODS FOR PROJECT";I;"?"
01720 PRINT "(INCLUDING INITIAL PERIOD)"
01730 INPUT P1
01740 LET P1=INT(P1)
01750 IF P1>0 AND P1<=20 THEN 01790
01760 PRINT "NUMBER OF PERIOD SHOULD BE FROM 1 TO 20"
01770 PRINT "INPUT AGAIN"
01780 GOTO 01730
01790 PRINT "PLEASE ENTER THE NET CASH FLOWS OF PROJECT";I
01800 LET D(I,21)=P1
01810 FOR J=1 TO P1
01820 INPUT D(I,J)
01830 NEXT J
01840 NEXT I
01850 RETURN
01860 REM ******************************************************
01870 REM   SUBROUTINE FOR PRINTING OUT THE DATA (ONE PROJECT)
01880 REM   ------------------------------------------------
01890 PRINT
01900 PRINT
01910 PRINT "YEAR";
01920 FOR I=1 TO D(1,21)
01930 PRINT TAB(I*8);I-1;
01940 NEXT I
01950 PRINT
01960 PRINT
01970 FOR I=1 TO V
01980 PRINT N$(I);
01990 FOR J=1 TO P
02000 PRINT TAB(J*8);A(I,J);
02010 NEXT J
02020 PRINT
02030 NEXT I
02040 FOR J=1 TO P
02050 PRINT TAB(J*8);" ------ ";
02060 NEXT J
02070 PRINT
02080 PRINT "NCF";
02090 FOR J=1 TO P
02100 PRINT TAB(J*8);D(1,J);
02110 NEXT J
02120 PRINT
02130 RETURN
02140 REM
02150 REM ***********************************************
02160 REM        SUBROUTINE FOR PRINTING OUT THE DATA
02170 REM        ----------------------------------
```

```
02180 PRINT
02190 LET M5=D(1,21)
02200 FOR I=2 TO K1
02210 IF D(I,21)>M5 THEN LET M5=D(I,21)
02220 NEXT I
02230 FOR I=1 TO M5
02240 PRINT TAB(16+(I-1)*9);"YEAR";I-1;
02250 NEXT I
02260 PRINT
02270 PRINT
02280 FOR I=1 TO K1
02290 PRINT "PROJECT";I;" : ";
02300 FOR J=1 TO D(I,21)
02310 PRINT TAB(15+(J-1)*9);D(I,J);
02320 NEXT J
02330 PRINT
02340 NEXT I
02350 PRINT
02360 RETURN
02370 REM **************************************************
02380 REM      SUBROUTINE TO CALCULATE NPV FOR GIVEN R
02390 REM      ---------------------------------------
02400 FOR I=1 TO K1
02410 LET Z=0
02420 FOR J=1 TO D(I,21)
02430 LET Z=Z+D(I,J)/(R/100+1)**(J-1)
02440 NEXT J
02450 LET Z=INT(100*Z+0.5)/100
02460 LET S(I,1)=Z
02470 NEXT I
02480 RETURN
02490 REM
02500 REM ****************************************************
02510 REM        SUBROUTINE TO CALCULATE PAYBACK PERIOD
02520 REM        --------------------------------------
02530 FOR I=1 TO K1
02540 LET T2=0
02550 LET S1=0
02560 LET C1=0
02570 FOR J=2 TO D(I,21)
02580 LET T2=J
02590 LET T1=S1
02600 LET S1=S1+D(I,J)
02610 IF S1<ABS(D(I,1)) THEN LET C1=C1+1
02620 IF S1=ABS(D(I,1)) THEN 02710
02630 IF S1>ABS(D(I,1)) THEN 02650
02640 NEXT J
02650 LET B1=C1+ABS(D(I,1)+T1)/D(I,T2)
02660 LET B1=INT(100*B1+0.5)/100
02670 REM ** STORE THE PAYBACK VALUE INTO FIFTH  COL. OF ARRAY S **
02680 IF C1=D(I,21)-1  THEN LET S(I,5)=999999
02690 IF B1<D(I,21)-1 THEN LET S(I,5)=B1
02700 GOTO 02720
02710 LET S(I,5)=C1+1
02720 NEXT I
02730 RETURN
```

```
02740 REM
02750 REM ******************************************************
02760 REM      THIS SUBROUTINE WILL CALCULATE AND STORE THE IRR
02770 REM      FOR THE CASH FLOWS BY USING 'BISECTION METHOD'
02780 REM
02790 PRINT "PLEASE ENTER THE ACCURACY FOR IRR"
02800 PRINT "FOR EXAMPLE, 0.01 MEANS CORRECT TO 2 SIG. FIGURES"
02810 INPUT E1
02820 LET E1=ABS(E1)
02830 FOR I=1 TO K1
02840 LET L1=-128
02850 LET R1=256
02860 LET M=(L1+R1)/2
02870 IF R1-M<=E1 THEN 02950
02880 LET V1=0
02890 FOR J=1 TO D(I,21)
02900 LET V1=V1+D(I,J)/(1+M/100)**(J-1)
02910 NEXT J
02920 IF V1>0 THEN LET L1=M
02930 IF V1<=0 THEN LET R1=M
02940 GOTO 02860
02950 REM ** STORE THE IRR VALUE TO THE 2ND COL. OF ARRAY S **
02960 LET M=INT(100*M+0.5)/100
02970 LET S(I,3)=M
02980 REM ** TEST THE ACCURACY OF IRR **
02990 LET V2=0
03000 FOR J=1 TO D(I,21)
03010 LET V2=V2+D(I,J)/(1+M/100)**(J-1)
03020 NEXT J
03030 LET S(I,16)=V2
03040 NEXT I
03050 RETURN
03060 REM
03070 REM ******************************************************
03080 REM      THIS SUBROUTINE WILL CALCULATE AND STORE THE P.I.
03090 REM      -------------------------------------------------
03100 FOR I=1 TO K1
03110 LET T1=(S(I,1)+ABS(D(I,1)))/ABS(D(I,1))
03120 LET T1=INT(100*T1+0.5)/100
03130 REM ** STORE THE P.I. VALUE TO THE 3RD COL. OF ARRAY S **
03140 LET S(I,4)=T1
03150 NEXT I
03160 RETURN
03170 REM
03180 REM **********************************
03190 REM   SUBROUTINE TO CALCULATE AVAI
03200 REM   ------------------------------
03210 FOR I=1 TO K1
03220 LET T1=0
03230 FOR J=2 TO D(I,21)
03240 LET T1=T1+D(I,J)
03250 NEXT J
03260 LET T1=T1*2/((D(I,21)-1)*ABS(D(I,1)))
03270 LET S(I,7)=INT(T1*100+0.5)
03280 NEXT I
03290 RETURN
```

```
03300 REM
03310 REM ****************************************************
03320 REM  SUBROUTINE TO PRINT OUT THE NPV,NAB,IRR,PI,PB,DPB,ARAI
03330 REM  ---------------------------------------------------
03340 PRINT
03350 PRINT "DISCOUNT RATE=";R;"%"
03360 PRINT "IRR IS CORRECTED TO";E1
03370 PRINT
03380 PRINT
03390 PRINT
03400 PRINT TAB(1);"PROJECT";TAB(10);"NPV";TAB(20);"NAB";
03410 PRINT TAB(30);"IRR(%)";TAB(38);"PI";TAB(46);"PB";
03420 PRINT TAB(54);"DPB";TAB(62);"ARAI(%)";TAB(71);"LIFE"
03430 PRINT
03440 FOR I=1 TO K1
03450 PRINT I;
03460 PRINT TAB(9);S(I,1);TAB(19);S(I,2);
03470 IF ABS(S(I,16))/ABS(D(I,1))<0.05 THEN 03510
03480 PRINT TAB(29);"UNFOUND";
03490 LET S(I,3)=-999999
03500 GOTO 03520
03510 PRINT TAB(29);S(I,3);
03520 PRINT TAB(37);S(I,4);
03530 IF S(I,5)=999999 THEN PRINT TAB(45);"NEVER";
03540 IF S(I,5)<>999999 THEN PRINT TAB(45);S(I,5);
03550 IF S(I,6)=999999 THEN PRINT TAB(53);"NEVER";
03560 IF S(I,6)<>999999 THEN PRINT TAB(53);S(I,6);
03570 PRINT TAB(61);S(I,7);TAB(70);D(I,21)-1;
03580 PRINT
03590 NEXT I
03600 RETURN
03610 REM ***********************************************
03620 REM               NPV AS A FUNCTION OF DISCOUNT RATES
03630 REM               ------------------------------------
03640 PRINT
03650 PRINT "TABLE OF NPV FOR DIFFERENT DISCOUNT RATES"
03660 PRINT "-----------------------------------------"
03670 PRINT
03680 PRINT
03690 PRINT "PROJECT";
03700 FOR I=1 TO R1
03710 PRINT TAB(10+(I-1)*10);R(I);"%";
03720 NEXT I
03730 PRINT "         ------------------------------------";
03740 PRINT "--------------"
03750 PRINT
03760 FOR I=1 TO K1
03770 PRINT I;
03780 FOR J=1 TO R1
03790 LET Z=0
03800 FOR K=1 TO D(I,21)
03810 LET Z=Z+D(I,K)/(R(J)/100+1)**(K-1)
03820 NEXT K
03830 PRINT TAB(10+(J-1)*10);Z;
03840 NEXT J
03850 PRINT
```

```
03860 NEXT I
03870 PRINT
03880 RETURN
03890 REM
03900 REM *************************************************
03910 REM          SUBROUTINE FOR SENSITIVITY ANALYSIS
03920 REM          -----------------------------------
03930 PRINT
03940 PRINT "             SENSITIVITY ANALYSIS"
03950 PRINT "             --------------------"
03960 PRINT
03970 PRINT "DO YOU WANT TO ADJUST CASH FLOWS ? (YES OR NO)"
03980 INPUT Q9$
03990 IF Q9$="NO" THEN 04490
04000 PRINT
04010 PRINT "YOU GIVE THE PERCENTAGE CHANGES IN CASH FLOWS"
04020 PRINT "THEN THE COMPUTER WILL CALCULATE THEIR EFFECTS ON NPV"
04030 PRINT
04040 PRINT "INPUT NUMBER OF CHANGES IN CASH FLOWS"
04050 PRINT "(MAX. IS 10)"
04060 INPUT R9
04070 LET R9=INT(R9)
04080 IF R9>0 AND R9<11 THEN 04120
04090 PRINT "INPUT SHOULD BE FROM 1 TO 10"
04100 PRINT "PLEASE TRY AGAIN"
04110 GOTO 04060
04120 PRINT "PLEASE INPUT THE % CHANGE IN CASH FLOW"
04130 PRINT " E.G. 10% DECREASE IN CASH FLOW IS ENTERED AS  -10"
04140 PRINT "      10% INCREASE IN CASH FLOW IS ENTERED AS   10"
04150 PRINT
04160 FOR I=1 TO R9
04170 INPUT C(I)
04180 NEXT I
04190 PRINT
04200 PRINT "     NOTE : DISCOUNT RATE IS ";R;"%"
04210 PRINT
04220 PRINT "     TABLE OF NPV FOR DIFFERENT CHANGES OF CASH FLOWS"
04230 PRINT"     ----------------------------------------------------"
04240 PRINT
04250 PRINT
04260 PRINT "                     % CHANGE IN CASH FLOW"
04270 PRINT
04280 PRINT "PROJECT";
04290 FOR I=1 TO R9
04300 PRINT TAB(10*I);C(I);"%";
04310 NEXT I
04320 PRINT "          -----------------------------------";
04330 PRINT "--------------------"
04340 PRINT
04350 FOR I=1 TO K1
04360 PRINT I;
04370 FOR J=1 TO R9
04380 LET Z=D(I,1)
04390 LET Q=(100+C(J))/100
04400 FOR K=2 TO D(I,21)
04410 LET Z=Z+Q*D(I,K)/(R/100+1)**(K-1)
```

```
04420 NEXT K
04430 LET Z=INT(Z*100+0.5)/100
04440 PRINT TAB(10*J);Z;
04450 NEXT J
04460 PRINT
04470 NEXT I
04480  PRINT
04490 PRINT
04500 PRINT "THE FOLLOWING TABLE WILL GIVE THE ANNUAL EQUIVALENT"
04510 PRINT "CASH FLOW WHICH WHEN DISCOUNTED AT";R;"% OVER"
04520 PRINT "PROJECT LIFE WILL GIVE       ZERO      NPV"
04530 PRINT "                             ------       "
04540 PRINT
04550 PRINT
04560 PRINT "     NOTE : DISCOUNT RATE IS ";R;"%"
04570 PRINT
04580 PRINT
04590 PRINT TAB(16);"BREAK-EVEN"
04600 PRINT TAB(16);"ANNUITY";TAB(28);"PROJECT LIFE"
04610 LET U=R/100
04620 FOR I=1 TO K1
04630 LET D(I,22)=1/U-1/(U*((1+U)**(D(I,21)-1)))
04640 NEXT I
04650 PRINT
04660 FOR I=1 TO K1
04670 LET T1=ABS(D(I,1))/D(I,22)
04680 LET T1=INT(100*T1+0.5)/100
04690 PRINT "PROJECT";I;" : ";TAB(15);T1;TAB(30);D(I,21)-1
04700 PRINT
04710 NEXT I
04720 RETURN
04730 REM ********************************************************
04740 REM              SUBROUTINE TO CALCULATE NET ANAUAL BENEFIT
04750 REM              ------------------------------------------
04760 LET U=R/100
04770 FOR I=1 TO K1
04780 LET D(I,22)=1/U-1/(U*((1+U)**(D(I,21)-1)))
04790 LET Z=S(I,1)/D(I,22)
04800 LET S(I,2)=INT(100*Z+0.5)/100
04810 NEXT I
04820 RETURN
04830 REM
04840 REM **********************************************************
04850 REM    SUBROUTINE TO CALCULATE DISCOUNTED PAYBACK PERIOD
04860 REM    -----------------------------------------------
04870 FOR I=1 TO K1
04880 LET T2=0
04890 LET S1=0
04900 LET C1=0
04910 FOR J=2 TO D(I,21)
04920 LET T2=J
04930 LET T1=S1
04940 LET S1=S1+D(I,J)/(1+R/100)**(J-1)
04950 IF S1<ABS(D(I,1)) THEN LET C1=C1+1
04960 IF S1=ABS(D(I,1)) THEN 05040
04970 IF S1>ABS(D(I,1)) THEN 04990
04980 NEXT J
```

```
04990 LET B1=C1+ABS(D(I,1)+T1)/(D(I,T2)/(1+R/100)**(T2-1))
05000 LET B1=INT(100*B1+0.5)/100
05010 IF C1=D(I,21)-1 THEN LET S(I,6)=999999
05020 IF B1<D(I,21)-1 THEN LET S(I,6)=B1
05030 GOTO 05050
05040 LET S(I,6)=C1+1
05050 NEXT I
05060 RETURN
05070 REM        *****  END OF PROGRAM   *****
05080 END
```

Computer Program 2:

Probability Analysis

```
00100 REM
00110 REM               PROBABILITY ANALYSIS
00120 REM               --------------------
00130 REM
00140 REM      THIS PROGRAM WILL CALCULATE THE MEAN AND
00150 REM      STANDARD DEVIATION OF A PROJECT NPV AND
00160 REM      PERFORM PROBABILITY ANALYSIS BY ASSUMING
00170 REM      THE DISTRIBUTION IS NORMALLY DISTRIBUTED
00180 REM
00190 REM      TWO INPUT FORMAT ARE ALLOWED
00200 REM
00210 REM      1.  INPUT THE PROB. DIST. OF THE PROJECT
00220 REM          (MAX. IS 10) AND CASH FLOWS FOR EACH
00230 REM          PERIOD (MAX. NO. OF STATE OF WORLD IS 10)
00240 REM
00250 REM      2.  INPUT THE MOST LIKELY PROJECT CASH FLOW,
00260 REM          MAX DEVIATION (BEST AND WORST) AND
00270 REM          THE PROBABILITY OF DEVIATION
00280 REM          (MAX. PERIOD IS 10)
00290 REM
00300 DIM D(100,2),R(10,2),T(61,2),L(10,3)
00310 READ Y$,N$,G$,L$
00320 DATA YES,NO,>,<
00330 REM  **  INPUT THE NORMAL DISTRIBUTION TABLE **
00340 GOSUB 01400
00350 PRINT "HOW MANY PERIODS ARE CONSIDERED ?"
00360 PRINT "(INCLUDING INITIAL PERIOD)"
00370 PRINT "(MAX. IS 10)"
00380 INPUT P
00390 LET P=INT(P)
00400 IF P>0 AND P<11 THEN 00450
```

```
00410 PRINT "NO. OF PERIOD SHOULD BE FROM 1 TO 10"
00420 PRINT "PLEASE INPUT AGAIN"
00430 GOTO 00380
00440 PRINT
00450 PRINT "ARE THE DATA THE SAME FOR ALL PERIODS ?"
00460 PRINT "(EXCEPT INITIAL PERIOD)"
00470 PRINT "PLEASE INPUT 'YES' OR 'NO'"
00480 INPUT Q$
00490 IF Q$<>Y$ AND Q$<>N$ THEN 00450
00500 IF Q$=N$ THEN 00550
00510 PRINT
00520 PRINT "YOU ONLY NEED TO INPUT THE INITIAL PERIOD"
00530 PRINT "AND ONE OTHER PERIOD"
00540 PRINT
00550 PRINT "WHICH INPUT FORMAT YOU WANT ?"
00560 PRINT "INPUT '1' FOR 'PROB. DIST.' OF CASH FLOW"
00570 PRINT "      '2' FOR 'MOST LIKELY AND DEVIATON OF CASH FLOW"
00580 INPUT Q1
00590 IF Q1<>1 AND Q1<>2 THEN 00550
00600 PRINT
00610 PRINT "NET CASH OUTFLOWS CARRY 'MINUS' SIGN"
00620 PRINT "         INFLOWS  CARRY 'PLUS' OR 'NO' SIGN"
00630 PRINT
00640 ON Q1 GOSUB 01480,01930
00650 PRINT "DO YOU WANT TO PRINT OUT THE DATA ?"
00660 PRINT "INPUT 'YES' OR 'NO'"
00670 INPUT E$
00680 IF E$<>Y$ AND E$<>N$ THEN 00650
00690 IF E$=N$ THEN 00710
00700 ON Q1 GOSUB 02210,02460
00710 ON Q1 GOSUB 02620,02840
00720 IF Q$=N$ THEN 00770
00730 FOR I=3 TO P
00740 LET R(I,1)=R(2,1)
00750 LET R(I,2)=R(2,2)
00760 NEXT I
00770 PRINT
00780 PRINT "THE EXPECTED RETURN AND S.D. FOR EACH PERIOD ARE :"
00790 PRINT
00800 PRINT
00810 PRINT "PERIOD";TAB(16);"EXP. RETURN";TAB(32);"S.D."
00820 PRINT
00830 FOR I=1 TO P
00840 PRINT TAB(3);I-1;TAB(15);R(I,1);TAB(30);R(I,2)
00850 NEXT I
00860 PRINT
00870 PRINT
00880 PRINT "PLEASE INPUT THE RISK-FREE INTEREST RATE"
00890 PRINT "(IN DECIMAL FORM)"
00900 INPUT H
00910 IF H<=0 OR H>1 THEN 00880
00920 PRINT
00930 PRINT "ARE THE CASH FLOWS IN DIFFERENT PERIODS"
00940 PRINT "INDEPENDENT  OR PERFECTLY CORRELATED ?"
00950 PRINT "-----------      --------------------"
00960 PRINT
```

```
00970 PRINT "PLEASE INPUT  '1'  FOR INDEPENDENT"
00980 PRINT "              '2'  FOR PERFECTLY CORRELATED"
00990 INPUT Q9
01000 LET Q9=INT(Q9)
01010 IF Q9<>1 AND Q9<>2 THEN 00930
01020 ON Q9 GOSUB 03120,03500
01030 PRINT "DO YOU WANT TO CONDUCT PROBABILITY ANALYSIS ?"
01040 PRINT "INPUT 'YES' OR 'NO'"
01050 INPUT A$
01060 IF A$<>Y$ AND A$<>N$ THEN 01020
01070 IF A$=N$ THEN 04410
01080 PRINT
01090 PRINT "                    PROBABILITY ANALYSIS"
01100 PRINT "                    --------------------"
01110 PRINT
01120 PRINT
01130 PRINT "PLEASE ENTER THE '<' OR '>' SIGN FIRST"
01140 PRINT "FOLLOWED BY COMMA(,) THEN THE FIGURES"
01150 PRINT "  ---------"
01160 PRINT
01170 PRINT "E.G.  IF YOU WANT TO KNOW THE PROBABILITY OF"
01180 PRINT "      NPV<1000, SAY, THEN INPUT AS"
01190 PRINT "                                  <,1000"
01200 PRINT
01210 INPUT S$,F
01220 GOSUB 03900
01230 PRINT "MORE PROBABILITY ANALYSIS ?"
01240 PRINT "PLEASE INPUT 'YES' OR 'NO'"
01250 INPUT B$
01260 IF B$=Y$ THEN 01120
01270 PRINT
01280 PRINT "DO YOU WANT TO RECONSIDER THE RISK FREE"
01290 PRINT "INTEREST RATE AND THE DEPENDENCE OF CASH FLOWS?"
01300 PRINT "PLEASE INPUT 'YES' OR 'NO'"
01310 INPUT O$
01320 IF O$=Y$ THEN 00880
01330 GOTO 04410
01340 REM
01350 REM ***************************************************
01360 REM *                                                 *
01370 REM *        SUBROUTINES OF THE PROGRAM               *
01380 REM *                                                 *
01390 REM ***************************************************
01400 REM          INPUT NORMAL DISTRIBUTION TABLE
01410 REM          -------------------------------
01420 FOR I=1 TO 61
01430 READ T(I,1),T(I,2)
01440 NEXT I
01450 RETURN
01460 REM
01470 REM ***************************************************
01480 REM       INPUT PROB. DIST. OF CASH FLOW
01490 REM       ------------------------------
01500 REM
01510 PRINT "HOW MANY 'STATES OF WORLD' FOR THE DISTRIBUTION ?"
01520 PRINT "(MAX. IS 10)"
```

```
01530 INPUT N
01540 LET N=INT(N)
01550 IF N>0 AND N<11 THEN 01590
01560 PRINT "NO. OF STATE OF WORLD SHOULD BE FROM 1 TO 10"
01570 PRINT "PLEASE INPUT AGAIN"
01580 GOTO 01530
01590 PRINT "              NOW INPUT THE PROB. DIST."
01600 PRINT
01610 PRINT "FOR EACH LINE,FIRST INPUT THE PROBABILITY"
01620 PRINT "AND THEN THE CORRESPONDING CASH FLOWS"
01630 PRINT
01640 PRINT "REMARK  :  NEED A COMMA(,) BETWEEN EACH DATA"
01650 PRINT "                    --------"
01660 PRINT
01670 PRINT "PERIOD '0' IS THE STARTING PERIOD (INITIAL INVESTMENT)"
01680 PRINT "IF INITIAL INVESTMENT IS CERTAIN, SAY, -1000"
01690 PRINT "THEN INPUT AS"
01700 PRINT "                     1,-1000"
01710 PRINT "AND PUT              0,0       TO THE OTHER STATE OF WORLD"
01720 PRINT
01730 LET P9=0
01740 IF Q$=Y$ THEN LET C9=2
01750 IF Q$=N$  THEN LET C9=P
01760 FOR I=0 TO 90 STEP 10
01770 IF P9>=C9 THEN 01900
01780 PRINT "PLEASE INPUT THE PROB. DIST. OF PERIOD   ";P9
01790 LET V1=0
01800 FOR J=1 TO N
01810 INPUT D(I+J,1),D(I+J,2)
01820 LET V1=V1+D(I+J,1)
01830 NEXT J
01840 IF V1=1 THEN 01880
01850 PRINT "SUM OF PROBABILITY NOT EQUAL TO  '1'"
01860 PRINT "PLEASE INPUT AGAIN"
01870 GOTO 01780
01880 LET P9=P9+1
01890 NEXT I
01900 RETURN
01910 REM
01920 REM ***************************************************
01930 REM    INPUT MOST LIKELY AND DEVIATION OF CASH FLOW
01940 REM    ------------------------------------------
01950 PRINT
01960 PRINT "FOR EACH LINE, FIRST INPUT THE MOST LIKELY "
01970 PRINT "CASH FLOW,FOLLOWED BY MAX. DEVIATION AND"
01980 PRINT "PROBABILTY OF DIVIATION AT LAST"
01990 PRINT
02000 PRINT "REMARK: COMMA(,) IS NEEDED BETWEEN INPUT OF EACH LINE"
02010 PRINT "        --------"
02020 PRINT
02030 PRINT "PERIOD '0' IS THE PERIOD OF INITIAL INVESTMENT"
02040 PRINT "IF INITIAL INVESTMENT IS CERTAIN WITHOUT DEV."
02050 PRINT "SAY, -1000, THEN INPUT AS "
02060 PRINT "                          -1000,0,0"
02070 PRINT
02080 IF Q$=Y$ THEN LET C9=2
```

```
02090 IF Q$=N$  THEN LET C9=P
02100 FOR I=1 TO C9
02110 PRINT" PLEASE INPUT DATA OF PERIOD";I-1
02120 INPUT L(I,1),L(I,2),L(I,3)
02130 IF L(I,3)>=0 AND L(I,3)<0.5 THEN 02170
02140 PRINT "PROBABILITY SHOULD BE BETWEEN 0 AND 0.5"
02150 PRINT "PLEASE INPUT AGAIN"
02160 GOTO 02110
02170 NEXT I
02180 RETURN
02190 REM
02200 REM *****************************************************
02210 REM          PRINTING OUT THE PROB. DIST.
02220 REM          ----------------------------
02230 PRINT
02240 PRINT TAB(12);"PROBABILITY";TAB(25);"NET CASH FLOW"
02250 PRINT
02260 LET P9=0
02270 IF Q$=Y$ THEN LET C9=2
02280 IF Q$=N$ THEN LET C9=P
02290 FOR I=0 TO 90 STEP 10
02300 IF P9>=C9 THEN 02420
02310 PRINT "PERIOD";P9;
02320 FOR J=1 TO N
02330 PRINT TAB(15);D(I+J,1);TAB(28);D(I+J,2)
02340 NEXT J
02350 PRINT TAB(12);"----------------------------"
02360 PRINT
02370 LET P9=P9+1
02380 NEXT I
02390 PRINT
02400 PRINT
02410 PRINT
02420 IF Q$=Y$ THEN PRINT"THE NEXT ";P-2;" PREIODS HAVE SAME DATA"
02430 RETURN
02440 REM
02450 REM *****************************************************
02460 REM     PRINTING OUT THE DATA OF MOST LIKELY CASH FLOW
02470 REM     -------------------------------------------------
02480 PRINT
02490 PRINT TAB(15);"MOST LIKELY";TAB(30);"MAX. DEV.";TAB(40);"PROB.'
02500 PRINT
02510 IF Q$=Y$ THEN LET K=2
02520 IF Q$=N$  THEN LET K=P
02530 FOR I=1 TO K
02540 PRINT "PERIOD";I-1;TAB(15);L(I,1);TAB(30);L(I,2);TAB(40);L(I,3
02550 NEXT I
02560 PRINT
02570 PRINT
02580 IF Q$=Y$ THEN PRINT "DATA OF OTHER PERIODS ARE THE SAME"
02590 RETURN
02600 REM
02610 REM *****************************************************
02620 REM   CAL. E.R. AND S.D. FOR EACH PERIOD (PROB. DIST.)
02630 REM   -----------------------------------------------
02640 LET P9=0
```

```
02650 IF Q$=Y$ THEN LET C9=2
02660 IF Q$=N$ THEN LET C9=P
02670 FOR I=0 TO 90 STEP 10
02680 IF P9>=C9 THEN 02810
02690 LET T9=0
02700 LET T8=0
02710 FOR J=1 TO N
02720 LET T9=T9+D(I+J,1)*D(I+J,2)
02730 NEXT J
02740 FOR J=1 TO N
02750 LET T8=T8+D(I+J,1)*(D(I+J,2)-T9)**2
02760 NEXT J
02770 LET R(P9+1,1)=T9
02780 LET R(P9+1,2)=SQR(T8)
02790 LET P9=P9+1
02800 NEXT I
02810 RETURN
02820 REM
02830 REM ***********************************************************
02840 REM   CAL. E.R. AND S.D. FOR EACH PERIOD (MOST LIKELY CASE)
02850 REM   ---------------------------------------------------------
02860 IF Q$=Y$ THEN LET K=2
02870 IF Q$=N$ THEN LET K=P
02880 FOR I=1 TO K
02890 LET R(I,1)=L(I,1)
02900 NEXT I
02910 FOR I=1 TO K
02920 LET T=L(I,3)
02930 IF T>0.0013 THEN 02960
02940 LET S8=3
02950 GOTO 03070
02960 LET C8=0
02970 FOR J=1 TO 61
02980 IF T(J,2)>T THEN LET C8=C8+1
02990 IF T(J,2)=T THEN 03020
03000 IF T(J,2)<T THEN 03040
03010 NEXT J
03020 LET S8=T(C8+1,1)
03030 GOTO 03070
03040 LET T8=(T(C8,2)+T(C8+1,2))/2
03050 IF T<T8 THEN LET S8=T(C8,1)
03060 IF T>=T8 THEN LET S8=T(C8+1,1)
03070 LET R(I,2)=L(I,2)/S8
03080 NEXT I
03090 RETURN
03100 REM
03110 REM **********************************************************
03120 REM      CAL. THE EXP. VALUE AND S.D. OF PROJECT NPV
03130 REM      ----------------------------------------
03140 REM            (ASSUMED PERIOD CASH FLOWS ARE INDEPENDENT)
03150 PRINT
03160 PRINT "        (ASSUMED PERIOD CASH FLOWS ARE INDEPENDENT)"
03170 PRINT
03180 LET V=0
03190 FOR I=1 TO P
03200 LET V=V+R(I,1)/(1+H)**(I-1)
```

```
03210 NEXT I
03220 LET X1=V
03230 LET V=0
03240 FOR I=1 TO P
03250 LET V=V+R(I,2)**2/(1+H)**(2*(I-1))
03260 NEXT I
03270 LET Y1=SQR(V)
03280 PRINT
03290 PRINT "THE RISK-FREE INTEREST RATE IS  ";H*100;"(%)"
03300 PRINT
03310 PRINT "THE EXPECTED VALUE OF THE PROJECT NPV IS  ";X1
03320 PRINT "                                          -------"
03330 PRINT
03340 PRINT "THE   S.D.      OF THE PROJECT NPV IS  ";Y1
03350 PRINT "                                          -------"
03360 PRINT
03370 PRINT
03380 PRINT"68% CONFIDENT THAT THE PROJECT NPV IS BETWEEN  ";
03390 PRINT X1-Y1;" AND ";X1+Y1
03400 PRINT
03410 PRINT"95% CONDIDENT THAT THE PROJECT NPV IS BETWEEN  ";
03420 PRINT X1-2*Y1;" AND ";X1+2*Y1
03430 PRINT
03440 PRINT"99% CONFIDENT THAT THE PROJECT NPV IS BETWEEN  ";
03450 PRINT X1-3*Y1;" AND ";X1+3*Y1
03460 PRINT
03470 RETURN
03480 REM
03490 REM ***************************************************
03500 REM      CAL. EXPECTED RETURN AND S.D. OF PROJECT NPV
03510 REM      --------------------------------------------
03520 REM    (ASSUMING PERIOD CASH FLOWS ARE PERFECTLY CORRELATED)
03530 PRINT
03540 PRINT "(ASSUMING PERIOD CASH FLOWS ARE PERFECTLY CORRELATED)"
03550 PRINT
03560 LET V=0
03570 FOR I=1 TO P
03580 LET V=V+R(I,1)/(1+H)**(I-1)
03590 NEXT I
03600 LET X2=V
03610 LET V=0
03620 FOR I=1 TO P
03630 LET V=V+R(I,2)/(1+H)**(I-1)
03640 NEXT I
03650 LET Y2=V
03660 PRINT
03670 PRINT "THE RISK-FREE INTEREST RATE IS  ";H*100;"(%)"
03680 PRINT
03690 PRINT
03700 PRINT "THE EXPECTED VALUE OF THE PROJECT NPV IS ";X2
03710 PRINT "                                         -------"
03720 PRINT
03730 PRINT "THE     S.D.      OF THE PROJECT NPV IS ";Y2
03740 PRINT "                                         -------"
03750 PRINT
03760 PRINT
```

```
03770 PRINT "68% CONFIDENT THAT THE PROJECT NPV IS BETWEEN   ";
03780 PRINT X2-Y2;" AND ";X2+Y2
03790 PRINT
03800 PRINT "95% CONFIDENT THAT THE PROJECT NPV IS BETWEEN   ";
03810 PRINT X2-2*Y2;" AND ";X2+2*Y2
03820 PRINT
03830 PRINT "99% CONFIDENT THAT THE PROJECT NPV IS BETWEEN   ";
03840 PRINT X2-3*Y2;" AND ";X2+3*Y2
03850 PRINT
03860 PRINT
03870 RETURN
03880 REM
03890 REM ****************************************************
03900 REM                 PROBABILITY ANALYSIS
03910 REM                 --------------------
03920 IF Q9=1 THEN LET Z=(F-X1)/Y1
03930 IF Q9=2 THEN LET Z=(F-X2)/Y2
03940 LET P5=9999
03950 IF S$=G$ AND Z>3  THEN LET P5=0
03960 IF S$=G$ AND Z<-3 THEN LET P5=0
03970 IF S$=L$ AND Z<-3 THEN LET P5=0
03980 IF S$=L$ AND Z>3  THEN LET P5=0
03990 IF P5=0 OR P5=1 THEN 04130
04000 IF Z>0 THEN LET Z9=Z
04010 IF Z<=0 THEN LET Z9=ABS(Z)
04020 LET C3=0
04030 FOR I=1 TO 61
04040 IF T(I,1)<Z9 THEN LET C3=C3+1
04050 IF T(I,1)=Z9 THEN 04080
04060 IF T(I,1)>Z9 THEN 04100
04070 NEXT I
04080 LET P5=T(C3+1,2)
04090 GOTO 04130
04100 LET T5=(T(C3,1)+T(C3+1,1))/2
04110 IF Z9<T5 THEN LET P5=T(C3,2)
04120 IF Z9>=T5 THEN LET P5=T(C3+1,2)
04130 IF S$=G$ AND Z>=0 THEN PRINT"PROB. OF NPV ";S$;F;"=";P5
04140 IF S$=G$ AND Z<0  THEN PRINT"PROB. OF NPV ";S$;F;"=";1-P5
04150 IF S$=L$ AND Z>=0 THEN PRINT"PROB. OF NPV ";S$;F;"=";1-P5
04160 IF S$=L$ AND Z<0  THEN PRINT"PROB. OF NPV ";S$;F;"=";P5
04170 PRINT TAB(19);"--------"
04180 PRINT
04190 PRINT
04200 RETURN
04210 REM
04220 REM ************************************************
04230 REM              DATA OF NORMAL DISTRIBUTION TABLE
04240 REM              --------------------------------
04250 DATA 0.00,0.5000,0.05,0.4801,0.10,0.4602,0.15,0.4404
04260 DATA 0.20,0.4207,0.25,0.4013,0.30,0.3821,0.35,0.3632
04270 DATA 0.40,0.3446,0.45,0.3264,0.50,0.3085,0.55,0.2912
04280 DATA 0.60,0.2743,0.65,0.2578,0.70,0.2420,0.75,0.2264
04290 DATA 0.80,0.2119,0.85,0.1977,0.90,0.1841,0.95,0.1711
04300 DATA 1.00,0.1577,1.05,0.1469,1.10,0.1357,1.15,0.1251
04310 DATA 1.20,0.1151,1.25,0.1056,1.30,0.0968,1.35,0.0885
04320 DATA 1.40,0.0808,1.45,0.0735,1.50,0.0668,1.55,0.0606
```

```
04330 DATA 1.60,0.0548,1.65,0.0495,1.70,0.0446,1.75,0.0401
04340 DATA 1.80,0.0359,1.85,0.0322,1.90,0.0287,1.95,0.0256
04350 DATA 2.00,0.0228,2.05,0.0202,2.10,0.0179,2.15,0.0158
04360 DATA 2.20,0.0139,2.25,0.0122,2.30,0.0107,2.35,0.0094
04370 DATA 2.40,0.0082,2.45,0.0071,2.50,0.0062,2.55,0.0054
04380 DATA 2.60,0.0047,2.65,0.0040,2.70,0.0035,2.75,0.0030
04390 DATA 2.80,0.0026,2.85,0.0022,2.90,0.0019,2.95,0.0016
04400 DATA 3.00,0.0013
04410 END
```

Computer Program 3:

Cost of Capital

```
00100 PRINT
00110 PRINT "             EVALUATION OF RISKY INVESTMENT"
00120 PRINT "             ------------------------------"
00130 PRINT
00140 PRINT "     THIS PROGRAM WILL EVALUATE A RISKY PROJECT"
00150 PRINT "     BY USING COMPANY'S AVERAGE COST OF CAPITAL"
00160 PRINT "     OR CAPITAL ASSETS PRICING MODEL APPROACH"
00170 PRINT "     FINALLY, AN ACCEPT/REJECT DECISION IS MADE"
00180 PRINT
00190 DIM C(20),D(20)
00200 GOTO 00390
00210 PRINT
00220 PRINT "HOW MANY PERIODS OF CASH FLOW CONSIDERED ?"
00230 PRINT "(INCLUDING INITIAL PERIOD,MAX. IS 20)"
00240 INPUT P
00250 LET P=INT(P)
00260 IF P<1 OR P>20 THEN 00230
00270 PRINT
00280 PRINT "PLEASE INPUT THE PROJECT'S CASH FLOWS"
00290 PRINT
00300 PRINT "NET OUTFLOWS CARRY 'MINUS' SIGN"
00310 PRINT "NET INFLOWS  CARRY  'PLUS' OR 'NO' SIGN"
00320 PRINT
00330 PRINT "EACH LINE ONLY INPUT 'ONE' CASH FLOW"
00340 PRINT
00350 FOR I=1 TO P
00360 INPUT C(I)
00370 NEXT I
00380 RETURN
00390 PRINT
00400 PRINT "WHICH METHOD TO CALCULATE THE DISCOUNT RATE ?"
```

```
00410 PRINT "PLEASE INPUT"
00420 PRINT "            '1' FOR COMPANY'S AVERAGE COST OF CAPITAL"
00430 PRINT "            '2' FOR CAPITAL ASSETS PRICING MODEL"
00440 INPUT Q1
00450 IF Q1<>1 AND Q1<>2 THEN 00410
00460 ON Q1 GOSUB 00780,01950
00470 PRINT
00480 PRINT "DO YOU WANT TO APPLY THE INFORMATION INTO A"
00490 PRINT "RISKY PROJECT (YES OR NO) ?"
00500 INPUT Q7$
00510 IF Q7$ = "NO" THEN 03420
00520 GOSUB 00220
00530 PRINT
00540 PRINT
00550 PRINT "THE PROJECT CASH FLOWS ARE :"
00560 PRINT
00570 FOR I=1 TO P
00580 PRINT C(I);"  ";
00590 NEXT I
00600 PRINT
00610 PRINT
00620 PRINT "THE DISCOUNT RATE IS "; R; "%"
00630 LET V=0
00640 FOR I=1 TO P
00650 LET V=V+C(I)/(1+R/100)**(I-1)
00660 NEXT I
00670 PRINT
00680 PRINT "THE NET PRESENT VALUE OF THE PROJECT IS";TAB(50);V
00690 PRINT
00700 IF V>0 THEN PRINT "NPV>0, SO THE PROJECT IS ACCEPTABLE"
00710 IF V<=0 THEN PRINT "NPV<=0, SO REJECT THE PROJCET"
00720 PRINT
00730 PRINT "****************************************************"
00740 REM
00750 REM ***** END OF MAIN PROGRAM *****
00760 GOTO 03420
00770 REM **************************************************
00780 REM           SUBROUTINE TO CALCULATE WACC
00790 REM           ----------------------------
00800 PRINT
00810 PRINT "      EVALUATE A RISKY PROJECT BY USING  'WACC'"
00820 PRINT "      -----------------------------------------"
00830 PRINT
00840 LET V1=V2=V3=V4=0
00850 REM ***** SHARE *****
00860 PRINT "WHAT IS THE NUMBER OF SHARES FOR THE COMPANY ?"
00870 INPUT S1
00880 PRINT "WHAT IS THE CURRENT PRICE PER SHARE ( IN POUNDS) ?"
00890 INPUT P1
00900 LET V1=S1*P1
00910 PRINT "WHAT IS THE REQUIRED RETURN OF EQUITY ?"
00920 PRINT "PLEASE INPUT  '1' IF INPUT BY USERS"
00930 PRINT "              '2' IF USING CONSTANT GROWTH FORMULA"
00940 INPUT F9
00950 IF F9 <>1 AND F9<>2 THEN 00920
00960 IF F9=2 THEN 01000
```

```
00970 PRINT "PLEASE INPUT THE REQUIRED RETURN OF EQUITY IN %"
00980 INPUT K1
00990 GOTO 01090
01000 PRINT "WHAT IS THE TREND OF DIVIDEND GROWTH ?"
01010 PRINT "FOR EXAMPLE, IF DIVIDEND GROW FROM 6P TO 14P"
01020 PRINT "IN 10 YEARS' TIME, THEN INPUT AS"
01030 PRINT"     0.06,0.14,10"
01040 INPUT D0,D9,Y1
01050 LET G=(D9/D0)**(1/Y1)-1
01060 LET K1=D9*(1+G)/P1+G
01070 LET K1=INT(100*K1+0.5)
01080 REM ***** CONSTANT GROWTH FORMULA *****
01090 PRINT "ANY DEBENTURE ISSUED ? (YES OR NO)"
01100 INPUT Q2$
01110 IF Q2$ <> "YES" AND Q2$<>"NO" THEN 01090
01120 IF Q2$="NO" THEN 01440
01130 REM ***** DEBENTURE *****
01140 PRINT "PLEASE INPUT TOTAL AMOUNT (IN POUNDS) OF"
01150 PRINT "DEBENTURE ISSUED"
01160 INPUT D2
01170 PRINT "WHAT IS THE INTEREST RATE OF THE DEBENTURES (%) ?"
01180 INPUT I2
01190 PRINT "PLEASE INPUT THE CURRENT PRICE OF THE DEBENTURES"
01200 PRINT "(BASE ISSUE PRICE IS ASSUMED TO BE 100)"
01210 INPUT P2
01220 LET V2=D2*P2/100
01230 PRINT "HOW MANY YEARS LATER THE DEBENTURES BE REDEEMED ?"
01240 INPUT Y2
01250 FOR I=2 TO Y2+1
01260 LET D(I)=-I2
01270 NEXT I
01280 LET D(1)=P2
01290 LET D(Y2+1)=D(Y2+1)-100
01300 REM *** NOW USE BISECTION METHOD TO FIND COST OF DEBT ***
01310 LET L2=-128
01320 LET R2=256
01330 LET M=(L2+R2)/2
01340 IF R2-M<=0.01 THEN 01420
01350 LET T2=0
01360 FOR J=1 TO Y2+1
01370 LET T2=T2+D(J)/(1+M/100)**(J-1)
01380 NEXT J
01390 IF T2>0 THEN LET R2=M
01400 IF T2<=0 THEN LET L2=M
01410 GOTO 01330
01420 LET M=INT(100*M+0.5)/100
01430 LET K2=M
01440 REM ***** BANK LOAN *****
01450 PRINT "ANY BANK LOAN IN THE CAPITAL STRUCTURE ? (YES OR NO)"
01460 INPUT Q3$
01470 IF Q3$<>"YES" AND Q3$<>"NO" THEN 01450
01480 IF Q3$="NO" THEN 01530
01490 PRINT "PLEASE INPUT THE AMOUNT (IN POUNDS) OF BANK LOAN"
01500 INPUT V3
01510 PRINT "WHAT IS THE INTEREST RATE OF THE LOAN (%) ?"
01520 INPUT K3
```

```
01530 REM ***** NEW SHARE *****
01540 PRINT "ANY NEW ISSUE OF SHARES ? (YES OR NO)"
01550 INPUT Q4$
01560 IF Q4$<>"YES" AND Q4$<>"NO" THEN 01540
01570 IF Q4$="NO" THEN 01670
01580 PRINT "WHAT IS THE TOTAL AMOUNT (EXCLUDED COST OF ISSUE)"
01590 PRINT "OF NEW ISSUE ?"
01600 INPUT V4
01610 PRINT "WHAT IS THE COST PER SHARE OF NEW ISSUE (IN PUUND) ?"
01620 PRINT "E.G. IF COST OF NEW ISSUE IS 4P PER SHARE, THEN INPUT"
01630 PRINT "     0.04"
01640 INPUT C4
01650 LET K4=D9*(1+G)/(P1-C4)+G
01660 LET K4=INT(100*K4+0.5)
01670 PRINT "PLEASE INPUT TAX RATE"
01680 PRINT "E.G. IF TAX RATE IS 40% THEN INPUT   '40'"
01690 PRINT "     IF NO TAX CONSIDERED THEN INPUT '0'"
01700 INPUT T
01710 LET U9=(1-T/100)
01720 LET W=(K1*V1+U9*K2*V2+U9*K3*V3+K4*V4)/(V1+V2+V3+V4)
01730 LET W=INT(100*W+0.5)/100
01740 LET R=W
01750 PRINT
01760 PRINT "****************************************************"
01770 PRINT "MARKET VALUE OF SHARES ";TAB(40);"=";V1
01780 PRINT "REQUIRED RETURN OF EQUITY";TAB(40);"=";K1;"%"
01790 PRINT
01800 PRINT "MARKET VALUE OF DEBT";TAB(40);"=";V2
01810 PRINT "REQUIRED RETURN OF DEBT AFTER TAX";
01820 PRINT TAB(40);"=";(1-T/100)*K2;"%"
01830 PRINT
01840 PRINT "MARKET VALUE OF BANK LOAN"; TAB(40);"=";V3
01850 PRINT "REQUIRED RETURN OF BANK LOAN AFTER TAX";
01860 PRINT TAB(40);"=";(1-T/100)*K3;"%"
01870 PRINT
01880 PRINT "MARKET VALUE OF NEW ISSUE OF SHARES";TAB(40);"=";V4
01890 PRINT "REQUIRE RETURN OF NEW ISSUE";TAB(40);"=";K4;"%"
01900 PRINT TAB(40);"---------"
01910 PRINT
01920 PRINT "WEIGHTED AVERAGE COST OF CAPITAL";TAB(40);"=";W;"%"
01930 RETURN
01940 REM ****************************************************
01950 REM                CAPM APPROACH
01960 REM                -------------
01970 PRINT
01980 PRINT
01990 DIM A(100,4)
02000 PRINT "WHICH METHOD YOU WANT TO CALCULATE PROJECT BETA ?"
02010 PRINT "INPUT        '1' FOR PROBABILITY ANALYSIS METHOD"
02020 PRINT "             '2' FOR ADJUSTING OBSERVED BETA METHOD"
02030 PRINT
02040 INPUT Q2
02050 IF Q2<>1 AND Q2<>2 THEN 02010
02060 ON Q2 GOTO 02080,03090
02070 REM **************************************************
02080 PRINT " PROBABILITY ANALYSIS TO CAL. PROJECT BETA (CAPM)"
```

```
02090 PRINT " ----------------------------------------------"
02100 DIM L(10,5)
02110 PRINT "HOW MANY STATES OF THE WORLD ARE CONSIDERED ?"
02120 PRINT "(MAX. IS 10)"
02130 INPUT N
02140 LET N=INT(N)
02150 PRINT "FOR EACH LINE, INPUT"
02160 PRINT "PROBABILITY,RETURN OF EXISTING PROJECT(%)"
02170 PRINT "RETURN OF NEW PROJECT(%),RETURN OF MARKET PORTFOLIO(%),"
02180 PRINT "RETURN OF RISK-FREE SECURITY (%)"
02190 LET C0=0
02200 FOR I=1 TO N
02210 INPUT L(I,1),L(I,2),L(I,3),L(I,4),L(I,5)
02220 LET C0=C0+L(I,1)
02230 NEXT I
02240 IF C0=1 THEN 02280
02250 PRINT "SUM OF PROBABILITIES NOT EQUAL TO '1'"
02260 PRINT "PLEASE INPUT AGAIN"
02270 GOTO 02190
02280 LET R2=R3=R4=F1=0
02290 FOR I=1 TO N
02300 LET R2=R2+L(I,1)*L(I,2)
02310 LET R3=R3+L(I,1)*L(I,3)
02320 LET R4=R4+L(I,1)*L(I,4)
02330 LET F1=F1+L(I,1)*L(I,5)
02340 NEXT I
02350 LET S2=S3=S4=C1=C2=0
02360 FOR I=1 TO N
02370 LET S2=S2+(L(I,2)-R2)**2*L(I,1)
02380 LET S3=S3+(L(I,3)-R3)**2*L(I,1)
02390 LET S4=S4+(L(I,4)-R4)**2*L(I,1)
02400 LET C1=C1+(L(I,2)-R2)*(L(I,4)-R4)*L(I,1)
02410 LET C2=C2+(L(I,3)-R3)*(L(I,4)-R4)*L(I,1)
02420 NEXT I
02430 LET S2=SQR(S2)
02440 LET S3=SQR(S3)
02450 LET S4=SQR(S4)
02460 LET P1=C1/(S2*S4)
02470 LET P2=C2/(S3*S4)
02480 LET B1=C1/(S4*S4)
02490 LET B2=C2/(S4*S4)
02500 LET D1=F1+(R4-F1)*B1
02510 LET D2=F1+(R4-F1)*B2
02520 PRINT
02530 PRINT "*****************************************************"
02540 PRINT
02550 PRINT "EXPECTED RISK-FREE RATE OF RETURN =";F1;"%"
02560 PRINT "EXPECTED MARKET RETURN            =";R4;"%"
02570 PRINT "S. D. OF MARKET RETURN            =";S4;"%"
02580 PRINT
02590 PRINT "EXISTING PROJECT"
02600 PRINT "----------------"
02610 PRINT
02620 PRINT "EXPECTED RETURN";TAB(50);"=";R2;"%"
02630 PRINT "S.D. OF RETURN" ;TAB(50);"=";S2;"%"
02640 PRINT "COVARIANCE WITH MARKET RETURN";TAB(50);"=";C1
```

```
02650 PRINT "CORRELATION COEFF. WITH MARKET RETURN";TAB(50);"=";P1
02660 PRINT "BETA VALUE";TAB(50);"=";B1
02670 PRINT "REQUIRED RATE OF RETURN";TAB(50);"=";D1;"%"
02680 PRINT
02690 PRINT
02700 PRINT "NEW PROJECT"
02710 PRINT "-----------"
02720 PRINT
02730 PRINT "EXPECTED RETURN";TAB(50);"=";R3;"%"
02740 PRINT "S.D. OF RETURN ";TAB(50);"=";S3;"%"
02750 PRINT "COVARIANCE WITH MARKET RETURN";TAB(50);"=";C2
02760 PRINT "CORRELATION COEFF. WITH MARKET RETURN";TAB(50);"=";P2
02770 PRINT "BETA VALUE";TAB(50);"=";B2
02780 PRINT "REQUIRED RATE OF RETURN";TAB(50);"=";D2;"%"
02790 PRINT
02800 IF R3>D2 THEN PRINT "PROJECT IS ACCEPTABLE"
02810 IF R3<=D2 THEN PRINT " PROJECT IS NOT ACCEPTABLE"
02820 LET R=D2
02830 PRINT
02840 PRINT "DO YOU WANT TO KNOW THE IMPACT OF THE NEW PROJECT"
02850 PRINT "ON THE COMPANY'S SYSTEMATIC RISK (TOTAL) ?"
02860 PRINT "          ---------"
02870 PRINT "PLEASE INPUT 'YES' OR 'NO'"
02880 INPUT Q5$
02890 IF Q5$<>"YES" AND Q5$<>"NO" THEN 02870
02900 IF Q5$="NO" THEN 03060
02910 PRINT "WHAT IS THE PROPORTION OF THE NEW PROJECT TO"
02920 PRINT "THE OVERALL COMPANY OPERATIONS ?"
02930 PRINT "(IN DECIMAL FORM)"
02940 INPUT L1
02950 IF L1>=1 THEN 02930
02960 LET B9=(1-L1)*B1+L1*B2
02970 LET D9=F1+(R4-F1)*B9
02980 PRINT
02990 PRINT
03000 PRINT "AFTER ACCEPTED THE PROJECT,";
03010 PRINT " COMPANY BETA BECOMES";TAB(55);B9
03020 PRINT "COMPANY'S AVERAGE REQUIRED RETURN (CAPM) BECOMES";
03030 PRINT TAB(55);D9;"%"
03040 PRINT
03050 PRINT
03060 GOTO 03410
03070 REM *********************************************************
03080 PRINT
03090 PRINT "   ADJUSTING OBSERVED BETA METHOD (CAPM APPROACH)"
03100 PRINT "   -----------------------------------------------"
03110 PRINT
03120 PRINT "PLEASE INPUT THE OBSERVED COMPANY BETA"
03130 INPUT B7
03140 PRINT "PLEASE INPUT THE DEBT/EQUITY RATIO"
03150 INPUT E7
03160 PRINT "PLEASE INPUT THE TAX RATE(%)"
03170 INPUT T7
03180 PRINT "PLEASE INPUT THE % OF GROWTH OPPORTUNITIES"
03190 PRINT "TO THE COMPANYS' TOTAL MARKET VALUE"
03200 INPUT P7
```

```
03210 PRINT "PLEASE INPUT THE % OF GROWTH OPPORTUNITIES"
03220 PRINT "BETA 'ABOVE' THE BETA OF TANGIBLE ASSETS"
03230 INPUT X7
03240 PRINT "PLEASE INPUT THE PROJECT REVENUE SENSITIVITY"
03250 PRINT" (RELATIVE TO THE COMPANY)"
03260 INPUT S7
03270 PRINT "PLEASE INPUT THE PROJECT OPERATIONAL GEARING FACTOR"
03280 PRINT" (RELATIVE TO THE COMPANY)"
03290 INPUT G7
03300 LET B9=(B7*S7*G7)/((1+(1-T7/100)*E7)*(1+P7*X7/10000))
03310 PRINT "PLEASE INPUT THE AVERAGE RISK-FREE RATE IN %"
03320 INPUT F7
03330 PRINT "PLEASE INPUT THE AVERAGE MARKET RETURN IN %"
03340 INPUT M7
03350 LET R=F7+(M7-F7)*B9
03360 PRINT
03370 PRINT "*****************************************************"
03380 PRINT
03390 PRINT "THE PROJECT BETA VALUE IS";TAB(50);B9
03400 PRINT "THE REQUIRED RETURN OR THE PROJECT IS";TAB(50);R;"%"
03410 RETURN
03420 PRINT
03430 PRINT "DO YOU WANT TO RE-RUN THE PROGRAM ? (YES OR NO)"
03440 INPUT Q8$
03450 IF Q8$="YES" THEN 00400
03460 END
```

Computer Program 4:

Simulation Model

```
00100 REM
00110 REM                    HERTZ SIMULATION MODEL
00120 REM                    ----------------------
00130 REM
00140 REM      THIS PROGRAM PERFORMS RISK ANALYSIS BY USING THE
00150 REM      HERTZ SIMULATION METHOD
00160 REM
00170 REM      USERS CAN INPUT DATA BY EITHER USING 'DATA STATEMENT'
00180 REM      OR INTERACTIVELY INPUT FROM TERMINALS
00190 REM
00200 REM
00210 REM      SAMPLE DATA ARE PROVIDED, PROGRAM IS READY TO RUN BY
00220 REM      ANSWING  'YES'  TO THE FIRST QUESTION
00230 REM
00240 REM      IF USERS WANT TO INPUT NEW SET OF DATA WITHOUT
00250 REM      INTERACTI   WITH COMPUTER,THEN THEY SHOULD DELETE
00260 REM      'OLD DATA' AND INSERT 'NEW DATA' STARTING FROM LINE
00270 REM                     04040  TO  04340
00280 REM      BEFORE EXECUTING THE PROGRAM AND ANSWER  'YES' TO THE
00290 REM      FIRST QUESTION
00300 REM
00310 REM      USERS CAN SPECIFY NEW RELATIONSHIPS BETWEEN VARLABLES
00320 REM               BY CHANGING THE STATEMENTS FROM
00330 REM                    01060  TO  01380
00340 REM
00350 DIM V(500),R(500),X(20,8),Y(20,8),X$(20),F(100),G(100)
00360 DIM H(20),Z(500),C(20),C$(20)
00370 RANDOMIZE
00380 REM
00390 REM ***** SET Z8=0 WILL DELETE 'RATE OF RETURN' ROUTINE *****
```

```
00400 REM ***** SET Z8=1 WILL USE THE'RATE OF RETURN' ROUTINE *****
00410 LET Z8=1
00420 PRINT "***** DISCOUNT RATE (Z9) IS ALREADY SET TO 10%   *****"
00430 PRINT "***** IF REQUIRE NEW DISCOUNT RATE, CHANGE LINE 00440"
00440 LET Z9=.10
00450 PRINT
00460 PRINT "***** IF USERS DO NOT WANT TO INPUT FROM TERMINAL"
00470 PRINT "***** CHANGE SAMPLE DATA 'BEFORE' RUNNING PROGRAM"
00480 PRINT "DO YOU WANT TO USE 'SAMPLE DATA '? (YES OR NO)" ;
00490 INPUT Q1$
00500 PRINT
00510 IF Q1$="YES" THEN 00590
00520 LET Q9=P0=Q0=0
00530 REM *****          INPUT DATA FROM TERMINAL      *****
00540 GOSUB 01560
00550 REM *****  INPUT MODEL *****
00560 GOTO 01040
00570 REM          *****  READ DATA FROM DATA BLOCK  *****
00580 REM **** NUMBER OF ITERATIONS (SAMPLE)  *****
00590 READ N2
00600 REM **** NUMBER OF INTERVALS IN HISTOGRAMS  ****
00610 READ S9
00620 REM **** NO. OF CONSTANTS IN MODEL(BUILD IN MODEL IS 0) ****
00630 READ N9
00640 IF N9=0 THEN 00700
00650 FOR I=1 TO N9
00660 REM **** INPUT NAME OF CONSTANTS, VALUE OF CONSTANT  ****
00670 READ C$(I),C(I)
00680 NEXT I
00690 REM **** NUMBER OF VARIABLES IN MODEL  ****
00700 READ N1
00710 FOR I=1 TO N1
00720 REM **** NAME OF VARIABLES, NO OF POSSIBLE OUTCOMES  ****
00730 READ X$(I),N(I)
00740 FOR J=1 TO N(I)
00750 REM **** UPPER LIMITS OF OUTCOMES ****
00760 READ X(I,J)
00770 NEXT J
00780 LET P2=0
00790 FOR J=1 TO N(I)
00800 REM **** PERIORS ON INTERVALS BETWEEN LIMITS ****
00810 READ Y(I,J)
00820 LET P2=P2+Y(I,J)
00830 NEXT J
00840 IF ABS(P2-1)<0.0001 THEN 00880
00850 PRINT"SUM OF PROB.  FOR ";X$(I);" DOES NO EQUAL TO  '1' "
00860 PRINT "PROGRAM TERMINATED,RERUN THE PROGRAM FOR NEW INPUT"
00870 STOP
00880 NEXT I
00890 GOTO 01040
00900 REM ******************************************************
00910 REM **** FUNCTION-RANDOMLY SELECT A VALUE FOR A FACTOR  ****
00920 REM **** GEVEN THE VALUE OF INTERVAL AND PROB. OF FACTOR****
00930 DEF FNR(M)
00940 LET S1=0
00950 LET R1=RND(X)
```

```
00960 FOR K9=1 TO N(M)
00970 LET S1=S1+Y(M,K9)
00980 IF R1>=S1 THEN 01010
00990 LET FNR=X(M,K9-1)+(RND(X)*(X(M,K9)-X(M,K9-1)))
01000 GOTO 01020
01010 NEXT K9
01020 FNEND
01030 REM ***********************************************************
01040 FOR I0=1 TO N2
01050 MAT F=ZER
01060 REM **** MODEL IS ENTERED FROM HERE  *****
01070 REM ---------------------------------
01080 REM **** NO OF YEARS OF LIFE          *****
01090 LET N3=INT(FNR(1)+0.5)
01100 REM **** MARKET SIZE IN PERIOD 0      *****
01110 LET A1=FNR(2)
01120 REM **** INVESTMENT CASH FLOW IN PERIOD 0 *****
01130 LET F(0)=-1*FNR(7)
01140 LET G1=1
01150 REM **** FOR EACH YEAR OF LIFE *****
01160 FOR I=1 TO N3
01170 REM **** MULTIPLICATIVE GROWTH RATE PERIOD I  *****
01180 LET G1=G1*(1+FNR(3))
01190 REM **** MARKET SIZE PERIOD I                 *****
01200 LET A2=A1*G1
01210 REM **** QUANTITY PERIOD I                    *****
01220 LET A3=A2*FNR(4)
01230 REM **** VALUE OF SALES PERIOD I              *****
01240 LET A4=A3*FNR(5)
01250 REM **** OPERATING COSTS PERIOD I             *****
01260 LET C1=FNR(6)
01270 REM **** IS VALUE>= QTY*OP.COST  *****
01280 IF A4>=A3*C1 THEN 01320
01290 LET A3=0
01300 LET A4=0
01310 REM **** TOTAL COST PERIOD I      *****
01320 LET A5=FNR(9)+A3*C1
01330 REM **** CASH FLOW PERIOD I       *****
01340 LET F(I)=A4-A5
01350 NEXT I
01360 REM **** ADD RESID. VALUE TO CASH FLOW  LAST PERIOD *****
01370 LET F(N3)=F(N3)+FNR(8)
01380 REM                     **** END OF MODEL ****
01390 FOR I=0 TO N3
01400 REM **** PREPARE FOR RATE OF RETURN SUBROUTINE       *****
01410 LET G(I+1)=F(I)
01420 NEXT I
01430 IF I0>1 THEN 01480
01440 REM **** PRINT OUT CASH FLOWS OF FIRST ITERATION  ****
01450 GOSUB 03930
01460 REM **** CALCULATE NPV,RATE OF RETURN,RATEIO OF NPV ****
01470 REM **** FOR EACH ITERATION                         ****
01480 GOSUB 02790
01490 NEXT I0
01500 REM **** PRINT OUT HISTOGRAM  ****
01510 GOSUB 03120
```

```
01520 IF Q1$="YES" THEN 04350
01530 LET Q9=1
01540 GOSUB 01560
01550 GOTO 01040
01560 REM          *****  INPUT FROM TERMINAL  *****
01570 IF Q9=1 THEN 02050
01580 READ Q,Q,Q,Q
01590 PRINT "HOW MANY CONSTANTS IN YOUR MODEL";
01600 PRINT "(ORIGINAL MODEL IS  '0')"
01610 INPUT N9
01620 IF Q9=0 THEN 01710
01630 PRINT
01640 PRINT "ENTER THE VALUES FOR THE FOLLOWING:"
01650 PRINT
01660 FOR I=1 TO N9
01670  READ C$(I),Q
01680  PRINT C$(I);
01690  INPUT C(I)
01700 NEXT I
01710 PRINT
01720 PRINT "HOW MANY RANDOM VARIABLE CATEGORIES IN YOUR MODEL";
01730 INPUT N1
01740 PRINT
01750 PRINT "ENTER THE 'MOST LIKELY','LOWEST' AND 'HIGHEST'"
01760 PRINT "ESTIMATE VALUES OF EACH VARIABLE IN THE MODEL"
01770 PRINT "SEPARATED BY COMMAS."
01780 PRINT "                ------"
01790 PRINT
01800 PRINT "BY ASSUMING THE RANDOM DISTRIBUTION IS NORMAL "
01810 PRINT "THE COMPUTER WILL GENERATE PROBABILITIES OF THE "
01820 PRINT "VARIABLES FOR A GIVEN RANGE "
01830 PRINT
01840 PRINT
01850 PRINT "***NOTE***USERS HAVE OPPORTUNITY TO CHANGE INPUT"
01860 PRINT "          FIGURES LATER ON"
01870 PRINT
01880 PRINT
01890 PRINT TAB(25);"MOST LIKELY,LOWEST,HIGHEST"
01900 PRINT
01910 LET Q2$="ABC"
01920 FOR I=1 TO N1
01930  LET N(I) = 5
01940  LET Y(I,1) = 0
01950 REM **** GET RID OF DATA IN 'DATA BLOCK' ****
01960 REM **** BUT RESERVE THE VARIABLE NAME   ****
01970  READ X$(I),Q1
01980  FOR J=1 TO Q1+Q1
01990   READ Q
02000  NEXT J
02010 REM **** MORE INPUT ****
02020  GO SUB 02440
02030 NEXT I
02040 LET Q0=P0=0
02050 PRINT "DO YOU WANT TO CHANGE ANYTHING";
02060 INPUT Q2$
02070 PRINT
```

```
02080 IF Q2$="NO" THEN 02340
02090 LET Q0=1
02100 PRINT "INDEX NUMBER OF ITEM TO CHANGE";
02110 INPUT I
02120 PRINT
02130 PRINT "DO YOU WANT NEW VALUES";
02140 INPUT Q3$
02150 PRINT
02160 IF Q3$="NO" THEN 02200
02170 PRINT "INPUT 5 NEW VALUES";
02180 INPUT X(I,1),X(I,2),X(I,3),X(I,4),X(I,5)
02190 PRINT
02200 PRINT "DO YOU WANT TO CHANGE PROBABILITY ?"
02210 INPUT Q3$
02220 PRINT
02230 IF Q3$="NO" THEN 02320
02240 LET P0=1
02250 PRINT "INPUT 4 NEW PROBABILITY";
02260 INPUT Y(I,2),Y(I,3),Y(I,4),Y(I,5)
02270 LET P2=Y(I,2)+Y(I,3)+Y(I,4)+Y(I,5)
02280 IF ABS(P2-1)<0.0001 THEN 02310
02290 PRINT "  SUM OF PROB. DOES NOT EQUAL TO  '1'"
02300 GOTO 02250
02310 PRINT
02320 GOSUB 02440
02330 GOTO 02050
02340 PRINT "HOW MANY TIMES DO YOU WANT TO ITERATE ?"
02350 PRINT "( 0 WILL STOP PROGRAM)"
02360 INPUT N2
02370 PRINT
02380 IF N2=0 THEN 04350
02390 PRINT
02400 PRINT "HOW MANY INTERVALS DO YOU WANT IN THE HISTOGRAMS";
02410 INPUT S9
02420 PRINT
02430 RETURN
02440 REM **MORE INPUT *****
02450 IF Q0=1 THEN 02570
02460 PRINT
02470 PRINT I;X$(I);TAB(24);
02480 INPUT X(I,3),X(I,1),X(I,5)
02490 PRINT
02500 IF X(I,1)<1 THEN 02540
02510 LET X(I,2)=X(I,1)+INT(((X(I,3)-X(I,1))/2)+0.5)
02520 LET X(I,4)=X(I,3)+INT(((X(I,5)-X(I,3))/2)+0.5)
02530 GOTO 02570
02540 LET X(I,2)=X(I,1)+((X(I,3)-X(I,1))/2)
02550 LET X(I,4)=X(I,3)+((X(I,5)-X(I,3))/2)
02560 REM  ***  VALUES *********
02570 PRINT TAB(2);X(I,1);TAB(17);X(I,2);TAB(32);X(I,3);TAB(47);
02580 PRINT X(I,4);TAB(62);X(I,5)
02590 IF Q2$="YES" THEN 02730
02600 IF Q0=1 THEN 02630
02610 IF P0=1 THEN 02730
02620 LET Y(I,2)=Y(I,5)=0.10
02630 LET Q2=Y(I,2)*(X(I,1)+((X(I,2)-X(I,1))/2))
```

```
02640 LET Q3=Y(I,5)*(X(I,4)+((X(I,5)-X(I,4))/2))
02650 LET Q4=X(I,2)+((X(I,3)-X(I,2))/2)
02660 LET Q5=X(I,3)+((X(I,4)-X(I,3))/2)
02670 LET Q6=1-Y(I,2)-Y(I,5)
02680 LET Q7=Q4-Q5
02690 LET Q8=(X(I,3)-Q2-(Q5*Q6)-Q3)/Q7
02700 LET Y(I,3)=Q8
02710 LET Y(I,4)=1-Q8-Y(I,2)-Y(I,5)
02720 REM **** PROBABILITY ****
02730 PRINT TAB(9);Y(I,2);TAB(24);Y(I,3);TAB(39);Y(I,4);
02740 PRINT TAB(54);Y(I,5)
02750 PRINT
02760 PRINT
02770 RETURN
02780 REM ****************************************************
02790 REM ** RATE OF RETURN AND PRESENT VALUE SUBROUTINES **
02800 REM ------------------------------------
02810 REM ** RATE OF RETURN **
02820 IF Z8=0 THEN 02990
02830 LET R1=R2=R3=0
02840 LET R4=INT(N3/2)
02850 LET R5=R1
02860 FOR I=1 TO N3+1
02870 LET R6=I-R4
02880 LET R7=-1*R6
02890 LET R2=(G(I)*(EXP(1)**(R5*R7)))+R2
02900 LET R3=((R7*G(I))*(EXP(1)**(R5*R7)))+R3
02910 NEXT I
02920 LET R1=R5-(R2/R3)
02930 LET R2=R3=0
02940 LET R8=R1-R5
02950 IF ABS(R8)>0.000005 THEN 02850
02960 LET R(I0)=(EXP(1)**R1)-1
02970 LET R(I0)=INT(10000*R(I0)+0.5)/10000
02980 REM ------------------------------------
02990 REM *** NET PRESENT VALUE ***
03000 LET R1=Z1=Z2=0
03010 FOR I=0 TO N3
03020 LET R1=R1+(F(I)/((1+Z9)**I))
03030 IF F(I)>0 THEN 03060
03040 LET Z1=Z1+(ABS(F(I))/((1+Z9)**I))
03050 GOTO 03070
03060 LET Z2=Z2+(F(I)/((1+Z9)**I))
03070 NEXT I
03080 LET V(I0)=R1
03090 LET Z(I0)=INT(10000*(Z2/Z1)+0.5)/10000
03100 RETURN
03110 REM *****************************************************
03120 REM ** SET UP FOR HISTOGRAM PRINT SUBROUTINE **
03130 IF Z8=0 THEN 03180
03140 PRINT "RATES OF RETURN FOR";N2;"SAMPLES"
03150 PRINT
03160 LET I1=1
03170 GOSUB 03310
03180 PRINT "NET PRESENT VALUES FOR";N2;"SAMPLES"
03190 PRINT
```

```
03200 LET I1=2
03210 MAT R=ZER
03220 MAT R=R+V
03230 GOSUB 03310
03240 PRINT "PROFITABILITY INDEX FOR ";N2;"SAMPLES"
03250 PRINT
03260 LET I1=3
03270 MAT R=ZER
03280 MAT R=R+Z
03290 GOSUB 03310
03300 RETURN
03310 REM *** PRINT HISTOGRAMS SUBROUTINE ***
03320 LET R1=R2=R(1)
03330 LET A9$="*"
03340 FOR I=2 TO N2
03350 IF R(I)=R1 THEN 03430
03360 IF R(I)<R1 THEN 03400
03370 IF R(I)=R2 THEN 03430
03380 IF R(I)>R2 THEN 03420
03390 GOTO 03430
03400 LET R1=R(I)
03410 GOTO 03430
03420 LET R2=R(I)
03430 NEXT I
03440 ON I1 GOTO 03450,03470,03450
03450 LET R3=INT(1000*((R2-R1)/(S9-1))+0.5)/1000
03460 GOTO 03510
03470 LET R3=INT(((R2-R1)/(S9-1))+0.5)
03480 IF R2<99999 THEN 03510
03490 PRINT "FOR ACTUAL VALUE MULTIPLY BY 1000"
03500 PRINT
03510 MAT H=ZER
03520 LET S4=S5=H1=0
03530 LET S1=R1
03540 FOR I=1 TO S9
03550 LET S2=S1+R3
03560 FOR J=1 TO N2
03570 IF R(J)>=S2 THEN 03620
03580 IF R(J)<S1 THEN 03620
03590 LET H(I)=H(I)+1
03600 LET S4=S4+R(J)
03610 LET S5=S5+R(J)**2
03620 NEXT J
03630 ON I1 GOTO 03640,03670,03640
03640 PRINT INT(S1*10**4+0.5)/10**4;TAB(11);"TO";
03650 PRINT TAB(18);INT(S2*10**4+0.5)/10**4;
03660 GOTO 03710
03670 IF R2<99999 THEN 03700
03680 PRINT INT(S1/1000+.5);TAB(11);"TO";TAB(18);INT(S2/1000+.5);
03690 GO TO 03710
03700 PRINT INT(S1+.5);TAB(11);"TO";TAB(18);INT(S2+.5);
03710 PRINT TAB(31);
03720 IF H(I)=0 THEN 03760
03730 FOR J=1 TO H(I)
03740  PRINT A9$;
03750 NEXT J
```

```
03760 PRINT TAB(55);H(I)
03770 LET S1 = S2
03780 LET H1 = H1 + H(I)
03790 NEXT I
03800 PRINT
03810 PRINT
03820 ON I1 GO TO 03830,03850,03830
03830 PRINT "MEAN";INT(10000*(S4/H1)+.5)/10000
03840 GO TO 03860
03850 PRINT "MEAN";S4/H1
03860 PRINT
03870 LET V4 = (S5/H1)-((S4/H1)**2)
03880 PRINT "STANDARD DEVIATION";INT(10000*SQR(V4)+.5)/10000
03890 PRINT
03900 PRINT
03910 PRINT
03920 RETURN
03930 REM   **** PRINT FIRST SET OF FLOWS ****
03940 PRINT "FLOWS FOR THE FIRST ITERATION FOR";N3+1;" PERIODS"
03950 PRINT
03960 PRINT "PERIOD","FLOW"
03970 PRINT
03980 FOR I=0 TO N3
03990  PRINT I,F(I)
04000 NEXT I
04010 PRINT
04020 PRINT
04030 RETURN
04040 DATA 100
04050 DATA 15
04060 DATA 0
04070 DATA 9
04080 DATA LIFE,5
04090 DATA 7,9,12,15,18
04100 DATA 0,0.2,0.4,0.3,0.1
04110 DATA MARKET SIZE,5
04120 DATA 100000,150000,200000,250000,340000
04130 DATA 0,0.2,0.2,0.4,0.2
04140 DATA MARKET GROWTH RATE,7
04150 DATA 0,0.01,0.02,0.03,0.04,0.05,0.06
04160 DATA 0,0.05,0.10,0.35,0.3,0.15,0.05
04170 DATA SHARE OF MARKET,6
04180 DATA 0.03,0.06,0.09,0.12,0.15,0.17
04190 DATA 0,0.1,0.15,0.4,0.3,0.05
04200 DATA SELLING PRICE,5
04210 DATA 300,330,370,400,450
04220 DATA 0,0.1,0.45,0.35,0.1
04230 DATA OPERATING COSTS,6
04240 DATA 250,270,300,310,330,350
04250 DATA 0,0.15,0.35,0.35,0.1,0.05
04260 DATA INVESTMENT,6
04270 DATA 7000000,8000000,9000000,9500000,10000000,10500000
04280 DATA 0,0.05,0.15,0.35,0.35,0.1
04290 DATA RESIDUAL VALUE,4
04300 DATA 3500000,4000000,4500000,5000000
04310 DATA 0,0.2,0.4,0.4
```

```
04320 DATA FIXED COST,6
04330 DATA 250000,275000,300000,325000,350000,375000
04340 DATA 0,0.1,0.3,0.3,0.2,0.1
04350 END
```

Appendix A

Present Value Tables

Appendix A: Present Value of £1.00 Due at the End of n Years*

n	1%	2%	3%	4%	5%	6%	7%	8%	9%	10%	n
1	0.99010	0.98039	0.97007	0.96154	0.95238	0.94340	0.93458	0.92593	0.91743	0.90909	1
2	0.98030	0.96117	0.94260	0.92456	0.90703	0.89000	0.87344	0.85734	0.84168	0.82645	2
3	0.97059	0.94232	0.91514	0.88900	0.86384	0.83962	0.81630	0.79383	0.77218	0.75131	3
4	0.96098	0.92385	0.88849	0.85480	0.82270	0.79209	0.76290	0.73503	0.70843	0.68301	4
5	0.95147	0.90573	0.86261	0.82193	0.78353	0.74726	0.71299	0.68058	0.64993	0.62092	5
6	0.94204	0.88797	0.83748	0.79031	0.74622	0.70496	0.66634	0.63017	0.59627	0.56447	6
7	0.93272	0.87056	0.81309	0.75992	0.71068	0.66506	0.62275	0.58349	0.54703	0.51316	7
8	0.92348	0.85349	0.78941	0.73069	0.67684	0.62741	0.58201	0.54027	0.50187	0.46651	8
9	0.91434	0.83675	0.76642	0.70259	0.64461	0.59190	0.54393	0.50025	0.46043	0.42410	9
10	0.90529	0.82035	0.74409	0.67556	0.61391	0.55839	0.50835	0.46319	0.42241	0.38554	10
11	0.89632	0.80426	0.72242	0.64958	0.58468	0.52679	0.47509	0.42888	0.38753	0.35049	11
12	0.88745	0.78849	0.70138	0.62460	0.55684	0.49697	0.44401	0.39711	0.35553	0.31863	12
13	0.87866	0.77303	0.68095	0.60057	0.53032	0.46884	0.41496	0.36770	0.32618	0.28966	13
14	0.86996	0.75787	0.66112	0.57747	0.50507	0.44230	0.38782	0.34046	0.29925	0.26333	14
15	0.86135	0.74301	0.64186	0.55526	0.48102	0.41726	0.36245	0.31524	0.27454	0.23939	15
16	0.85282	0.72845	0.62317	0.53391	0.45811	0.39365	0.33873	0.29189	0.25187	0.21763	16
17	0.84438	0.71416	0.60502	0.51337	0.43630	0.37136	0.31657	0.27027	0.23107	0.19784	17
18	0.83602	0.70016	0.58739	0.49363	0.41552	0.35034	0.29586	0.25025	0.21199	0.17986	18
19	0.82774	0.68643	0.57029	0.47464	0.39573	0.33051	0.27651	0.23171	0.19449	0.16351	19
20	0.81954	0.67297	0.55367	0.45639	0.37689	0.31180	0.25842	0.21455	0.17843	0.14864	20
21	0.81143	0.65978	0.53755	0.43883	0.35894	0.29415	0.24151	0.19866	0.16370	0.13513	21
22	0.80340	0.64684	0.52189	0.42195	0.34185	0.27750	0.22571	0.18394	0.15018	0.12285	22
23	0.79544	0.63414	0.50669	0.40573	0.32557	0.26180	0.21095	0.17031	0.13778	0.11168	23
24	0.78757	0.62172	0.49193	0.39012	0.31007	0.24698	0.19715	0.15770	0.12640	0.10153	24
25	0.77977	0.60953	0.47760	0.37512	0.29530	0.23300	0.18425	0.14602	0.11597	0.09230	25

*Note:** $PV = £1/(1 + r)^n$.

Appendix A (*cont'd*): Present Value of £1.00 Due at the End of *n* Years

n	11%	12%	13%	14%	15%	16%	17%	18%	19%	20%	*n*
1	0.90090	0.89286	0.88496	0.87719	0.86957	0.86207	0.85470	0.84746	0.84034	0.83333	1
2	0.81162	0.79719	0.78315	0.76947	0.75614	0.74316	0.73051	0.71818	0.70616	0.69444	2
3	0.73119	0.71178	0.69305	0.67497	0.65752	0.64066	0.62437	0.60863	0.59342	0.57870	3
4	0.65873	0.63552	0.61332	0.59208	0.57175	0.55229	0.53365	0.51579	0.49867	0.48225	4
5	0.59345	0.56743	0.54276	0.51937	0.49718	0.47611	0.45611	0.43711	0.41905	0.40188	5
6	0.53464	0.50663	0.48032	0.45559	0.43233	0.41044	0.38984	0.37043	0.35214	0.33490	6
7	0.48166	0.45235	0.42506	0.39964	0.37594	0.35383	0.33320	0.31392	0.29592	0.27908	7
8	0.43393	0.40388	0.37616	0.35056	0.32690	0.30503	0.28487	0.26604	0.24867	0.23257	8
9	0.39092	0.36061	0.33288	0.30751	0.28426	0.26295	0.24340	0.22546	0.20897	0.19381	9
10	0.35218	0.32197	0.29459	0.26974	0.24718	0.22668	0.20804	0.19106	0.17560	0.16151	10
11	0.31728	0.28748	0.26070	0.23662	0.21494	0.19542	0.17781	0.16192	0.14756	0.13459	11
12	0.28584	0.25667	0.23071	0.20756	0.18691	0.16846	0.15197	0.13722	0.12400	0.11216	12
13	0.25751	0.22917	0.20416	0.18207	0.16253	0.14523	0.12989	0.11629	0.10420	0.09346	13
14	0.23199	0.20462	0.18068	0.15971	0.14133	0.12520	0.11102	0.09855	0.08757	0.07789	14
15	0.20900	0.18270	0.15989	0.14010	0.12289	0.10793	0.09489	0.08352	0.07359	0.06491	15
16	0.18829	0.16312	0.14150	0.12289	0.10686	0.09304	0.08110	0.07078	0.06184	0.05409	16
17	0.16963	0.14564	0.12522	0.10780	0.09393	0.08021	0.06932	0.05998	0.05196	0.04507	17
18	0.15282	0.13004	0.11081	0.09456	0.08080	0.06914	0.05925	0.05083	0.04367	0.03756	18
19	0.13768	0.11611	0.09806	0.08295	0.07026	0.05961	0.05064	0.04308	0.03669	0.03130	19
20	0.12403	0.10367	0.08678	0.07276	0.06110	0.05139	0.04328	0.03651	0.03084	0.02608	20
21	0.11174	0.09256	0.07680	0.06383	0.05313	0.04430	0.03699	0.03094	0.02591	0.02174	21
22	0.10067	0.08264	0.06796	0.05599	0.04620	0.03819	0.03162	0.02622	0.02178	0.01811	22
23	0.09069	0.77379	0.06014	0.04911	0.04017	0.03292	0.02702	0.02222	0.01830	0.01509	23
24	0.08170	0.06588	0.05322	0.04308	0.03493	0.02838	0.02310	0.01883	0.01538	0.01258	24
25	0.07361	0.05882	0.04710	0.03779	0.03038	0.02447	0.01974	0.01596	0.01292	0.01048	25

Appendix A (*cont'd*): Present Value of £1.00 Due at the End of *n* Years

n	21%	22%	23%	24%	25%	26%	27%	28%	29%	30%	
1	0.82645	0.81967	0.81301	0.80645	0.80000	0.79365	0.78740	0.78125	0.77519	0.76923	1
2	0.68301	0.67186	0.66098	0.65036	0.64000	0.62988	0.62000	0.61035	0.60093	0.59172	2
3	0.56447	0.55071	0.53738	0.52449	0.51200	0.49991	0.48819	0.47684	0.46583	0.45517	3
4	0.46651	0.45140	0.43690	0.42297	0.40960	0.39675	0.38440	0.37253	0.36111	0.35013	4
5	0.38554	0.37000	0.35520	0.34111	0.32768	0.31488	0.30268	0.29104	0.27993	0.26933	5
6	0.31863	0.30328	0.28878	0.27509	0.26214	0.24991	0.23833	0.22737	0.21700	0.20718	6
7	0.26333	0.24859	0.23478	0.22184	0.20972	0.19834	0.18766	0.17764	0.16822	0.15937	7
8	0.21763	0.20376	0.19088	0.17891	0.16777	0.15741	0.14776	0.13878	0.13040	0.12259	8
9	0.17986	0.16702	0.15519	0.14428	0.13422	0.12493	0.11635	0.10842	0.10109	0.09430	9
10	0.14864	0.13690	0.12617	0.11635	0.10737	0.09915	0.09161	0.08470	0.07836	0.07254	10
11	0.12285	0.11221	0.10258	0.09383	0.08590	0.07869	0.07214	0.06617	0.06075	0.05580	11
12	0.10153	0.09198	0.08339	0.07567	0.06872	0.06245	0.05680	0.05170	0.04709	0.04292	12
13	0.08391	0.17539	0.06780	0.06103	0.05498	0.04957	0.04472	0.04039	0.03650	0.03302	13
14	0.06934	0.06180	0.05512	0.04921	0.04398	0.03934	0.03522	0.03155	0.02830	0.02540	14
15	0.05731	0.05065	0.04481	0.03969	0.03518	0.03122	0.02773	0.02465	0.02194	0.01954	15
16	0.04736	0.04152	0.03643	0.03201	0.02815	0.02478	0.02183	0.01926	0.01700	0.01503	16
17	0.03914	0.03403	0.02962	0.02581	0.02252	0.01967	0.01719	0.01505	0.01318	0.01156	17
18	0.03235	0.27289	0.02408	0.02082	0.01801	0.01561	0.01354	0.01175	0.01022	0.00889	18
19	0.02673	0.02286	0.01958	0.01679	0.01441	0.01239	0.01066	0.00918	0.00792	0.00684	19
20	0.02209	0.01874	0.01592	0.01354	0.01153	0.00983	0.00839	0.00717	0.00614	0.00526	20
21	0.01826	0.01536	0.01294	0.01092	0.00922	0.00780	0.00661	0.00561	0.00476	0.00405	21
22	0.01509	0.01259	0.01052	0.00880	0.00738	0.00619	0.00520	0.00438	0.00369	0.00311	22
23	0.01247	0.01032	0.00855	0.00710	0.00590	0.00491	0.00410	0.00342	0.00286	0.00239	23
24	0.01031	0.00846	0.00695	0.00573	0.00472	0.00390	0.00323	0.00267	0.00222	0.00184	24
25	0.00852	0.000693	0.00565	0.00462	0.00378	0.00310	0.00254	0.00209	0.00172	0.00152	25

Appendix A (*cont'd*): Present Value of £1.00 Due at the End of *n* Years

n	31%	32%	33%	34%	35%	36%	37%	38%	39%	40%	*n*
1	0.76336	0.75758	0.75188	0.74627	0.74074	0.73529	0.72993	0.72464	0.71942	0.71429	1
2	0.58272	0.57392	0.56532	0.55692	0.54870	0.54066	0.53279	0.52510	0.51757	0.51020	2
3	0.44482	0.43479	0.42505	0.41561	0.40644	0.39754	0.38890	0.38051	0.37235	0.36443	3
4	0.33956	0.32939	0.31959	0.31016	0.30107	0.29231	0.28387	0.27573	0.26788	0.26031	4
5	0.25920	0.24953	0.24029	0.23146	0.22301	0.21493	0.20720	0.19980	0.19272	0.18593	5
6	0.19787	0.18904	0.18067	0.17273	0.16520	0.15804	0.15124	0.14479	0.13865	0.13281	6
7	0.15104	0.14321	0.13584	0.12890	0.12237	0.11621	0.11040	0.10492	0.09975	0.09486	7
8	0.11530	0.10849	0.10214	0.09620	0.09064	0.08545	0.08058	0.07603	0.07176	0.06776	8
9	0.08802	0.08219	0.07680	0.07179	0.06714	0.06283	0.05882	0.05509	0.05163	0.04840	9
10	0.06719	0.06227	0.05774	0.05357	0.04973	0.04620	0.04293	0.03992	0.03714	0.03457	10
11	0.05129	0.04717	0.04341	0.03998	0.03684	0.03397	0.03134	0.02893	0.02672	0.02469	11
12	0.03915	0.03574	0.03264	0.02984	0.02729	0.02498	0.02287	0.02096	0.01922	0.01764	12
13	0.02989	0.02707	0.02454	0.02227	0.02021	0.01837	0.01670	0.01519	0.01383	0.01260	13
14	0.02281	0.02051	0.01845	0.01662	0.01497	0.01350	0.01219	0.01101	0.00995	0.00900	14
15	0.01742	0.01554	0.01387	0.01240	0.01109	0.00993	0.00890	0.00798	0.00716	0.00643	15
16	0.01329	0.01177	0.01043	0.00925	0.00822	0.00730	0.00649	0.00578	0.00515	0.00459	16
17	0.01015	0.00892	0.00784	0.00691	0.00609	0.00537	0.00474	0.00419	0.00370	0.00328	17
18	0.00775	0.00676	0.00590	0.00515	0.00451	0.00395	0.00346	0.00304	0.00267	0.00234	18
19	0.00591	0.00512	0.00443	0.00385	0.00334	0.00290	0.00253	0.00220	0.00192	0.00167	19
20	0.00451	0.00388	0.00333	0.00287	0.00247	0.00213	0.00184	0.00159	0.00138	0.00120	20
21	0.00345	0.00294	0.00251	0.00214	0.00183	0.00157	0.00135	0.00115	0.00099	0.00085	21
22	0.00263	0.00223	0.00188	0.00160	0.00136	0.00115	0.00098	0.00084	0.00071	0.00061	22
23	0.00201	0.00169	0.00142	0.00119	0.00101	0.00085	0.00072	0.00061	0.00051	0.00044	23
24	0.00153	0.00128	0.00107	0.00089	0.00074	0.00062	0.00052	0.00044	0.00037	0.00031	24
25	0.00117	0.00097	0.00080	0.00066	0.00055	0.00046	0.00038	0.00032	0.00027	0.00022	25

Appendix B

Annuity Tables

Appendix B: Present Value of Annuity of £1.00 for *n* Years*

n	1%	2%	3%	4%	5%	6%	7%	8%	9%	10%	*n*
1	0.9901	0.9804	0.9709	0.9615	0.9524	0.9434	0.9346	0.9259	0.9174	0.9091	1
2	1.9704	1.9416	1.9135	1.8861	1.8594	1.8334	1.8080	1.7833	1.7591	1.7355	2
3	2.9410	2.8839	2.8286	2.7751	2.7232	2.6730	2.6243	2.5771	2.5313	2.4868	3
4	3.9020	3.8077	3.7171	3.6299	3.5459	3.4651	3.3872	3.3121	3.2397	3.1699	4
5	4.8535	4.7134	4.5797	4.4518	4.3295	4.2123	4.1002	3.9927	3.8896	3.7908	5
6	5.7955	5.6014	5.4172	5.2421	5.0757	4.9173	4.7665	4.6229	4.4859	4.3553	6
7	6.7282	6.4720	6.2302	6.0020	5.7863	5.5824	5.3893	5.2064	5.0329	4.8684	7
8	7.6517	7.3254	7.0196	6.7327	6.4632	6.2098	5.9713	5.7466	5.5348	5.3349	8
9	8.5661	8.1622	7.7861	7.4353	7.1078	6.8017	6.5152	6.2469	5.9852	5.7590	9
10	9.4714	8.9825	8.5302	8.1109	7.7217	7.3601	7.0236	6.7101	6.4176	6.1446	10
11	10.3677	9.7868	9.2526	8.7604	8.3064	7.8868	7.4987	7.1389	6.8052	6.4951	11
12	11.2552	10.5753	9.9539	9.3850	8.8632	8.3838	7.9427	7.5361	7.1607	6.8137	12
13	12.1338	11.3483	10.6349	9.9856	9.3935	8.8527	8.3576	7.9038	7.4869	7.1034	13
14	13.0038	12.1062	11.2960	10.5631	9.8986	9.2950	8.7454	8.2442	7.7861	7.3667	14
15	13.8651	12.8492	11.9379	11.1183	10.3796	9.7122	9.1079	8.5595	8.0607	7.6061	15
16	14.7180	13.5777	12.5610	11.6522	10.8377	10.1059	9.4466	8.8514	8.3125	7.8237	16
17	15.5624	14.2918	13.1660	12.1656	11.2740	10.4772	9.7632	9.1216	8.5436	8.0215	17
18	16.3984	14.9920	13.7534	12.6592	11.6895	10.8276	10.0591	9.3719	8.7556	8.2014	18
19	17.2261	15.6784	14.3237	13.1339	12.0853	11.1581	10.3356	9.6036	8.9501	8.3649	19
20	18.0457	16.3514	14.8774	13.5903	12.4622	11.4699	10.5940	9.8181	9.1285	8.5136	20
21	18.8571	17.0111	15.4149	14.0291	12.8211	11.7640	10.8355	10.0168	9.2922	8.6487	21
22	19.6605	17.6580	15.9368	14.4511	13.1630	12.0416	11.0612	10.2007	9.4424	8.7715	22
23	20.4559	18.2921	16.4435	14.8568	13.4885	12.3033	11.2722	10.3710	9.5802	8.8832	23
24	21.2435	18.9139	16.9355	15.2469	13.7986	12.5503	11.4693	10.5287	9.7066	8.9847	24
25	22.0233	19.5234	17.4131	15.6220	14.0939	12.7833	11.6536	10.6748	9.8226	9.0770	25

Note: *A = $\{1 - 1/(1 + r)^n\}/r$

Appendix B (*cont'd*: Present Value of Annuity of £1.00 for *n* Years

n	11%	12%	13%	14%	15%	16%	17%	18%	19%	20%	*n*
1	0.0009	0.8929	0.8850	0.3772	0.8696	0.8621	0.8547	0.8475	0.8403	0.8333	1
2	1.7125	1.6901	1.6681	1.6467	1.6257	1.6052	1.5852	1.5656	1.5465	1.5278	2
3	2.4437	2.4018	2.3612	2.3216	2.2832	2.2459	2.2096	2.1743	2.1399	2.1065	3
4	3.1024	3.0373	2.9745	2.9137	2.8550	2.7982	2.7432	2.6901	2.6386	2.5887	4
5	3.6959	3.6048	3.5172	3.4331	3.3522	3.2743	3.1993	3.1272	3.0576	2.9906	5
6	4.2305	4.1114	3.9976	3.8887	3.7845	3.6847	3.5892	3.4976	3.4098	3.3255	6
7	4.7122	4.5638	4.4226	4.2883	4.1604	4.0386	3.9224	3.8115	3.7057	3.6046	7
8	5.1461	4.9676	4.7988	4.6389	4.4873	4.3436	4.2072	4.0776	3.9544	3.8372	8
9	5.5370	5.3282	5.1317	4.9464	4.7716	4.6065	4.4506	4.3030	4.1633	4.0310	9
10	5.8892	5.6502	5.4262	5.2161	5.0188	4.8332	4.6586	4.4941	4.3389	4.1925	10
11	6.2065	5.9377	5.6869	5.4527	5.2337	5.0286	4.8364	4.6560	4.4865	4.3271	11
12	6.4924	6.1944	5.9176	5.6603	5.4206	5.1971	4.9884	4.7932	4.6105	4.4392	12
13	6.7499	6.4235	6.1218	5.8424	5.5931	5.3423	5.1183	4.9095	4.7147	4.5327	13
14	6.9819	6.6282	6.3025	6.0021	5.7245	5.4675	5.2293	5.0081	4.8023	4.6106	14
15	7.1909	6.8109	6.4624	6.1422	5.8474	5.5755	5.3242	5.0916	4.8759	4.6755	15
16	7.3792	6.9740	6.6039	6.2651	5.9542	5.6685	5.4053	5.1624	4.9377	4.7296	16
17	7.5488	7.1196	6.7291	6.3729	6.0472	5.7487	5.4746	5.2223	4.9897	4.7746	17
18	7.7016	7.2497	6.8399	6.4674	6.1280	5.8178	5.5339	5.2732	5.0333	4.8122	18
19	7.8393	7.3658	6.9380	6.5504	6.1982	5.8775	5.5845	5.3162	5.0700	4.8435	19
20	7.9633	7.4694	7.0248	6.6231	6.2593	5.9288	5.6278	5.3527	5.1009	4.8696	20
21	8.0751	7.5620	7.1016	6.6870	6.3125	5.9731	5.6648	5.3837	5.1268	4.8913	21
22	8.1757	7.6446	7.1695	6.7429	6.3587	6.0113	5.6964	5.4099	5.1486	4.9094	22
23	8.2664	7.7184	7.2297	6.7921	6.3988	6.0442	5.7234	5.4321	5.1668	4.9245	23
24	8.3481	7.7843	7.2829	6.8351	6.4338	6.0726	5.7465	5.4509	5.1822	4.9371	24
25	8.4217	7.8431	7.3300	6.8729	6.4641	6.0971	5.7662	5.4669	5.1951	4.9476	25

Appendix B (*cont'd*): Present Value of an Annuity of £1.00 for *n* Years

n	21%	22%	23%	24%	25%	26%	27%	28%	29%	30%	*n*
1	0.8264	0.8197	0.8130	0.8065	0.8000	0.7937	0.7874	0.7813	0.7752	0.7692	1
2	1.5095	1.4915	1.4740	1.4568	1.4400	1.4235	1.4074	1.3916	1.3761	1.3609	2
3	2.0739	2.0422	2.0114	1.9813	1.9520	1.9234	1.8956	1.8684	1.8420	1.8161	3
4	2.5404	2.4936	2.4483	2.4043	2.3616	2.3202	2.2800	2.2410	2.2031	2.1662	4
5	2.9260	2.8636	2.8035	2.7454	2.6893	2.6351	2.5827	2.5320	2.4830	2.4356	5
6	3.2446	3.1669	3.0923	3.0205	2.9514	2.8850	2.8210	2.7594	2.7000	2.6427	6
7	3.5079	3.4155	3.3270	3.2423	3.1611	3.0833	3.0087	2.9370	2.8682	2.8021	7
8	3.7256	3.6193	3.5179	3.4212	3.3289	3.2407	3.1564	3.0758	2.9986	2.9247	8
9	3.9054	3.7863	3.6731	3.5655	3.4631	3.3657	3.2728	3.1842	3.0997	3.1090	9
10	4.0541	3.9232	3.7993	3.6819	3.5705	3.4648	3.3644	3.2689	3.1781	3.0915	10
11	4.1769	4.0354	3.9018	3.7757	3.6564	3.5435	3.4365	3.3351	3.2388	3.1473	11
12	4.2785	4.1274	3.9852	3.8514	3.7251	3.6060	3.4933	3.3868	3.2859	3.1903	12
13	4.3624	4.2028	4.0530	3.9124	3.7801	3.6555	3.6381	3.4272	3.3224	3.2233	13
14	4.4317	4.2646	4.1082	3.9616	3.8241	3.6949	3.5733	3.4587	3.3507	3.2487	14
15	4.4890	4.3152	4.1530	4.0013	3.8593	3.7261	3.6010	3.4834	3.3726	3.2682	15
16	4.5364	4.3567	4.1894	4.0333	3.8874	3.7509	3.6228	3.5026	3.3896	3.2832	16
17	4.5755	4.3908	4.2190	4.0591	3.9099	3.7705	3.6400	3.5177	3.4028	3.2948	17
18	4.6079	4.4187	4.2431	4.0799	3.9279	3.7861	3.6536	3.5294	3.4130	3.3037	18
19	4.6346	4.4415	4.2627	4.0967	3.9424	3.7985	3.6642	3.5386	3.4210	3.3105	19
20	4.6567	4.4603	4.2786	4.1103	3.9539	3.8083	3.6726	3.5458	3.4271	3.3158	20
21	4.6750	4.4756	4.2916	4.1212	3.9631	3.8161	3.6792	3.5514	3.4319	3.3198	21
22	4.6900	4.4882	4.3021	4.1300	3.9705	3.8223	3.6844	3.5558	3.4356	3.3230	22
23	4.7025	4.4985	4.3106	4.1371	3.9764	3.8273	3.6885	3.5592	3.4384	3.3254	23
24	4.7128	4.5070	4.3176	4.1428	3.9811	3.8312	3.6918	3.5619	3.4406	3.3272	24
25	4.7213	4.5139	4.3232	4.1474	3.9849	3.8342	3.6943	3.5640	3.4423	3.3286	25

Appendix B (*cont'd*)(Present Value of an Annuity of £1.00 for *n* Years

n	31%	32%	33%	34%	35%	36%	37%	38%	39%	40%	*n*
1	0.7634	0.7576	0.7519	0.7463	0.7407	0.7353	0.7299	0.7246	0.7194	0.7143	1
2	1.3461	1.3315	1.3172	1.3032	1.2894	1.2760	1.2627	1.2497	1.2370	1.2245	2
3	1.7909	1.7663	1.7423	1.7188	1.6959	1.6735	1.6516	1.6302	1.6093	1.5889	3
4	2.1305	2.0957	2.0618	2.0290	1.9969	1.9658	1.9355	1.9060	1.8772	1.8492	4
5	2.3897	2.3452	2.3021	2.2604	2.2200	2.1807	2.1427	2.1058	2.0699	1.9352	5
6	2.5875	2.5342	2.4828	2.4331	2.3852	2.3388	2.2936	2.2506	2.2086	2.1680	6
7	2.7386	2.6775	2.6187	2.5620	2.5075	2.4550	2.4043	2.3555	2.3083	2.2628	7
8	2.8539	2.7860	2.7208	2.6582	2.5982	2.5404	2.4849	2.4315	2.3801	2.3306	8
9	2.9419	2.8681	2.7976	2.7300	2.6653	2.6033	2.5437	2.4866	2.4317	2.3790	9
10	3.0091	2.9304	2.8553	2.7836	2.7150	2.6495	2.5867	2.5265	2.4689	2.4136	10
11	3.0604	2.9776	2.8987	2.8236	2.7519	2.6834	2.6180	2.5555	2.4956	2.4383	11
12	3.0995	3.0133	2.9314	2.8534	2.7792	2.7084	2.6409	2.5764	2.5148	2.4559	12
13	3.1294	3.0404	2.9559	2.8757	2.7994	2.7268	2.6576	2.5916	2.5286	2.4685	13
14	3.1522	3.0609	2.9744	2.8923	2.8144	2.7403	2.6698	2.6026	2.5386	2.4775	14
15	3.1696	3.0764	2.9883	2.9047	2.8255	2.7502	2.6787	2.6106	2.5457	2.4839	15
16	3.1829	3.0882	2.9987	2.9140	2.8337	2.7575	2.6852	2.6164	2.5509	2.4885	16
17	3.1931	3.0971	3.0065	2.9209	2.8398	2.7629	2.6899	2.6202	2.5546	2.4918	17
18	3.2008	3.1039	3.0124	2.9260	2.8443	2.7668	2.6934	2.6236	2.5573	2.4941	18
19	3.2067	3.1090	3.0169	2.9299	2.8476	2.7697	2.6959	2.6258	2.5592	2.4958	19
20	3.2112	3.1129	3.0202	2.9327	2.8501	2.7718	2.6977	2.6274	2.5606	2.4970	20
21	3.2174	3.1158	3.0227	2.9349	2.8519	2.7734	2.6991	2.6285	2.5616	2.4979	21
22	3.2173	3.1180	3.0246	2.9365	2.8533	2.7746	2.7000	2.6294	2.5623	2.4985	22
23	3.2193	3.1197	3.0260	2.9377	2.8543	2.7754	2.7008	2.6300	2.5628	2.4989	23
24	3.2209	3.1210	3.0271	2.9386	2.8550	2.7760	2.7013	2.6304	2.5632	2.4992	24
25	3.2220	3.1220	3.0279	2.9392	2.8556	2.7765	2.7017	2.6307	2.5634	2.4994	25

Index